We have just experienced the worst financial crash the world has seen since the Great Depression of the 1930s. While real economies in general did not crash as they did in the 1930s, the financial parts of the economy certainly did, or, at least, came very close to doing so. Hundreds of banks in the USA and Europe have been closed by their supervisory authorities, forcibly merged with stronger partners, nationalized or recapitalized with taxpayers' money. Banks and insurance companies had, by mid-2010, already written off some $2,000 billion in credit write-downs on loans and securities. In this book, Johan Lybeck draws on his experience as both an academic economist and a professional banker to present a detailed yet non-technical analysis of the crash. He describes how the crisis began in early 2007, explains why it happened, and shows how it compares to earlier financial crises.

JOHAN A. LYBECK has worked as Managing Director of Finanskonsult AB (Stockholm) and Risk Analysis SA (Brussels) for the last twenty-five years. As an academic, he has been, inter alia, a chaired professor of economics, associate professor of econometrics and adjunct professor of finance. His banking career includes jobs as Senior Vice President of Swedbank (Stockholm), in charge of financial strategy, and Chief Economist at Matteus Bank. He holds a PhD degree in Economics (University of Michigan, 1971) and a "fil. lic." in Political Science (University of Gothenburg, 1986).

A Global History of the Financial Crash of 2007–2010

JOHAN A. LYBECK

CAMBRIDGE
UNIVERSITY PRESS

University Printing House, Cambridge CB2 8BS, United Kingdom

Published in the United States of America by Cambridge University Press, New York

Cambridge University Press is part of the University of Cambridge.

It furthers the University's mission by disseminating knowledge in the pursuit of education, learning and research at the highest international levels of excellence.

www.cambridge.org
Information on this title: www.cambridge.org/9781107648883

First published 2011
3rd printing 2013

Printed in the United Kingdom by Clays, St Ives plc.

A catalogue record for this publication is available from the British Library

ISBN 978-1-107-01149-6 Hardback
ISBN 978-1-107-64888-3 Paperback

Contents

Figures

Tables

Preface

By 2010, the world has finally recuperated from a financial crisis which has been – by far – the worst economic episode to occur since the Great Depression in the 1930s. It definitely merits the label "crash" rather than "crisis," hence the title of this book. To paraphrase the Keynesian economist Hyman Minsky, who formulated the best explanations for why financial systems have a built-in, endogenous tendency to land themselves in trouble, "it" did happen again![1] While the real economies in general did not crash as they did in the 1930s, the financial parts of the economy certainly did, or at least came very close to doing so. The crash in the financial system also triggered the simmering sovereign debt crisis in the so-called PIIGS countries (Portugal, Ireland, Italy, Greece and Spain).

Hundreds of banks in the USA and Europe have been closed by their supervisory authorities, forcibly merged with stronger partners, nationalized or recapitalized with taxpayers' money. By mid-2010, banks and insurance companies had already written off some $2,000 billion ($2 trillion) in credit write-downs on loans and securities. Several hundred billion dollars were yet to come. An estimate from the International Monetary Fund (IMF) in April 2009 threatened that the ultimate loss to the world's banks might well exceed $4,000 billion, an indication of the perceived seriousness of the situation at that point in time, at the very height of the crisis. The forecast total losses were later scaled down to $2,800 billion in October 2009, and to $2,200 billion in October 2010. These sums may be compared with a world gross domestic product (GDP) of some $58,000 billion in 2009. Dividing one number by the other, we find that global write-downs have been almost 4 percent of world GDP. We shall find, however, that they were very unevenly spread among countries, with the USA and the UK

---

[1] Minsky, *Can "It" Happen Again?*. We will return in Chapter 3 to Minsky's theories of financial instability and systemic crises.

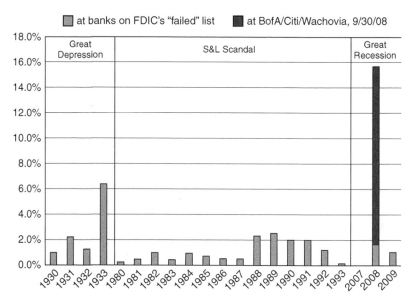

Figure 0.1 Deposits in failed banks (% of nominal GDP)
Source: FDIC and Federal Reserve Board

bearing the brunt of the costs. On average, the world banking system lost almost half of the capital base it possessed at the beginning of the crash in 2007.

As Figure 0.1 shows, at the lowest point of the Great Depression in 1933, US banks with deposits corresponding to 6 percent of GDP failed. Over the four worst years in the 1930s, banks with deposits totaling 10 percent to GDP went bankrupt. The number of failed banks was huge; no fewer than 4,004 banks went belly up in one single year, 1933. In the 1980s, a large number of savings and loan associations and mutual savings banks (so-called thrifts) in the USA went bankrupt, the graph showing that over the decade as a whole, those failed banks held deposits corresponding to some 15 percent of GDP. During 2007–9, 168 US banks failed, holding deposits of just over 3 percent of GDP (see Figures 0.1 and 0.2), lower even than during the thrift crisis in the 1980s. If we add the three large banks saved by government intervention (Citigroup, Bank of America and Wachovia Bank, the latter now a part of Wells Fargo Bank), however, the figure would have risen to 16 percent of GDP in 2008.

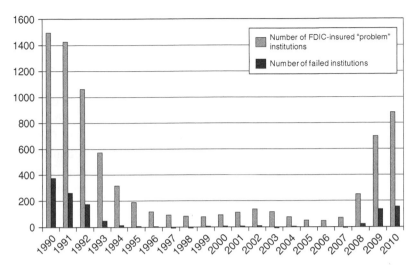

Figure 0.2 FDIC-insured "problem" institutions
Source: FDIC

In 2009, 140 banks failed, and a similar number had gone under up to the third quarter of 2010, though they were all relatively small. Their deposits still amounted to around 1 percent of the GDP of the USA each year.[2] Apart from outright failed banks, over 700 US banks were still on the Federal Deposit Insurance Corporation (FDIC) list of banks with severe problems at the end of 2009 (rising to 829 banks in the second quarter of 2010), as contrasted with some 250 just a year before (Figure 0.2).

In the UK, only four banks or building societies have needed public support and have been wholly or partially nationalized. But on the list we find the Royal Bank of Scotland (RBS) and Lloyds TSB (renamed Lloyds Banking Group after its merger with Halifax Bank of Scotland [HBOS]). Measured by total assets, at the end of 2007, before the crisis, they were number one and number eight among the banks in the world, number one and number four in the UK.[3]

---

[2] Total deposits in American banks were $10.4 trillion at the end of 2009; GDP was $14.4 trillion in 2009. Hence the 1.1 percent of GDP translates to 1.5 percent of total deposits for those who prefer looking at it that way.

[3] Lloyds Banking Group is measured pro forma since the companies were only merged in January 2009.

The background to the crisis we have just been through lies in over-heated housing markets in countries located far apart, such as the USA, the UK, Ireland, Iceland, Spain and Australia. But how could this have happened? Why did no one, or almost no one, give any warning as to what was about to happen? How could a relatively small part of the economy, the mortgage market, create such gigantic effects on the total economies, raise unemployment rates to double digits and almost over-turn whole sovereign countries, such as Iceland, Ireland and Greece? Why did the problems spread from the above-mentioned countries to countries that had not seen excessive house price inflation, such as Germany and France? Why were the Asian countries, in the main, sheltered from these problems? And how could the financial sector pay its executives tens of millions of dollars in individual salaries and bonuses while the companies themselves bled?

These are examples of some of the major questions addressed by this book. But it also delves deeply into details and explains what subprime loans, Fannie Mae and TARP are, to mention just a few of the terms and concepts that have appeared daily in the media during the crisis. The book describes how the crisis began in early 2007 and how it evolved, and tries to explain why. The book also makes comparisons with earlier financial crises, such as the US thrift crisis in the 1980s, and the Japanese, Russian-LTCM, Asian and Nordic crises in the 1990s. The earlier financial crises most reminiscent of today's, those of 1907 and 1929, are analyzed in detail.

If the crisis had been limited to losses on mortgage loans, it would not have attained the extent that it did. It would have been a crisis similar to the US thrift crisis or the Nordic crises, with losses in the range of 8–10 percent of the loan stock and costs to the taxpayer of a few percent of GDP; certainly painful for the economy, but not life-threatening to the economic system itself. What was new in the recent crisis was that risks had been shifted from the original lending banks (in the USA in partic-ular) to a number of actors all over the world: to other banks like the German Landesbanken and the Agricultural Bank of China, to name but a few; to insurance companies such as the US AIG, the German Allianz and the French AXA; to hedge funds, pension funds and even wealthy (and many times not so wealthy) individuals, who were per-suaded by asset managers, such as the Swiss bank UBS or the Norwegian asset manager Acta, to buy what are now commonly called "toxic assets."

Since no one knew where new problems might arise, confidence between the actors on the financial markets evaporated. No one knew who was stuck with "the old maid." The perceived increase in counter-party risk led to a loss of confidence; and at the next stage, liquidity, that important lubricant for the daily evening-out of claims and liabilities in the interbank market, disappeared overnight. This crisis began fundamentally as a liquidity crisis, where assets could no longer be sold, because there was no market where prices could be determined with any degree of precision, and no new loans were made. In this respect, it was similar to the earlier crises of 1907 and 1929, both of which also started as liquidity squeezes. Only later in the crisis did credit risk enter the story.

There is a clear similarity between the loss of liquidity and a "bank run." When the general public loses confidence in the safety of their deposits, they hasten to withdraw them – that is, they do not lend to that particular bank. If there is panic involved, it becomes a run on the bank. Similarly, in the wholesale market between banks, the interbank market, one does not lend to a bank which is known to have problems.

The book presents in detail the regulatory framework on the financial markets, and presents and discusses the changes in regulation and supervision that have been introduced as a result of the crash. Higher capital requirements and higher quality of capital in order to reduce the speculative possibilities form an important ingredient. In the present crisis, some of the major banks in the world, such as UBS in Switzerland and Deutsche Bank in Germany, had gearing ratios of total assets to equity capital of above seventy! It is also necessary to provide better scrutiny and regulatory approval of products and marketing methods directed at consumers, especially as concerns mortgage loans. Some countries have proposed to tax banks, either to pay for the past crisis (USA) or to build up a fund to finance future bank bailouts (Sweden, Germany, France, Austria), or simply to lower profitability in the banking sector while increasing tax revenues (the UK, Hungary). Better coordination between the supervisory authorities has been proposed in the USA as well as in the European Union. Also needed are restrictions on the ability to speculate in house price inflation – for example, by setting maximum ratios of loan-to-value, such as already existed in countries like Denmark, France and Germany, and were introduced in the UK and Sweden. Better education and higher personal responsibility should also be required of those who market and sell loans, as already exists in the securities market.

Increased regulation comes at a price. JPMorgan Chase (presently the world's second largest bank measured by equity capital) estimated in February 2010 that the various proposed measures would cost the major banks in the world some $220 billion in additional capital and would lower their pre-tax profitability on equity from 20 to 5 percent. To restore profits to their earlier level, prices to the customer would have to be raised by an average of 33 percent.

The book will show how the banking community succeeded in watering down most of these costly proposals to a more manageable size, allowing them to continue business as usual in pre-crisis formats and basically with pre-crisis regulation. The political attempts to attack the banks' "too-big-to-fail" syndrome have so far failed miserably.

This book attempts to reach a wide audience. Everybody does not need to read everything in the book! Someone who is satisfied with a description of how and why the financial crisis came about gets his or her share (every chapter ends with a list of "points to remember"), as well as those who want a deeper analysis of what actually happened, and why. Much material has been placed in appendices in order not to clutter up the narration in the chapter text. There are many references to literature for those who want more information.

Those who, like me and so many others, are furious with the greed that has become a prevalent feature on the financial markets get some more meat on the bones, but also an attempt to modulate the stigmatization of the "crooks" (see front cover). Politicians, and hence ultimately common citizens, as well as shareholders, bear their part of the blame for allowing the financial system to get out of hand and develop the excesses that we have witnessed.

A large number of books have been written on the great financial crisis of 2007–10. Some of them complement the present book and are highly recommended.[4] Many of these will be referred to again and quoted in the text later on.

---

[4] Acharya and Richardson, eds., *Restoring Financial Stability*; Brownell, *Subprime Meltdown*; Cooper, *The Origin of Financial Crises*; Ferguson, *The Ascent of Money*; Foster and Magdoff, *The Great Financial Crisis*; Gorton, *Slapped by the Invisible Hand*; Johnson and Kwak, *13 Bankers*; Kaufman, *The Road to Financial Reformation*; Milne, *The Fall of the House of Credit*; Read, *Global Financial Meltdown*; Reinhart and Rogoff, *This Time Is Different*; Roubini, *Crisis Economics*; Shiller, *The Subprime Solution*; Taylor, *Getting Off Track*; Wolf, *Fixing Global Finance*.

Acknowledgments

A number of friends have been kind enough to read and comment on this book, in its English or Swedish versions. I would like to thank, in particular, Ingrid Bonde (formerly Director-General of the Swedish Financial Supervisory Authority, now CEO of AMF Pension), Sir Callum McCarthy (formerly head of the British Financial Services Authority), Martin Guri (Chief Equity Strategist, Nordea Bank Markets), Peter Jennergren (Professor of Finance, Stockholm School of Economics), Johanna Lybeck Lilja (State Secretary for Financial Markets, Swedish Ministry of Finance), Bo Lundgren (Director-General, the Swedish National Debt Office), Göran Nirdén and Lars Söderlind (the Swedish Financial Supervisory Authority), Björn Wahlroos (Professor of Economics, Chairman of Sampo O/Y, Finland and Chairman, Nordea Bank, Stockholm), Arvid Wallgren (Department for Financial Markets and Institutions, Swedish Ministry of Finance) and Staffan Viotti (Professor of Finance and Chief Advisor to the Governor of the Central Bank of Sweden), as well as several anonymous referees. None of them, or anyone else but myself, is responsible for remaining errors and misconceptions, nor for any of the views or proposals presented.

Abbreviations

ABCP	asset-backed commercial paper
ABS	asset-backed security
ADR	American depository receipt
AIB	Allied Irish Banks
AIF	alternative investment fund
AIG	American International Group
AMA	advanced measurement approach
APF	Asset Purchase Facility
ARM	adjustable rate mortgage
ATS	Alternative Trading System
BCCI	Bank of Credit and Commerce International
BEA	Bureau of Economic Analysis (US Department of Commerce)
BIS	Bank for International Settlements
BofA	Bank of America
CBO	Congressional Budget Office
CCB	China Construction Bank Corp.
CCP	central counter-party
CDO	collateralized debt obligation
CDS	credit default swap
CEBS	Committee of European Banking Supervisors
CEIOPS	Committee of European Insurance and Occupational Pensions Supervisors
CESR	Committee of European Securities Regulators
CFO	Chief Financial Officer
CFTC	Commodity Futures Trading Commission
CIC	China Investment Corporation
CLN	credit-linked note
CME	Chicago Mercantile Exchange
CMO	collateralized mortgage obligation
CoCo bonds	contingent convertible Core Tier 1 securities

COP	Congressional Oversight Panel
CP	commercial paper
CPFF	Commercial Paper Funding Facility
CPSS	Committee on Payment and Settlement Systems
CRR	capital resources requirement
CSD	Central Securities Depository
Danat-bank	Darmstädter und Nationalbank
DeKa	Deutsche Kapitalanlage Deutsche Girozentrale
DGS	depository guarantee scheme
DIDMCA	Depository Institutions Deregulation and Monetary Control Act
DIF	Deposit Insurance Fund
DKK	Danish krone
DTCC	Depository Trust and Clearing Corporation
DTI	debt-to-income ratio
DvP	Delivery vs Payment
EBA	European Banking Authority
EBC	European Banking Committee
EBRD	European Bank for Reconstruction and Development
EBS	Educational Building Society
ECAI	External Credit Assessment Institutions
ECB	European Central Bank
ECN	enhanced capital note
ECOFIN	Economic and Financial Affairs Council
ECOSOC	Economic and Social Committee
EDF	exchange-traded fund
EEA	European Economic Area
EFTA	European Free Trade Association
EIB	European Investment Bank
EIOPA	European Insurance and Occupational Pensions Authority
EMCF	European Multilateral Clearing Facility
EPS	earnings per share
ESC	European Securities Committee
ESFS	European System of Financial Supervision
ESMA	European Securities and Markets Authority
ESRB	European Systemic Risk Board
FAIF	funds of alternative investment fund

Fannie Mae/FNMA	Federal National Mortgage Association
FASB	Financial Accounting Standards Board
FAT	financial activity tax
FDIC	Federal Deposit Insurance Corporation
Fed	Federal Reserve Bank
FHA	Federal Housing Administration
FHFA	Federal Housing Finance Agency
FHLMC/Freddie Mac	Federal Home Loan Mortgage Corporation
FICC	Fixed Income Clearing Corporation
FINRA	Financial Industry Regulatory Authority
FIRREA	Financial Institutions Reform, Recovery and Enforcement Act
FNMA/Fannie Mae	Federal National Mortgage Association
FOMC	Federal Open Market Committee
FPC	Financial Policy Committee
FRA	forward rate agreement
FRB	Federal Reserve Board
Freddie Mac/FHLMC	Federal Home Loan Mortgage Corporation
FROB	Fondo de Reestructuración Ordenada Bancaria
FSA	Financial Services Authority
FSB	Financial Stability Board
FSCS	Financial Services Compensation Scheme
FSLIC	Federal Savings and Loan Insurance Corporation
FSOC	Financial Stability Oversight Council
GAO	General Accounting Office (Government Accountability Office from 2004)
GDP	gross domestic product
Ginnie Mae/GNMA	Government National Mortgage Association
GMAC	General Motors Acceptance Corporation (Ally Financial Inc. since 2009)
GNMA/Ginnie Mae	Government National Mortgage Association
GSE	government-sponsored enterprise
HGAA	Hypo Group Alpe Adria
HSBC	Hongkong and Shanghai Banking Corporation
HUD	Department of Housing and Urban Development
IASB	International Accounting Standards Board
IBCA	International Bank Credit Analyst

IBJ	Industrial Bank of Japan
ICE Europe	InterContinental Exchange
ICG	individual capital guidance
IMF	International Monetary Fund
IOSCO	International Organization of Securities Commissions
IPO	initial public offering
IRB	internal ratings-based approach
IRR	interest rate risk
IRS	interest rate swap
ISDA	International Swaps and Derivatives Association
ISE	International Securities Exchange
ISK	Icelandic krone
KfW	Kredietanstalt für Wiederaufbau
KOP	Kansallis Osake Pankki
LBBW	Landesbank Baden-Württemberg
LTCB	Long-Term Credit Bank of Japan
LTCM	Long-Term Capital Management
LTV	loan-to-value
MBS	mortgage-backed security
MIFID	Markets in Financial Instruments Directive
MMIFF	Money Market Investor Funding Facility
MMMF	Money Market Mutual Fund Liquidity Facility
MTF	multilateral trading facility
NAB	National Australia Bank
NAM	National Association of Manufacturers
NAMA	National Asset Management Agency (Ireland)
NAV	net asset value
NBER	National Bureau of Economic Research
NRSRO	Nationally Recognized Statistical Rating Organization
NSCC	National Securities Clearing Corporation
OCC	Office of the Comptroller of the Currency
OECD	Organisation for Economic Cooperation and Development
OTC	over-the-counter
OTS	Office of Thrift Supervision
PAC	Prompt Corrective Action

PDCF	Primary Dealer Credit Facility
P/E	price-earnings (ratio)
PIIGS (countries)	Portugal, Ireland, Italy, Greece, Spain
PPIP	Public Private Investment Program
PvP	Payment vs Payment
RCB	Resolution and Collection Bank Corporation
REIT	real estate investment trust
REMIC	real estate mortgage investment conduit
repo	repurchase agreement
RFC	Reconstruction Finance Corporation
RTC	Resolution Trust Corporation
SEC	Securities and Exchange Commission
SEF	swap execution facility
SEK	Swedish krona
SIGTARP	Special Inspector General for the Troubled Asset Relief Program
SIV	structured investment vehicle
SNB	Schweizerische Nationalbank
SoFFin	SonderFonds Finanzmarktstabilisierung
SPV	special-purpose vehicle
SRO	self-regulatory organization
TAF	Term Auction Facility
TALF	Term Asset-Backed Securities Loan Facility
TARP	Troubled Assets Relief Program
TCE	tangible common equity/true core equity
TLGP	Temporary Liquidity Guarantee Program
TRORS	total rate of return swap
TRS	total return swap
TSLF	Term Securities Lending Facility
UBF	Union Bank of Finland
UBS	Union Bank of Switzerland
UCITS	Undertakings for Collective Investments in Transferable Securities
UKFI	UK Financial Investments
VaR	Value at Risk
WaMu	Washington Mutual
WestLB	Westdeutsche Landesbank

1 | Introduction

The ups and downs of the business cycle

Despite all the claims about the demise of the business cycle, it lives on. Every five years, the economies of the developed world experience a recession of varying intensity. In popular terms, a recession is defined as two consecutive quarters with falling gross domestic product (GDP). To be more precise, a recession in the USA occurs whenever a specifically appointed group of researchers at the National Bureau of Economic Research (NBER) says so. The decision they take depends not only on the growth rate, but also the unemployment rate and other factors.

Since the first recession was identified in 1854, thirty-two full business cycles had occurred before the present one, the average cycle thus having a duration of 4.6 years. The downturn (recession phase) lasted on average 17 months and the upturn (expansion phase) for 38 months. The latest identified low points in the cycle in the USA took place in March 1975, July 1980, March 1991 and November 2001. The 10-year uninterrupted expansion between 1991 and 2001 is unique, since the period lacks a clearly defined recession, even though the growth rate slowed in the middle of the period. The expansion from the autumn of 2001 was also much longer-lasting than usual. According to the NBER, the recent recession started in December 2007, after a 6-year expansion phase. But the latest recession has also been longer than average. It ended in June of 2009, according to an announcement by the NBER in September 2010. This would mean a recession of 18 months, the longest downturn since the 43-month Great Depression, and longer than the 16-month oil-price-induced contractions of 1973–5 and 1981–2.

A stable macroeconomy induces more financial risk-taking

One of the contentions in this introduction and the next two chapters is that the long period of stable and unusually high growth rates led to a false sense of security on the financial markets. Uncertainty, as measured by the volatility index of stock market prices or interest rate spreads of risky assets ("junk bonds") versus government bonds or prices of credit default swaps (CDS contracts; to be discussed in much more detail later), fell to unprecedented levels during this long, benevolent period.

This false sense of security and well-being led governments, as well as banks, investors and ordinary consumers, to speculative behavior of gigantic proportions. The result, as growth became negative and asset markets crashed, was a huge debt burden, leading to defaults and bankruptcies of overborrowed households and corporations (GM, Chrysler ...), as well as banks in a number of countries (Lehman Brothers and Washington Mutual in the USA; Northern Rock and RBS in the UK; Hypovereinsbank and Landesbank Sachsen in Germany; Fortis Bank in the Benelux; Erste Bank in Austria; Anglo Irish Bank in Ireland; Roskilde Bank in Denmark), and indeed also sovereign states (Iceland, Greece ...). Even the USA has not been immune; the ratio of debt to GDP is set to surpass 100 percent in 2012, according to forecasts from the International Monetary Fund (IMF). This has never happened before in peacetime.

Yet it is surprising that the risk of an oncoming financial crisis was seen as low or even non-existent by almost all observers. We know from history that every other registered recession has been accompanied by or created by or given rise to a financial crisis – which is the chicken and which is the egg has varied from time to time. In the thorough analysis in his classic book *Manias, Panics and Crashes*, Charles P. Kindleberger identified thirty-eight serious financial crises in the world from 1618 to 1998, of which eleven occurred during the last 100 years, starting with the crisis of 1907, hence a financial crisis every 10 years on average. In the mid-1970s, the crisis was occasioned by currency fluctuations connected with the breakdown of the Bretton Woods regime of fixed exchange rates, aggravated by the rise in oil prices (OPEC I). The bankruptcy of the German Herstatt Bank in 1974 is the most well-known bank collapse of this period. The middle of the 1980s saw the US bank and thrift crisis, after a wave of deregulations allowed banks to move away from their traditional home markets, towards new products, new markets and new customers. The result was a bubble, particularly in commercial property. When it imploded, almost 4,000 banks were knocked down; the then seventh largest bank in the USA, Continental Illinois, was nationalized in

1984. We had to wait until September 2008, and the bankruptcy of the savings bank Washington Mutual (the 39th largest bank in the world and also number 7 in the USA), for an even larger bank collapse. From the beginning of 2007 until the third quarter of 2010, over 300 US banks or savings banks were closed, placed under public conservatorship, recapitalized by the government or merged with stronger partners with the support and encouragement of the supervisory authorities, together with three of the largest and best-known investment banks, Bear Stearns, Merrill Lynch and Lehman Brothers. The number of failed banks may seem small from a historical perspective, but, as we will discover, we find in their midst five of the fifteen largest US banks in 2007, the year the crisis started.

Kindleberger does not discuss the financial crises in the Nordic countries since they were regional in character. They are analyzed in this book, however, not least since "the Swedish way" (i.e. total nationalization rather than a limited capital injection and part ownership) has become in vogue in the debate on solutions to the recent financial crisis. Kindleberger wound up his book with the Asian banking crises in 1997, which, though regional, were much more severe than any of the other crises studied in this book, with the exception of that of Iceland today.[1] The next crisis was the Russian insolvency in August 1998. In itself, this was a minor event, given the (then) small size of the Russian economy. But the Russian problems revealed and highlighted the existence of a new financial phenomenon, so far relatively unknown, the so-called "shadow banking system," and, in particular, hedge funds. A hedge fund called Long-Term Capital Management (LTCM) experienced serious problems. The fund, led by, inter alios, two winners of the Nobel Prize in Economics, had speculated that credit risks were waning, and hence that spreads between interest rates on such assets as Italian vs German bonds, Russian vs US dollar-denominated bonds, mortgage bonds vs sovereigns, would fall. The Russian collapse led to widening instead of diminishing spreads and the fund lost great amounts of money. At the end, its capital was down to $600 million, to support assets of $129 billion and a leverage (gearing ratio) of 215! On top of this, LTCM had positions in derivatives, mainly interest swaps and moreover mostly uncollateralized, of $1,250 billion, corresponding to one-tenth of the entire world market for rate swaps.

---

[1] Kindleberger and Aliber, *Manias, Panics and Crashes*.

The most exhaustive recent survey of financial crises, by Reinhart and Rogoff, identifies a great number (296 to be exact) of financial crises in sixty-six countries over a span of 800 years.[2] Their book is a must-read for any serious student of financial panics. Their focus in the main part of the book is on government defaults in developing economies (including today's developed countries at earlier stages in their history), and is thus not of primary relevance for the financial crisis of today, which has been almost exclusively a rich-country phenomenon, where no sovereign country has gone openly bankrupt (so far, that is; Greece or Ireland may have defaulted after this book went to the printers).

Reinhart and Rogoff also study the 138 banking crises occurring after the Second World War. Again, their main interest is the effect of a banking crisis on the sovereign country's growth rate and an increase in government budget deficit and debt. Interestingly enough, however, they show that banking crises in developed and developing nations have two features in common. One of their main findings, for instance, is that a surge in capital imports is prevalent in the run-up to banking crises. As we shall see in Chapter 8, this was indeed a major feature of the Southeast Asian crises in the 1990s (mainly Thailand, South Korea and Indonesia). But the recent crises in countries like the USA, the UK or Spain can also be said to be connected with a huge amount of capital imports, since the countries in question were running large-scale current account deficits.

The other feature common to banking crises in both developed and developing nations is a surge in the price of property, residential and/or commercial. We will come back to these two important features in the following chapters.

A financial crisis can only be triggered by factors unknown to (most) market participants. If these factors were known, there would have been no crisis, since the market would have adjusted itself to the circumstances. This does not mean that warning signals were not visible to the informed observer, only that the majority were happily ignorant. While some well-known academic seers, such as Professor Robert Shiller of Yale University, Professor Daniel Roubini of the Stern School of Business at the New York University and Dr. Henry Kaufman (former Chief Economist of the investment bank Salomon Brothers), warned of

---

[2] Reinhart and Rogoff, *This Time Is Different*.

the oncoming storm, they were treated like Cassandras and ignored.[3] Comforting words came from the Federal Reserve Chairman Alan Greenspan and his successor Ben Bernanke, as well as from the Secretary of the Treasury under President George W. Bush, Henry "Hank" Paulson, not least trustworthy to the general public, since he came from the position of CEO of the most respected Wall Street firm, Goldman Sachs.

Paulson stated in August 2007 that the problem in the mortgage sector, due to failing subprime mortgages (to be defined in Chapter 4), was "largely contained." Four months later, Countrywide Financial, the largest mortgage bank in the USA, was on the brink of failure and was absorbed into Bank of America. The year before, Countrywide had had a market share of 20 percent of all outstanding residential mortgage loans in the USA. In July 2008, after the failure of the fifth largest investment bank, Bear Stearns, and the seventh largest mortgage bank, IndyMac, Paulson said: "It's a safe banking system, a sound banking system. Our regulators are on top of it. This is a very manageable situation." He continued a month later by stating that the government had no intention of injecting fresh capital into the two semi-public mortgage giants Fannie Mae and Freddie Mac (which are so-called government sponsored enterprises, or GSEs), responsible for half the mortgage market in the USA. Within a month, both had to be taken into government conservatorship and given potentially $400 billion in new capital, while the largest investment bank, Merrill Lynch, was saved only by being bought by Bank of America. Another of the five largest investment banks, Lehman Brothers, was allowed to go bankrupt, and the largest insurance company in the world, AIG, was saved only by government intervention and direct loans from the Federal Reserve.

You can fool some people all of the time . . .

Unfortunately, people want to be comforted and have a built-in tendency to trust their elected officials. As emphasized by Robert Shiller and George Akerlof (Nobel Prize winner in 2001), in their highly readable book on the "animal spirits" that guide human behavior,

---

[3] We will meet them again many times in later chapters. Cassandra was the daughter of King Priam of Troy. Possessed with prophetic powers, she had been cursed by the lovesick but spurned Apollo, so that no one would believe her.

confidence in one's fellow human beings is as contagious as a disease and may arise or vanish in the most mysterious ways.[4] Akerlof has also stressed the importance of information asymmetry, when investors/ buyers know much less about the product being sold than the issuer/ seller.[5] Indeed, Goldman Sachs was sued by the Securities and Exchange Commission (SEC) in April 2010 for selling and marketing products to unsuspecting clients, products that the employees in the firm privately called "junk," and did not tell investors buying the product that Goldman Sachs themselves were selling the bonds short – that is, speculating in a falling price of these securities.[6] Goldman Sachs has also been sued for breach of trust by private investors, such as the German Landesbank Baden-Württemberg.

The adages that "some people can be fooled all of the time" and "all the people can be fooled some of the time" are of course hardly new.[7] Akerlof and Shiller would have done well to quote the Scottish journalist Charles Mackay, whose book *Extraordinary Popular Delusions and the Madness of Crowds* really told the whole story of the present financial folly in the year 1841, well over 160 years before it broke out:

We find that whole communities suddenly fix their minds upon one object, and go mad in its pursuit; that millions of people become simultaneously impressed by one delusion, and run after it, till their attention is caught by some new folly more captivating than the first ... Money, again, has often been a cause of the delusion of multitudes. Sober nations have all at once become desperate gamblers, and risked almost their existence upon the turn of a piece of paper ... Men, it has been well said, think in herds; it will be seen that they go mad in herds, while they only recover their senses slowly, and one by one.[8]

---

[4] Akerlof and Shiller, *Animal Spirits*, p. 56.
[5] The classic article is Akerlof, The market for "lemons." A "lemon" is slang for a lousy car with a shiny exterior.
[6] The case was settled in July 2010, with Goldman Sachs paying a record fine of $550 million.
[7] But, as Milton Friedman famously reminded us, "you cannot fool all the people all of the time." All three quotes are originally from Abraham Lincoln.
[8] Mackay, *Extraordinary Popular Delusions*. The quote is from the preface to the 1852 edition. The book is eminently readable, describing and deriding not only John Law and his Mississippi scheme, the South Sea Bubble and tulipomania in Holland, but also such frenzies as the crusades in the eleventh and twelfth centuries and the witch hunts of the sixteenth and seventeenth centuries.

In the situation ruling just before the outbreak of the most recent financial crisis, it was well-known that the housing markets in some countries were loan-financed to a greater extent than in other countries. In the USA, housing loans in 2007 amounted to an equivalent of 75 percent of GDP. In the UK, the equivalent figure was 83 percent of GDP, to be contrasted with only 18 percent of GDP in Italy, 30 percent in France and 54 percent in Germany. These data were, of course, published and known. What was less well known was that some 10 percent of the amount outstanding and 20 percent of new loans granted in the USA were so-called subprime loans, extended to persons with earlier instances of payment delinquencies and/or low incomes in relation to the size of the loan. Often these people had bought the house on pure speculation, with no downpayment at all. Indeed, the US National Association of Realtors found that in 2005 and 2006, 40 percent of those who bought their first house took out mortgages with no downpayment whatsoever. They also benefited from initial beneficially low rates of interest, so called "teaser rates," which were to be adjusted after a few years. It was the resetting of these advantageous interest rate terms at the end of 2006 that was to trigger the "subprime crisis."

But the unknown did not stop here. For another new factor was a characteristic feature of the financial crisis of 2007–10. Earlier banking crises had been local – a bank with excessive or risky lending went bust. This time round, the delinquent loans turned up in the most unexpected places. The reason was that the vast majority of mortgage loans in the USA, and some in the UK, had been "securitized" – that is, sold off in the form of mortgage-backed securities (MBSs) or collateralized debt obligations (CDOs) to companies formally independent from the bank (structured investment vehicles, or SIVs), which, in turn, had financed the purchase by borrowing at short term (for instance, on asset-backed commercial paper, or ABCP). The securities purchased had often been given the highest possible rating (AAA/Aaa) by rating companies such as Standard & Poor's or Moody's, with, as it would turn out, vastly unrealistic assumptions as to borrowers' low rate of default, and also a vastly overstated confidence in the insurance written to safeguard such bonds and guarantee their payments, CDSs. Not only banks, but also insurance companies such as AIG, then the largest insurance company in the world, landed themselves on the brink of bankruptcy by means of such products. All the major insurance companies in the USA that specialized in guaranteeing mortgage products (so-called "monolines") vanished.

The outstanding stock of mortgage loans in the USA amounted to just over $10,000 billion at the end of 2008, the year crisis struck. Bonds issued with these mortgages as underlying collateral were equivalent to over four-fifths of this sum. Since the bonds were (mostly) AAA-rated but still had a higher yield than government bonds, they were attractive investments not only for US investors but for investors worldwide, in particular, pension funds, which are precluded by law from investing in low-rated securities. The three main Icelandic banks had purchased US mortgage bonds and other foreign currency securities for an amount corresponding to five times Iceland's GDP! All three banks were later nationalized. The German savings bank Landesbank Sachsen, owned and guaranteed by the state of Sachsen, had purchased US mortgage-related securities for $26 billion; the bank's equity corresponded to $1 billion. Under threat of bankruptcy, the bank was merged with the larger Landesbank Baden-Württemberg, while the residents of the relatively poor, former East German state of Sachsen were stuck with the bill for the excesses, amounting to €650 per inhabitant, irrespective of age. Not to be outdone, also state-guaranteed Westdeutsche Landesbank in Düsseldorf bought US mortgage bonds for $114 billion on a capital base which amounted to $10 billion. More examples will be given in the body of the book later on.

How much will this cost banks and taxpayers?

From the beginning of 2007 through mid-2010, the world's banks have written off well over $1,700 billion for actual or expected credit losses related to the housing market, corresponding to almost half of their capital at the end of 2007. Many banks have written off sums much larger than their capital, though they have been recapitalized by their owners and/or by the government in the process. Insurance companies add some $300 billion to these losses. The IMF estimated in April 2009 that the final bill might amount to over $4,000 billion (lowered to a new estimate of $3,400 billion in September 2009 and to $2,200 billion in October 2010). (See Figure 1.1.)

Realized write-downs through mid-2010 were, as seen in the graph (left-hand scale), about $700 billion in the USA, $350 billion in the UK, $400 billion in the euro area, with minor amounts in other European countries and Asia. But given the delinquent assets in question, the rate

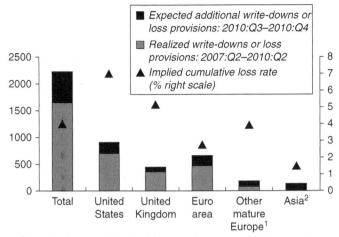

¹Includes Denmark, Iceland, Norway, Sweden and Switzerland.
²Includes Australia, Hong Kong SAR, Japan, New Zealand and Singapore.

Figure 1.1 Realized and expected write-downs or loss provisions for banks (by region, $ billion and % of loans)
Source: International Monetary Fund, *Global Financial Stability Report* (October 2010)

of loss is seen to be (right-hand scale) 6.5 percent in the USA, 5 percent in the UK, 2.5 percent in the euro area, 4 percent in other European countries (such as Switzerland, Denmark and other Nordic countries), but only 1.5 percent in Asia.

In capital injections, loans and guarantees from the various states, banks have received potential sums of over $20,000 billion ($20 trillion), a figure that may be compared with total GDP in the USA and the European Union put together, of $32,000 billion in 2008 (Figure 1.2). We will come back to more detailed data later. It should be noted that the figures in Figure 1.2 understate the full amount of government support, since they do not include the deposit guarantee system, despite the fact that the various sovereign states guarantee depositors should the accumulated insurance funds prove insufficient. With these guarantees included, the total amount of support exceeded the level of GDP in both the USA and the UK.

Actual gross costs to the taxpayer have been much lower, some $51 billion in the USA, according to a Treasury forecast from October 2010. For the UK, the loss was set at £117 billion (according to the National

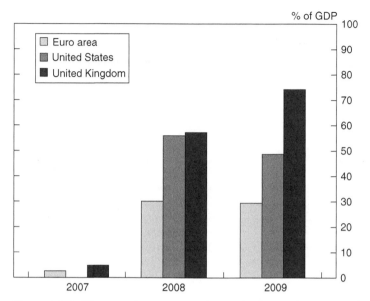

Figure 1.2 Public sector interventions during the financial crisis (% of GDP)
Source: Bank of England, *Financial Stability Report* (December 2009)

Audit Office) in December 2009).[9] The British Treasury calculated at the same time that the final cost might be only £10 billion, down from earlier estimates of between £20 billion and £50 billion. The Treasury lowered the estimate still further to a net loss of just £2.4 billion in June 2010.

Well over a million jobs have been lost in the financial sector worldwide.

Recapitalization by taxpayers, issues of fresh equity and a return to profitability actually allowed banks to raise their capital standards, even during the crisis. Figure 1.3 shows Tier 1 capital (to be defined in more detail later, but basically equal to equity) in relation to risk-weighted assets in the major European countries. The ratio actually rose somewhat in 2008, and even more so in 2009, to reach 12 percent in the UK. This may be contrasted with the legal minimum of just 4 percent.

---

[9] National Audit Office, Maintaining financial stability.

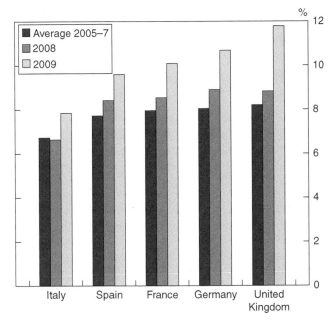

Figure 1.3 Tier 1 capital ratios for selected European banking systems, 2005–2009
Source: Bank of England, *Financial Stability Report* (June 2010)

The development in the USA has been similar, as shown in Figure 1.4. Tier 1 ratios on average have been raised from 9–10 percent to above 11 percent.

The macroeconomic scenario

It will be evident from this book that we have escaped from the worst financial crisis since the 1930s relatively unscathed. Those who are inclined to think that the macroeconomic picture is also reminiscent of the Great Depression should think again. In today's crisis, the unemployment rate in the USA climaxed at just above 10 percent, to be compared with 25 percent in the 1930s. Still, the IMF has calculated that the combination of the financial crash and the debt crisis has led to a loss of 30 million jobs worldwide.

GDP fell by 2.4 percent in the USA in 2009, compared with a fall of 25 percent 80 years ago. The UK was somewhat more affected, with

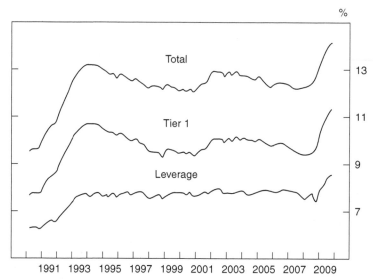

Figure 1.4 Tier 1 and total capital ratios in the USA, 1989–2009
Note: Leverage ratio is Tier 1 capital over total (unweighted) assets, to be presented later.
Source: *Federal Reserve Bulletin* (May 2010)

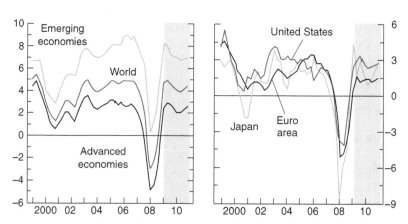

Figure 1.5 Growth rates of real gross domestic product, selected areas, 2000–2011
Source: International Monetary Fund, *World Economic Outlook* (October 2010)

GDP falling by 4.9 percent in 2009. The crisis has been much deeper in developed countries than in emerging economies. (See Figure 1.5.) The inflation rate hovers around zero, whereas the 1930s saw the price level fall by a quarter.

Other differences pertain to the housing market. Some 10 percent of all US borrowers were delinquent in mid-2010 – that is, more than 30 days overdue on their payments.[10] Some 5 percent were seriously delinquent – that is, more than 90 days overdue. In 1934 half of mortgage borrowing was delinquent. Foreclosures – that is, forced auctions of houses where the owners were delinquent – affected 13 percent of all borrowers in 1933, compared to some 5 percent today (through October 2010).

The other major difference from the Great Depression is that governments and central banks – albeit with some lag – have reacted in the main quite correctly this time round (with the notable exception of the decision to let the investment bank Lehman Brothers fail, unexpectedly and uncontrollably). It helped having a Chairman of the Federal Reserve Board who gained his academic laurels by analyzing the mistakes made under the Depression! Monetary policy has been eased by lower interest rates, by easier terms of lending, by lending also to non-banks such as AIG, and by purchases of government bonds and other financial assets, even mortgage bonds and commercial paper. States have extended capital injections and guarantees to banks, as well as to other companies deemed to be "too big to fail" (AIG, General Motors, Chrysler). Fiscal policy has been activated for the largest investments in infrastructure in 50 years, and taxes have been lowered. Moreover, discussions and coordinated policies between countries ("jaw-jaw" rather than "war-war," to quote Winston Churchill) have avoided what was probably the single most important factor behind the Great Depression, trade wars and "beggar-my-neighbor" policies.

---

[10] The 30-day delinquency rate was 7 percent for prime loans, but 25 percent for subprime loans.

2 | Financial crises in the USA and Europe, but not in Asia

Origins of the crises

A financial crisis is, by definition, unexpected. If it were anticipated, it would not occur. There will appear a sudden flare of fire, even though there might have been some smoke visible before. Today's financial crisis, the worst in 80 years, had been smoldering since the end of 2006. But "the firemen" had been on guard and prevented the flames from blazing forth. The central banks, guided by the actions of the Federal Reserve, had lowered their target interest rates in order to enable banks to lower their lending rates in turn, in particular with regard to housing. They had also injected gradually larger amounts of liquidity into the system. The Fed Funds rate, which is the major monetary policy weapon of the US central bank, was 5.25 percent in the beginning of 2007. Two years later it had been lowered to basically zero (and in the autumn of 2010, that is where it still is). This is the lowest central bank lending rate recorded over the 95 years that the central bank has existed (for the "Fed" was actually only founded in 1913, after the great crisis of 1907). Other major central banks, such as the Bank of England and the European Central Bank (ECB), were only paces behind.

In a smoothly functioning economy, banks lend to one another in the interbank market. These loans are extremely short-term, most often just for a day (or rather for a night), evening out liquidity imbalances in the system. A bank with excess reserves lends money to a bank that is short on cash. So long as the banks regard one another as being perfectly safe, the interbank rate will lie marginally above the rate at which banks may borrow in the central bank. At the beginning of 2007, before the crisis, the spread between the Fed Funds rate and 1-month Euro-dollar in the interbank market was 5–10 basis points (0.05–0.10 percentage points). The Fed Funds rate was 5.25 percent and the interbank rate 5.30–5.35 percent. The events during 2007 and spring 2008 (to be described later in this chapter) persuaded the Fed to lower its rate to 2 percent, while the spread widened somewhat; the interbank rate in July to August 2008 was around 2.65 percent. On September 18, confidence evaporated in the entire system, sending the interbank rate from 3.75 percent to 6 percent on a single day, tantamount to saying that banks no longer trusted each other and basically refused to lend. (See Figure 2.1.)

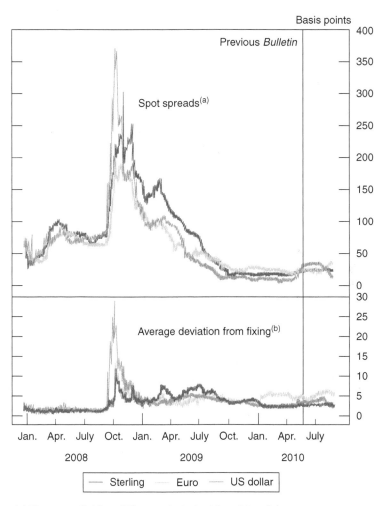

(a) Three-month Libor-OIS spreads derived from Libor fixings
(b) Average absolute deviation of individual panel members' 3-month
    Libor submissions from the Libor fixing

Figure 2.1 Spread between 3- and 6-month interbank rates and expected central bank lending rates (OIS spread)
Source: Bank of England, *Quarterly Bulletin* (2010: III), Chart 4

What had happened was that one of the major investment banks in the USA, Lehman Brothers, with a history dating back to 1850, had suspended payments and sought protection from its creditors under chapter 11 in the US Bankruptcy Code. The bank had total assets of $691 billion, making the bankruptcy by far the largest ever in the world, much larger than the collapse of Washington Mutual, at $328 billion, or the $63 billion in assets connected with the failure of the energy company Enron in 2001, or the $104 billion in WorldCom the year after. Lehman's stock price fell by 90 percent over the day to virtually zero.

The main driving force behind the events was that the central bank, which earlier that year had supported two other investment banks in difficulty and helped them merge with stronger partners (indeed Merrill Lynch was saved during the weekend of 13–14 September, only the day before the Lehman crash), this time refused to assist. One might be excused for thinking that Lehman would have been regarded as "too big to fail," that the central bank would normally have supported its liquidity, since the bank was of systemic importance to the entire financial system.

Or maybe it was all just a misunderstanding. The regulatory authorities may have assumed that the rising problems over the year and its effect on investment banks such as Bear Stearns and Merrill Lynch would have led other actors such as Lehman to decrease their risk-taking. Hence the big bank no longer posed a problem, they may have thought. But Lehman and the other big banks had instead drawn the conclusion that saving (the relatively small) Bear Stearns in the spring meant that the Federal Reserve and the other supervisory authorities regarded all the major investment banks as "too big to fail." Hence no actions were taken, and business continued as usual. Citibank's former CEO, "Chuck" Prince, expressed the matter very succinctly in 2007, just before he was ousted from his position: "When the music stops, in terms of liquidity, things will get complicated. But as long as the music is playing, you've got to get up and dance. We're still dancing."[1]

Maybe the authorities also wanted to make a scapegoat out of Lehman Brothers, as a warning to the others. Many economists, as well as members of Congress, had warned of the dire consequences to follow should the central bank always save banks in trouble. This

[1] Interview in the *Financial Times*, July 9, 2007.

would lead to a situation of even more risk-taking from the banks in the future, a reaction economists call "moral hazard." Or maybe the decision not to intervene was caused by personalities. The CEO and Chairman of the Board of Lehman, Richard S. Fuld, Jr., called "the Gorilla," insisted up to the very day of bankruptcy that "his" bank had no problems that it could not solve on its own. Fuld was in 2007 the best-paid banker in the world. His salary was a meager $0.6 million, but his bonus for that year amounted to $73 million.[2]

Lehman Brothers was an investment bank, not a commercial bank or a savings bank with direct lending to housing or taking deposits from the public. Yet the bank had a severe exposure to so-called subprime loans (which will be presented in greater detail in Chapter 4), since Lehman was one of the major participants in the process called securitization which transformed these mortgage loans into securities. Not only other banks which were Lehman's counter-parties in all these operations suffered, but so did hundreds of hedge funds that had invested in Lehman's bonds and also used Lehman as their major counter-party in derivatives operations such as CDSs, and also as their chief bank for funding.

Exposures created by investments in mortgage-related securities had often been protected by credit insurance (CDSs will be presented in greater detail in Chapter 5). The failure of Lehman led to the next crisis a few days later, when the then largest insurance company in the world and the eighteenth largest company in the world, American International Group (AIG), got into trouble. The company had a leading position as writer – that is, guarantor – of CDSs, not least to Lehman's customers. AIG was by itself also a major investor in mortgage-related bonds, so-called CDOs, issued by Lehman and others. Lehman's bankruptcy triggered a lowering (downrating), on September 16, of the official creditworthiness, or rating, of AIG by both major rating companies, Moody's and Standard & Poor's. This in turn led to demands from its counter-parties that AIG post another $18 billion in collateral for its CDS contracts, something which the company was unable to do.[3] AIG's application for creditor protection under chapter

---

[2] The inside story of events leading up to the failure of Lehman Brothers is well told in Sorkin, *Too Big to Fail*.

[3] Indeed, until March 2005, AIG was rated AAA and did not have to post any collateral at all on its CDS positions.

11 on Wednesday September 17 was the triggering event in the explosion of mistrust. The interbank rate rose the next day by several percentage points, as we saw in Figure 2.1. An index showing how banks assessed the credit risk of their counter-parties trebled over the day. Yet it had already risen tenfold from the beginning of 2007 to fall 2008.

In its capacity as "lender of last resort," the Federal Reserve normally lends only to banks who are members of the Federal Reserve System. But under the Federal Reserve Act, the Fed may, under "unusual and exigent circumstances," lend to "any individual or partnership or corporation," as long as the loans are secured "to the satisfaction" of the Fed (Section 13 [3]). Using this authority for the first time since the 1930s, the Fed extended a credit line of $85 billion to AIG. The loan was secured by warrants on almost 80 percent of AIG's stock. But the loan was not sufficient to calm the markets. When compared with the total size of the CDS market – $57,325 billion in notional outstanding in the middle of 2008 – it was a drop in the ocean. Even comparing with the total credit risk – that is, after netting and correction for double counting – in the CDS market of over $3,000 billion, it was nothing. Lehman's outstanding CDS contracts alone were estimated to cost several hundred billions of dollars to settle.[4] That the amount was insufficient is also evident from the fact that in mid-November 2008, the amount of help to AIG was raised to $152.5 billion in capital injections and loans. And in March 2009, the amount was raised by a further $30 billion, to a total of $182.5 billion. A sum corresponding to 1.3 percent of the entire GDP of the USA was handed in aid to a single privately owned company.

What to find in the rest of this book

By spring 2009, the actions taken by the central banks and governments, as described in the appendix to this chapter and in Chapter 6 (liquidity enhancements) and Chapter 7 (capital injections), had almost restored liquidity in the interbank market to the level when it all had begun 6 months before. The spread between the Fed Funds rate and 1-month Euro-dollar had reverted to 25–40 basis points, marginally higher than what was considered normal two years earlier. In the rest

---

[4] As will be discussed later, AIG paid $93 billion to counter-parties in early 2009 to settle some of the contracts outstanding, mostly on CDS contracts.

of the present chapter, we will give the reader a chronological narration of the evolving crisis and the reactions by the authorities – central banks, governments, supervisory authorities – to counteract the worst financial crisis that the world had seen since 1907. Even if the macroeconomic environment during the Great Depression of 1929–33 was in much more serious trouble than is the case today, the crisis of 1907 is still the one most reminiscent of today's crisis, with its loss of confidence between agents on the financial markets, and hence breakdown of the interbank market and consequent lack of liquidity.

Today's financial crisis was triggered by problems in the housing markets of countries such as the USA, the UK, Australia, Spain, Ireland and Iceland, when "bubbles" created by house prices which had more than doubled collapsed. But in parallel with falling prices on residential property (to which we return in Chapter 3 and 4), the stock markets also fell all over the world. From a peak in October 2007, total capitalization on the world's stock markets collapsed from over $63,000 billion to $28,600 billion at the low point in February 2009.[5] The NASDAQ index fell by over 50 percent, and developing markets' indices by vastly larger percentages. Interestingly enough, the falls in stock prices were of about the same magnitude as those experienced in the implosion of the "dotcom" bubble in 2000–2, despite widely different macroeconomic conditions. At the peak in March 2000, the price-earnings (P/E) ratio on the broad US index S&P 500 had risen to above 40, and to over 400 (sic) on NASDAQ.[6] The average P/E number over the last 120 years in the USA is around 15. A correction was inevitable and long overdue. This time round, evaluations were quite normal, marginally above the historical average, yet the markets collapsed under the double impact of the financial crisis and the resulting recession.

There is another, more important, difference between the stock market bubble of 2000 and the housing bubble of 2007. Thanks to the fact that the excessive values on the stock markets had not, other than marginally, been followed by increased borrowing from households, the bubble could be pricked with only minor effects on the real

[5] Data are given by the World Federation of Exchanges at www.world-exchanges.org/WFE/home.Asp
[6] Robert Shiller provides the data and background to this bubble in his acclaimed book *Irrational Exuberance*. Updates can be found at www.irrationalexuberance.com

economy. Only one quarter, the third quarter of 2001, saw negative growth in the USA, and this was due more to the terrorist attacks on the World Trade Center on September 11 than to falling share prices. In annual terms, GDP growth receded to 0.8 percent and unemployment rose to 6.3 percent. This time, the bubble has been heavily mortgaged, a fact to which we will return in Chapter 4. The consequence was a much more severe downturn when households were forced to dampen their consumption in order to raise their savings rates. Growth was sharply negative in most OECD (Organisation for Economic Cooperation and Development) countries in 2009. Unemployment in the USA had risen above the peak of 2003 and peaked at 10 percent, the highest level in 25 years. Still, this is *not* a repeat performance of the Great Depression, something which is discussed in Chapters 6 and 8.

While the major uncertainty on the money markets occurred in September to October 2008 and has since rescinded, the stock market took a new hit on the gradually worsening economic news in 2009. Stock markets dived 35 percent during the money market collapse, and another 25 percent in January to February 2009. This fall is not unique; it has happened before and will happen again. What *was* new were the dramatic ups and downs on the stock markets, 10 percent up one day and 10 percent down the next. This volatility was the result of the interaction of the financial crisis with the macroeconomic recession. Figure 2.2 shows the increase in the VIX volatility to figures above

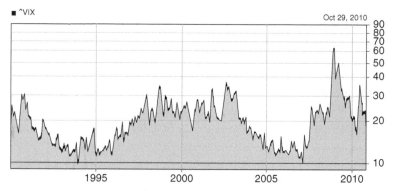

Figure 2.2 Implicit volatility (%) in the option on the S&P future on Chicago Board Options Exchange (CBOE), January 1990–October 2010
Source: Yahoo

90 percent on individual days in October 2008. This may be compared with 45 percent, even when terrorists crashed into the World Trade Center on September 11, 2001.[7]

But the graph also shows the extremely low volatility levels of around 10 percent, both in the mid-1990s and 10 years later. Volatility and risk are two sides of the same coin. To say that volatility was unusually low is therefore identical to saying that the price of risk was unusually low. The low price on risk led to a higher level of risk-taking, and the consequence was the stock market bubble that collapsed in 2000 and the housing bubble which imploded in 2007. The role of the central bank(s) in fertilizing these bubbles will be taken up in Chapter 6.

Chapter 3 will combine theory and practice as concerns the various measures of risk. Which have been the most useful definitions in theory of terms such as risk and financial crisis, and were the warning signals provided by the theories ignored?

Chapter 4 will describe how the housing market for so-called sub-prime and Alt-A loans grew like a rolling snowball in the beginning of the new century. But not only mortgage loans grew dramatically. Over 80 percent of all US mortgage loans outstanding at the end of 2008 had been securitized and transformed into MBSs and CDOs, often backed up by derivatives such as credit-linked notes (CLNs) and CDSs. This development is described in Chapter 5, as is the story how such bonds and derivatives found their way into the portfolios of banks, insurance companies, hedge funds, pension funds and individuals, not only in the USA but also in Europe. Asian banks, wiser after their own crisis in 1997 (discussed in Chapter 8), have been much more reticent than their European colleagues.

So what was the problem and which solutions have been attempted? As we shall see later on, the interventions by the central banks have in the main consisted of giving the markets liquidity support of various kinds. This was necessary since the deposit insurance programs were either insufficient or not trusted, leading to "runs" on several banks in the USA as well as in the UK. This was also a feature of the crises of 1907 and 1929. On top of raising the amounts covered by the deposit insurance schemes, governments have also had to guarantee other

---

[7] Volatility is taken to mean the standard deviation of daily percentage changes in stock prices, in annualized terms.

bank liabilities, in particular interbank loans, in order to get lending going again. These actions are described below and in Chapter 6.

After the banking crises in the 1970s and 1980s, governments and supervisory authorities sought to better supervise and control risk-taking by banks. Capital adequacy (solvency) requirements have been the most active ingredient in these policies, specifying minimum relationships between a bank's capital and its (risk-weighted) assets. The capital regulatory framework called Basel I has been introduced in over a hundred countries around the world, and has contributed to a greater understanding of credit risk and raised capital levels, thereby making the present crisis milder than it might otherwise have been.

In the next step, Basel II, introduced in the European Union from 2007, sought to create a better correspondence between actual risks and capital. An important part in the grading of risk levels was (and is) the use of ratings by such rating companies as Moody's, Fitch and Standard & Poor's. There are, however, a number of question marks surrounding these new rules. A first question concerns whether internal models for the calculation of risks are proper. These models were designed to assess risk on a daily basis (the famous "4:15 report" at JPMorgan in the 1990s being their intellectual origin), and to allocate economic capital to various banking activities according to their return versus risk (Sharpe ratios). It is to be doubted that these models are suitable for the evaluation of the adequacy of capital in a severe downturn, where so-called stress tests are more to the point. The second question concerns the procyclicality of solvency requirements and ratings – that is, the question of whether or not these policy measures actually increase volatility during the business cycle. When asset prices rise during the upturn phase, marking these assets to market ("fair value") creates capital to be used for lending or investments. When the downturn comes and asset prices fall, the process is reversed and capital is "destroyed," just at the time when it is most needed to cover the widening losses in the loan book.

The rule book may itself lead banks into a situation where the only alternative in the end is a recapitalization by the state or outright nationalization of problem banks. All this is treated and analyzed in Chapters 7 and 9. Maybe the socialists of the 1960s were right in deeming that capitalism and the market mechanism could not be allowed to rule the behavior of banks; hence financial institutions should be permanently under state ownership to prevent their speculative excesses![8] The picture on the front cover of this book is a vivid description of the distrust (and perhaps even disgust) that many citizens feel in their relationship with banks and bankers, and their perceived dictum that "greed is good."[9]

Banks' assets may be held in either of two books. The "banking book" contains assets that are to be held until maturity. In that case, the bank has no market risk – that is, the risk that the price of the asset moves during its lifetime – but only the credit risk that the borrower may not be able to repay the debt at maturity. In the "trading book" is held everything that the bank plans to buy and sell during the lifetime of the asset. These assets must be marked to market, generally every day, or at even shorter intervals. In a crisis situation such as we have just been through, such bonds were trading at prices well below par; frequently there were no (reliable) prices at all. The question of whether this principle of marking to market also increases volatility is discussed in Chapter 7, as are the proposed rules on mark-to-market accounting by the International Accounting Standards Board (IASB).

As was pointed out in Chapter 1, it is always necessary to put things in perspective. The world did not founder in 1907 or 1929, and it did not founder this time either. Chapter 8 makes comparisons between the financial crisis of today and some of the earlier crises: the US thrift crisis of the 1980s, the drawn-out Japanese financial crisis, and the Nordic, Asian and Russian crises in the 1990s. What similarities and differences do we see? How much did they cost taxpayers in the end? What might this crisis cost ultimately?

Chapter 9 presents the changes that have been proposed and introduced as regards the regulation and supervision of financial institutions worldwide. Some of these have been national, some undertaken within the European Union and some finally discussed within the Financial

---

[8] Some of these socialists are still alive and kicking. One of the leading figures of the French Socialist Party (PS), Ségolène Royal, her party's candidate in the presidential election of 2007, has proposed that the French banking system be nationalized, just as president François Mitterrand did in 1982 on coming to power. In their book *The Great Financial Crisis*, George Bellamy Foster and Fred Magdoff view the financial crisis in a Marxist perspective à la Baran-Sweezy, and come up with socialism as the only viable solution to today's financial problems and the greed of bankers.

[9] The quote is from the movie *Wall Street*, and earlier widely proclaimed by the financial entrepreneur Michael Milken, the man who made "junk bonds" popular.

Stability Board (at the Bank for International Settlements, or BIS), and decided on by the G-20 group of large economies.

A major change relates to increasing the quantity and quality of bank capital. The introduction of Basel II and the allowance of internal models for risk evaluation would have led to diminished capital bases of 25–50 percent in major international banks. Instead, banks will face sharply raised capital quotas under Basel III, on three accounts. First, supervisors will focus on tangible common equity (also called true core equity, or TCE, which, in principle, is equal to common stock and reserves), rather than total Tier 1 or Tier 2 capital. This minimum ratio is raised from 2 to 4.5 percent. In order to guarantee this minimum, a "conservation buffer" of 2.5 percent is added, making the effective rate 7 percent. Banks below this level will face restrictions on dividend and bonus payments. Other buffers under discussion (and hence not yet decided by October 2010) are counter-cyclical buffers of up to 2.5 percent.

Second, there will be a complementary leverage ratio as in the USA, even though European banks are screaming bloody murder. This is not surprising, since their ability to leverage (assets/capital) will be limited to a maximum of thirty-three times, whereas banks such as the giants UBS and Deutsche Bank were leveraged over seventy times when this crisis broke out.

Third, there may be additional capital charges under Pillar 2 of Basel II and III for banks that are judged to create systemic risk (with regard to their total absolute size, or size relative to the banking system or to their home country or interrelationship with other banks), as well as banks having remuneration systems that are judged to be conducive to short-term positioning and excessive risk-taking. Under discussion in BIS is an additional buffer of 1–2 percent placed on banks deemed to be thus systemically important. We will find that Switzerland has on its own raised the required TCE capital requirement for its two major banks to 10 percent, anticipating international agreements.

A second change comes in the form of better reporting on liquidity, as well as satisfying higher requirements on liquidity. Here the UK Financial Services Authority (FSA) presented an excellent proposal in its September 2009 policy statement "Strengthening liquidity standards," followed up by the Basel Committee's Financial Stability Board in December 2009, "International framework for liquidity risk measurement, standards and monitoring." Since the present crisis started as a liquidity squeeze, it is imperative that something similar be adopted in other countries too, not least in the USA.

As regards bonuses, far too much political capital has been spent on this side issue. The bonuses, excessive as they certainly were, did not create the crisis. Indeed, Lehman followed the "new" prescriptions already in 2007–8 – that is, multi-year bonuses paid primarily in stock rather than cash. It did not prevent the demise of the company. It is also instructive to note that of the US bankers subject to restrictions on pay (in AIG, Citibank, and so on), half the number of affected persons had already left by the end of 2009, to pursue their careers in unrestricted institutions with better pay prospects. We see also the problems in Citi and AIG in attracting qualified CEOs with the existing pay restrictions. Indeed, AIG suffered through four CEOs in 2 years. A similar situation may be occurring in UK banks.

Another requirement is to demand better transparency in derivatives, especially CDSs. However, it does not appear that the required shift to CCP (central counter-party) clearing will be sufficiently encompassing, since only "standardized" contracts will be compulsorily cleared. This leaves participants free to trade in all sorts of non-standardized over-the-counter (OTC) contracts. Also end-users (non-financial corporations) are exempted. And even if banks will be better supervised than before, what will governments do when a major hedge fund (such as LTCM was) or corporation fails? (Remember, both GM and Chrysler were bailed out in this crisis.)

A fifth change regards better transparency in securitization. Banks will also be forced to retain a sufficiently large portion of loans originated, at least 5 percent of originations, so that they share the risk. Mortgage lenders like Countrywide retained only a few percent of the loans, the rest being sold on to investors in the form of CDOs.

A sixth issue concerns better control over tax havens, private equity funds and hedge funds. Obviously, this is a highly popular measure that politicians love to attack, but neither of these phenomena was behind the financial crash that we have just been through.

A seventh and much more important issue concerns how to diminish "moral hazard" by preventing banks from becoming "too big to fail." Here the UK and the Netherlands have (with the help of the EU Commission) gone a long way by beginning the break-up of RBS, Lloyds, Northern Rock and Fortis. But what to do with behemoths such as HSBC (Hongkong and Shanghai Banking Corporation) and

Barclays that did not receive government aid and hence are not under the sway of the government? And when will Switzerland do something about UBS (which has total assets of five times Swiss GDP), and the US something about Citibank? In the USA it appears that "the bigger the better" is still the way of life. A return of Glass-Steagall, separating commercial and investment banking activities, as suggested by Mervyn King (Governor of the Bank of England) and Paul Volcker (ex-Chairman of the Federal Reserve) is a non-starter; remember that Lehman was an investment bank, yet its failure almost collapsed the world's financial system.

Moral hazard has actually been increased and extended as a result of the present crisis in that not only banks but also insurance companies (AIG) and auto firms (GM, Chrysler) have been bailed out at the taxpayers' expense. Hence the next crisis (for there will certainly be one in the not-so-distant future) risks being much wider in scope than the present one, as more and more firms in all kinds of activities may regard themselves as being "too big to fail," believing that they will be rescued by the government, should the need arise.

Let me end with a final word on supervision. In the European Union, micro-prudential supervision will be conducted, as now, mainly by the home-country national financial supervisory authorities, but coordinated within the European Banking Authority (EBA), the European Insurance and Occupational Pensions Authority (EIOPA) and the European Securities and Markets Authority (ESMA), based in London, Frankfurt and Paris respectively. These coordinating bodies, together with the ECB and the European System of Central Banks and the European Commission, will also monitor macro-prudential risks in the so-called European Systemic Risk Board (ESRB), chaired by the President of the ECB.

In the USA, the main problem of supervision has been its fragmentation. The Federal Reserve, the Office of the Comptroller of the Currency (OCC), the Office of Thrift Supervision (OTS), the Federal Deposit Insurance Corporation (FDIC), the National Credit Union Administration, the Federal Housing Finance Agency (FHFA), the SEC, the Commodity Futures Trading Commission (CFTC), as well as the fifty state Departments of Financial Institutions and Insurance Departments, all have their separate or overlapping jurisdictions. Indeed, for insurance companies there has so far been no federal supervision. The Obama administration has enacted only minor changes. The

OCC and the OTS are to be merged and a new agency for consumer protection set up. A national insurance supervisor is to be created. Whether all these new regulatory authorities will create a positive or negative change remains to be seen.

There remains, however, the basically unresolved question of cross-border banking supervision. The Financial Stability Board (FSB) identified thirty financial groups worldwide that are considered to create systemic risk and should be supervised cross-border:

- Five US banks: Goldman Sachs, JPMorgan Chase, Morgan Stanley, Bank of America Merrill Lynch, Citigroup;
- One Canadian bank: Royal Bank of Canada;
- Four UK banks: HSBC, Barclays, RBS, Standard Chartered (Lloyds Banking Group, including HBOS, is missing for some reason);
- Two Swiss banks: UBS and Credit Suisse;
- Two French banks: Société Générale and BNP Paribas (the largest bank by capital, Crédit Agricole, has solely domestic operations);
- Two Spanish banks: Santander and BBVA;
- Two Italian banks: UniCredit, Banca Intesa San Paolo;
- One German bank: Deutsche Bank;
- One Dutch bank: ING;
- Four Japanese banks: Mizuho, Sumitomo Mitsui, Nomura, Mitsubishi UFJ;
- Six insurance groups: Axa (France), Aegon (Netherlands), Allianz (Germany), Aviva (UK), Zurich Financial Services (Switzerland) and Swiss Re (Switzerland) (for some reason, AIG is missing).

It is difficult to see that the new bodies created in the EU for micro- and macro-supervision, or in the USA, will resolve the question of cross-border supervision. How will they be able to supervise any major international bank, present in hundreds of countries? Lehman was working under 2,895 legal names when it crashed! How will any supervisor be able to get a handle on such organizations? The way forward may be to shift focus completely, from home-country control to host-country control. This will require banks to work as subsidiaries in each country rather than as branches, as is the case now. It means that each subsidiary will have its own capital base in each country and will be supervised by the local financial supervisory authority. Hence each will also be small enough to be let go. All these regulatory issues are presented and discussed in Chapter 9 of the book.

The concluding chapter of the book will be a bit more contentious than the body of the text, discussing to what extent proposals for new regulation and supervision will be sufficient to prevent a new crisis of the dimensions that we have just lived through.

Points to remember

- The financial crisis started in the USA during the first half of 2007, when several mortgage banks went bankrupt.
- In September, BNP Paribas closed the possibility to withdraw money from some of its bond funds, since market prices could no longer be established for US mortgage-related bonds.
- In September, a major British mortgage bank, Northern Rock, was subjected to a "bank run." Despite assistance from the Bank of England, it had to be placed under public conservatorship and was later nationalized.
- Several German *Landesbanken* revealed problems, despite the fact that they are owned and guaranteed by the German state.
- Despite rising credit write-downs, the situation did not seem alarming, given very satisfactory levels of capital in most banks.
- Stock markets continued upwards for most of the year and prices did not peak until October 2007.
- During spring 2008, US house prices started to fall for the first time since the Great Depression.
- During the spring and summer of 2008, problems increased in the US banking system. The investment bank Bear Stearns merged with a commercial bank at the instigation of the Federal Reserve and other regulatory authorities. One of the larger savings banks, IndyMac, was placed under the conservatorship of the FDIC and later nationalized. The two government-sponsored mortgage enterprises Fannie Mae and Freddie Mac, which together guarantee over half the market for residential mortgages, were placed under conservatorship of their regulatory authority, the FHFA.
- In September 2008, panic set in when the investment bank Lehman Brothers filed for protection under chapter 11. The world's largest insurance company AIG received liquidity support from the Federal Reserve, which took most of its stock as collateral.
- The market uncertainty – which banks are next to reveal losses and which will be deemed too big to fail or be allowed to collapse like

Lehman? – led to a collapse of the interbank market and vastly higher interest rates.

- In the USA, the Treasury proposed to recapitalize banks with public funds. The Troubled Assets Relief Program (TARP), was set at $700 billion.
- The savings bank Washington Mutual, the seventh largest bank in the USA, was seized by its regulatory authority. With assets of over $300 billion, it was then the largest bank collapse ever.
- The authorities in Benelux took over and nationalized Fortis bank.
- The Icelandic supervisory authority seized control of the three largest banks, Kaupthing, Glitnir and Landsbanki, which together had liabilities ten times the size of Iceland's GDP.
- October 2008 saw the greatest weekly fall in share prices since 1929. Volatility on the US stock markets reached the highest level ever recorded.
- The coverage of deposit insurance was doubled in the USA as well as in Europe. Some countries provided limitless coverage.
- Many countries in Europe injected capital into their troubled banks. The state became majority shareholder in such banks as the RBS and Hypo Real Estate in Germany. Anglo-Irish Bank in Ireland, Fortis Bank in the Netherlands and Fionia Bank in Denmark were nationalized, to name but a few.
- Iceland received an emergency loan from the IMF. It was the first developed country in 25 years to receive such support. Ukraine, Hungary and Latvia later also received IMF funding.
- In the middle of 2010, the world's banks had written off over $1,700 billion in credit losses since the crisis started, to which figure comes some $300 billion in losses in insurance companies such as AIG. On the other hand, they had raised a similar sum in new equity, although one-third has come from governments.

Appendix 2.1
Chronology of events: January 2007–June 2011

February 5, 2007	The mortgage bank Mortgage Lenders Network in the USA becomes the first victim of the subprime crisis.
April 2, 2007	New Century Financial, the largest subprime lender in the USA, files for protection under chapter 11.

June 7, 2007	The US investment bank Bear Stearns disallows withdrawals from two of its funds which have invested in US CDOs, the value of which has fallen sharply.
July 19, 2007	The Dow Jones stock market index exceeds 14,000 for the first time ever.
August 6, 2007	American Home Mortgage, the tenth largest mortgage bank in the USA, files for protection under bankruptcy laws.
August 9, 2007	The largest French bank, BNP Paribas, closes three of its funds for withdrawals, since the market for CDOs based on mortgages can no longer provide reliable prices.
August 10, 2007	To alleviate the lack of liquidity in the interbank market, the major central banks inject money into the system: the Federal Reserve $43 billion, the ECB $215 billion (equivalent) and the Bank of Japan $8 billion (equivalent).
August 16, 2007	Countrywide Financial, the largest US mortgage bank, narrowly avoids bankruptcy by receiving emergency loans of $11 billion from a consortium of banks.
August 28, 2007	The regional German savings bank, Landesbank Baden-Württemberg, takes over its colleague, Landesbank Sachsen, which would otherwise have gone bankrupt on account of its investments in US mortgage-related CDOs.
August 31, 2007	Ameriquest, the largest remaining subprime lender, goes bankrupt. Citigroup takes over its deposits and healthy assets.
September 1–3, 2007	In the annual central bank conference in Jackson Hole, Wyoming, Yale professor Robert Shiller predicts that house prices in the USA may fall by 50 percent over the next couple of years.
September 3, 2007	The German investment bank IKB, majority-owned by the German federal state via

	Kreditanstalt für Wiederaufbau, reports a loss of over $1 billion on account of US mortgage-related bonds.
September 13, 2007	BBC reports that the Bank of England has secretly given the mortgage bank Northern Rock liquidity support to the tune of £21 billion. The news leads to a run on the bank the next day, the first bank run in the UK since 1830.
September 18, 2007	The Federal Reserve continues its decreases of the Fed Funds rate, which brings the rate from 5.25 percent to 1 percent in a year.
September 28, 2007	Netbank, one of the largest internet banks in the USA, is closed by its supervisor, the OTS. It becomes the largest savings bank failure since the 1980s. Its deposits are taken over by ING Direct.
October 2, 2007	The Swiss bank UBS reports credit write-downs of $3.6 billion on account of losses on US mortgage-related bonds.
October 5, 2007	The largest US investment bank, Merrill Lynch, makes reservations for credit losses of $5.6 billion for the third quarter alone.
October 8, 2007	The Dutch bank ABN AMRO is bought by a consortium consisting of the Benelux bank Fortis, the Spanish Grupo Santander and RBS, which divide up the bank among them.
October 9, 2007	The Dow Jones share index tops at index level 14,165. The low point of 6,627 is reached in March 2009, after a fall of 53 percent in 17 months.
October 15, 2007	Citigroup, the largest bank in the USA, reports a write-down of $8.5 billion for the third quarter.
October 15, 2007	A consortium of US banks and investment banks plan to create a government-supported "super fund" of $100 billion in order to buy mortgage bonds, thereby supporting their

	prices. The plan collapses on December 24, on account of the falling prices on these bonds and the impossibility of assessing what the reasonable price would be.
October 30, 2007	The Chairman and CEO of Merrill Lynch, Stan O'Neill, is forced to resign. Despite the company's credit write-downs of $2.3 billion for the third quarter, he receives a severance payment (a "golden parachute") of $161 million, on top of his normal annual salary of $48 million.
October 31, 2007	Deutsche Bank makes reservations for credit write-downs of $3 billion (equivalent).
November 1, 2007	Credit Suisse reports a write-down of $1 billion (equivalent).
November 1, 2007	The Federal Reserve injects $41 billion in liquidity, the largest operation since 9/11 in 2001.
November 5, 2007	Citigroup is forced to make a new reservation of $11 billion. Its CEO and Chairman, Charles "Chuck" Prince, resigns. His severance payment is "only" $12 million in cash, the rest being paid in stock, which would eventually become virtually worthless as the price per share falls from $36 on the day of his resignation to below $1 at the lowest point.
November 8, 2007	The investment bank Morgan Stanley reports losses related to subprime loans of $3.7 billion.
November 9, 2007	Wachovia, the fourth largest bank in the USA, reports write-downs of $1.7 billion.
November 13, 2007	Bank of America, the largest bank in the USA by deposits, writes down $3 billion in credit losses.
November 14, 2007	The credit crisis reaches Europe, whose largest bank (by capital), HSBC, makes a credit write-down of $3.4 billion (equivalent). Most of it referred to its US subsidiary.

November 15, 2007   Barclays, the second largest bank in the UK by assets and number three by capital, makes write-downs of $2.6 billion (equivalent).

November 20, 2007   The US mortgage bank "Freddie Mac", Federal Home Loan Mortgage Corporation, a GSE, is forced to take a credit write-down of $1.2 billion. It issues new stock worth $6 billion to private investors.

November 26, 2007   HSBC reports having given its investment fund for structured products (SIV) a support loan of $45 billion to cover write-downs on its investments in CDOs and CDSs.

November 27, 2007   The sovereign wealth fund of Abu Dhabi buys shares in Citigroup for $7.5 billion, thereby becoming the bank's largest shareholder.

December 4, 2007   The US mortgage bank "Fannie Mae", Federal National Mortgage Association, also a GSE, issues new stock worth $7 billion.

December 6, 2007   RBS, the biggest bank in the UK and the world by assets, writes down $2.5 billion (equivalent) in credit losses.

December 10, 2007   UBS is forced to reserve another $10 billion for credit losses.

December 12, 2007   The Federal Reserve starts to lend under the Term Auction Facility (TAF) program. The program also involves the Bank of Canada, the Bank of England, the ECB and the Schweizerische Nationalbank (SNB).

December 19, 2007   Morgan Stanley reports another $9.4 billion in credit write-downs and receives $5 billion in new capital from the Chinese sovereign wealth fund China Investment Corporation (CIC), corresponding to approximately 10 percent of its share capital.

January 9, 2008   The investment bank Bear Stearns reports write-downs related to subprime loans of $1.9 billion. Its Chairman and CEO, James

	Cayne, resigns, selling his shares in the company for $61 million. A year earlier, they had been worth over $1 billion.
January 11, 2008	Countrywide Financial, the largest mortgage bank in the USA, is purchased by Bank of America for $4 billion. In 2006, Countrywide had had a market share of 20 percent of all outstanding residential mortgage loans in the USA.
January 15, 2008	Citigroup writes down credits for $18 billion for the fourth quarter of 2007.
January 17, 2008	Merrill Lynch writes down an additional $14.1 billion.
January 24, 2008	The National Association of Realtors in the USA reports the first fall in house prices to have occurred since the Depression.
January 25, 2008	Douglass National Bank in Missouri becomes the first bank to become insolvent in the New Year. Another twenty-four banks would follow later that year.
January 31, 2008	The insurance company MBIA, whose main business is credit insurance (it is a monoline), reserves $2.3 billion for expected losses.
February 8, 2008	Deutsche Bank makes further write-downs of $3.2 billion (equivalent).
February 19, 2008	The French bank Société Générale issues new stock worth €5.5 billion in order to cover losses of €4.9 billion made by one single trader, Jérôme Kerviel. The larger part of the loss was incurred when the bank decided to close unauthorized positions in stock index futures amounting to €50 billion in three days, thereby creating a huge impact on prices. Mr. Kerviel was later sentenced to five years in prison and obligated to pay the bank's loss. The bank also wrote down $3.2 billion (equivalent) for credit losses related to US mortgage products.

February 19, 2008	Credit Suisse reports an additional write-down of $2.85 billion (equivalent) on account of erroneous prices used to value its portfolio of CDOs.
February 22, 2008	The British mortgage lender Northern Rock is nationalized, meaning that its £100 billion in liabilities are added to the British national debt, which thereby increases from 37 to 45 percent of GDP. The holding company UK Financial Investments (UKFI) is created for the purpose of being the formal owner of nationalized banks.
March 3, 2008	HSBC adds $13.8 billion (equivalent) to its reservations.
March 11, 2008	The Federal Reserve introduces the program Term Securities Lending Facility, whereby primary dealers (the counter-parties to the Fed in open market operations) can exchange less liquid bonds for government bonds.
March 17, 2008	The US bank JPMorgan Chase buys the investment bank Bear Stearns. The initially agreed price of $236 million, or $2 per share, was raised to $10 per share a few days later, due to angry shareholders. Still, the price had been at a level of $133 per share during the previous year. The Federal Reserve issues a non-recourse loan[10] to JPMorgan Chase of up to $29 billion, to guarantee potential future losses of the bank's holdings of subprime-backed securities.
March 18, 2008	Federal Reserve begins its Primary Dealer Credit Facility (PDCF), by which all their primary dealers can borrow from the Fed, whether commercial banks, investment banks or broker/dealers.

[10] "Non-recourse loan" means that if the underlying collateral – mortgage debt, in this case – were to become insufficient because of a fall in its value, the lender – in this case, the Federal Reserve – could not seize other assets.

April 1, 2008	UBS makes further write-downs of $19 billion, and Deutsche Bank of $3.9 billion (equivalent).
April 1, 2008	Lloyd Blankfein, CEO of Goldman Sachs, says that "we're closer to the end than the beginning" of the global credit crisis, words echoed on May 1 by Hank Paulson, the US Secretary of the Treasury.
April 17, 2008	Merrill Lynch writes down a further $4.5 billion.
April 18, 2008	Citigroup follows, with write-downs of $12 billion.
April 21, 2008	The Royal Bank of Scotland writes down $9.4 billion (equivalent) and issues new stock worth £12 billion ($19 billion).
May 12, 2008	HSBC writes down $3.2 billion (equivalent) for the first quarter.
May 15, 2008	Barclays follows suit with $2 billion (equivalent).
June 6, 2008	The investment bank Lehman Brothers gives notice that it needs $6 billion in additional capital.
July 11, 2008	IndyMac, the largest savings bank in the Los Angeles area and the seventh largest mortgage bank in the USA, is seized by its supervisor FDIC. The name of the bank stands for the Independent National Mortgage Corporation and tries to mimic the semi-public Freddie Mac, with which it has no connections. It becomes the fourth largest banking collapse in US history. The bank had total assets of $32 billion, and the cost to the FDIC to bail out depositors was calculated at $4–8 billion. It had specialized in so-called Alt-A mortgages, as well as jumbo mortgages, loans too big to sell to Fannie Mae or Freddie Mac. The nationalized bank was sold in January 2009 to a private equity consortium.

July 13, 2008	The Treasury and the Federal Reserve save the GSEs Fannie Mae and Freddie Mac by guaranteeing their liabilities and giving them temporary borrowing facilities.
July 23, 2008	The Federal Housing Administration Rescue Bill is adopted by Congress to help Fannie Mae and Freddie Mac.
July 31, 2008	Deutsche Bank sees write-downs of $8 billion (equivalent) for the first half of 2008.
August 31, 2008	The German insurance company Allianz sells its subsidiary Dresdner Bank to Commerzbank for €9.8 billion; Dresdner writes down $1.3 billion (equivalent) in bad loans.
September 7, 2008	The US government seizes Freddie Mac and Fannie Mae, which are placed in public conservatorship under the FHFA. They get a capital injection of a maximum of $100 billion each. The US government will control up to 79.9 percent of the share capital in both organizations.
September 7, 2008	Silver State Bank in Nevada becomes the 11th victim in 2008 of the banking crisis.
September 14, 2008	The largest US investment bank Merrill Lynch is bought by Bank of America for $50 billion, or $29 per share, a 70 percent premium over the latest closing price of $17 per share. At year-end 2006, the share price had been $256.
September 15, 2008	The investment bank Lehman Brothers seeks protection under chapter 11. With $639 billion in assets, it is easily the biggest bankruptcy ever. Its US "good" assets will later be purchased by Barclays for $1.75 billion, and its Asian operations by Nomura Securities.
September 15, 2008	The Federal Reserve extends markedly the range of securities acceptable as collateral.
September 16, 2008	The Federal Reserve extends a bridge loan of up to $85 billion to the insurance company

AIG and takes the majority (79.9 percent) of its stock as collateral. Its share price had fallen by 65 percent in one single day of trading the day before.

September 17, 2008   Lloyds TSB agrees to purchase the mortgage bank HBOS for £12 billion.

September 18, 2008   The Federal Reserve extends its swap arrangements with other central banks (Bank of England, ECB, SNB, Bank of Sweden) to $247 billion.

September 18, 2008   The UK's FSA forbids the short selling of shares in financial corporations.

September 19, 2008   US Secretary of the Treasury Hank Paulson outlines a program of support for the banking system known as TARP (Troubled Assets Relief Program). $700 billion will be spent to recapitalize banks or purchase mortgage-related assets. At the same time, short selling of banking shares is outlawed. The amount covered by deposit insurance is temporarily raised from $100,000 to $250,000 (made permanent in July 2010).

September 19, 2008   The Federal Reserve starts purchasing ABCP. Financial as well as non-financial paper qualifies, provided it has a rating of not lower than A1 (Standard & Poor's), F1 (Fitch) or P-1 (Moody's). By 19 November, $272 billion of paper had already been bought.

September 21, 2008   The two remaining large investment banks, Morgan Stanley and Goldman Sachs, are accepted as bank holding companies by the Federal Reserve. This implies that the Fed rather than the SEC is their main supervisor in the future and gives them the borrowing rights of commercial banks. Also, they can participate in the TARP program.

September 22, 2008   The largest bank in Japan, Mitsubishi UFJ, buys stock in Morgan Stanley for $9 billion,

	corresponding to 21 percent of the share capital. Later on, the investment is converted to preference shares.
September 24, 2008	The billionaire Warren Buffet's Berkshire Hathaway buys 9 percent of the stock in Goldman Sachs, preferred stock with a dividend of 10 percent, with an option for a further 5 percent. At the same time, Goldman issues new stock for an additional 5 percent of its capital.
September 25–26, 2008	The OTS seizes the largest savings bank in the USA, which is also the sixth largest bank in the country, Washington Mutual, placing it in conservatorship under the FDIC. With assets of more than $300 billion, it is the largest bank failure in US history. Next day, JPMorgan Chase purchases the banking activities for $1.9 billion, while the holding company seeks protection under chapter 11. The CEO of Washington Mutual resigns after only 17 days in his post, with salary and severance pay of $19.1 million, amounting to over $1 million in salary per working day.
September 28, 2008	The Benelux authorities nationalize Fortis Bank for a sum of €11.2 billion paid to the existing shareholders.
September 29, 2008	The Federal Reserve increases to $620 billion the amounts placed at the disposal of some foreign central banks by means of swap arrangements: Bank of Canada, Bank of Japan, Bank of England, Bank of Denmark, Bank of Norway, Bank of Sweden, SNB and the ECB.
September 29, 2008	The US House of Representatives rejects the government's TARP plan, which leads to a collapse in share prices: Dow Jones −7.0 percent, NASDAQ −9.1 percent and S&P 500 −8.8 percent in a single day.

September 29, 2008   The UK nationalizes the mortgage lender
                            Bradford & Bingley, after a run on the bank
                            cost it tens of millions of pounds. The bank
                            gets a bridge loan from the Bank of England
                            of £17.9 billion ($32.5 billion). The branch
                            offices and deposits are sold to Abbey
                            National (owned by the Spanish bank
                            Grupo Santander) for £612 million, while
                            the troubled mortgage book is taken over
                            by the state.

September 29, 2008   The fourth largest bank in the USA,
                            Wachovia, agrees to be taken over by
                            Citigroup for $2.2 billion in cash. The FDIC
                            will support losses of up to $12 billion. A
                            week later, however, Wells Fargo bids
                            $15.1 billion (in stock), a bid which more-
                            over does not require the support by the
                            FDIC. Wells Fargo wins, despite a court chal-
                            lenge by Citigroup.

September 29, 2008   The Icelandic Glitnir bank receives support
                            funding of $864 million (equivalent) from
                            the central bank.

September 29, 2008   The major mortgage bank in Germany,
                            Hypo Real Estate, gets financial support of
                            €35 billion from a consortium consisting of
                            the ECB, the Bundesbank and some commer-
                            cial banks. A week later, the loan volume is
                            raised to €50 billion, of which €20 billion is
                            from the Bundesbank.

September 30, 2008   The French-Belgian bank Dexia (ex-Crédit
                            Local and Crédit Communal) gets an injection
                            of new capital of €6.4 billion ($9.2 billion) by
                            the French, Luxembourg and Belgian states.
                            In return, the EU Commission decrees it has to
                            sell assets in Spain, Italy and Slovakia, and
                            shrink its balance sheet by 35 percent.

September 30, 2008   Ireland is the first country in the European
                            Union to extend its deposit insurance to

cover an unlimited amount. Greece follows suit. The European Commission claims that this action is in violation of the free movement of capital, but cannot act when a few days later some other countries, including Germany, follow the example.

September 30, 2008   "The National Debt Clock" on Times Square in New York registers $10 trillion ($10,000,000,000,000,000).

October 1, 2008   The Senate of the USA votes in favor of a revised version of the TARP program; the House follows suit on October 3.

October 3, 2008   President Bush signs the Economic Stabilization Act, authorizing the spending of $700 billion under TARP.

October 3, 2008   The Netherlands buys the Dutch part of Fortis Bank for €16.8 billion, in violation of the agreement of September 28, angering Belgium.

October 3, 2008   Wachovia and Wells Fargo announce their merger. (See above, September 29.)

October 5, 2008   BNP Paribas purchases the Belgian and Luxembourg parts of Fortis for €11 billion in new stock, making Belgium the largest shareholder of BNP, with 12 percent, and BNP Paribas the biggest bank by deposits in the euro area. The deal is blocked, however, by a court order, on the initiative of angry shareholders, and is not approved until April 2009.

October 6–10, 2008   The largest fall in stock prices over a week since the Depression occurs. Dow Jones falls −22.1 percent and Standard & Poor's −18.2 percent during the week. In London, FTSE 100 falls by −21.1 percent; in Frankfurt DAX falls by −21.6 percent; and in Tokyo Nikkei 225 falls by −24.3 percent.

October 6, 2008   The Federal Reserve raises the amount of credit granted to member banks to $900

	billion. It also starts paying interest on the banks' reserves in the central bank.
October 6, 2008	Bank of America makes some changes in the terms and condition for loans to 400,000 customers taken over from Countrywide Financial, thus avoiding being sued for predatory pricing.
October 6, 2008	The Danish government guarantees all bank deposits. However, banks must themselves build up a fund of $6.5 billion (equivalent) to save banks in trouble.
October 7, 2008	Lending by the Federal Reserve to its member banks rises to $1.3 trillion.
October 7, 2008	The Federal Reserve allows commercial paper to be used as collateral for borrowings from the Fed. Potentially, this means that the Fed is guaranteeing a market of $2,400 billion.
October 7, 2008	The Financial Supervisory Authority of Iceland takes over the banks Landsbanki and Glitnir; the Swedish subsidiary of the latter is sold to HQ Bank and its Norwegian subsidiary to the SpareBank 1 Group.
October 7, 2008	The European Union raises the minimum coverage in the deposit guarantee scheme from €20,000 to €50,000.
October 8, 2008	A number of central banks lower their interest rates in a concerted action: the Federal Reserve, the Bank of England, the Reserve Bank of Canada, the Bank of Sweden, SNB, the ECB and the People's Bank of China.
October 8, 2008	The Icelandic Financial Supervisory Authority nationalizes the largest bank, Kaupthing. Its British subsidiary, Singer & Friedlander, is nationalized by the UK.
October 11, 2008	The leaders of the seven major countries in the world (G-7) meet in Washington, but no concrete decisions are taken.

October 13, 2008	The French president Sarkozy promises to guarantee French banks' borrowing up to €320 billion and sets aside €40 billion for recapitalizing the banking system.
October 13, 2008	The Spanish Prime Minister Zapatero promises to guarantee banks' borrowing up to €100 billion.
October 13, 2008	The Netherlands will guarantee bank borrowing for €200 billion and set up a fund for recapitalization of banks of €20 billion.
October 13, 2008	Germany follows up with €400 billion in guaranteed bank borrowing and €100 billion for recapitalization of banks.
October 13, 2008	The British government announces injections of capital in RBS, Lloyds TSB and HBOS totaling £37 billion, of which £20 billion is in RBS and £17 billion in the merged Lloyds TSB-HBOS (renamed the Lloyds Banking Group). The state will thereby become a majority owner of RBS, with 60 percent of the share capital.
October 13, 2008	Denmark establishes a state-owned institution for failed and nationalized banks. Two years later, it owned, inter alia, Roskilde Bank, Fionia Bank, EBH Bank and some savings banks.
October 13, 2008	ECB announces that it will lend an indefinite amount at the refi rate of interest (the main lending rate of the ECB).
October 13, 2008	The Federal Reserve extends the swap arrangements with the above-mentioned central banks to the amounts demanded, without limitations. This means that these central banks can lend an infinite amount also in dollars.
October 14, 2008	The Japanese bank Mitsubishi UFJ purchases 21 percent of Morgan Stanley, an investment of $9 billion, of which $7.8 billion is in

preferred but convertible stock at a dividend of 10 percent, and $1.2 billion is in preferred non-convertible shares. Since both the USA and Japan were closed for Columbus Day, payment was made by the largest check ever written, for $9 billion ($9,000,000,000).

| October 14, 2008 | Nine major US banks receive a combined $125 billion in new capital under the TARP program: JPMorgan Chase ($25 billion), Wells Fargo ($25 billion), Citigroup ($25 billion), Bank of America ($15 billion), Merrill Lynch ($10 billion), Goldman Sachs ($10 billion), Morgan Stanley ($10 billion), Bank of New York Mellon ($3 billion), State Street Bank ($2 billion). |

| October 14, 2008 | FDIC guarantees new interbank loans of up to $1,400 billion, against a fee of between 0.5 and 1.0 percent, depending on the bank's capital strength. |

| October 16, 2008 | The Swiss bank UBS reaches an agreement with its central bank SNB, whereby $60 billion in illiquid US mortgage bonds are shifted to a "bad bank," capitalized by SNB but run by UBS. |

| October 19, 2008 | The Dutch state injects €10 billion of new capital into ING Groep. |

| October 20, 2008 | The Swedish government proposes a plan for "safeguarding the stability of the financial system." New bank borrowing is guaranteed up to SEK 1,500 billion ($190 billion) against a fee. Only Swedbank joins the program initially; SEB joins in April 2009. |

| October 20, 2008 | France wants to give its banks capital support of €10.5 billion: Crédit Agricole (€3 billion), BNP Paribas (€2.5 billion), Société Générale (€1.7 billion), Crédit Mutuel (€1.2 billion), *caisses d'épargne* (savings banks; €1.1 billion) and Banque Populaire (€950 |

	million). The program is initially stopped by the EU Commission, however, on grounds of distorted competition, but is later accepted.
October 21, 2008	The Federal Reserve sets up the Money Market Investor Funding Facility (MMIFF), whereby money market funds may separate out their "toxic assets" to a special structured investment vehicle, guaranteed by the Federal Reserve Bank of New York.
October 24, 2008	The volatility index VIX on the Standard & Poor's 500 index reaches 90 percent, its highest value ever.
October 24, 2008	Iceland receives a loan from the IMF of $2.1 billion. It is the first developed nation to borrow from the IMF since the UK did so in 1976.
October 24, 2008	PNC Financial Services buys National City, which otherwise would have gone bankrupt. The bank was one of the major lenders in the subprime market.
October 26, 2008	The IMF gives Ukraine a loan amounting to $16.5 billion.
October, 28 2008	The IMF, the EU and the World Bank lend a total of $24.8 billion to Hungary.
October 29, 2008	The ECB announces that its lending operations have risen to €773.7 billion, or an equivalent of exactly $1 trillion ($1,000,000,000,000), excluding the lending in dollars under the swap arrangement with the Federal Reserve.
October 31, 2008	Barclays Bank avoids using the government support program by issuing £7 billion ($11.8 billion) in preference shares (at an interest rate of 14 percent) to investors in Abu Dhabi and Quatar. Protests from shareholders make it doubtful if the issue will be accepted.
November 1, 2008	Freedom Bank in Florida becomes the 17th bankrupt bank in 2008 and is placed under

	conservatorship, its deposits being taken over by Fifth Third Bank in Michigan.
November 3, 2008	Germany's largest bank, Commerzbank, which had recently bought Dresdner Bank, gets a capital injection of €8.2 billion by the German state. Deutsche Bank avoids government support by switching accounting principles, thereby avoiding marking some assets to market.
November 7, 2008	The FHFA decides to temporarily raise the limit for mortgage loans underlying the CDOs or MBSs that Fannie Mae and Freddie Mac can purchase or guarantee from $417,000 to $625,500. Other loans are "jumbos" and disallowed for investment.
November 8, 2008	Security Pacific Bank in Los Angeles becomes the year's 19th victim of the banking crisis.
November 9, 2008	The financial crisis spreads to the Baltic countries when the supervisory authority in Latvia nationalizes the second largest bank, Parex, paying the nominal sum of $5 (equivalent) for the entire bank.
November 10, 2008	The support to AIG is extended and changed after losses of $24.5 billion for the third quarter are reported. The insurance company gets a capital injection of $40 billion under TARP and the credit line is increased to $112.5 billion.
November 10, 2008	The credit card company American Express becomes a bank and can henceforth get access to TARP money.
November 10, 2008	HSBC announces credit write-downs for the third quarter of $4.3 billion, and altogether $38 billion since the start of the crisis.
November 10, 2008	Fannie Mae takes losses of $21.4 billion for the third quarter; the bank forecasts becoming insolvent by the end of the year, forcing capital injections under the $100 billion available for capital support.

November 10, 2008	The Federal Reserve refuses to say which banks are the borrowers of its lending programs, now totaling almost $2 trillion. The decision is challenged in court by the news agency Bloomberg.
November 11, 2008	The EU Commission establishes a working party to harmonize financial supervision among the member countries.
November 11, 2008	Fannie Mae eases terms for hard-hit borrowers. They may get a reduction of the rate of interest or the amount borrowed, provided they are more than 90 days delinquent and the sum of interest and amortization exceeds 38 percent of their disposable income.
November 12, 2008	The Treasury Department makes a U-turn concerning how the $700 billion of TARP money is to be spent. Purchases of mortgage-related securities are no longer contemplated, but the entire sum is to be used to recapitalize financial institutions and help homeowners directly.
November 14, 2008	Freddie Mac writes down $20 billion for the third quarter and seeks an injection of $13.8 billion out of the $100 billion granted by the government.
November 15, 2008	By buying the small bank Federal Trust in Florida for $10 million, the insurance company Hartford Financial Services, one of the largest in the USA, transforms itself into a banking conglomerate, thereby being able to access money from the Federal Reserve's TAF. It also calculates on receiving $1 billion to $3 billion in new capital under TARP.
November 15, 2008	The leaders of G-20 gather in Washington to discuss the economic and financial crisis, but take no decisions.
November 19, 2008	Citibank transfers CDOs worth over $17 billion from its SIV onto its own books. Its

share price drops by 23 percent the next day, and by 60 percent for the week. The market for CDSs indicates a 24 percent probability that Citigroup will become bankrupt.

November 21, 2008 The Treasury announces that a total of $36.5 billion in TARP money has been paid to forty-four medium-sized banks.

November 23, 2008 The FDIC, the Federal Reserve and the Treasury save Citigroup by giving it a further $20 billion in capital. They will also guarantee $306 billion of "toxic assets." Citi will take the first $37 billion of the losses, and thereafter the FDIC will bear 90 percent of further losses. The authorities are paid by receiving $27 billion of preference shares, yielding 8 percent interest. The share price of Citigroup rises 62 percent on the news.

November 25, 2008 The Federal Reserve agrees to take on $800 billion in risk by purchasing bonds. It will buy up to $100 billion in bonds issued by Fannie Mae or Freddie Mac, and up to $600 billion in MBSs guaranteed by Fannie Mae or Freddie Mac. Moreover, under its new program, Term Asset Backed Securities Loan Facility (TALF), the Fed will buy up to $200 billion of AAA-rated bonds or paper guaranteed by the Small Business Administration and containing loans to education, car loans and credit card loans. The result is a marked decrease in the 30-year mortgage rate of interest, from 6.38 percent to 5.70 percent.

November 27, 2008 Three former top executives of the Swiss bank UBS voluntarily repay bonuses received to the tune of $58 million (equivalent).

December 8, 2008 The EU Commission decides to accept the French plan for recapitalizing its banks, as well as the proposal from Austria.

December 9, 2008	The Chairman of the Federal Reserve, Ben Bernanke, writes a letter to Congress stating that the Federal Reserve Act will not allow it to act as "lender of last resort" to the auto industry.
December 12, 2008	Sanderson State Bank in Texas becomes the 28th victim of the crisis, and the final and the 25th for the year 2008.
December 12, 2008	A court in Belgium stops the purchase by BNP Paribas of Fortis, awaiting shareholders' approval.
December 15, 2008	The UK lowers the fees for banks using its £250 billion guarantee program, also extending the guarantee to 5 years from 3 years.
December 15, 2008	Ireland proposes to use up €10 billion to recapitalize its six biggest banks.
December 18, 2008	Credit Suisse takes the innovative step of paying this year's bonuses in illiquid US CDOs of doubtful value.
December 19, 2008	The Belgian government is forced to resign on account of the "Fortis affair."
December 24, 2008	General Motors Acceptance Corporation (GMAC) is transformed into a bank and gets an immediate capital injection from TARP of $5 billion.
December 29, 2008	Merrill Lynch, which is to become a part of the Bank of America by the end of the year, pays out $4 billion in bonuses, one month earlier than normal.
December 31, 2008	The Austrian authorities seize control of Bank Medici, which had invested its own and client money in the bankrupt investment firm owned by Bernard Madoff.
January 2, 2009	The bankrupt IndyMac is sold by its conservator the FDIC to a private equity group led by Dune Capital Management and J. C. Flowers.
January 8, 2009	Commerzbank, which has already received €8.2 billion in new capital, gets another €10

	billion to ensure that its solvency ratio does not fall short of 10 percent, even after the purchase of Dresdner Bank from the insurance company Allianz. The state becomes the largest shareholder of the bank, with a 25 percent stake.
January 15, 2009	The Senate votes to release the second half of the $700 billion allocated under TARP.
January 15, 2009	Bank of America, which already has received $25 billion of TARP money, gets a further $20 billion, plus a guarantee for $118 billion in "toxic assets," on and off balance. Bank of America will take the first $10 billion in losses, and thereafter the FDIC and the Treasury will take half of the rest.
January 16, 2009	The Irish government nationalizes Anglo-Irish Bank.
January 16, 2009	Merrill Lynch repays $550 million to investors in its stock. Thus the company avoids being sued for "issuing false and misleading statements about collateralized debt obligations and other assets backed by subprime mortgages, artificially inflating Merrill Lynch's shares."
January 16, 2009	National Bank of Commerce in Illinois and Bank of Clark County in Washington are closed by the FDIC, the first victims of the New Year. They will be followed into bankruptcy by 138 more banks in 2009.
January 19, 2009	The British government extends its ownership of the Royal Bank of Scotland by exchanging preference shares for common stock. The stake owned by the government increases from 58 to almost 70 percent. Simultaneously, a new program is set up under which the government takes 90 percent of losses on the portfolios of "toxic assets," provided that banks promise to increase their lending.

January 20, 2009	The French government injects a further €10.5 billion into the six largest banks, provided their top managers abstain from bonuses.
January 22, 2009	John Thain, former CEO of Merrill Lynch, is fired by Bank of America as it turns out that he has (a) purposely underestimated the losses for the fourth quarter in order to complete the merger, these losses turning out to be $15.4 billion; (b) given the top managers of Merrill Lynch bonuses worth $4 billion one month earlier than usual, three days before the completion of the merger; (c) redecorated his personal Merrill Lynch office for $1.2 million while losses exploded.
January 27, 2009	The New York's district attorney Andrew Cuomo issues a subpoena to John Thain in order to discover the circumstances surrounding the bonus payments.
January 29, 2009	President Obama criticizes Wall Street bonus payments for 2008 of a total of $17.4 billion, to be compared with $34.3 billion and $33 billion respectively for the two preceding years.
February 2, 2009	The Bank of England begins to purchase corporate bonds, syndicated loans and commercial paper with top rating for a maximum of £50 billion.
February 3, 2009	Sweden announces a plan to use up to SEK 50 billion ($6.3 billion) to recapitalize banks. The participants are placed under restrictions not to raise salaries or give bonuses to top management.
February 4, 2009	President Obama decides that banks receiving support from the government must limit the top management's salary to a maximum of $500,000. Amounts above may be given in the form of shares, to be sold only when all government support has been repaid.

February 10, 2009	The new Treasury Secretary of the USA, Tim Geithner, presents a plan for how the residual TARP money is to be spent. A combination of private and public initiatives will purchase delinquent loans of up to $1,000 billion from the banking system. The proposal is considered too vague in not answering the question whether undercapitalized banks will be nationalized or closed. US stock markets fell by 5 percent on the proposal.
February 23, 2009	British Prime Minister Gordon Brown proposes that in the future mortgage loans are to be restricted to 95 percent of the value of the property – that is, buyers must put at least 5 percent down in cash.
February 24, 2009	Share prices of Bank of America and Citigroup rise by over 20 percent after the statement by the Fed Chairman Ben Bernanke that the supervisory authorities do not plan to nationalize banks in crisis, but continue to support them by purchases of preference shares.
February 24, 2009	The authorities seize the ninth largest bank in Denmark, Fionia Bank in Odense, which gets capital support of DKK 1 billion. It is the third Danish bank to be nationalized during the crisis.
February 25, 2009	The US begins an investigation of the nineteen largest banks, those with assets above $100 billion, in order to ascertain by means of stress tests whether they will need to hold more capital.
February 26, 2009	The Royal Bank of Scotland reports a loss of over £40 billion for 2008, the biggest loss ever reported by a British company.
February 26, 2009	RBS, 70 percent owned by the British government, utilizes the state guarantee to insure £325 billion of assets. RBS will take the first £19.5 billion in losses, plus 10 percent of the residual. The fee to the government of £6.5 billion in stock may lead to the state owning

	80 percent of the bank when the preference shares are converted to common stock. Moreover, a "bad bank" is set up to handle assets worth a nominal £540 billion.
February 26, 2009	The partly nationalized US mortgage bank Fannie Mae reports a loss for the fourth quarter of $25.2 billion, bringing the loss for the full year to $58.7 billion. The bank needs $15.2 billion in new capital from the state to avoid equity from becoming negative.
February 27, 2009	The US government and Citigroup agree that up to $25 billion of preference shares held by the government are converted to common stock, raising the stake of the government in the bank to 36 percent. Citi's share price falls by an identical number of percentage points on the news.
March 2, 2009	The insurance company AIG, which has already received $152.5 billion in support (capital and loans), gets another $30 billion from the Fed. At the same time, the state converts its $70 billion of preference shares to common stock in order to strengthen its control over the company. The loss for the year 2008 is reported at almost $100 billion, the largest loss ever reported by any company in the world.
March 6, 2009	The ECB prolongs for an unspecified period of time the possibility to borrow infinite amounts at the refi rate of interest.
March 6, 2009	BNP Paribas and the Belgian state reach a new agreement concerning Fortis. BNP will purchase 75 percent of the nationalized bank. Non-performing assets worth €11.4 billion are to be shifted to a "bad bank" capitalized by the Belgian state. The Fortis holding company will become, in essence, an insurance company with the rest of the Fortis assets. The deal is approved at a general meeting of shareholders on April

28, despite shoes being thrown at the members of the management present.

March 6, 2009 — Lloyds TSB signs an agreement with the British government, similar to the earlier RBS deal. Assets worth £260 billion will be guaranteed by the state. Lloyds will take the first £25 billion in losses and 10 percent of the rest. The fee to the government in the form of preference shares will lead to a government stake of 77 percent of the bank once the preference shares are converted into common stock; until then the state's share is 43 percent.

March 9, 2009 — The remaining major bank in Iceland, Straumur-Burdaras, is seized by the supervisory authority.

March 10, 2009 — Italy's fourth largest bank, Banco Populare, becomes the first to apply for government support. The bank issues to the state €1.45 billion in bonds which may be converted into non-voting preference shares.

March 12, 2009 — The other US GSE mortgage bank Freddie Mac reports a loss for the fourth quarter of $23.9 billion, the loss for the entire 2008 being a staggering $50.1 billion. The bank gets a further capital injection of $30.8 billion under the Senior Preferred Stock Purchase Agreement set up to recapitalize Fannie and Freddie.

March 11, 2009 — The Swiss bank UBS reports the largest loss in Swiss corporate history, over 27 billion Swiss francs for 2008.

March 18, 2009 — The Federal Reserve announces a doubling of its purchases of mortgage bonds and other securities issued by Freddie Mac, Fannie Mae and other "agencies," to a maximum of $1.45 trillion. The Fed will also purchase throughout the year $300 billion of long-term government bonds. The 10-year bond yield falls by 50 basis points on the news.

March 20, 2009	The German parliament (Bundestag) adopts legislation enabling the nationalization of banks even when opposed by a minority of shareholders. The concrete bank in question concerns the mortgage bank Hypo Real Estate. This would be the first time since 1931 that the German state has nationalized a bank. A week later, the government buys a first stake, €60 million for 9 percent of the bank. The government already owned a majority stake, 50 percent of the capital plus one share.
March 23, 2009	Tim Geithner, US Treasury Secretary, makes a more concrete proposal on how banks are to be rid of their "toxic assets," the Public Private Investment Program (PPIP). A number of competing funds are to be set up, financed by both private and public capital. These will buy up to $1,000 billion of assets. The government will make an initial capital injection of $100 billion from TARP, to which will be added guarantees to private investors' borrowing by the FDIC.
March 26, 2009	Tim Geithner proposes new legislation that would place hitherto unsupervised hedge funds, private equity funds and OTC derivatives under supervision. The FDIC and the Fed are also to get the authority to close down financial companies, even if they are not banks, provided they are judged to be of systemic importance.
March 27, 2009	Omni National Bank of Georgia is closed by its supervisor, bringing to forty-nine the number of banks closed since the beginning of 2007.
March 29, 2009	Spain is forced to its first bank support operation, giving a loan of €9 billion to the savings bank Caja Castilla & La Mancha.
April 2, 2009	The US FASB (Financial Accounting Standards Board) suspends the principle of

mark-to-market and gives the banks the opportunity to use their own judgment and their own models in valuing assets for which there are no established market prices. This is deemed to reduce by at least 20 percent the necessary write-downs for the first quarter.

April 2, 2009   The leaders of the G-20 countries, meeting in London, agree on measures to combat the economic and financial crisis. Included are new regulations concerning hedge funds, private equity funds and OTC derivatives such as CDSs. The European Commission proposes that funds with assets above €100 million be put under supervision. The G-20 also agrees on "principles for sound compensation practices" to avoid "perverse incentives" that contributed to the financial crisis. The principles include adjusting compensation to better take into account risks, deferring a portion of bonus payouts and linking the size of the bonus pool to the firm's overall performance.

April 3, 2009   Nordea becomes the first bank in Sweden to be recapitalized by the government. It was not intended by the bank, however. The Swedish state, through the National Debt Office, decided to invest in the new issue of shares by using the Stabilization Fund rather than the budget. The state's stake in the bank will remain at 20 percent.

April 22, 2009   The IMF forecasts that the total write-downs in banks and insurance companies may reach over $4 trillion, of which only some $1,500 billion have been realized so far. Of these, two-thirds involve the USA and one-third Europe, with Asian countries having minimal exposure.

April 30, 2009   Chrysler Corporation, the third largest auto manufacturer in the USA, files for protection

	under chapter 11, having been unable to strike a deal with its bond holders.
April 30, 2009	Efforts to stabilize the financial system could cost the US taxpayer up to $1,900 billion, or over 13 percent of GDP, the IMF estimates. This is over three times as much as the cost of the thrift crisis of the 1980s. Of these costs, the direct support through TARP would cost $450 billion, the FDIC guarantees $800 billion and the Fed purchases add another $600 billion.
May 6, 2009	Standard & Poor's downgrades the ratings of five of Germany's seven *Landesbanken*. They have been reported to hold €816 billion of "toxic assets."
May 7, 2009	The ECB joins the Federal Reserve and the Bank of England in purchasing bonds. €60 billion will be devoted to buying mainly covered mortgage bonds, in Germany called *Pfandbriefe*. The Bank of England raises the volume of its bond purchases to £125 billion.
May 7, 2009	Results of the stress test of nineteen US banks conducted by the Federal Reserve and the FDIC reveal that they need an additional $74.6 billion in capital. Bank of America alone needs $33.9 billion, Wells Fargo $13.7 billion, GMAC $11.5 billion and Citigroup $5.5 billion. Nine of the banks, among them Goldman Sachs and JPMorgan Chase, were judged to already have sufficient capital.
May 7, 2009	American Express Bank, one of the nineteen banks deemed to be sufficiently capitalized, becomes the first bank to apply for permission to repay the TARP funds received.
May 19, 2009	The FDIC's borrowing limit from the Treasury is raised to a temporary $500 billion as the insurance fund dwindles to $13 billion.
May 21, 2009	Standard & Poor's gives the UK a Negative Outlook in its rating, the result of a

government debt predicted to attain 100 percent of GDP and a total support to the financial sector of £1,400 billion in capital support, guarantees and loans.

May 22, 2009   While seventeen small US banks have so far repaid the TARP money, Old National Bancorp. in Indiana becomes the first to repurchase the warrants given to the Treasury to give taxpayers some upside when banks recover.

May 27, 2009   The US government's Aaa credit rating is stable, "even with a significant deterioration" in the nation's debt, Moody's Investors Service says, signaling confidence in a rebound from the recession. Standard & Poor's added that its recent negative outlook for the British AAA rating should not be construed as a warning to the USA.

June 8, 2009   Ten big banks are authorized to repay $68 billion of TARP funds, being judged sufficiently stable without government support. JPMorgan Chase repaid $25 billion to TARP, while Goldman Sachs Group Inc. and Morgan Stanley repaid $10 billion each.

Among other banks, U.S. Bancorp. repaid $6.6 billion, Capital One Financial Corp. $3.6 billion, American Express $3.4 billion, BB&T Corp. $3.1 billion, Bank of New York Mellon $3 billion, State Street $2 billion and Northern Trust $1.57 billion. They will also have to buy back some $5 billion of warrants at "fair value" to repay the taxpayers' risk in TARP.

June 10, 2009   Spain sets up a €9 billion rescue fund for the banking sector, in particular aimed at the ailing savings banks, *cajas de ahorro*. The fund may leverage itself tenfold and hence inject up to €90 billion in capital into the banks.

June 10, 2009	Germany extends its "bad bank" to encompass the regionally owned *Landesbanken*, which have shown little interest in the scheme.
June 17, 2009	The Obama administration announces proposals for changing financial oversight in the USA. Among them is the merger of the OTS and the OCC, creating a single supervisor for all nationally chartered banks, as well as the creation of a Consumer Financial Protection Agency.
June 18, 2009	The Swiss National Bank threatens to limit the size of Swiss banks, which would affect Credit Suisse and UBS in particular.
July 1, 2009	Freddie Mac and Fannie Mae receive permission to refinance residential mortgages up to a limit of 125 percent loan-to-value, this in an effort to stem the rising wave of foreclosures.
July 6, 2009	The ECB begins the first of its promised purchases in the market, buying €60 billion of covered bonds.
July 8, 2009	The British Secretary of the Treasury unveils proposals following the Turner Review for making banks more stable, including capital provisioning during the business cycle and increasing resources for macro-prudential supervision.
July 9, 2009	The International Swaps and Derivatives Association (ISDA) rules that the non-payment of interest by the British mortgage bank Bradford & Bingley is a "credit event," triggering payment on credit default swaps worth $416 million. The nationalized lender had refused to pay interest.
July 13, 2009	The European Commission and the Basel Committee on Banking Supervision propose to double the capital charge that banks face on their proprietary trading. They also toughen capital charges on resecuritization,

proposing a risk weight of 1,250 percent (that is, 100 percent of the asset, since the normal risk weight is 8 percent) for repackaged securities, unless banks can show that the risk has really been shifted.

July 14, 2009   The IASB proposes new rules for the reporting of fair value. If an instrument such as a government bond has a predictable flow of revenues, it may be carried on the books by a mechanism that smoothes out market fluctuations in value. Items with unpredictable cash flows, like derivatives, will still be carried at current market value.

July 15, 2009   The FDIC and the Federal Reserve push for tougher measures to curb the size and risk-taking of the largest financial firms in the USA. The FDIC will propose slapping fees on the biggest bank holding companies to the extent that they carry on activities, such as proprietary trading, outside of traditional lending.

July 21, 2009   Neil Barofsky, Special Inspector General for the Treasury's TARP, claims in a report that, potentially, the US government may have to spend $23.7 trillion (almost twice the level of GDP) if all existing programs were to be used to the maximum. Barofsky's estimates include $2.3 trillion in programs offered by the Federal Deposit Insurance Corp., $7.4 trillion in TARP and other aid from the Treasury, and $7.2 trillion in federal money for Fannie Mae, Freddie Mac, credit unions, Veterans Affairs and other federal programs. Total money actually spent is less than $2 trillion.

July 22, 2009   Goldman Sachs becomes the first bank to free itself from all TARP limitations as it repurchases warrants for $1.1 billion, on top of having repaid the $10 billion preferential share infusion.

July 23, 2009	Sheila Bair, Chairman of the Federal Deposit Insurance Corporation, suggests that Congress should create a Financial Company Resolution Fund, funded by the banks themselves, just like deposit insurance, to provide working capital and cover unanticipated losses when government steps in to unwind a failed firm. It would impose charges on large or complex institutions that create potential risks to the financial system, thereby providing an economic incentive for an institution not to grow too large.
August 6, 2009	Morgan Stanley, having repaid its TARP funds of $10 billion in June, joins Goldman Sachs in also repurchasing the warrants held by the US government, thereby freeing it from all obligations connected with the program. Including dividends, it has paid the government $1.26 billion, a 20 percent annualized return on the government's investment the previous fall.
August 6, 2009	The Bank of England decides to increase its asset purchases from £125 billion to £175 billion.
August 7, 2009	The closure of Community First Bank of Oregon brings to exactly one hundred the number of US banks or savings banks closed since the beginning of the financial crisis in early 2007.
August 9, 2009	The IMF calculates the total "cost" of the global banking crisis at $11.9 trillion, over 20 percent of world GDP, $10.2 trillion of which will hit developed nations, and only $1.7 trillion developing nations. The cost includes capital injections, as well as loans and guarantees and liquidity support by central banks.
August 12, 2009	With the financial crisis abating, the Federal Reserve decides to end its purchases of

open-market paper by October. Or to cite the
Federal Open Market Committee (FOMC)
statement: "to provide support to mortgage
lending and housing markets and to improve
overall conditions in private credit markets,
the Federal Reserve will purchase a total of
up to $1.25 trillion of agency mortgage-
backed securities and up to $200 billion of
agency debt by the end of the year [2009]. In
addition, the Federal Reserve is in the process
of buying $300 billion of Treasury securities.
To promote a smooth transition in markets
as these purchases of Treasury securities are
completed, the Committee has decided to
gradually slow the pace of these transactions
and anticipates that the full amount will be
purchased by the end of October."

August 17, 2009
The Federal Reserve extends in time the TALF
program, with a capacity of as much as $1
trillion. It will expire on June 30, 2010 for
newly issued commercial mortgage-backed
securities, instead of on December 31, 2009.

August 20, 2009
UBS becomes the first European bank to free
itself from government control as the Swiss
government sells all its shares in the bank,
reaping a profit of over 1 billion Swiss francs
in the process.

August 24, 2009
A US District Court Judge orders the Federal
Reserve to release the names of all counter-
parties in the eleven liquidity support programs it runs, totaling some $2,000 billion.
The Federal Reserve claims that releasing the
names of individual banks may subject them
to runs by nervous depositors.

August 25, 2009
French banks and the government agree on
principles for bonus payments, to be suggested
also to the G-20 meeting. Only one-third of
bonus payments due may be paid for the first

year, the rest saved until the next two years and clawed back if losses occur, one-third of the deferred payments to be made in stock rather than cash. A "pay general" is appointed to supervise the system, Michel Camdessus, a former Governor of the Banque de France and Managing Director of the IMF.

September 4, 2009   The US Treasury Department says that $70 billion of TARP money has been repaid by receiving banks.

September 7, 2009   The Basel Committee proposes changes to the Basel II framework, to be implemented by 2011. Tier 1 capital should in principle include only common stock and retained earnings, goodwill, hybrids, and so on, being deducted. At least half of Tier 1 capital should be TCE, the Tier 1 ratio raised to 8 percent from 4 percent. A maximum leverage ratio of 25, defined as unweighted assets over capital, should be introduced as a complement to the Basel II risk-based assessments. Counter-cyclical capital requirements ("dynamic provisioning") should be added to existing Pillar 1 requirements. Systemically important banks may be subjected to extra capital charges. The whole is obviously named Basel III.

September 8, 2009   The rating company Moody's reassures the Aaa-rated large countries (USA, France, Germany, UK, Spain) that they do not risk being downgraded, despite rising budget deficits and debt levels. In June 2010, Moody's changes its mind and warns Spain of being downrated (which it is, to Aa1).

September 17, 2009   Ireland becomes the first country to actually implement a "bad bank," which will acquire the toxic assets of the main commercial banks. The National Asset Management Agency (NAMA) will pay €54 billion to take over a

	nominal €77 billion of toxic assets with a market value of €47 billion. Critics say that the 35 percent discount amounts to an actual subsidy of the banks involved.
September 29, 2009	BNP Paribas becomes the first European bank to repay the government's infusion of capital after having raised €4.3 billion in a new issue of common stock.
September 29, 2009	The FDIC asks its member banks to prepay $45 billion of future assessments until 2012 in order to bolster its reserve ratio. Among the biggest payers would be Bank of America ($3.5 billion), Wells Fargo ($3.2 billion), JPMorgan Chase ($2.4 billion) and Citigroup ($1.2 billion).
October 2, 2009	The European Union reports results from stress-testing the twenty-two largest banks in the area. Even under adverse conditions, no bank's Tier 1 ratio will fall below 6 percent, and the average will be 8–9 percent, depending on assumptions. (New stress tests were conducted in July 2010; see below.)
October 9, 2009	The new German Conservative-Liberal government proposes to strip the financial supervisory authority *Bundesanstalt für Finanzdienstleistungsaufsicht* (Bafin) of its banking supervisory powers and combine them with the Bundesbank's macro-prudential supervision. The Conservatives in the UK similarly promise to abolish the FSA and give its powers to the Bank of England, should they win the next election in May 2010.
October 19, 2009	After months of political haggling, Iceland agrees to borrow £2.35 billion from the UK and €1.2 billion from the Netherlands to cover its deposit-insurance liabilities to depositors in the failed *Landsbanki* Icesave.

October 21, 2009	Bank of England Governor Mervyn King breaks ranks with the government in suggesting that big banks be broken up along commercial bank/investment bank lines, a proposal already aired by the former Chairman of the Federal Reserve Board Paul Volcker.
October 26, 2009	The European Commission requires that Dutch bank ING, which has received €15 billion in state support, divest itself of its insurance and investment management units, as well as its US arm ING Direct USA. Fears that similar requirements may be put on other recipients of state aid, such as Lloyds and RBS, lead to a fall in European bank shares.
October 30, 2009	Nine banks are seized by the authorities in the USA in the largest one-day sweep during this crisis, bringing the total since the start of 2007 to 143 failed banks.
November 1, 2009	The US commercial lender CIT, a major lender to small and medium-sized enterprises, files for bankruptcy. With assets of $60 billion, it is one of the biggest bankruptcies in US history. Taxpayers stand to lose $2.3 billion in TARP money, CIT being the largest bank to go bankrupt after having been bailed out by the Treasury.
November 3, 2009	RBS is forced to sell off its insurance division and some bank branches, after decisions from the European Commission's Competition Commissioner and the UK Treasury. The bank will sell some branches in England and Wales, as well as its NatWest branches in Scotland. RBS also agrees to put £282 billion of assets into the government's Asset Protection Scheme and take an additional £25.5 billion of investment from the Treasury. As a result, the government will increase its stake in RBS to 84.4 percent. RBS will increase the first loss

on the assets protected under the government insurance program to about £60 billion, from the £42.2 billion initially agreed.

November 3, 2009   Lloyds Banking Group says it plans to raise £22 billion in the UK's biggest rights issue ever and denies the government majority control of the country's largest mortgage lender (after the purchase of HBOS). Lloyds will not take part in the government's asset protection scheme, which would have increased the UK's stake to about 62 percent from today's 43.5 percent. Lloyds will sell a retail banking unit, with a 4.6 percent share of the current account market, and 19 percent of the group's mortgage balances to gain Commission approval for the previous year's £17 billion bailout. The government will invest an additional £5.8 billion by taking up its rights in the Lloyds share sale.

£7 billion will be issued in the form of enhanced capital notes (ECNs), also known as contingent convertible Core Tier 1 securities (CoCo bonds). These bonds will automatically be converted to equity should Lloyd's Core Tier 1 ratio fall below 6 percent.

Both RBS and Lloyds also agree to sell their units only to smaller or new competitors.

November 9, 2009   The Federal Reserve announces that of the ten banks ordered in May to raise new capital, after stress tests had shown them to be undercapitalized, only GMAC Financial Services has failed to comply with its target and might be recapitalized by returned TARP funds. The other nine banks raised a total of $71 billion in fresh capital.

November 12, 2009   Ireland, the only country so far to set up a "bad bank" for toxic assets, NAMA, is expected to take over assets of €54 billion from the Irish

	banks (book value €77 billion), equivalent to one-third of Ireland's GDP.
November 13, 2009	Sheila Bair, Chairwoman of the Federal Deposit Insurance Corporation, says that, in retrospect, injecting government money into the largest US banks was not a good thing.
November 20, 2009	The American Mortgage Bankers Association reports a record number of mortgage delinquencies and foreclosures. The percentage of borrowers with at least one payment overdue more than 90 days rose to 14.4 percent in the third quarter. Also, 23 percent of all house owners, 10.7 million households, live in houses where the mortgage exceeds the value of the property.
November 20, 2009	The Dutch government announces plans to inject a further €4.4 billion into the merging banks Fortis Bank Nederland and ABN AMRO, both of which are nationalized. The total injection of capital will then amount to €24 billion.
November 23, 2009	The Chinese regulatory authority tells the country's five major banks to raise their capital adequacy ratio to 13 percent, as compared to around 11 percent at present and the regulatory minimum of 8 percent.
November 24, 2009	The German federal government agrees to inject €4 billion in new capital into the ailing savings bank Westdeutsche Landesbank (WestLB). If converted to common stock, it will give Germany a 49 percent ownership in the bank. WestLB also agrees to offload some €85 billion in toxic assets to a "bad bank," with losses underwritten by the bank's owners, the state of Nordrhein Westfalen and the local savings banks.
November 24, 2009	Lloyds Banking Group (Lloyds TSB-HBOS) issues the world's largest ever rights issue, at

£13.5 billion, thereby avoiding having to pay £15 billion to the state for the insurance of toxic assets. The government's stake in the bank will remain at 43.5 percent. On top of shares, the bank also issues £7.5 billion of Coco bonds, which will automatically convert to equity should Lloyds' Core Tier 1 ratio fall below 6 percent.

November 30, 2009   The FSB identifies thirty financial groups worldwide that are considered to create systemic risk and should be supervised cross-border.

November 30, 2009   Bank of Ireland and Allied Irish Banks (AIB) sell a combined value of €28 billion of toxic securities to the country's "bad bank," NAMA.

December 2, 2009   The European Union finance ministers agree to set up three coordinating agencies for microprudential supervision. Under a compromise, countries acting through the auspices of the Economic and Financial Affairs Council (ECOFIN) can set aside decisions of the three bodies by simple majority of countries. There will also be a European Systemic Risk Board, comprising the central banks, the three supervisory bodies and the EU Commission.

December 3, 2009   Bank of America repays the $45 billion for itself and for Merrill Lynch received from TARP, thereby freeing the bank from hampering pay restrictions. Of these, $19.3 billion came from a record issue of preferred shares.

December 4, 2009   The UK Secretary of the Treasury sharply cuts the amount expected to be lost in financial support to the banking system, from the £20–50 billion estimated earlier, to £10 billion. The major reason is the decision by Lloyds Banking Group not to participate in the government's guarantee scheme for toxic securities, the government's share of Lloyds thereby remaining at 43 percent. The major participant in the scheme, RBS, 84 percent owned by the government, has reduced its participation in the scheme by £43 billion to £282 billion.

December 9, 2009   The British Chancellor of the Exchequer, Alistair Darling, imposes a one-time tax for 2009 on bankers' bonuses above £25,000. The tax is to be paid by the banks as a surcharge on income. Coming on top of the increase in the British top marginal tax rate, from 40 to 50 percent on incomes over £150,000, the measure threatens an exodus of bankers from London. France, however, decides to follow on the bonus tax on incomes over €7,500. In the USA, the government's "pay czar," Kenneth Feinberg, has set a limit of $500,000 for executives in the companies still receiving support from TARP: Citigroup, AIG, GM and GMAC. Chrysler and its finance company have no employees reaching the limit. Two senators have proposed a 50 percent tax on 2009 bonuses above $400,000 at firms that have received more than $5 billion in government assistance, but the measure does not win a majority in the Senate.

December 9, 2009   Bank of America repays in full its $45 billion TARP support in order to escape from government-imposed pay limitations.

December 10, 2009   Anticipating new rules from BIS and the EU, the UK's FSA proposes more stringent rules for banks' proprietary trading. The new rules are estimated to cost British banks an additional £29 billion in Core Tier 1 capital.

December 11, 2009   The Dutch bank ING repays €5.6 billion of the total support received of €10 billion in capital support and €21.6 billion in guarantees on US mortgage-related assets.

December 11, 2009	In its first auction of warrants received by the Treasury under TARP, warrants on stock in JPMorgan generate a profit of $936 million to the Treasury.
December 11, 2009	The US House of Representatives votes a comprehensive package of financial reform, including the creation of a new supervisory authority for consumer credits. The narrow vote of 223 for and 202 against makes it probable that it would fail to gain a majority in the Senate in its present form.
December 14, 2009	Citigroup repays $20 billion of support given under TARP in order to escape from the imposed pay limits. It also terminates the guarantee given on $301 billion of toxic assets.
December 14, 2009	Austria nationalizes the country's sixth largest bank, Hypo Group Alpe Adria (HGAA), majority-owned by Landesbank Bayern, which will receive €1 for its 67 percent ownership.
December 15, 2009	Wells Fargo also repays its $25 billion in TARP support, becoming the last of the big US banks to exit the TARP program.
December 18, 2009	The Basel Committee publishes a proposed set of regulations for banks. Among the changes is the phase-out of hybrid capital in Tier 1, focusing on True Core Tier 1 (common equity and retained earnings). Other proposals involve liquidity ratios, a global leverage ratio and counter-cyclical capital buffers (the proposal is analyzed in greater detail in Chapters 7 and 9).
December 29, 2009	GMAC receives an additional $3.8 billion from TARP, on top of the $12.5 billion already received. The US government owns 56 percent of the lender, the rest being owned by Cerberus, a private-equity firm.
January 5, 2010	The Icelandic saga continues as the president unexpectedly vetoes the payment of €3.8

	billion to 320,000 Icesave investors in the UK and the Netherlands, forcing the question to a referendum.
January 7, 2010	The regulatory authorities in the USA release an advisory to depository institutions on sound practices in managing interest rate risk (IRR).
January 14, 2010	The US administration proposes a fee on all financial institutions (banks and insurance companies) with assets over $50 billion. It would encompass around thirty-five banks and fifteen insurance groups. The fee would be set at 0.15 percent on assets minus Core Tier 1 capital and insured deposits. Over 10 years, the fee is estimated to collect $90 billion. The stated purpose is to recover losses on TARP. An objection is that most banks have already repaid their TARP contributions with profit to the Treasury, the remaining losses being capital injected into AIG, the two auto firms and their finance companies, and the Affordable Housing Program. Hence banks are essentially being asked to pay twice. The US initiative is said to copy a Swedish scheme to build a "stability fund" of 2.5 percent of GDP. The Swedish fee is levied at all banks and set at 0.036 percent of liabilities.
January 21, 2010	President Obama takes the financial sector by surprise by proposing restrictions on banks' proprietary trading and ownership of hedge and equity funds, as well as absolute size (the "Volcker rule").
February 1, 2010	The Federal Reserve closes the ABCP Money Market Mutual Fund (MMMF) Liquidity Facility, the Commercial Paper Funding Facility (CPFF), the PDCF and the TSLF, as well as the temporary liquidity swap arrangements between the Federal Reserve and other

central banks. The Federal Reserve is also in the process of winding down its TAF: $50 billion in 28-day credit will be offered on February 8 and $25 billion in 28-day credit will be offered at the final auction on March 8. The anticipated expiration date for the TALF remains set at June 30 for loans backed by new-issue commercial mortgage-backed securities, and March 31 for loans backed by all other types of collateral.

February 23, 2010 — Austria decides to follow the USA in imposing a levy on banks, set at 0.07 percent of total assets, in order to finance the cost of the financial aid given to banks, including the nationalization of HGAA and Kommunalkredit. The levy plans to raise €500 million.

March 2, 2010 — The insurance company AIG, which has received support from the Treasury and the Federal Reserve totaling $182 billion, agrees to sell its Asian subsidiary AIA to Prudential for $35 billion, $25 billion of which will be used to repay the Fed. As a result, AIG's shares rise over the day by more than 4 percent, while those of Pru fall by 11 percent on the first day and another 8 percent the day after. Later, the shareholders of Pru reject the deal, which falls through, with AIG refusing to renegotiate the deal at a lower price. A few days later, AIG agrees to sell its foreign life insurance unit to MetLife Inc. for about $15 billion in cash and stock, $9 billion of which will be used to repay the government.

March 2, 2010 — London-based investment banks ignore the government's efforts to hold down bonus payments, preferring to pay the 50 percent surcharge tax rather than losing qualified staff. Barclays increases its payments of salary and bonuses in 2009 by 93 percent vis-à-vis 2008, and RBS by 73 percent, despite the latter being majority-owned by the British state. The tax is now expected to bring in four times as much revenue as the government originally planned.

March 3, 2010 President Obama sends to Congress a formalized proposal of the so-called Volcker rule. In an addition, banks would be forbidden to acquire other banks if the new entity has more than 10 percent of total US bank liabilities. An exception is made if the acquired bank is in default. It should be pointed out that both JPMorgan and Bank of America already exceed a similar restriction based on relative deposits, with no reaction from the authorities.

March 3, 2010 Bank of America sells the bailout warrants connected with TARP at a total of over $1.5 billion, the biggest such sale yet. This dwarfs the $1.1 billion raised from a similar warrant sale by Goldman Sachs and $950 million by JPMorgan Chase.

March 6, 2010 In a referendum, Icelandic voters overwhelmingly (93-2) reject the deal negotiated by the government regarding repayment to the Netherlands and the UK concerning Icesave depositors.

March 17, 2010 Regulatory authorities in the USA issue new guidelines on the management of liquidity risk. The authorities are the Federal Reserve, the FDIC, the OTS, the National Credit Union Administration and the Conference of State Bank Supervisors. The guidelines are discussed further in Chapters 5 and 8.

March 24, 2010 Denmark abolishes the unlimited guarantee for deposits, but raises the former limit to €100,000, double the minimum requirement of the EU. The government also underscores that in Denmark it is the financial sector itself, and not the state, that bears the primary responsibility for saving banks in trouble.

March 29, 2010   The French arm of the clearing house LCH. Clearnet starts the clearing of euro-denominated corporate CDS contracts in competition with the London subsidiary of the InterContinental Exchange (ICE Europe).

March 30, 2010   NAMA, the Irish "bad bank," starts buying toxic assets from banks. In all, it plans to buy loans for €81 billion ($107 billion), applying an average "haircut" of 47 percent – that is, loans will be purchased for about half of their nominal value. In combination with raised capital adequacy requirements ahead of changes enforced by BIS (minimum Core Tier 1 ratio of 8 percent, minimum equity Core Tier 1 ratio of 7 percent), this leads to banks having to raise more capital: AIB €7.4 billion, Bank of Ireland €2.7 billion, Irish Nationwide €2.6 billion, the Educational Building Society (EBS) €0.9 billion and the nationalized Anglo Irish Bank Corp. may need €18.3 billion. Share prices in the first two banks fell sharply, by 20 percent in AIB and by 10 percent in the Bank of Ireland. AIB could risk having to have government ownership of 70 percent, and Bank of Ireland 40 percent. Nationwide and EBS are to be nationalized completely. Bank of Scotland and Fortis have already left their Irish market joint ventures.

March 31, 2010   The Federal Reserve ends its program for support of the mortgage market, under which it has purchased $1.43 trillion of mortgage and agency bonds.

April 1, 2010   WestLB becomes the first German bank to announce that it will be selling toxic assets to the federal "bad bank" scheme, in total loans

| | worth a nominal €77 billion. WestLB is also the only one of the *Landesbanken* in trouble (the others are HSH Nordbank, BayernLB and Landesbank Baden-Württemberg) to have accepted a federal bail-out, the others having been recapitalized by the respective states, their owners. |

April 16, 2010   The SEC takes the market by surprise by charging the Goldman Sachs Group Inc. with fraud in connection with repackaging and selling CDOs linked to subprime mortgages. In its lawsuit, the SEC alleged that Goldman structured and marketed a synthetic collateralized debt obligation (Abacus 2007-AC1) that hinged on the performance of subprime residential mortgage-backed securities. It alleges that Goldman did not tell investors "vital information" about Abacus, including the fact that a hedge fund by the name of Paulson & Co. was involved in choosing which securities would be part of the portfolio. It also alleges that Paulson took a short position against the CDO in a bet that its value would fall. According to the SEC, the marketing materials for the CDO showed that a third party, ACA Management LLC, chose the securities underlying the CDO. The SEC said that Paulson & Co. paid Goldman $15 million to structure and market the CDO, which closed on April 26, 2007. Little more than 9 months later, 99 percent of the portfolio had been downgraded. The Goldman Sachs stock fell by over 12 percent during the day, Citigroup by 7 percent and Bank of America Merrill Lynch by 5 percent.

April 17, 2010   The Central Bank of China increased to 50 percent the minimum downpayment in purchasing a new home, up from 40 percent.

April 21, 2010	General Motors announces that GM has repaid the remaining $5.8 billion in loans from the USA and Canada. The US government still owns a 61 percent stake in the company (and Canada 11 percent), after GM received over $61 billion in aid after its 2009 bankruptcy.
April 26, 2010	The countries in the G-20 group meet without being able to agree other than in general terms on the need to improve both the quantity and quality of capital. In particular, the countries disagree on the need for a US-type overall leverage ratio of a maximum twenty-five times (opposed in particular by Germany, where Deutsche Bank was leveraged seventy-one times), as well as a bank bailout tax (opposed in particular by Canada and Australia, where bank bail-outs were not necessary).
April 30, 2010	The European Commission issues a set of recommendations for remuneration in the financial sector.
May 1, 2010	China raises the cash reserve requirement for large banks to 16.5 percent, to combat excessive house price inflation.
May 3, 2010	Greece sets aside €10 billion to support its banking system as the austerity plan forces it to cut government expenditure by 13 percentage points of GDP in 3 years.
May 5, 2010	The Swedish Financial Supervisory Authority (Finansinspektionen) decides that new mortgages, as well as increases in existing mortgages, must not exceed 85 percent of the market value of the property. This makes Sweden the first country to introduce explicit ceilings on loan-to-value after the crisis. Germany, France and Denmark already have such limits.

May 9, 2010	The Federal Reserve restarts its emergency currency-swap tool by providing as many dollars as needed to the ECB, the Bank of England and SNB, allowing them to provide the "full allotment" of US dollars as needed. The swaps are authorized through January 2011.
May 17, 2010	The ECB reveals that it has bought €16 billion of Eurozone bonds in the first such attempt to create liquidity, a move that was heavily criticized by the two German members of the Governing Council. By early June, the volume had risen to €40 billion.
May 19, 2010	Germany decides to go it alone and ban the selling of naked default swaps – that is, the situation of buying insurance without having the underlying risk. The ban encompasses EU government bonds as well as the shares in certain German banks. Germany's Euro partners, not having been informed of the move, are deeply offended.
May 20, 2010	The US Senate votes to overhaul financial regulation, a bill that must now be reconciled with that taken by the House of Representatives.
May 23, 2010	Bank of Spain seizes control over the ailing Cajasur d'Andalusia, run by the Catholic Church. The initial cost is calculated at €500 million.
May 26, 2010	The European Commission proposes a levy on banks, to be paid upfront into a stability fund to insure against future financial failures. Germany calculates that its banks would pay around €1 billion per year. The UK and France oppose that plan, arguing that the existence of a fund will create moral hazard, encouraging higher risk levels. The UK also argues that the proposal must be agreed by unanimity in the ECOFIN Council, since it is a

	matter of taxation. This would guarantee that the plan fails.
May 26, 2010	The US FASB proposes that a much larger proportion of bank assets in the future be carried at "fair" – that is, market – values. This would apply not only to derivatives, but also to many loan categories, such as credit card debts, corporate lending, unsecured loans, some mortgage debt. Banks would report on a separate line the more smoothly developing "amortized cost."
June 2, 2010	The European Commission proposes that rating companies operating in the EU countries be supervised by the new EU-wide regulatory body, the ESMA.
June 5, 2010	Finance ministers from the G-20 countries fail to agree on a global bank tax to finance future interventions, leaving each country to go it alone. In particular, Japan, Australia and Canada, which have not had to support their banks in the financial crisis, as well as Brazil and India among the developing nations, are against the idea.
June 7, 2010	Finance ministers agree on a common stabilization fund for the euro countries (plus Sweden and Poland), encompassing €750 billion in potential support to countries in difficulty. Each country will share proportionately to GDP in the funding of a special-purpose vehicle (SPV) located in Luxembourg. Sharper sanctions will be applied to countries which repeatedly break the budgetary rules. The fund should be compared with claims on Portugal, Spain and Greece held by financial institutions, amounting to some €2,000 billion.
June 16, 2010	The newly elected Conservative-Liberal British government proposes a complete overhaul of financial regulation and supervision. The FSA

is to be abolished. Its personnel and functions will reappear as the Prudential Regulatory Authority, an independent division of the Bank of England. As in the USA, a Consumer Protection and Markets Authority (now named the Financial Conduct Authority) is to be set up, outside the Bank of England. Executive power will lie in the Financial Policy Committee, a body parallel to the present Monetary Policy Committee. Both committees will be chaired by the Governor of the Bank of England.

June 22, 2010

The new British government proposes a levy on banks which would tax their balance sheets starting in January 2011, generating £2 billion of revenue per year. The tax will be set at 0.04 percent in 2011, increasing thereafter to 0.07 percent. The levy will apply to UK banks as well as the subsidiaries and branches of overseas banks. Firms will only be liable for the levy when their relevant aggregate liabilities exceed £20 billion. The proposal may be compared with the existing Swedish "stability fund," into which all banks pay 0.036 percent of their liabilities, with the exclusion of such subordinated liabilities that count as Tier 2 capital. The difference, however, is that the British levy will go directly into the budget, not to build up a fund. The levels may be compared with the 0.15 percent that the USA proposes to level on its fifty biggest banks, but the US tax is levied on liabilities minus equity and minus all FDIC-insured deposits. The UK tax will be levied at total liabilities minus core capital and insured deposits. Liabilities with more than 1-year maturity would be taxed at half-rate.

June 25, 2010

A committee with members from both the US Senate and the House of Representatives succeeds in compromising the two bills passed by the respective houses in the form of the Dodd-Frank Bill, which needs to be taken by the two chambers.

June 27, 2010   The leaders of the G-20 countries meeting in Toronto make very little headway towards financial reform. Higher standards for capital and liquidity (Basel III) are agreed in principle, but their introduction is postponed. There will be no global bank tax, with some countries going their own way (UK, Germany, Austria, France and Sweden). Achieving a common set of global accounting principles also appears to fail, as the international IASB and the US FASB fail to agree.

June 30, 2010   The US House of Representatives passes by 237 to 192 the bill H.R. 4173 Restoring American Financial Stability Act of 2010, also called the Dodd-Frank Bill. (See July 15, 2010 for Senate passing the bill.)

June 30, 2010   The European Union agrees on new rules for remuneration in banks as well as hedge funds. At least 40 percent (or 60 percent for large bonuses) of the bonus must be postponed for 3 to 5 years, and the payment upfront must be limited to half the amount, the rest being paid in stock. The cash portion is thus reduced to 20–30 percent of the total. Some EU countries already have similar rules, following the previous recommendation by the EU Commission, K (2009) 3159.

July 1, 2010   The US Treasury Department announces that it has sold in the market part of its holdings in Citigroup, bringing down its stake from at most 36 percent to 18 percent of equity. The price per share, $4.03, gives the taxpayer a handsome profit, since at the bottom of the crisis, the shares were worth $1.

July 9, 2010	Spain's troubled savings banks (*cajas*) will be allowed to sell half their equity to private investors in the future to recapitalize their losses.
July 15, 2010	The US Senate adopts the Dodd-Frank Bill for the reform of financial regulation (The Wall Street Reform and Consumer Protection Act) by 60 to 39, passed by the House of Representatives on June 30. (It will be discussed below in various chapters, especially Chapters 9 and 10.)
July 22, 2010	The Congressional Budget Office (CBO) calculates that the two mortgage giants Fannie Mae and Freddie Mac, placed in conservatorship under the government, having already cost $145 billion in new capital, might cost the taxpayer a total of $389 billion by 2019.
July 23, 2010	The stress testing of ninety-one European banks is published. All but seven banks pass the test, implying that their Tier 1 capital ratio will exceed 6 percent even in a stressed situation.
July 26, 2010	The Basel Committee on Banking Supervision agrees rules for a new leverage ratio (Tier 1 capital over total asset including off-balance-sheet items) of 3 percent, meaning a maximum gearing of thirty-three (rather than the twenty-five originally proposed).
August 23, 2010	Ireland's NAMA reveals that it is paying just 38 percent of the nominal value of assets acquired from Anglo-Irish Bank, implying a 62 percent mark-down.
September 2, 2010	HSBC warns that it might relocate to Hong Kong if an attempt is made to break up the bank. Its Chief Executive has been based in Hong Kong since January 2010.
September 12, 2010	The new higher capital requirements under Basel III were revealed by the Basel

Committee, to be decided on by the G-20 group of countries. Focusing on Core Tier 1 capital, basically equity and reserves, the new rules demand an increase of the absolute minimum, from 2 percent to 4.5 percent. In order to guarantee this minimum, a conservation buffer of 2.5 percent is added, making the effective rate 7 percent. Banks below this level will face restrictions on dividend and bonus payments. Other buffers under discussion are a counter-cyclical buffer of up to 2.5 percent (as used already in Spain) and an additional buffer of 1–2 percent placed on banks deemed to be systemically important ("too big to fail"). The total Tier 1 ratio is raised from 4 to 6 percent, while the total capital ratio is maintained at 8 percent (excluding the conservation buffer). The new rules will be phased in gradually. The 4.5 percent minimum must be attained by January 1, 2015, while the buffer capital has until 2019. The new liquidity standard also has to be fulfilled by 2015. The use of hybrid capital in Tier 1 capital will be phased out, with an adjustment period stretching until 2023.

September 15, 2010   The European Commission proposes new rules for trading. First, rules on short selling of shares and government bonds require dealers to reveal to the authorities any short position above 0.2 percent of issued capital, and to the market if the position is larger than 0.5 percent. A new authority also provides the legal means of banning short selling altogether in certain securities at times of market unrest. Second, in order to push trades in OTC derivatives such as CDSs to exchanges, or at least to central clearing, after the trade, new capital requirements will require far higher capital demands for trades cleared bilaterally.

September 22, 2010   The EU Parliament votes in favor of the new system of financial regulation and supervision in the European Union, making possible the start on January 1, 2011 of the European Banking Authority (EBA, London), the European Securities and Markets Authority (ECMA, Paris) and the European Insurance and Occupational Pensions Authority (EIOPA, Frankfurt), as well as the European Systemic Risk Board (ESRB, Frankfurt).

September 22, 2010   The SEC and the CFTC present a plan for how derivatives trading, especially in CDSs, will take place after the implementation of the Dodd-Frank Bill. They envisage 20–30 exchanges called swap execution facilities (SEFs), with compulsory centralized clearing, as is already the case for options trading in the USA, with clearing of trades from different venues in the Options Clearing Corporation.

September 30, 2010   The government of Ireland gives notice that it might have to inject more capital into Allied Irish Banks (AIB), increasing the state's share from 18.7 percent to possible majority control. The government has already spent €33 billion to prop up its banking system, of which €22 billion went into AIB, which is already majority-owned. The total might rise to €50 billion, the finance minister warns.

September 30, 2010   The bailed-out insurance company AIG and the US government agree that the government's holding of preferred stock ($49.1 billion) be converted to common shares, to be sold on the open market over an 18- to 24-month period. This will reduce the share of stock held by present private shareholders from 20 to 7.9 percent.

October 1, 2010	The US Treasury notifies that it has reduced its stake in Citigroup to 12 percent by selling 1.5 billion ordinary shares at a profit of just over $1 billion.
October 4, 2010	Switzerland proposes a sharp increase in the capital requirements for their two largest, systemically important banks, UBS and Credit Suisse. By 2019, they would have to hold at least 10 percent TCE (as compared with the 7 percent proposed by the Basel group) and 19 percent total capital (as compared with 8 percent today and 10.5 percent proposed by Basel). Of the TCE, at least 5.5 percent has to be in common equity, while the residual may be CoCo bonds. The government will not, however, recommend the break-up of banks nor limit the size of operations such as proprietary trading.
October 5, 2010	Landesbank Baden-Württemberg sues Goldman Sachs for $37 million lost in a CDO investment built on subprime loans. The CDO (Davis Square Funding VI) was characterized as "safe, secure and nearly risk free," while Goldman itself bought protection through CDSs linked to the failure of the Davis securities.
October 21, 2010	The eight funds created under the PPIP to buy toxic assets from banks reports a 36 percent return on the Treasury's money, showing the increased stability in the economy and tighter credit spreads. Unfortunately, the total sum involved is a meager $7 billion.
October 21, 2010	The British Treasury calculates that the levy on banks in the UK will yield an estimated £2.5 billion by 2012. For all banks, liabilities of up to £20 billion will be untaxed, meaning large institutions get hit harder. Since international banks with a UK presence will be

	taxed on their UK operations, there is a risk of double taxation on banks from other countries having adopted a bank levy, such as Germany, France, Austria and Sweden.
October 22, 2010	The FHFA calculates that the two GSEs Fannie Mae and Freddy Mac may need a total of $363 billion in taxpayer aid. Of this amount, $148 billion has already been drawn. The calculation may be compared with the more pessimistic figure of $390 billion emanating from the CBO, and the more optimistic figure of $160 billion from the White House Office of Management and Budget.
October 26, 2010	The European Union agrees on new rules for hedge funds and private equity funds. Capital and disclosure requirements will be placed on "alternative investment funds," while there will be created a common EU passport for EU as well as outside providers, but only from 2018.
November 1, 2010	The US Treasury Department announces that the troubled insurance company AIG will draw $22 billion in unspent TARP funds, which allows it to repay in full credits extended by the Federal Reserve. In this way, taxpayers rather than Fed will reap the profits.
November 2, 2010	In US elections, the Republican party gains control of the House of Representatives and picks up sufficient seats in the Senate to block Democratic proposals. It will enable them to influence the more than 240 rules necessary to fully implement the Dodd-Frank financial legislation. Hence the outcome for such rules as capital standards, especially as concerns big banks, derivatives trading and clearing, and banks' proprietary trading is unclear.
November 3, 2010	The FOMC decided that a further monetary stimulus being needed, the Fed would

purchase another $600 billion in marketable securities until summer 2011, having already bought $1,700 billion from September 2008, when the liquidity problems became acute. The move has been criticized by several well-known economists, such as Alan Greenspan (former Chairman of the Federal Reserve) and Martin Feldstein (former head of the NBER).

November 3, 2010   General Motors, 61 percent owned by the US government, plans an issue of common stock that will lower the government's share to 43 percent.

November 5, 2010   China starts a market for CDSs called credit risk mitigation. However, you can only buy protection if you have the underlying asset. Central clearing will be compulsory.

November 9, 2010   The FDIC proposes two changes to the way fees for deposit insurance are calculated. First, fees will be charged on a much larger base, assets minus tangible capital, but the rates lowered correspondingly. Second, fees will be risk-based by means of forward-looking scorecards rather than capital adequacy. The change will impact the largest banks most, and, in particular, the ex-investment banks Morgan Stanley and Goldman Sachs, with few deposits.

November 16, 2010   Despite a budget deficit of over 10 percent of GDP, Moody's confirms that the US Aaa rating is not in danger this year or the next, but could be in the longer run.

November 28, 2010   Ireland, the IMF and the European Union agree on a loan to shore Ireland's banking system. Of a total of €85 billion, €35 billion will be used to recapitalize banks, aiming for a Core Tier 1 ratio of 12 percent, and €50 billion to restore the consequences for the budget of the blanket guarantee of banks' deposits. As a consequence, AIB will join Anglo-Irish Bank in being totally nationalized, while the government will become a majority owner of the Bank of Ireland. The interest rate is at 5.8 percent – some 3 percentage points above German levels.

December 6, 2010	The US government sold off its remaining shares in Citigroup Inc. for $4.35 each, marking an exit from ownership in the bailed-out banking giant, with a $12 billion gross profit for taxpayers.
December 9, 2010	Iceland strikes a new deal with the Netherlands and the UK concerning the Icesave accounts. While acknowledging the debt of €4 billion, the rate of interest to be paid is lowered to 3.3 percent, from the 5.55 percent in the previous agreement. This deal still has to be approved by Parliament and the President of Iceland, as well as by a referendum. (The new deal is again voted down in a referendum on April 9, 2011, with a margin of 59-40, meaning that the dispute goes to the European Free Trade Association court.)
December 15, 2010	The Basel Committee calculates that 263 European banks would have needed an additional €602 billion in equity capital had the new Basel III 7 percent rule on TCE been in force in 2009. They also calculated that the world's major banks needed to have an additional $1,730 billion in liquid assets to fulfill the new liquidity ratio due by 2015.
December 30, 2010	The Irish government injects €3.7 billion into AIB, raising the government's stake from 18.7 percent to 93 percent. The result is a sharp drop in its share price, –23 percent over the day. From the start of the crisis, the share price has declined almost 99 percent.

January 4, 2011   Bank of America agrees to pay $2.6 billion to Freddie Mac and Fannie Mae, as compensation for faulty information on loans sold by Countrywide, the lender that Bank of America acquired in 2008.

January 7, 2011   The German *Landesbanken* agree to sell their investment banking unit DeKaBank to their part-owners, the local savings banks, for €2.3 billion. The savings banks already own half of DeKa (Deutsche Kapitalanlage) and will now acquire the rest.

January 10, 2011   The Basel Committee on Banking Supervision agrees on counter-cyclical capital buffers. A country may require its banks to hold up to 2.5 percent extra Core Tier 1 capital (that is, 9.5 instead of 7 percent) if its ratio of credit to GDP is deemed excessive. Other countries are required to follow suit. If the UK applies the full 2.5 percent and a US bank has 20 percent of its operations in the UK, the USA would be required to raise its capital demand on this bank by 0.5 percentage points.

January 12, 2011   The Congressional Oversight Panel for the Troubled Asset Relief Program (COP) estimates that TARP will end up costing the taxpayer only $15 billion, compared with initial estimates as high as $350 billion. Auto industry bailout costs are lowered from $40 billion to $19 billion.

                          Citigroup, which received $45 billion in capital and a guarantee for $301 billion of impaired assets, has exited both programs, with a gain to the taxpayer of $12 billion.

January 13, 2011   The bailed-out insurance company AIG retires its Federal Reserve credit line and converted the Treasury's preferred stock to common stock. The 92 percent public stake in AIG will be sold on the market gradually.

January 20, 2011	Investors of over €5 billion of subordinated debt in the almost fully nationalized AIB are offered 30 percent of face value in a buy-back.
January 21, 2011	Spain announces plans for the ailing savings bank sector (*cajas*). Problem savings banks are to be converted into commercial banks and, if needed, recapitalized by the state bank resolution fund (*Fondo de Reestructuración Ordenada Bancaria*, or FROB). Estimates of the capital necessary lie in the range of €25 billion to €50 billion, 3–5 percent of GDP. First out is the Barcelona-based Caixa, which, transformed into a commercial bank, would have a Core Tier 1 ratio of 10.9 percent, becoming the tenth largest bank in Europe by capital. All Spanish banks have to have a core ratio of 8 percent, as contrasted with a minimum of 7 percent under Basel III.
January 28, 2011	The Bank of England releases a research paper under which the optimal capital ratio of banks is set at 50 percent of risk-weighted assets and 17 percent of total assets, rather than 7–9.5 percent and 3 percent respectively under Basel III.
February 6, 2011	As yet another indication that the financial crisis is not over, the Danish Amagerbanken, the fifth biggest bank in Denmark, went bankrupt and was taken over by the government agency *Finansiel stabilitet*. Since the blanket guarantee of deposits and bonds was abolished in September 2010, bond holders as well as uninsured depositors were likely to lose money.
February 8, 2011	The British government temporarily increased the charge on banks to 0.1 percent on short-term liabilities, and to 0.05 percent for long-term liabilities for March and April, after which months the rate will return to the previously set

	0.075 percent rate for short-term and 0.0375 percent for long-term liabilities. The temporary increase is expected to yield an additional £800 million for an annual total of £2.5 billion.
February 16, 2011	WestLB, having received unacceptable support from the German federal government in setting up a "bad bank," is proposed to be split in several parts and put up for sale or wound down.
February 16, 2011	Companies in the USA with more than $50 billion in assets, where at least 85 percent of their revenue stems from financial transactions, are to be regarded as systemically important financial institutions and hence subject to decisions by the FSOC.
February 17, 2011	German banks' subordinated debt of a total of €24 billion is downgraded by the rating firm Moody's Investor Services, after a change in German legislation allows authorities to impose losses on investors in these securities, even without bankrupting the bank. Deutsche Bank and Commerzbank are among the banks involved.
February 18, 2011	The FDIC reports that so far this year 22 banks have been closed, compared with 140 failures in 2009 and 157 in 2010.
February 18, 2011	The newly created Financial Policy Committee (FPC) in the Bank of England is created by the interim naming of eleven members, headed by the Bank of England Governor Mervyn King as Chairman. The FPC has the authority to order an increase in banks' capital adequacy requirements, to limit bank lending, to increase collateral requirements or to place more restrictive loan-to-value demands on mortgages.
February 18, 2011	Investors rush to purchase the proposed $2 billion of CoCo bonds issued by Credit Suisse. The issue was oversubscribed eleven

	times. The issue was the first in Switzerland after the authorities set the required Core Tier 1 capital ratio at 19 percent. Only Rabobank in the Netherlands and Lloyds Banking Group in the UK had so far issued CoCos.
February 23, 2011	Thomas Hoenig, President of the Federal Reserve Bank of Kansas City, says in a speech that the largest financial institutions, those being "too big to fail," should be broken up.
March 10, 2011	The Bank of Spain estimates that its banks may need additional capital of €15 billion, concentrated to the major savings banks, such as Bankia (formed by Caja Madrid and six smaller banks), Novacaixagalicia and Catalunya Caixa. Moody's sets the shortfall at €40 billion to €50 billion. Spain also decrees that its banks must attain a Core Tier 1 ratio of 8 percent for listed banks and 10 percent for unlisted banks by September 2011.
March 10, 2011	The new stress test by the EBA of ninety-one European banks appears to be just as irrelevant as last year's exercise. First, the assumed economic downturn is very mild (for example, an assumed fall in the euro area GDP of 0.5 percent in 2011, 15 percent fall in European equity markets). Second, the floor of failure/pass is set at a low 5 percent Core Tier 1 capital. Third, only effects of sovereign holdings on trading-book assets are included; no effects on banking-book assets assumed. Hence the test does not include credit risk, only market risks. Commodity prices and commercial real estate shocks are not included. Also the fact that the results will be published limits the value of the exercise.
March 11, 2011	Sweden aims at directing its banks to hold 12 percent Core Tier 1 capital, and banks of

systemic importance perhaps 15 percent, rather than the 7 percent plus a counter-cyclical buffer of 2.5 percent agreed under the Basel III arrangements.

March 16, 2011	The US FDIC sues the former Chief Executive and other top executives of the failed Washington Mutual, accusing the leaders of the then largest savings bank in the USA of reckless lending.
March 19, 2011	Goldman Sachs is given permission to repurchase the $5 billion of preferred shares bought by Warren Buffet's company Berkshire Hathaway during the crisis.
March 22, 2011	Sweden, Luxembourg and Italy criticize the proposed ban on naked short selling of EU government bonds, arguing that it will diminish liquidity and thus raise volatility and interest costs.
March 23, 2011	The Basel Committee on Banking Supervision is considering requiring banks "too big to fail" to hold an additional 3 percentage points Core Tier 1 capital. The proposed rule is sharply criticized by the banking community, especially the Institute of International Finance and its Chairman, Josef Ackermann from Deutsche Bank.
March 29, 2011	US regulators propose that when banks securitize mortgage credits, they have to retain at least 5 percent "skin in the game," unless the underlying house purchase has been made with at least a 20 percent cash downpayment.
March 31, 2011	After concluding stress tests, Irish banks have been told to raise an additional €24 billion in capital, bringing the total to €70 billion (almost 50 percent of GDP), to be compared with the €35 billion envisaged in the EU rescue plan for Ireland. AIB must raise an additional €13 billion, and the Bank of Ireland €5

billion. It appears likely that, like Anglo Irish Bank, they will find themselves nationalized.

April 1, 2011
The US Treasury calculates a $24 billion profit on the aid that it and the Federal Reserve have extended to the banking system. The Fed's mortgage bond investments are expected to bring a $110 billion profit, offset by losses of $73 billion on guarantees to Fannie Mae and Freddie Mac.

April 9, 2011
In a referendum, the population of Iceland again rejects the agreement with the UK and the Netherlands concerning Icesave, despite milder payment conditions.

April 11, 2011
The Independent Commission on Banking (the Vickers Commission) in the UK proposes that the biggest banks should hold 10 percent Core Tier 1 equity capital.

May 5, 2011
Out of the €78 billion granted in aid from the EU and the IMF, €12 billion will be used to capitalize Portuguese banks, according to the agreement. Banks will have to attain a 9 percent Core Tier 1 ratio by the end of 2011, and 10 percent by the end of 2012.

May 9, 2011
In the first quarter of 2011, 28 percent of US homeowners had negative equity – that is, the value of the house was less than the amount of the mortgage. In Las Vegas, the corresponding ratio was 85 percent.

May 26, 2011
The EU Commission proposes to ease some of the ingredients of Basel III for the benefit of EU banks. They can continue to issue hybrid capital longer than previously agreed, and make use of more than the agreed maximum of 10 percent (of the total capital base) in their insurance subsidiaries.

June 1, 2011
The EU proposes to harmonize capital requirements, thereby preventing member states from imposing higher true core equity

	ratios than 10 percent. It also prolongs the period during which hybrid capital will be allowed in Tier 1 capital.
June 3, 2011	The US Treasury Department sells its remaining shares in Chrysler to Fiat. After this transaction, Chrysler has repaid all but $1.3 billion of the $12.5 billion received in support from the US government.
June 6, 2011	The German Financial Supervisory Authority BaFin criticizes the forthcoming EU-wide stress tests of banks, since they exclude the Tier 1 hybrid capital that the German *Landesbanken* have in the form of guarantees from their owners, the German states.
June 6, 2011	Seven EU member states (the UK, Spain, Sweden, Slovakia, Estonia, Lithuania, Bulgaria) protest against the proposal from the EU Commission that true core Tier 1 ratios be maximized at 7 percent for banks (and at 10 percent for systemically important institutions), in contrast with the normal EU way of setting minimum standards.

3 | *Could today's financial crisis have been foreseen?*

Can financial crises be predicted?

This chapter will contain both theory and empirics. In relation to the other chapters in the book, it may feel theoretical, at least at the beginning. The reader who is more interested in today's crisis, and the suggested remedies for how future crises are to be avoided or alleviated, may skip this chapter and go directly to Chapter 4, without losing the main thread of the argument.

The crucial question in this chapter regards the possibility to predict and thereby avoid financial crises. Could today's crisis have been foreseen, given known facts? With the results of the present crisis at hand, can we more easily predict and hence counteract the next crisis?

We saw earlier that Reinhart and Rogoff found that two common features of most of the 138 financial crises that have occurred since the Second World War were, first, speculative capital inflows to counteract deficits in the current account (that is, national overspending), and second, bloated prices on residential and/or commercial property.[1]

Some observers have claimed that a fundamental precondition for avoiding a financial crisis is conducting a credible monetary policy aimed at price stability. The current crisis, which had its roots in the USA, would thus be a result of the Fed's failed inflation fight. We shall see below that there were a number of indicators pointing to the fact that the financial economy and the pricing of financial instruments were being subjected to gradually increasing strains, even though the "normal" inflation rate in the price of goods and services was under control (at least if we focus on "core prices," which exclude the prices of food and energy). We will see later in Chapter 6 that the Fed reacted to the

---

[1] Reinhart and Rogoff, *This Time Is Different*.

dotcom crisis in 2000 by lowering the Fed Funds rate to 1 percent, which set the stage for the next bubble, in property prices.

Bubbles in housing prices appeared in countries like the UK and Australia, despite the fact that these two countries raised their interest rates far above the rest of the industrialized world: to almost 6 percent in the UK and to over 7 percent in Australia. Still house prices rose by 130 percent in the UK and by 95 percent in Australia between 1998 and 2004, with corresponding problems as the bubbles burst, which the bankruptcies of Northern Rock and Bradford & Bingley evince. In Australia the mortgage banks have fared better. National Australia Bank (NAB), however, has taken over Wizard Home Loans, a subsidiary of GE Money Bank, with mortgage-related problems.

Within Euroland, the interest rate policy of the ECB could not target problems in individual countries, a general problem with a common currency in countries that really do not constitute what economists call an "optimal currency area." Some countries, such as Germany, Italy and Portugal, would have needed a looser monetary policy than that conducted by the ECB to get growth going. Other countries with exploding property prices, like Ireland and Spain, would have needed much higher interest rates. To this general problem should be added the fact that the ECB did not (and still does not) want to target asset prices, only the prices of goods and services. Hence the refi rate (corresponding to the US Federal Funds rate) stopped at 4.25 percent, and hence property prices rose by 146 percent in Spain and by 129 percent in Ireland between 2000 and 2006.

As we shall see throughout this book, financial crises have usually been triggered by events outside the control of the financial sector itself. The thrift crisis in the USA, and the Nordic, Asian and Japanese crises were all the sequels to political deregulations, and the Russian crisis in 1998 (and 2008) was the consequence of falling oil prices. The unique common denominator in the crises of 1907, 1929 and 2007 is that they appear to have arisen spontaneously, without any clearly defined exogenous factor to blame. It is as if the economic system itself derailed, the crises being not exogenous but endogenous, created by and within the financial system itself.

Reinhart and Rogoff claim, however, and perhaps rightly, that today's crisis should also be seen as a result of deregulation, since "new unregulated or lightly regulated financial entities [hedge funds, private equity funds, SIVs, insurance companies, together commonly called the shadow banking system, as well as rating companies] have come to play a much larger role in the financial system, undoubtedly enhancing stability against some kinds of shocks, but possibly increasing vulnerabilities against others."[2]

The questions to be asked are these:

- Is there a *theory* which can explain these seemingly spontaneous crises?
- Can we find *explanatory variables* in these theories, statistically observable, which may serve as warning signals of an approaching crisis?

It is tempting to see the oncoming crisis in a deterministic world, where physics can help economists interpret the future, in particular where there is an abrupt breaking point, such as the Lehman crash in 2008 constituted:

It has been proposed that financial crashes correspond to a special type of critical transition: one that shows so-called log-periodic behavior. Such critical points arise within certain models in statistical physics, and they have a distinctive signature. This kind of system is prone to oscillatory, periodic fluctuations – in an economic context they would be analogous to periodic business cycles. But log-periodic variations are not like the regular oscillations of a light wave or a tuning fork. Instead, the peaks and troughs of the waves get steadily closer together. At the critical point itself they pile up on top of one another. The approach to such a critical transition is therefore signaled in advance by peaks and dips that follow one after the other at ever shorter intervals – a series of accelerating wobbles that herald catastrophe.[3]

Many of the graphs shown below, in particular on volatility, could be interpreted in this log-normal way, with gradually increasing fluctuations signaling an oncoming crisis.

What are "systemic risk" and "systemic crisis"?

The economic literature has attempted to give a number of definitions of the concepts "systemic risk" and "systemic crisis." Read the definitions below and focus on the mentioned variables.

---

[2] Reinhart and Rogoff, Is the 2007 US sub-prime financial crisis so different?
[3] Ball, *Critical Mass*, p. 291.

Macro-definition 1:

- A demand for reserve money so intense that the demand could not be satisfied for all parties simultaneously in the short run.
- A liquidation of credits that have been built up in the boom.
- A condition in which borrowers who in other situations were able to borrow without difficulty become unable to borrow on any terms – a credit crunch or a credit market collapse.
- A forced sale of assets because liquidity structures are out of line with market-determined asset values, causing further declines in asset values – the bursting of a price "bubble."
- A sharp reduction in the value of banks' assets, resulting in the apparent or real insolvency of many banks and accompanied by some bank collapses and possibly some runs.[4]

This definition stresses that it is the *lack of liquidity* that is behind the problems, and it is only when banks start selling assets and refusing credits that a more general crisis develops. The asset sales create a domino effect, leading to a general fall in the value of the banks' assets and thus to a solvency crisis. Variables to look for are those related to liquidity and the functioning of the interbank market. Today's crisis is definitely of this character, but what signs could we find of the appearing crisis?

Macro-definition 2:

Systemic risk refers to the risk or probability of breakdowns in the entire system, as opposed to breakdowns in individual parts or components, and is evidenced by co-movements (correlation) among most or all of its parts.[5]

The problem with this definition is that it is only afterwards that one may observe whether the different parts in the financial system have moved in tandem or in disparate ways. At least until the end of 2007 in the present crisis, one could claim that problems lay in individual banks, not in the financial system itself. Remember that the world stock markets continued to attain new record levels until October 2007.[6]

---

[4] Sundararajan and Baliño, *Banking Crises*, pp. 2ff.
[5] Kaufman and Scott, What is systemic risk?
[6] The S&P 500 topped on October 9, 2007 at index 1,565.

Macro-definition 3:

1. There has been a marked increase in short-term borrowing.
2. ... increasing willingness to finance at floating interest rates and to shorten the maturity of borrowings.
3. ... recent failure of the equity market to provide a net new source of capital for business.
4. The last danger signal associated with this rapid swelling of debt is the fragility of many of our financial institutions. Their assets and liabilities have risen much more quickly than their capital accounts.[7]

Now we are getting somewhere! It is quite natural for borrowers to want to fix maturities at long terms in order to lower their risk. But when this is no longer possible, they have to shorten maturities, borrowing on commercial paper instead of on bonds. The fact that it is much easier to get a high short rating (for example, P-1) than a long rating (Aaa–Aa) also points to the advantage of shortening maturities for risky borrowers. Variables to look for are thus increased borrowing on short instruments by households and businesses, an increase in total liabilities of financial institutions, and increased difficulty for companies to issue new shares.

Macro-definition 4:

The later stages of the boom are characterized by optimistic expectations as to the future yield of capital-goods, sufficiently strong to offset their growing abundance and their rising costs of production and, probably, a rise in the rate of interest also. It is of the nature of organized investment markets, under the influence of purchasers largely ignorant of what they are buying and speculators who are more concerned with forecasting the next shift of market sentiment than with a reasonable estimate of the future yield of capital-assets, that, when disillusion falls upon an over-optimistic and over-bought market, it should fall with sudden and even catastrophic force.[8]

Keynes is very clear in pinpointing the characteristics of a bubble, namely that buyers are relatively unaware of what it is they are really buying and not very interested, provided they have the time to make a quick buck before the market collapses. The main point in the definition is the focus on optimism – that is, the development of a bubble is in

---

[7] Kaufman, *Interest Rates*, pp. 37ff.
[8] Keynes, *The General Theory of Employment, Interest and Money*, pp. 315ff.

reality euphoria founded on the apparent growth, strength and stability of the economy. Second, this euphoria, and hence the bubble, are not the result of external forces, but are naturally imbedded into the capitalist system and the dynamics of the business cycle.

Macro-definition 5:

During the expansion phase of a long swing, or alternatively over a period in which only mild recessions occur, systematic changes in the financial structure occur. These reflect the financial aspects of high rates of growth by leading sectors, revaluation of assets to allow for growth expectations and the growing financial layering at the same time as ultimate liquidity grows slowly if at all. Financial institutions and usages evolve, both in response to market forces and as a result of administrative processes and legislation. Thus the exact course of financial variables over the phase of the longer waves differs greatly among the various observed cycles . . .

The financial panic is made possible by the changes in the financial structure that take place during the long-swing expansion. One element in the development of an "unstable" financial system is the rise in balance-sheet payments relative to final gross income for the income producing units[9]

And:

Every disaster, financial or otherwise, is compounded out of initial displacements or shocks, structural characteristics, and human error. The theory developed here argues that the structural characteristics of the financial system change during periods of prolonged expansion and economic boom, and that these changes cumulate to decrease the domain of stability of the system. Thus, after an expansion has been in progress for some time, an event that is not of unusual size or duration can trigger a sharp financial reaction.

Displacements may be the result of system behavior or human error. Once the sharp financial reaction occurs, institutional deficiencies will be evident. Thus, after a crisis it will always be possible to construct plausible arguments – by emphasizing the triggering events or institutional flaws – that accidents, mistakes, or easily corrected shortcomings were responsible for the disaster.[10]

It was Hyman Minsky who picked the tidbits from the Keynesian cake and brought his "general theory" further. Under the expansion phase of the cycle, not only will investors be lulled into security and change their behavior towards risk, the institutions themselves will be changing. An example is the explosion of securitized products in the latest

---

[9] Minsky, Longer waves in financial relations, pp. 324–35.
[10] Minsky, *Can "It" Happen Again?*, pp. 117–18.

boom, leading the advance of the "shadow banking system." As Minsky emphasizes, one can expect changes to be more profound if the expansion phase has lasted longer. We may recall from the earlier discussion that the US economy grew strongly and almost continuously from 1991 to 2008. Minsky also points out that it is the size of the financial economy in relation to the real economy that will create future instability. Not only Iceland and Ireland, but also the USA and the UK, make good examples, as we shall see, where the size of the financial parts of the economy has exploded in relation to the real, underlying economy.

In the next part of the quote, Minsky develops the effect on individuals. Human beings, being human, are responsible for having created, by their own mistakes, the ensuing instability, but they will always try to find an excuse, an event beyond their control, which they claim to be the trigger behind the events. We may carry the thought further. During a long period of well-being, organizations become more lax in their control of costs. Magnificent office buildings arise and customers are treated to luxurious golf trips or taken to lunch in three-star restaurants.[11] Shareholders and board members are tempted to give generous bonuses to those who are perceived to be responsible for the general well-being, and those who are thereby favored will have incentives to continue in the same direction. All is well as long as there is money.

Systemic crises may also be given a macro-micro dimension:

> Systemic risk is the probability that cumulative losses will accrue from an event that sets in motion a series of successive losses along a chain of institutions comprising a system ... That is, systemic risk is the risk of a chain reaction of falling interconnected dominos.[12]

Falling dominoes have indeed been evident in the current crisis. Think of the following dominoes (compare the chronology in Appendix 2.1):

---

[11] On a personal note, I vividly remember being taken to lunch in London in 1989 or 1990, at Le Gavroche, arguably the best restaurant in central London, by a company called Gamlestaden Research, which, despite its name, traded in financial futures and options. I was surprised at the invitation, since I was a stray guest with no particular connection with the firm. After a delicious lunch, I inwardly predicted their imminent downfall. The parent company, the finance company Gamlestaden, was indeed one of the first to succumb to the Swedish financial crisis in 1991.

[12] Kaufman (ed.), *Research in Financial Services*, p. 47.

Mortgage Lenders, American Home Mortgage, Landesbank Sachsen, Ameriquest, IKB, Northern Rock, Netbank, Countrywide, Bear Stearns, IndyMac, Freddie Mac and Fannie Mae, Lehman Brothers, Merrill Lynch, AIG, HBOS, Washington Mutual, Fortis, Bradford & Bingley, Wachovia, Hypo Real Estate, Dexia, Landsbanki, Glitnir and Kaupthing, RBS, Lloyds TSB, Anglo-Irish Bank, HGAA, Roskilde Bank . . .

That a gambler who has lost tries to get even by placing gradually larger bets is a well-known phenomenon. That was the way Leeson bankrupted Barings Bank in 1995, and that was how Jérôme Kerviel made a large hole in the balance sheet of Société Générale in 2007. But the banks' managements have also sought revenge in taking larger and larger risks. Sometimes they have even received help from their supervisors. The Office of Thrift Supervision is perhaps the best example of misuse of power, when its leading supervisor allowed IndyMac and some other ailing Californian savings banks to date an infusion of capital earlier than it was actually received in order to avoid their compulsory liquidation.

What empirical conclusions can we draw from these theories?

From the above literature we find the following warning signs:

- sharp (unmotivated?) increases in the value of stocks, property and commodities;
- a household savings ratio approaching zero or even becoming negative;
- borrowing and debt service ratios in households which rise markedly;
- assets and liabilities in the banking sector that rise as a percentage of GDP;
- increased share of short-term borrowing in households, corporations and banks;
- increasing deficit in the current account;
- a long period of stable growth with no major setbacks;
- unusually low risk premium (volatility, credit spreads, CDS spreads) which lead to a higher risk appetite.

In the following I will show some graphs, which, taken together, should have given any observer a clear indication of the problems that were on the way. The problem was that in the height of the euphoria, nobody or

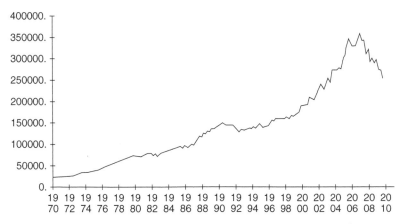

Figure 3.1 House prices in the western USA ($), 1970–2010
Source: Economagic Time Series

almost nobody looked in the right direction, or at least not sufficiently far in the right direction.[13]

House prices in the western USA, the area most ravaged by speculative excesses, started to rise rapidly in 2000. From a median price of $200,000, it had risen to $356,000 by 2006 – a rise of 78 percent. The Case-Shiller index (to which we will return in Chapter 4) showed house prices during this period rising by 118 percent in Phoenix (Arizona), 124 percent in San Diego (California) and 125 percent in Las Vegas (Nevada). Only Miami (Florida), with an increase of 167 percent in these 6 years, was even worse. And the region's banks would suffer as a consequence.

The great regional differences in price increases should have sounded an alarm bell about future problems in the region. It is not mere chance that the financial crisis would affect most deeply such banks and financial groups as IndyMac (California), Washington Mutual (California and Washington), Security Pacific (California), First Heritage Bank (California), PFF Bank and Trust (California), First National Bank

---

[13] Nassim Nicholas Taleb, a Lebanon-born "quant" on Wall Street, with an American Ph.D. in Finance, has recently shown how decision-makers in financial organizations were misled by the normal distribution, without regard for improbable but possible events falling outside the tails of the normal distribution, events which he calls "black swans." See Taleb, *The Black Swan* and also Chapter 7 in this book.

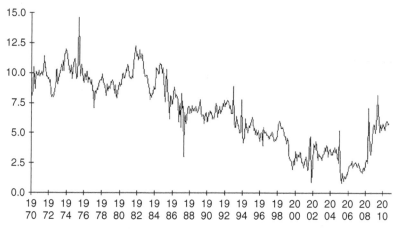

Figure 3.2 Household savings ratio in the USA (%), 1970–2010
Source: Economagic Time Series

(Nevada), Silver State Bank (Nevada), Sanderson State Bank (Texas), Franklin Bank (Texas), and many more to follow during 2009 and 2010.

The household savings ratio (savings as a percentage of disposable income) has shown a falling trend in the USA since 1982. During 2005–7 the ratio was even negative during some quarters, as households used their "home equity" to finance consumption, hence being able to consume more than they earned.[14] The same warnings signs were evident in Australia, where the savings ratio fell from 7 percent in 1996 to negative numbers for 2002–5. The UK saw a similar development, with the savings ratio falling from 10 percent in 1996 into negative territory 10 years later. The development is highly reminiscent of what had happened in Sweden 15 years earlier, with a savings ratio that fell from 10 percent in 1980 to –2.5 percent in 1988, the year before the financial crisis started.

From the beginning of the 1960s until the beginning of the 1980s, household liabilities were a relatively constant fraction of GDP, at 40–45 percent. The stability is even more surprising when we recall that this was a period of substantial volatility in share prices, interest rates, GDP

---

[14] While no negative numbers are shown in the graph, which builds on National Accounts data, there was a negative savings rate in 2007 according to the Flow of Funds accounts. The reason for the difference is a discrepancy between the two ways to calculate savings, either as income minus expenditures (National Accounts data) or as an increase in assets minus liabilities (Flow of Funds data).

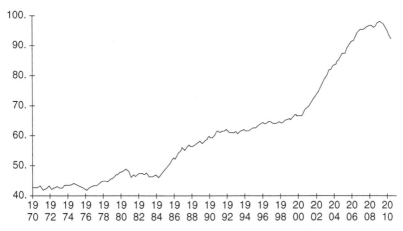

Figure 3.3 Household liabilities in the USA (% of GDP), 1970–2010
Source: Economagic Time Series

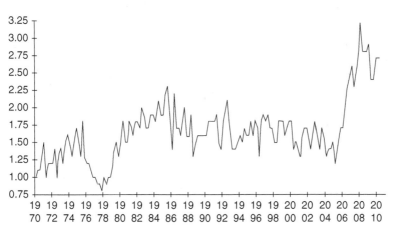

Figure 3.4 Share of empty/abandoned single-family houses in the USA (%),
1970–2010
Source: Economagic Time Series

growth rates and unemployment. From 1981, a process set in which
doubled the indebtedness to 96 percent at the end of 2007. One may be
forgiven for thinking that this long, uphill road should have triggered
some kind of reaction from politicians and supervisory authorities. It did
not. Figure 3.3 also shows the process accelerating from 2000.

The share of empty houses is a clear indication of supply and demand
in the housing market. From the mid-1980s until 2004, the vacancy

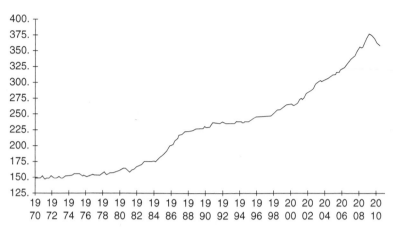

Figure 3.5 Total credit market liabilities in the USA (% of GDP), 1970–2010
Source: Economagic Time Series

ratio in the western USA was quite stable, at around 1.5 percent, the same level as in the country as a whole. From that point onwards, the ratio doubled to over 3 percent in just 3 years, as people abandoned houses that they could no longer afford and had not been able to sell.

It is natural in a mature economy that the process of intermediation increases – that is, banks and other financial institutions take up a gradually larger part of the economy. During the years under study, total credit market liabilities in the USA rose from 150 percent of GDP in 1982 to over 350 percent 25 years later, with a clear acceleration in the last few years. In just 4 years, from 2003 to 2007, total credit market liabilities outstanding rose from $34,647 billion to $50,051 billion (according to the Board of Governors of the Federal Reserve System, Flow of Funds data for the USA). This reflects the tendencies discussed in the following chapters, where financial assets were sold from one part of the chain to the next, and onwards. The development was similar in the UK, with financial sector liabilities growing from 30 to well over 200 percent of GDP between 1987 and 2007. In Iceland, gross liabilities of the financial sector rose to 1,500 percent of GDP.

Among the factors indicating a future financial crisis, we found earlier that shortening of maturities was one of the most important. Issues of commercial paper (CP) in the USA rose from levels of $500–600 billion in 2004 to around $800 billion in 2007, for both financial and non-financial sectors. During the same period, the amount of asset-backed

CP (ABCP) rose from $600 billion to $1,200 billion, only to collapse in 2008. Another worrying factor was the rising share of loans with variable rate of interest (adjustable rate mortgages, or ARMs). From a low of 11 percent of all new lending, it rose to 33 percent in 2004. The share of ARMs in subprime loans was almost 100 percent.[15]

The USA "manufactures" the world's most important reserve currency, the dollar. A gradually larger world trade needs to be financed by more dollars. In contrast to most other nations, the USA not only may but should have a permanent deficit in its current account, supplying the world with dollars. This "natural" (that is, sustainable) deficit has been calculated by the Peterson Institute for International Economics to perhaps 2 percent of GDP. As the figures below show, the actual deficit attained almost $900 billion, corresponding to over 6 percent of GDP in 2006, but this has since halved, as a result of the improved competitiveness (in particular vis-à-vis the Asian currencies) and falling internal demand.

A deficit in the current account is tantamount to saying that the country is using the rest of the world's surplus savings. The current account is, by definition, the sum of the savings balance in the private sector (saving minus investment) and that of the public sector. A deficit is thus an indication that demand in the country exceeds production and needs to be financed with other countries' savings. Hence it is hardly surprising that we find similar developments in all countries with overheated property markets. In Australia, the current account deficit grew to –6 percent of GDP in 2004. Ireland reached the same relative deficit, but only in 2008. In Spain, the current account deficit continued to grow until 2007, when it reached –10 percent of GDP. In the UK, the deficit finally peaked at –3.8 percent of GDP in 2007.

There is, however, a marked difference between these countries. The pound, like the Australian dollar, floats, and hence a deficit is the sovereign problem of that particular country. To resolve the deficit problem, the pound obediently fell from €1.50 per pound in 2007 to close to parity at the end of 2008, only to recover somewhat in 2009 and 2010. Similarly, the Australian dollar fell from almost parity with the US dollar in August 2008 to 0.65 in December – that is, a fall of 35 percent.

---

[15] In the name of fairness, it should be pointed out that the choice of fixed or variable rates of interest is also a matter of tradition. In the UK, over 90 percent of new mortgages were ARMs (or floating rate, to use the British terminology) in 2007.

Ireland and Spain, however, are a part of Euroland, which means that their individual deficits are no longer relevant for the exchange rate. Thanks to German surpluses, the current account of Euroland is basically in balance.

Figures 3.7 and 3.8 point to the (apparent) stability in the US economy over the last 25 years. After the latest oil price crisis in 1979, and

Figure 3.6 Current account balance in the USA ($ billion), 1970–2010
Source: Economagic Time Series

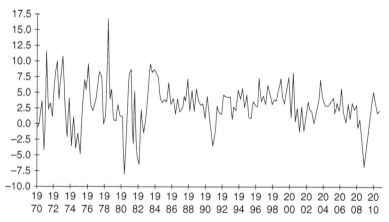

Figure 3.7 Gross domestic product in the USA (% quarterly change at annual rates), 1970–2010
Source: Economagic Time Series

the instability created by the (failed) monetary policy experiment 1979–82,[16] the growth rate became much more stable. In the 25 years until 2007, real GDP grew by 3.1 percent per year on average. Only one year, 1991, saw a small fall in GDP. In the 2001 recession, only one quarter's growth was negative. This apparent stability came to an abrupt end when GDP fell (at annual rates) by –5.4 percent in the fourth quarter of 2008 and by –6.4 percent in the first quarter of 2009.

Figure 3.8 depicts uncertainty on the financial markets. In the 1990s, volatility was abnormally low, hence encouraging banks, individuals

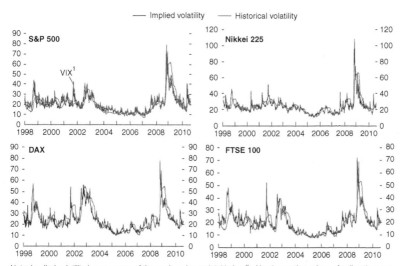

Note: Implied volatility is a measure of the equity price variability implied by the market prices of call options on equity futures. Historical volatility is calculated as a rolling 100-day annualized standard deviation of equity price changes. Volatilities are expressed in % rate of change
[1]VIX is the Chicago Board Options Exchange volatility index. This index is calculated by taking a weighted average of implied volatility for the eight S&P 500 calls and puts.

Figure 3.8 Implied and actual volatility in the S&P 500 index (USA), Nikkei 225 (Japan), DAX (Germany) and FTSE 100 (UK) (%), 1998–2010
Source: International Monetary Fund, *World Economic Outlook* (October 2010), Appendix, Figure 7

---

[16] This policy implied targeting money supply instead of interest rates. This resulted in the Fed Funds rate moving from 7 to 23 percent, with daily movements of up to 4 percentage points. In the real economy, GDP growth varied from +17.5 percent to –7.5 percent from quarter to quarter – a total catastrophe! The experiment was abandoned in 1982.

and corporations to take on more risk. The result was the dotcom crisis. Despite the fall of share prices, and despite the terrorist attacks in September 2001, volatility again fell back from 2003, encouraging speculative excesses, this time in securities markets linked to housing.

From the fall of 2007, volatility started rising and reached an all-time high of 70–90 percent in October 2008, and of over 100 percent in Japan. By summer 2010, it had fallen back to an almost normal 20 percent, only to rise again to 40 percent on account of the government debt problems in the USA and the UK, and especially in the PIIGS countries.

The interconnectedness of global financial markets is clearly shown in the highly parallel movement of volatility in these four stock markets.

Points to remember

- A systemic crisis is a financial crisis affecting the entire financial system, not just an individual bank.
- Signs of an approaching systemic crisis may be such factors as large increases in asset prices, a household savings ratio falling towards zero or becoming negative, increases in household borrowing and payments ratios as a percentage of disposable income, increases in credit market liabilities as a fraction of the economy, increased share of short-term borrowing by households, corporates and banks, unusually low risk premiums leading to speculative behavior.
- An important factor concerns regional differences. The accelerating house price increases in some US states, such as California, Arizona, Nevada and Florida, should have raised an alarm. It was no chance that the crisis hit mainly banks and financial groups in these states.
- The US household savings ratio fell from 10 percent to negative numbers, just like in Australia and the UK (and Sweden in 1988).
- US households doubled their borrowing as a fraction of GDP in 20 years. Interest payments and amortizations as a fraction of disposable income also rose sharply. Vacancies increased as people abandoned homes they could no longer afford.
- Total US credit market debt rose from 150 percent of GDP to 350 percent between 1982 and 2007, with a clear acceleration in the years from 2000.
- An increasing part of borrowing was short-term CP, while the share of mortgages with adjustable (floating) interest rates rose from 11 percent to 33 percent.

- The risk premium was abnormally low in both the mid-1990s and the period just preceding the financial crisis. This was evident from the VIX volatility, from CDS spreads and from the difference between bonds with different risk levels.
- All this was visible and well known, but no one, or almost no one, gave a warning. Perhaps nobody listens to academic economists since they are not in the market, while those economists who are in the market keep quiet on account of solicitude for their organizations (and their jobs!). In a classical Ponzi scheme, investors realize prices are excessive, but believe that they are so close to the market center of information that they will have time to exit before the bubble bursts.[17]

[17] Personally I had noted the price increases on properties in the USA, the UK, Ireland, Spain and Australia, and the unsustainable relationship between household borrowing and income. I had foreseen price falls and banking problems in these countries. However, the strong world economy, and the fact that price-earnings ratios on most stock markets were quite normal, led me to the conclusion that other countries and the global economy as a whole would be only marginally affected. The error in the analysis was a grave underestimation of the transfer of risk that had taken place, to unknown actors and unknown countries, with the result that the confidence in the entire world financial sector evaporated overnight with the Lehman and AIG bankruptcies.

4 | The US housing market and the subprime crisis

Speculation and bubbles are eternal, only the object varies

A bubble will always follow its own rhythm, fundamentally unchanged in character throughout the centuries, from speculation in tulip buds in Holland in the seventeenth century, to today's speculation in US, British, Irish and Spanish house prices. The first phase is usually engineered by an exogenous event which enables speculation in higher future prices. Financial bubbles have most often followed deregulations, which create new possibilities but also new risks, of which the financial actors have not always been aware. The thrift crisis in the USA in the 1980s, the Japanese, Asian and Nordic crises of the 1990s, and today's crisis all bear traits of this type. We will return to their history in Chapter 8. Many want to see the changed legislation of 1999, which repealed the separation between commercial banking, investment banking and insurance (the Glass-Steagall Act of 1933), as one of the main drivers behind the subprime crisis.

As pointed out earlier, the move from organized and regulated credit markets in banks and investment banks to the "shadow banking system," with the ensuing loss of supervision, may also be characterized as an act of deregulation, albeit unintended. Some important financial units escaped supervision altogether, such as the London-based financial products division of the US insurance company AIG.

But we should not forget the growth of information technology (IT), creating a burst of productivity which was the major reason for the high and steady GDP growth rates between 1992 and 2007, but which alas has also had its drawbacks. One is the subprime crisis. Not only did the stable macro-environment lure investors into risky investments, but without IT, lenders and borrowers would not have been able to meet on the internet without physical contact; without IT, it would not have been possible to gather the amount of information necessary to separate different layers of customers into prime and subprime; and without IT, financial engineering ("the quants") would not have been able to create all these mathematically complex products such as CDOs and CDSs, to which we will return in the next chapter, and the rating agencies would not have been able to give these bonds an AAA rating without mathematically complex (if often inadequate!) models.

The new phenomenon, in this case subprime lending, generates a temporary but excessive increase in revenues and profits which furthers the speculative frenzy. Asymmetric information gives the seller of the products an advantage in knowledge about these products (remember the "lemon"!). Being aware of the drawbacks, the seller hides these facts from the buyers, in particular since the seller stands to gain personally from this knowledge. As the bubble rises, some more knowledgeable buyers become aware that prices are excessive and will fall, but believe that they themselves will be able to make a profit before selling in time (a pyramid game or Ponzi scheme). The sales by these insiders lead to the beginning of a fall in prices, which accelerates and becomes a panic when everybody starts running in the same direction.[1]

An extreme case of a Ponzi scheme was uncovered during December 2008. Bernard Madoff was a well-known and respected broker and investment manager, and former Chairman of NASDAQ. He reported a remarkably high and steady return on investments year after year, which in itself should have raised suspicions. In reality, all new money coming in was used to repay people wanting to sell and to give a stable dividend to remaining clients. In fact, he had not made a single transaction in 11 years; all reports to customers were faked. For this reason, investors could not get an online update of their investments, but had to rely on (fictitious) reports on paper. When the bluff was exposed, an amount in the order of $65 billion was missing.

Greed was rampant everywhere during the subprime years (the exact definition of "subprime" is given later in the chapter). There

---

[1] In his book *Irrational Exuberance*, Robert Shiller discusses the psychology behind financial bubbles. The latest edition has a new chapter on the housing market. See also the recent book by Akerlof and Shiller, *Animal Spirits*.

was greed among all those who took out equity loans on their houses to raise their consumption standards. There was even more greed among all those who bought a house on pure speculation, without ever intending to live there. There was greed among the mortgage brokers who sold their customers products with initial low rates of interest ("teaser rates"), which were reset to much higher levels a couple of years later. Two-thirds of all US mortgages during the build-up of the bubble were granted through a broker on the internet, with no physical contact between the lending bank and the borrower. There was greed among those banks that lent money to unknown risky customers in subprime loans, and then shifted the risk to others by securitizing the loans. There was greed among all those intermediaries in banks and investment banks who made heaps of money by repackaging these mortgage-backed securities (MBSs) into products that could attract a wider range of investors all around the world (collateralized debt obligations, or CDOs). There was greed among the rating companies that basically acceded to the banks' demands for high ratings in order to retain their business. And, finally, there was greed among all those investors who bought these CDOs, investing several times their equity, everything from German savings banks and Icelandic and Chinese commercial banks, to hedge funds and investment advisors and investment managers like UBS, who foisted onto their customers bonds which have since become virtually worthless.

Whether crimes were committed in the process will be something for the courts to sort out over the coming years. A number of subprime borrowers claim that they were swindled and did not understand the products they were sold. Likewise, just like after the Enron bankruptcy, class action suits have appeared in the courts, where bankers are sued for misleading information, breach of trust, and so on.[2]

---

[2] A class action suit has been entered, inter alios, against the former CEO of bankrupted Countrywide Financial Services, Angelo Mozilo, who sold shares in the company to the tune of $291.5 million, just before the crash. He has agreed to pay a fine of $22.5 million, and repay $45 million of illicit capital gains. In July 2009, the former head of the German bank IKB was charged with breach of trust. The case brought by the SEC against Goldman Sachs was referred to earlier (see pages 75–6).

Government pressures

An extenuating circumstance for those responsible in the financial sector is that politicians as well as supervisors were pushing banks to increase lending, in particular to the less privileged. The 1974 Equal Credit Opportunity Act in the USA expressly forbids a bank to refuse someone a loan on account of race, color, origin, sex, marital status or age. Nor may the bank take into consideration whether a certain disposable income emanates from salary, self-employed income or subsidies. The fact that the incomes of self-employed persons are generally more variable than those of salaried persons may thus not be taken into account. Nor must the bank ask whether a woman receives alimony from a former husband for herself or for children. The fact that one lacks a fixed telephone, and hence is not listed in the phone book, may not be a part of the decision. Neither may a bank reduce a woman's future income to take account of the fact that she will likely stay at home with the children over some years, nor ask her if she plans to have (more) children.

The Federal Reserve and other banking supervisors are required under law (The Community Reinvestment Act of 1977) to evaluate once a year the lending of each bank, according to geographical distribution by zip code. If it turns out that the bank is underexposed to a certain zip code area with predominantly slum quarters, the bank must prove to the Federal Reserve for each individual loan, including rejected applications, that its criteria were not discriminatory. One may suspect that the banks, even knowing better, accepted some highly doubtful loan applications rather than trying to explain their actions to the Fed.

On several occasions, politicians have also influenced the semi-public mortgage banks Fannie Mae and Freddie Mac to purchase bonds with subprime loans as underlying assets. The Clinton administration did this in 1999 and the Bush administration in 2004. President Bush called his initiative "The American Dream."[3] In 2008, no less than 56 percent of all new mortgages acquired or guaranteed by Fannie Mae and Freddie Mac went to so-called "affordable housing." On the surface, the push was eminently successful. Homeownership in the USA increased from 65.7 percent of the population in 1997 to 68.9 percent

---

[3] George W. Bush, press release, September 2, 2004: "Increasing Affordable Housing and Expanding Home Ownership."

in 2005. The increase was especially marked in western USA, for households under the age of 35, for those with lower-than-average income, and for Blacks and Hispanics.[4] The problems in the housing sector and the forced sales of homes (foreclosures) had brought the rate down to 66.9 percent by the third quarter of 2010.

Legislation also promoted (and still does) irresponsible behavior, since the bank's collateral consists exclusively of the mortgaged house and no other assets or incomes of the borrower. Should the house become worth less than the mortgage (a situation applying to almost one out of four US homeowners in 2010), the borrower may simply abandon the house, sending the keys to the bank. The bank has no right to further claims. Hence the borrower-speculator gets the gain if prices rise and the bank takes the loss if prices fall. Or rather, the bank accepts the situation since it has securitized the credit anyway and hence carries no further risk. And it earned a fee in the process.

A further protection of (sometimes irresponsible) house buyers is offered by the so-called homestead laws. While the Federal law from 1862 was repealed in the 1970s, legislation still exists in some states to protect homeowners from a bank seeking to foreclose the mortgage and sell the house on account of delinquent payment of interest and/or amortization. In Massachusetts, for instance, the law allows homeowners to protect their property up to $500,000 of the value of their primary residence, per family, against subsequent attachment, levy on execution or sale to satisfy debts.

A highly profitable sector paid absurdly high salaries and bonuses

The financial sector in the USA accounted for 5.6 percent of total employment in 2006, the year before the crisis, according to the Bureau of Labor Statistics, up from 5.2 percent 10 years earlier. The high productivity in the sector gave it a somewhat larger share in GDP, 7.7 percent. That same year, the financial sector made profits of $462 billion, corresponding to 33 percent of total corporate profits.[5] The

---

[4] Shiller, *The Subprime Solution* and A market to prop up, *Financial Times*, March 23, 2010.

[5] Both sets of data emanate from the Bureau of Economic Analysis (BEA), which is the agency under the Commerce Department that produces the national accounts.

share of total profits had been only 5 percent in the years directly after the Second World War, rising gradually to 15 percent in the mid-1990s, and then suddenly doubling its share of total corporate profits in the next 10 years, only to fall abruptly in 2008 with the imploding bubble. Similar figures apply to the UK, where financial services accounted for 10.1 percent of GDP in 2007, but 27.5 percent of corporate taxes.

Even internationally, profitability was high. According to *The Banker* (July 2008, July 2009 and July 2010), return on capital was 19.9 percent in 2004, 22.7 percent in 2005, 23.4 percent in 2006 and a still high 20 percent in 2007. These figures are averages for the world's 1,000 largest banks, hence not including (then) investment banks such as Merrill Lynch or Bear Stearns.[6] In 2008, profitability fell to 2.7 percent and then recuperated somewhat to 8.2 percent in 2009.

Chapter 8 will show that the take-off in banking profits (and salaries) from around 1980, and the explosion around the year 2000, is intimately linked with the process of deregulation, which began with the Depository Institutions Deregulation and Monetary Control Act of 1980 and the Garn–St. Germain Depository Institutions Act of 1982, culminating with the abolishing of the Glass-Steagall Act (which separated investment banking from commercial banking) by the Gramm-Leach-Bliley Act of 1999.

Profitability led to high remuneration, in particular in the form of annual bonuses. The New York banks paid out bonuses of $17.4 billion in the crisis year 2008, which may be compared to $33 billion in 2007 and $34.3 billion in 2006. As shown in Figure 4.1, the 2008 figure corresponds to $100,000 per employee, had the money been distributed equally, which of course it was not. The ten best-paid at Merrill Lynch shared bonuses of $209 million, of which the best-paid, the head of investment banking, received a bonus of $34 million (over and above his normal salary). This was a year when Merrill Lynch itself lost $27 billion . . .

Table 4.1 shows salaries and bonuses for some selected bank CEOs in 2007, the year in which the financial bubble started to burst.

---

[6] As we shall see later, the five major US investment banks have since either converted into bank holding companies (Goldman Sachs and Morgan Stanley), been absorbed by commercial banks (Merrill Lynch and Bear Stearns) or gone bankrupt (Lehman Brothers).

Table 4.1 *Compensation for selected bank CEOs ($ million), 2007*

Name	Bank/company	Annual salary	Bonus etc.
Dick Fuld	Lehman Brothers	0.60	73.1
Lloyd Blankfein	Goldman Sachs	0.75	71.2
James Dimon	JPMorgan Chase	1	27.8
Kenneth D. Lewis	Bank of America	1.5	23.8
James Cayne	Bear Stearns	3	17.1
John Thain	Merrill Lynch	0.7	15
Martin Sullivan	AIG	1	13.3
John Stumpf	Wells Fargo	0.75	11.8
John Mack	Morgan Stanley	0.8	8.1[1]
Vikram Pandit	Citigroup	0.25	New as CEO
Daniel Bouton	Société Générale	1.75	2.8
Sir Fred Goodwin	Royal Bank of Scotland	26[2]	5.8
Josef Ackermann	Deutsche Bank	1.6	18

Note: Those shown in bold have since lost their jobs.
[1] But he received $40 million in bonus the year before.
[2] The reason for this enormous figure is the accumulated pension rights that he received on leaving the bank.
Source: Forbes, Bloomberg and annual accounts from Société Générale, RBS and Deutsche Bank.

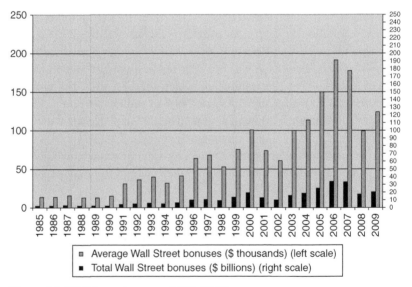

Figure 4.1 Wall Street bonuses, 1985–2009
Source: Office of the New York State Comptroller

Vikram Pandit had replaced the fired Chuck Prince as CEO of Citigroup in November 2007, which explains his lack of bonus for this year.[7] Prince had had a salary of $15 million, to which was added a severance payment of $94 million. Pandit, however, got a one-off payment of $165 million at the start of his employment, since Citigroup bought the hedge fund, Old Lane Partners, of which he was the manager. The paid price of $800 million for a fund which managed only $4.5 billion may seem a high price to pay, even for a high-level recruitment. Merrill Lynch's earlier CEO, Stanley O'Neill, does not figure in the table, since he had just left the company in October 2007 with a severance payment of $161 million.

Richard S. Fuld, Jr. was, as the table shows, the highest-paid financial CEO this year. On top of his bonus, Fuld had also received Lehman stock to the value of $158 million when he was fired. This became worthless, however, with the bankruptcy. The compensation (salary and bonus) received by Fuld during his 14 years at Lehman amounted to a total of $466 million. The average American works far more hours than the average European, 1,777 hours in 2004 according to the OECD, which corresponds to 36 hours per week, since Americans seldom take more than two weeks' vacation. If we assume that Mr. Fuld worked 80 hours a week (a normal weekly load for an investment banker!), he was still paid an average $8,320 per hour during these 14 years. This is 554 times the salary of $15 per hour paid to the average US worker.[8] If he worked normal business hours, his hourly income would be a 1,000 times that of the average worker.

Nor did the crisis of 2008 slow CEO remuneration. Lloyd Blankfein of Goldman Sachs had to halve his income, but still received $43 million in salary and stock. Kenneth Chenault, Chairman and CEO of American Express, which has recently become a bank, also earned $43 million. Third on the list was Citigroup's Vikram Pandit, with $38 million. Fourth was James Dimon of JPMorgan Chase, with $36 million. State Street's Ronald Logue earned $25 million. The insurance company AIG, which broke the record by losing almost exactly $100 billion in 2008, and has

---

[7] The Chief Executive Officer(CEO) in a US bank is normally the Chairman of the Board.

[8] This relationship is not limited to the financial sector. In the year 2000, the average CEO in a major listed company made 525 times the wage of a manufacturing worker, as against 42 times in 1980, according to Batra, *Greenspan's Fraud*, p. 222.

received government support of $182.5 billion, still paid its CEO Martin Sullivan over $13 million. Bank of New York Mellon's Robert Kelly, Wells Fargo's John Stumpf and Bank of America's Kenneth Lewis had to make do with around $10 million each.

Executive pay in 2009 depended on whether the bank had taken federal support or not, a question to which we return in Chapter 7. A sound bank like Wells Fargo could afford to pay its CEO John Stumpf a total of $21 million, of which $13 million was in stock. This was a doubling over the former year. James Dimon of JPMorgan Chase saw his salary fall to $9 million, of which the larger part was in stock. Lloyd Blankfein of Goldman Sachs saw a further fall from 2008 to just $10 million, most of which was stock awards.[9]

In this chapter and the next, I will tell the story of how the housing bubble could create such fantastic salaries.

The US and European housing markets and corresponding mortgages

Today's financial crisis has its major roots in the US housing market. Excepting minor notches in the price curve in 1971 and 1991, house prices had risen uninterruptedly since the Great Depression in the 1930s. Since price decreases had never been experienced, the possibility of a fall did not occur in people's minds. The price rise had not been very fast, but steady. In the 30 years from 1963 to 1993, the price of the average house rose 50 percent (1.5 percent per year) in real terms – that is, correcting for the inflation in the price of goods and services. But then house price inflation accelerated. From 1993 to the peak at the beginning of 2006, the average house more than doubled in value in nominal terms, from $125,000 to $257,000. This corresponds to 6 percent per year nominally and 2.5 percent per year in real terms on average over these 13 years. (See Figure 4.2.)

The price fall during the next 3 years brought the price of the median house in early 2010 back to the level at the end of 2003, $220,000, no more, no less, and prices have begun to rise again during the rest of 2010. Only those who bought their home during the bubble years have suffered – but they were many.

[9] See also Post-crisis: a less rewarding experience, *Financial Times*, August 23, 2010.

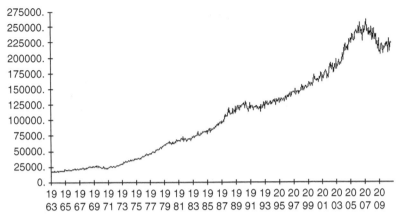

Figure 4.2 The median price of houses in the USA, 1963–2010
Source: Economagic Time Series

There were, however, vast regional differences. If the average house cost $257,000 at the peak, inflation in house prices had been larger in the parts of the country experiencing the greatest rise in population, especially California, Arizona, Nevada and Florida. In the western USA, the average price peaked at $357,000 and had thereafter fallen by –29 percent to the middle of 2010. The corresponding fall for the USA as a whole was "only" –22 percent.

An index of house prices frequently quoted in the press, the Case-Shiller index, fell from the middle of 2006 until mid-2010 by –32 percent. This index, however, has the limitation that it is dominated by houses in the major cities where the price falls have been larger than elsewhere. During these 4 years, the average price in Las Vegas (Nevada) fell by –56 percent, in Phoenix (Arizona) by –52 percent, in Miami (Florida) by –48 percent, and in San Diego (California) by –35 percent.

The development in house prices according to the Case-Shiller indices is shown in Figure 4.3.[10]

We must also remember that homeownership is much more common in the USA and in the Anglo-Saxon countries in Europe than on the European mainland, which implies that changes in house prices have

---

[10] The Case-Shiller indices are unique in that they hold the stock of houses constant. Each house is followed through its life cycle, so to speak.

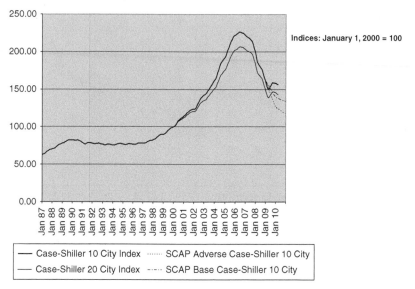

Figure 4.3 US house prices according to Case-Shiller, 1987–2010
Source: Bank of England, *Financial Stability Report* (June 2010), page 25

greater impacts on consumers and on the economy. According to Niall Ferguson, 65 percent of Americans owned their own homes in 2000.[11] In Europe, Spain led at over 90 percent, followed by Ireland at 83 percent and the UK with 69 percent. This may be contrasted with 60 percent in Sweden and 54 percent in France, but only 43 percent in Germany. The US figure for homeownership peaked at 69 percent in 2007, only to fall back to 67 percent in 2010.[12]

Another factor which is typical of the US housing market is the importance of speculation. It has been calculated that 28 percent of all residential house purchases in 2005 and 22 percent in 2006 were undertaken on pure speculation by persons who never intended to live in the house they had purchased or even to use it as a secondary home.[13] A building company claimed that 85 percent of all newly built condominiums in Miami were bought on speculation. This phenomenon has been almost totally lacking in Europe, at least outside Ireland and Spain. For obvious reasons, it is more difficult to abandon a house when the

[11] Ferguson, *The Ascent of Money*, p. 233.   [12] Kapner, US housing.
[13] Greenspan, *The Age of Turbulence*, p. 231.

price becomes less than the value of the mortgage if you live in the house with your family and work nearby. If you do not live there, you can just walk away. In the USA, as noted earlier, the bank has no right to further claims on you if you leave the house – that is, the collateral – to the bank.

Internationally, there have been major differences in the development of house prices. As shown in Table 4.2, increases in house prices occurred mostly in those countries now experiencing falling prices and financial problems. Apart from the Anglo-Saxon countries, the worst impact has been along the Spanish Mediterranean coast, where the building boom collapsed, affecting both building companies and banks. Building permits in Spain fell by 90 percent from the peak in a single year, and many houses still remain uncompleted.

Table 4.2 *Price changes on residential property (%), 1997–2010*

	1997–2007	2007–8	2008–9	2009–10[1]
Ireland	251	–10	–19	–17
Great Britain	211	–15	9	3
Spain	189	–3	–6	–3
USA 10 cities in Case-Shiller	171	–19	0	3
Australia	149	–4	14	18
France	139	–3	–4	6
Sweden	138	–2	6	9
Belgium	131	3	–3	7
Denmark	121	–11	–13	3
USA 20 cities in Case Shiller	120	–18	–3	2
New Zealand	116	–9	1	3
USA average	103	–4	–5	–5
Netherlands	102	–5	–2	4
Italy	98	1	–4	–3
Canada	65	0	1	5
Switzerland	18	4	6	5
Japan	–32	–3	–4	–4
Germany	n/a	1	0	5

[1] Third quarter over third quarter.
Source: *The Economist*, October 25, 2007, March 21, June 6, September 15, 2009, April 17, 2010, October 23, 2010; Organisation for Economic Cooperation and Development, *Economic Outlook*, 86 (November 2009); and the Case-Shiller index, via www.standardandpoors.com/home/en/us

It is apparent from Table 4.2 that the USA does not lead the international league of house price inflations. The major increases in the USA have taken place in the ten cities represented in the Case-Shiller index rather than in the country as a whole.

House price inflation has been very dependent on a rapid rise in borrowing. Table 4.3 shows the increasing indebtedness of US households during the last 15 years. During a period (1997–2007) when house prices doubled, home mortgages increased by a factor of 3, from $3,818 billion to $10,539 billion, or by almost $7,000 billion. As seen in Table 4.3, home mortgages account for the major part of household liabilities and also increased their share of the total from 65 to 73 percent. Other credits, mainly credit card debt, doubled during the 10 years.

As a comparison, one may note that the GDP of the USA was $8,332 billion in 1997, $14,078 billion in 2007 and $14,256 billion in 2009 (all according to the BEA in the Commerce Department). Hence household mortgage debt in relation to GDP increased from 46 percent in 1997 to 75 percent in 2007, but fell back to 72 percent in 2009.

Table 4.3 *Household liabilities in the USA ($ billion)*

	Mortgages	Consumer credit	Other	Total
1996	3,578	1,214	654	5,446
1997	3,818	1,272	735	5,825
1998	4,157	1,347	805	6,309
1999	4,531	1,446	911	6,888
2000	4,902	1,593	969	7,464
2001	5,379	1,703	958	8,040
2002	6,036	2,000	800	8,836
2003	6,894	2,103	868	9,865
2004	7,835	2,220	974	11,029
2005	8,874	2,321	989	12,184
2006	9,865	2,416	1,163	13,444
2007	10,539	2,555	1,273	14,367
2008	10,498	2,594	1,174	14,266
2009	10,335	2,479	1,255	14,069
2010:II	10,150	2,419	1,344	13,913

Source: Board of Governors of the Federal Reserve System, Flow of Funds data, Table L.100, various issues

The figure may also be compared with total financial and non-financial wealth (net of liabilities) of households of $51,427 billion at the end of 2008, according to the Flow of Funds. Falling house prices and stocks had led to a fall of almost $13,000 billion in household net worth in 2008, or −20 percent. The net worth of households has since come back up a bit, but at $53,500 billion in June 2010 still stood much lower than peak levels. The value of household real estate had peaked at $24,972 billion in 2006 and stood at $18,807 billion in June 2010, having first fallen by 30 percent and then increased somewhat from its bottom in the first quarter of 2009.

All new loans have not gone into equity loans in existing houses. New houses have been built. During the years 1996–2007, new homes worth $3,364 billion were completed (according to the BEA). This means that half of the new lending financed new homes and half went into existing houses. During these 10 years, homeowners still took out a total of $9,000 billion, according to a study by Martin Feldstein of the NBER (part of these loans having been amortized over the years). During the peak year 2006, home equity loans accounted for 10 percent of household consumption.[14]

The combination of falling house prices and a high level of initial indebtedness implies that for many homeowners the value of the mortgage now exceeds the value of the house. At the end of 2008, almost one in five (18 percent) US homeowners experienced negative equity in their homes. This figure had risen to 23 percent by the first half of 2010. Some affected states were way above the national average: Nevada 70 percent, Arizona 52 percent, Florida 48 percent, Michigan 39 percent, California 34 percent, whereas the figure was only 3 percent in Oklahoma and 4 percent in New York.[15] Nevada also leads the nation in having 50 percent of houses where the relative size of the negative equity is at least 25 percent. Arizona, Florida, California and Michigan are at ranges between 20 and 25 percent.[16]

For the USA as a whole, the relationship between the size of the mortgage and the value of the home (loan-to-value, or LTV) was only

---

[14] Feldstein, Housing, credit markets and the business cycle.
[15] Source: http://thinkingonthemargin.blogspot.com/2010/05/negative-home-equity-by-state.html
[16] *The Economist*, October 23, 2010.

42 percent in 2003, rose to 67 percent at the height of the crisis in March 2009, but fell back to 62 percent in March 2010.

In 2006, the nominal GDP of the USA amounted to $13,398 billion (seasonally adjusted in annual terms). Home mortgages were $9,865 billion. This implies that home mortgages were 74 percent of GDP. As appears from Table 4.4, this figure is much higher than the average in the European Union, but lower than in countries such as the Netherlands, Denmark and the UK. The difference between the European countries is marked. In countries such as Belgium, Greece and Italy, with high personal savings, you do not mortgage your home (or at least not very much). There were also legal restrictions or conventions that limit the size of the loan in relationship to the value of the house. This limit was 95 percent in Sweden (the same as now proposed for the UK, while Sweden has lowered it to 85 percent), 80 percent in Denmark, 75 percent in France and 60 percent in Germany. German banks are also required to evaluate the collateral every year so that the limit is not exceeded.

Table 4.4 *The relationship between home mortgages and GDP (%), 1997 and 2006*

Country	1997	2006
USA	46	74
EU	–	49
Denmark	71	101
Netherlands	49	98
Great Britain	55	83
Ireland	24	70
Spain	21	59
Sweden	49	57
Germany	49	51
Finland	29	44
Belgium	25	36
France	20	32
Greece	5	29
Austria	–	24
Italy	7	19

Source: European Mortgage Federation, Hypostat, November 2007 and own calculations for the USA

Table 4.4 also bears witness to the remarkable changes that have taken place during the last 10 years. Countries like Ireland and Spain trebled the ratio of mortgages to GDP. One could perhaps argue that the reason was the low initial level, and also the fact that they lagged the EU in living standards (GDP per capita) in the 1990s. But the rich Netherlands doubled its share to almost 100 percent. Countries like Denmark and the UK increased their share by 30 percentage points, just like in the USA (which, given that nominal GDP was also growing, corresponds to the trebling of the stock, as seen above).

Subprime and Alt-A (self-cert) loans

Even more remarkable than the trebling of the overall stock of mortgages in the USA was the increase in such mortgage lending that for different reasons was not regarded as prime: subprime and Alt-A loans.[17] These loans exploded from virtually nothing at the turn of the century to at most $1,300 billion or 12 percent of all mortgages. They made up an even higher share of new lending, 20 percent in 2006.

The evaluation of clients' creditworthiness is made with the aid of FICO scores, named after the company in Minneapolis (Fair Isaac Corporation) which started to develop the model 50 years ago. The FICO score starts at 300 and reaches 850. A FICO score below 600 implies a risk of failure of 51 percent, and a score between 600 and 649 a failure risk of 31 percent. A borrower needs to have a FICO score of at least 700 in order to qualify for prime status. The typical prime loan has a FICO score of 725; the typical subprime loan has a score of 628.[18]

These data apply to the situation just before the crisis. By 2010, the standards had had to be lowered on account of the worsening economic situation of most borrowers, and the border between prime and subprime had been set at 640 rather than 700.

FICO scores depend to a high degree on the payment history of the borrower (failures, late payments). This factor is given a weight of 35 percent in the calculation. If, for instance, you start by having a decent FICO score of 724, and then become more than 30 days late with your payments, your FICO score falls to 678. If the payment is more than

---

[17] The classic description of the subprime market and its securitizations is Ashcraft and Schuermann, Understanding the securitization of subprime mortgage credit.
[18] Goodman *et al.*, *Subprime Mortgage Credit Derivatives*, p. 12.

90 days overdue, the borrower is delinquent and the FICO score falls to 660. The borrower is reclassified from prime to subprime. Other factors taken into account are the period over which the customer's history has been established (a weight of 15 percent), the size of the loan in relation to the market value of the house (which must be no more than 80 percent for a prime loan), the borrower's income (a weight of 30 percent) and his or her use of credit cards (a weight of 10 percent; no more than 30 percent of the credit available must be utilized). The number of credit cards, however, is regarded as a positive factor since it shows that the person is responsible! The last 10 percent depends on the employment situation of the borrower.

Even persons with low FICO scores may borrow, but it costs, as is evident from these examples. (See Table 4.5.) An especially risky type of loan with FICO scores in the 500s is called a NINJA loan (No income, no job or assets).

Characteristic features of subprime loans are thus low FICO scores. But there are two other kinds of non-prime loans – that is, loans that are not prime, prime being necessary for the securitized loans to be purchased by or guaranteed by the semi-public mortgage bank giants Fannie Mae and Freddie Mac (which will be presented in greater detail in the next chapter). One type of non-prime loans is Alt-A loans (called self-cert loans in the UK), where the borrower may have decent FICO scores, but where documentation is missing. One reason may be that the person is self-

Table 4.5 *FICO scores, interest rate on a 15-year mortgage of $300,000 and monthly payment on a 36-month car loan, July 2010*

FICO score	Mortgage rate (%)	Monthly payment, typical car loan ($)
Prime		
760–850	4.344	1,492
700–759	4.566	1,532
680–699	4.743	1,564
660–679	4.957	1,603
640–659	5.387	1,682
Subprime		
620–639	5.933	1,786

Source: www.myfico.com

employed and hence has no employment contract or steady income to show. Another reason may be that there are things that you do not want your bank to know about. For this reason, Alt-A loans are often labeled "liar loans." Only from 2009 has there been a change in Federal Reserve regulations, forcing lenders to evaluate the ability of borrowers to repay interest and amortization out of their income or other assets than the mortgaged house. These rules also require mortgage lenders to ensure that subprime borrowers establish the means to pay for property taxes and insurance. New legislation from 2010 also forbids mortgage kickbacks, by which mortgage brokers have the incentive to steer the customer into loans with higher interest rates, thereby increasing their own reward.

The other category of non-prime is "jumbo loans," where borrowers usually have excellent FICO scores (being rich!), but where the loan is too large (above \$417,000) for Fannie Mae or Freddie Mac to accept.

The borrowers' ability to repay is, for obvious reasons, a distinguishing factor between the categories. This is measured by the ratio of payments to disposable income, payments including interest, amortization, insurance and property taxes. This factor is called debt-to-income (DTI). A prime loan will normally have a DTI of 25–30 percent, whereas the DTI for a subprime loan may exceed 40 percent.

Yet another distinguishing feature has been choice of interest. Most US mortgages will still be of the classical type, 30 years to maturity and the rate of interest fixed for the duration. Almost all prime loans will have a 15- to 30-year fixed rate. This is advantageous to the borrower when yields fall, since he or she can renegotiate the rate of interest to lower levels. Alt-A loans and subprime loans, however, have been mostly adjustable rate mortgages (ARMs). The most common interest rate reset for a subprime loan has been "2/28" – that is, the rate is fixed at a low level for the first 2 years (teaser rates), but then reset every year for the next 28 years at LIBOR plus a margin, which may amount to 600 basis points or more. Given the situation during fall 2007, this means that a subprime loan given in 2005 with a rate of interest of 3–4 percent was reset to an adjustable rate of 13 percent or more. No wonder borrowers started failing!

Delinquency and foreclosures

The effect of falling house prices in a situation with initial high borrowing was, not unexpectedly, economic problems for many borrowers. The average subprime loan taken during the peak year, 2006, had an initial loan-to-value ratio of 88 percent. It did not take much before the mortgage was greater than the value of the house. The situation of borrowers was not made easier by the rapidly declining economic situation. During the recession, which lasted until June 2009 according to the NBER, the US economy lost more than 8 million jobs and the unemployment rate rose to over 10 percent.

A loan where interest and amortization are more than 30 days overdue is called delinquent. If the payment is 90 days overdue, the loan (or rather the borrower) is seriously delinquent. After 120 days, most states allow the lender to foreclose – that is, to seize the property and sell it at an auction to the highest bidder. Note, however, the importance of homestead legislation in some states such as Massachusetts, which prevents banks from foreclosing properties.

The share of delinquent loans in total mortgages was a rather constant 2 percent at the beginning of the century, actually falling to just over 1 percent in 2005. (See Figure 4.4.) In 2006, the delinquency rate

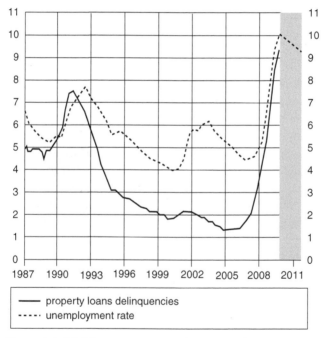

Figure 4.4 US delinquency rates and the unemployment rate, 1987–2011
Source: European Central Bank, *Financial Stability Review* (June 2010)

started rising abruptly and reached 10 percent during the first quarter of 2010 (according to data released by the National Delinquency Survey). The figure is the highest for the 33 years for which statistics have been collected. There were also vast regional differences. Florida was the worst affected state, with 26 percent of homeowners being delinquent, and Nevada was second, with 25 percent delinquency. According to the Mortgage Bankers Association, it appears that this might mark the peak of the crisis. At least the falling unemployment rates in Figure 4.4 give some hope.

The Federal Reserve Bank of New York has an interesting interactive map on its home page, where you can point at any county in the entire USA and read the 90-day delinquency rate. The national average in the fourth quarter of 2009 was 5.6 percent. You may observe figures of 1–2 percent in the inner parts of the country and on the Eastern Seaboard. The lowest value I detected was 0.7 percent. This may be contrasted with delinquency ratios of 10–20 percent in many counties in Florida, southern California, Arizona and Nevada. Among the highest values I found were 16.6 percent in Clark county, Nevada (which includes Las Vegas), and 23.1 percent in Dade county, Florida (which includes Miami).[19]

The difference between prime and non-prime loans is very marked. The share of prime loans that were delinquent at the end of 2009 was 3.5 percent, compared with an average of all loans of 5.6 percent. For all subprime loans the rate was almost 14 percent, and for subprime loans with ARM rates it was over 16 percent. For subprime loans taken during the peak year 2006, the share of delinquent loans was already 50 percent 2 years later and has continued to rise. (See Figure 4.5.)

Payment delinquencies are followed, with a lag, by foreclosures. A total of 3.2 million homeowners were somewhere in the foreclosure process in 2008, rising to 3.9 million in 2009. Over 1 million houses were sold at auctions in 2009 alone, at prices 25–30 percent below market values. The number of properties subject to foreclosures and distressed sales increased from 0.4 percent of all mortgages outstanding in the first quarter of 2007 to 4.58 percent in the fourth quarter of 2009.[20] Some states, such as California, have sought to slow down this

---

[19] See http://data.newyorkfed.org/creditconditionsmap
[20] According to the Mortgage Bankers Association.

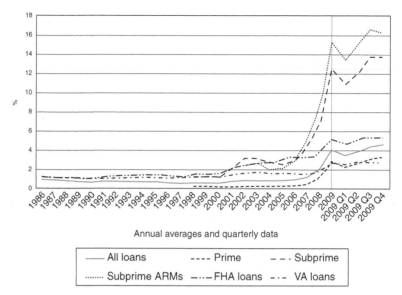

Annual averages and quarterly data

—— All loans	‑‑‑‑ Prime	‑ ‑ ‑ · Subprime
········ Subprime ARMs	—·‑·— FHA loans	‑ ·‑ VA loans

Figure 4.5 Ninety-day delinquency rates for different categories of loans, 1986–2009
Source: US Department of Housing and Urban Development

development by requiring contact and negotiations between borrower and lender before legal action is taken. This cut in half the number of cases in the state where foreclosure is the final result. Foreclosures peaked in the first quarter of 2009 and have since fallen back somewhat. Still, over 1 percent of all US homes were subject to a newly started foreclosure procedure in 2010, down from 1.3 percent in 2009.

Changing the banking landscape

The crisis has led to dramatic changes in the financial landscape. From the beginning of 2007 until June 2010, 254 US banks and three investment banks have been closed or seized by their supervisory authority or forcibly merged with a stronger partner. Many banks were recapitalized at the taxpayers' expense. We will return in Chapter 7 to these injections of capital. The figure 254 may seem minute in comparison with the 4,000 banks that went bankrupt during the thrift crisis in the 1980s or, even worse, the almost 10,000 banks that went bust during the Depression. The difference is that this time even the largest institutions have been affected. The banks shown in bold in Table 4.6 have disappeared. This

Table 4.6 *US banks under change, ranked after deposits ($ billion),*
June 30, 2007

Bank	Domicile	Deposits	What happened?
Bank of America	Charlotte, North Carolina	596	The biggest bank in the USA by assets. Merged with Nations Bank in 1997, US Trust in 2006 and LaSalle Bank Corp. in 2007. Completed the purchase of Countrywide Financial on July 1, 2008 for $4.1 billion, which gave the Bank of America a market share in mortgages of some 25 percent. On September 15, 2008, Bank of America bought the investment bank Merrill Lynch for $50 billion.
JPMorgan Chase	New York City, New York	440	JPMorgan Chase is the result of mergers between Chase Manhattan Bank, JPMorgan and Bank One, also including older entities such as Chemical Bank, Manufacturers Hanover, First Chicago Bank and National Bank of Detroit. JPMC purchased the investment bank Bear Stearns on June 2, 2008, for $10 per share, and, on September 25, 2008, bought the biggest savings bank in the USA, Washington Mutual, which had been seized by the OTS and put under the conservatorship of the FDIC.

Table 4.6 (*cont.*)

Bank	Domicile	Deposits	What happened?
Wachovia Bank	Charlotte, North Carolina	315	**Bought Golden West Financial in 2006. Purchased on October 12, 2008 by Wells Fargo Bank for $15.1 billion, which exceeded a bid from Citigroup of $2.2 billion. Moreover, the Wells Fargo deal required no support from the FDIC.**
Wells Fargo Bank	San Francisco, California	264	The only AAA-rated major bank in the USA. On October 12, 2008, Wells Fargo bought Wachovia Bank for $15.1 billion in own stock.
Citibank	New York City, New York	210	The holding company Citigroup is the world's largest financial conglomerate, the result of the 1998 merger between Citibank and the Travelers Group.
Washington Mutual	**Seattle, Washington**	**207**	**Sold by the FDIC on September 25, 2008, to JPMorgan Chase for $1.9 billion.**
Sun Trust Bank	Atlanta, Georgia	115	Partly owned by Coca-Cola. On November 2, 2007, Sun Trust bought GB&T Bancshares for $154 million.
US Bancorp.	Minneapolis, Minnesota	113	The ninth largest bank in the USA
Regions Bank	Birmingham, Alabama	88	Bought bankrupt Integrity Bank on August 29, 2008
Branch Banking and Trust Corp., BB&T	Winston Salem, North Carolina	84	Bought Coastal Federal Bank in 2007

Table 4.6 (*cont.*)

Bank	Domicile	Deposits	What happened?
National City Bank	Cleveland, Ohio	82	After a series of aggressive purchases (Wayne Bank 2004, Allegiant Bank 2005, Fidelity Bank 2006, Harbor Federal Savings Bank 2006, MidAmerica Bank 2007), National City was itself bought on October 24, 2008 by PNC Financial Services for $5.2 billion, with the aid of TARP money.
HSBC Bank USA	New York City, New York	75	The only foreign-owned bank of the ten largest US banks. The base was MarineMidland Bank, purchased by HSBC in 1980, and Republic National Bank, bought in 1999. In 2007, HSBC was the largest bank in the world measured by capital (but only the fifth largest measured by assets).
World Savings Bank	San Francisco, California	73	The holding company, Golden West Financial, was bought in 2006 by Wachovia Bank for $24.3 billion. It appears in the table because the bank itself had not been integrated into the buying bank by early 2008.
Countrywide Bank	Calabasas, California	60	The largest US mortgage bank, it was sold to Bank of America on July 1, 2008, for $4.1 billion.

Note: Banks shown in bold went bankrupt or were merged.
Source: The Banker, July 2008, bank accounts, own calculations

Table 4.7 *The largest US mortgage originators, 2007*

Name	Rank	Mortgage loans ($ billion)	Market share (%)
Countrywide	1	179	16.8
Wells Fargo	2	120	11.2
Chase Home Finance	3	92	8.6
Citi and Citi Mortgage	4	87	8.1
Bank of America	5	83	7.8
Washington Mutual	6	61	5.7
Wachovia	7	43	4.0
Residential Capital (GMAC)	8	42	3.9
Indy Mac	9	34	3.2
Sun Trust	10	26	2.4
Sum of these ten			71.7

Source: Board of Governors of the Federal Reserve System, Flow of Funds, and Mortgage Bankers Association

applies to five of the fourteen largest banks by deposits in 2007. Moreover, three of the five major investment banks vanished (Merrill Lynch, Bear Stearns and Lehman Brothers), the two remaining (Goldman Sachs and Morgan Stanley) having been transformed into commercial bank holding companies.

The table should be read in conjunction with Table 4.7, which shows the main mortgage lenders in the USA and their market share. Five of the top ten (shown in bold), with a combined market share of over 30 percent, went bankrupt or were absorbed into other organizations.

The terminology as concerns housing finance is confusing, since the US concept "mortgage banking" need not refer to a bank protected by deposit insurance. They would not be included in the list of bankrupt banks either. Rather, they are legally set up as real estate investment trusts (REITs), financing themselves by commercial paper in order to give a mortgage. These mortgages are then securitized, leaving the stream of interest and amortizations to be sent on to the ultimate investor. A mortgage bank will therefore carry the mortgage on its books only temporarily.

Of the organizations that went bankrupt during the crisis, many were of this type – for example, American Home Mortgage Investment Corporation or New Century Financial Corporation. Indeed, of the twenty-five largest providers of subprime and Alt-A loans in the peak year 2006, fourteen were non-banks and hence unregulated. Together they accounted for almost half of the total amount lent.[21] Only with the adoption of the Secure and Fair Enforcement Mortgage Licensing Act of 2008 did Congress enact minimum standards for the licensing and registration of mortgage lenders.

Washington Mutual, however, was a bank, or, to be more precise, an incorporated savings bank, its liabilities being covered by deposit insurance. Other holding companies contained both banking and non-banking subsidiaries. The holding company Countrywide Financial Services (today a subsidiary of Bank of America) contained one subsidiary for mortgage banking, which gave and securitized mortgages but was *not* a bank. Its sister, the savings bank Countrywide Bank, had a national banking license, supervised by the OTS and the Federal Reserve, financing mortgage lending by its own deposits. Together they were by far the largest mortgage lender in the USA, with one-quarter of the entire US market for residential mortgages. Another subsidiary in the group was licensed as a broker-dealer, financed by issuing commercial paper, trading and underwriting mortgage-backed securities. Thus one subsidiary in the Countrywide Financial Services group underwrote issues of another subsidiary – a very risky construction as it would turn out when the lights went out in January 2008.

Delinquencies in Europe

In Europe, the situation in general appears to be much less dramatic than in the USA. Unfortunately, by October 2010, Eurostat had still only published complete data up to 2008.[22] They show a quite different picture from that in the USA. The statistics on "arrears on mortgage payments" indicate basically unchanged problems. For the euro area, the percentage in arrears is virtually constant from 2004 to 2008, rising from 3.6 to 3.9 percent. Germany is at a flat 2.5 percent for all the years.

---

[21] Pozen, *Too Big to Save*, p. 16.

[22] The European Mortgage Federation and Hypostat do not have any data on delinquencies, nor do the Bank of England or the Financial Services Authority.

Greece shows somewhat more problems, with the rate rising to 5.6 percent in 2008 (but no data for 2009). In Spain, the delinquency rate doubled to 5.3 percent in 2009.

The total picture is served in Figure 4.6, showing the percentage of households with mortgages and having "problems" paying interest. The rate rose somewhat from 2006 to 2008 (the latest data), but was still lower than in the 1990s. As one could expect from Table 4.2, however, there were large differences between countries, as shown in the table at the bottom of Figure 4.6. Some countries had virtually no problems at all (Germany?), and some countries had 18 percent "problem borrowers" (Greece?). Unfortunately, the publication does not indicate the relationship between having "problems" and being formally delinquent.

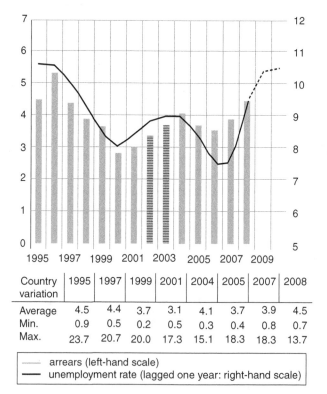

Country variation	1995	1997	1999	2001	2004	2005	2007	2008
Average	4.5	4.4	3.7	3.1	4.1	3.7	3.9	4.5
Min.	0.9	0.5	0.2	0.5	0.3	0.4	0.8	0.7
Max.	23.7	20.7	20.0	17.3	15.1	18.3	18.3	13.7

——— arrears (left-hand scale)
——— unemployment rate (lagged one year: right-hand scale)

Figure 4.6 Households holding a mortgage facing servicing problems (%), 1995–2008

Source: European Central Bank, *Financial Stability Review* (June 2010)

Anyway, it should be expected that delinquencies are much lower in Europe than in the USA. As well-expressed in a recent study on bankruptcy regimes in the major European economies, "[T]he US focuses on providing a fresh start and a clean slate for consumers. European insolvency legislation mostly aims to satisfy the claims of the creditors."[23] In the USA, you can walk away from the house and the mortgage. In Europe, the bank in most countries has the right to your other assets in a bankruptcy, even though you will have the right to some income and some assets that are necessary for your survival.

Points to remember

- The US mortgage market represents some 75 percent of GDP, which is higher than the EU average, but lower than in countries such as Ireland, Spain, Denmark, the Netherlands and the UK.
- Five-sixths of all US residential mortgages have been securitized, shifting the credit risk from the bank to the investor via an SIV.
- Many houses were bought on speculation by people never intending to live there. Legislation encouraged such behavior, since by leaving the house to the bank a borrower had no further liabilities.
- Houses could be purchased with no cash down, even by people with earlier payment problems or low or unknown incomes. The categories subprime and Alt-A loans encompassed 20 percent of new lending in 2006 and 10 percent of the stock of mortgages.
- Price increases on housing have been largest in the western USA and in Florida. In Europe, price increases, and hence problems, have been largest in Ireland, the UK and Spain.
- With falling house prices, loans today are worth more than the house in one-quarter of all US houses.
- In the first half of 2010, some 10 percent of US mortgages were delinquent. For subprime loans the share was 20 percent, and for subprime loans taken in the peak year 2006, 50 percent.
- Over 4 million US homeowners have been subject to legal foreclosures.
- The consequence of bank credit losses has been bankrupted banks. Since the beginning of 2007, 306 US banks have been forcibly merged with stronger banks or closed (up to the third quarter of 2010). Five

[23] Gerhardt, Consumer bankruptcy regimes and credit default.

of the fourteen largest banks and three of the largest investment banks have merged with stronger partners or gone belly up.

- Since bankruptcy regimes differ markedly, Europe has not been cursed by delinquencies to the same extent as the USA.
- In the UK, two of the major mortgage banks, Northern Rock and Bradford & Bingley, have been nationalized, and another mortgage bank, HBOS, has been merged with Lloyds TSB.
- Other banks with a mortgage banking focus have needed state intervention. This applies to, inter alia, the French-Belgian Dexia Bank, the German Hypo Real Estate and *Landesbanken*, the Austrian Erste Bank and the several of the Spanish savings banks, the *cajas* (*caixas* in Catalan).

5 | *Securitization and derivatives spread the crisis around the world*

MBSs and CDOs

Until the mid 1980s, a lending bank had several roles to play in the lending game. It held the contact with the customer and had made the evaluation of the customer's creditworthiness – that is, his or her ability to repay. It collected interest and amortizations from the borrower. It had also funded the loan, most often by its own short-term deposit taking. Since the deposit interest rate was most likely variable, while the lending rate was fixed, it had a built-in interest rate (maturity) risk which had to be handled. It also had a liquidity risk if depositors wanted their money back on top of the obvious credit risk on the borrower.[1]

The first transaction to move the credit risk from the originating bank to investors was actually already undertaken in 1970. In February of that year, the government-owned Government National Mortgage Association (GNMA, "Ginnie Mae") issued mortgage-backed securities (MBSs) backed up by a portfolio of underlying residential mortgages. This first deal led to a formal explosion of credits being securitized.[2]

The procedure when a portfolio of mortgages is securitized is shown in simplified form in Figure 5.1. Appendix 5.1 presents and discusses a more detailed story. Each individual underlying loan is scrutinized by a rating agency (such as Moody's or Standard & Poor's) in order to evaluate not only the economic situation of each borrower, but also their geographic and social diversification and other characteristics. The portfolio of loans is thereafter sold to a company, a special-purpose

---

[1] Problems of liquidity and bank runs are discussed in Chapter 6.
[2] For literature on credit derivatives, see, for example, Anson *et al.*, *Credit Derivatives*; Bank for International Settlements, *Semi-annual OTC Derivatives Statistics*; Chaplin, *Credit Derivatives*; Goodman *et al.*, *Subprime Mortgage Credit Derivatives*.

vehicle (SPV), or structured investment vehicle (SIV), created for the very purpose, legally separate from the bank, which funds the purchase by issuing bonds or paper to investors. The bank will obviously still have its liquidity risk on deposits, but it has got rid of the credit risk and the maturity risk (depending on what it used the proceeds of the sale to invest in). It will still collect interest and amortizations, passing these through to the SPV while retaining a fee for its services. A trustee may supervise the process. Frequently, an asset manager is hired to check that the quality of the underlying assets is not impaired, also helping to sell the repackaged product to investors. There may also be swaps to change the currency and the maturity of the underlying credit. The borrowers may, for instance, pay the bank fixed interest in dollars, while the investors (in Japan, say) want their yields in floating-rate yen.

Appendix 5.1 gives further information on the securitization process, in particular concerning the conflicting interests of the involved parties and also focused on subprime loans as underlying assets.

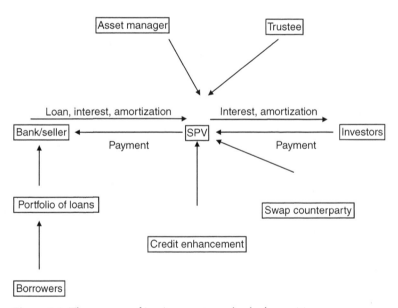

Figure 5.1 The process of issuing mortgage-backed securities

An important element in the process is credit enhancement. In the early days, this was most often achieved by buying a straight insurance on the underlying portfolio of loans. Later it became common to issue securities in different tranches. One reason may be to attract different types of investors. Banks may be interested in purchasing MBSs with short maturities, while a pension fund or an insurance company prefers longer maturities. More common is to issue several tranches according to credit risk. The issuing bank or investment bank may reserve, say, 10 percent of the loan portfolio for its own book, which is the first to go if something goes wrong. With the overhaul of banking legislation in the USA, as well as in the European Union in 2010, it is required to retain at least 5 percent. The most risky part of the bond issue, called equity, is next in turn. In this way, the safest part of the issue, perhaps 80 percent of the total, called the super senior tranche, may get an AAA-rating, while intermediate tranches (called senior tranche, junior tranche and mezzanine, and maybe more tranches) may get ratings from AA+ to BBB-, with increasing levels of risk (ratings are presented further in Chapter 7).

There are a number of reasons why banks would want to securitize credits:

- *Cheaper funding.* By attracting investors from all over the globe, funding is diversified and may be cheaper than taking deposits or issuing commercial paper. The issuing SPV will also most often have a better rating than the bank itself, which also lowers the rate that must be paid.
- Utilize *comparative advantages.* The bank, in particular a local savings bank, knows its customers but may lack knowledge about the capital market and its products, and hence where and how to best fund its investments.
- *Lower capital charges.* According to the solvency rules (Basel I), a mortgage has a capital charge of 50 percent – that is, half of the normal 8 percent minimum capital-asset relationship. A highly rated MBS only draws 20 percent. (Basel I and II are presented and discussed in Chapter 7.) It should be emphasized that as a result of the financial crisis, these percentages are about to change with the new Basel III framework.
- A *safe profit.* The bank has no remaining risk, but still collects a fee for its services in origination.

- *Increased growth.* By selling the credits, the bank gets funding to support further expansion. Indeed, the rapid growth of many banks during the last 20 years would have been impossible without securitization.
- *Investors* seek to invest in bonds which have higher returns than sovereigns, but still have a very high rating.

One can take the process one step further and issue bonds where the components are not mortgages but MBSs. These may be collateralized mortgage obligations (CMOs) or real estate mortgage investment conduits (REMICs). To mark the fact that other assets than mortgages may be the underlying, one would generally use the generic term collateralized debt obligations (CDOs).

Funds investing in bonds of different maturities and risk tranches are often called SIVs. These may take on maturity risk by issuing asset-backed commercial paper (ABCP), while holding a portfolio of CDOs with longer maturities. All the bank-independent SIVs that operated in this manner (Cheyne Investment Management, with a base of $6.5 billion; Whistlejacket, with $7.1 billion; Victoria Finance, with $6 billion; Sigma Finance, with $27 billion, and so on) went bankrupt during the crisis. In October 2008, when the sole remaining SIV, Sigma, applied for bankruptcy, an entire industry, with $400 billion in assets and liabilities, had disappeared. They had all been AAA-rated 2 years earlier.

The bank-owned SIVs have normally been saved by their owners. Citibank announced in November 2008 that it had closed some SIVs and taken subprime-related CDOs at a market value of $17 billion onto its own books. The bonds had been worth $87 billion 1 year earlier, and had hence fallen in value by 80 percent, a clear indication of the graveness of the situation. Citi already had some $20 billion of CDOs with subprime as underlying. The bank was forced to admit that there were still some $120 billion in CDOs remaining in other subsidiaries, which probably had to be shifted onto the bank's own books. The consequence was an immediate drop in Citigroup's share price of 23 percent during the day and 60 percent during the week.

Table 5.1 shows the extent of global issues of CDOs and the share of Citibank. In 2007, Citi was the largest issuer, with a market share worldwide of 10 percent. Each issue could yield the issuing bank a fee of perhaps 2.5 percent, which was a risk-free revenue, provided that the

Table 5.1 *Global issues of CDOs and those issued by Citibank ($ billion)*

Year	Global volume	Issued by Citibank
2000	68	4
2001	78	6
2002	83	5
2003	87	6
2004	158	9
2005	251	20
2006	521	41
2007	482	49
2008: I–III	54	5
2008	62	
2009	4	
2010: I	0.6	

Source: New York Times, November 22, 2008; *Financial Times*, June 10, 2010

bank did not retain any of the securities on its own books or in subsidiary SIVs. Table 5.1 indicates clearly that a market issuing CDOs worth almost $500 billion in 2007 had basically ceased to exist 2 years later.

New rules being considered both in the USA and the European Union would require any originating bank to retain at least 5 percent of the securitized volume.[3] Also much more stringent capital requirements connected with securitizations will be introduced. We will come back to discuss these changes in more detail below.

Ginnie Mae, Fannie Mae and Freddie Mac

Ginnie Mae, Fannie Mae and Freddie Mac have played a decisive role in the structuring of the market for residential mortgage credit in the USA, and in the explosion of MBSs. The Government National Mortgage Association (GNMA, or Ginnie Mae) has been part of the US state since

---

[3] US House of Representatives HR 1728 (May 7, 2009); Directive 2009/111 EC, new article 122a in the Capital Requirements Directive (CRD) (see http://eur-lex.europa.eu/LexUriServ/LexUriServ.do?uri=OJ:L:2009:302:0097:0119:EN:PDF). The European rules will enter into force by 2011.

1968 and its liabilities are therefore liabilities of the USA, backed by its full credit. Nowadays, Ginnie Mae does not issue its own MBSs, but will repackage mortgage loans by certain approved borrowers and, for a fee of 6 basis points, will guarantee these MBSs. The loans are those given by the Federal Housing Administration or the Department of Veteran Affairs, which explains the low risk.

Fannie Mae and Freddie Mac are the two dominating actors on the US MBS market. The Federal National Mortgage Association (FNMA, or Fannie Mae) was formed in 1938, but converted into a private company in 1968, with Ginnie Mae taking over its former role. The Federal Home Loan Mortgage Corporation (FHLMC, or Freddie Mac) was started 2 years later in order to create some competition in the market. Both are called government-sponsored enterprises (GSEs), which means that they are (or rather, were) privately owned corporations where the state had dictated the Articles of Association and where the state may take a stake if necessary (as indeed it became). In 2008, the two together had guaranteed over half of the outstanding stock of residential mortgages in the USA.

Originally, both Fannie and Freddie were restricted to buying or guaranteeing MBSs containing only prime mortgages. From 1995 onwards, they were subjected to increasing political pressure in order to make cheap housing available to low-income earners and the rules were gradually loosened. At the same time, volumes increased sharply.

Gross issues and amounts outstanding of agency bonds – that is, MBSs and CMOs issued by FNMA and FHLMC or guaranteed by GNMA, FNMA and FHLMC – and other issuers, respectively, are shown in Table 5.2. Bonds issued by these agencies still swamp outstanding government bonds (a situation that the present large budget deficits will no doubt rectify in due course!).

In 2009, mortgage bonds worth $1,957 billion were issued to attain a level of $9,188 billion outstanding. This may be compared with issues by the federal government of government bonds and Treasury notes worth $1,447 billion, to attain a level of total publicly held federal debt outstanding of $7,782 billion.

We saw earlier that total outstanding residential mortgages amounted to $10,335 billion at the end of 2009. Of these, $9,188 billion had been securitized, corresponding to 89 percent of all residential mortgages. Of this figure, the two agencies accounted for some $6,800 billion, and others for $2,400 billion.

Table 5.2 *Issued and outstanding mortgage bonds in the USA (MBSs and CMOs), agency and other issuers ($ billion), 1999–2010*

	Agency		Others		Total
	Issued	Outstanding	Issued	Outstanding	Outstanding
1999	885	2,944	141	390	3,334
2000	582	3,156	102	410	3,566
2001	1,455	3,632	218	495	4,127
2002	1,985	4,084	289	602	4,686
2003	2,726	4,496	441	743	5,239
2004	1,372	4,398	855	1,533	5,931
2005	1,321	4,951	901	2,262	7,213
2006	1,215	5,713	917	2,922	8,635
2007	1,372	5,948	774	3,195	9,143
2008	1,299	6,384	45	2,718	9,102
2009	1,925	6,835	32	2,353	9,188
2010	624	6,855	2	2,278	9,133[a]
	(Jan–March)	(March 31)	(Jan–March)	(March 31)	

[a] New regulations contained in Financial Accounting Standards 166 and 167 impact the classification of agency securities vs securities issued by GSE after March 2010, making comparisons with later data difficult. See Board of Governors of the Federal Reserve System, Flow of Funds, Tables L.1 and L.124. Total outstanding mortgage bonds were $8,941 billion in June 2010, according to the latest published SIFMA data as the book went into production.
Source: Securities Industry and Financial Markets Organization and Board of Governors of the Federal Reserve System, Flow of Funds

We may also notice the marked rise in mortgage bonds issued without government guarantee, from virtually nothing at the turn of the century to over 3,000 billion in 2007. It is here that we find the explosion in such instruments as subprime, Alt-A, jumbos and MBSs created with these loans as underlying. The sad consequences for the dominating actors on this market, Washington Mutual, Countrywide and many others, have already been discussed. Three-quarters of all new subprime loans were securitized in 2006, the peak year. The gradual decline in 2007, and the collapse of the market for mortgage bonds without government guarantee in 2008 and 2009, are evident. In 2006, the two agencies had a market share of newly issued mortgage bonds of 57 percent. This ratio rose to 98 percent in 2009, as privately issued bonds vanished more or less completely, investors demanding the safety that only the US government could provide. At the beginning of 2010, the share of the GSEs rose even higher, to 99.7 percent.[4]

Not only mortgages but any other asset may be securitized: car loans, credit card debt, leasing debt, and so on. The general term for all those liabilities is asset-backed securities (ABSs), which also includes MBSs, CMOs, and so on). Since the underlying loans are short-term, they are usually funded on paper rather than on bonds – asset-backed commercial paper (ABCP).

Securitization has been a much more common feature in the USA than in Europe. The total amount outstanding at the end of 2008 in ABSs in the USA was around $10,000 billion, of which the majority, as we have seen, had residential mortgages as underlying. In Europe, the outstanding amount was only some $2,000 billion (equivalent). While over 85 percent of all residential mortgages in the USA had been securitized at the end of 2008, the corresponding figure in the UK was 18 percent. Hence, in the UK, the main problem hit the originating mortgage banks like Northern Rock and Bradford & Bingley, while in the USA, the crisis hit mostly banks, funds and insurance companies that had invested in or guaranteed the mortgage bonds created from the underlying mortgages.

The increased focus on cheap housing for all Americans, especially from 2004, put pressure on Fannie and Freddie to buy or guarantee securities with subprime or Alt-A loans as underlying. In 2008, the two companies held around $600 billion in securities with non-prime as underlying; indeed, they held half the outstanding stock of Alt-A loans.

At the end of 2007, Fannie Mae had a share capital of $44 billion, Freddie Mac $26.7 billion. This was quickly exhausted when the subprime crisis hit. Uncertainty regarding whether they would be saved by the government or not led to a 90 percent fall in their stock price. On September 7, 2008, both agencies were placed in conservatorship under their supervisor, the Federal Housing Finance Agency (FHFA). The state thereby accepted responsibility for their liabilities. This led to an

---

[4] In order to be absolutely correct, it should be emphasized that the obligations of Fannie and Freddie did not carry a formal government guarantee, in contrast to those of Ginnie. This guarantee came forth only in the fall of 2008, as they were taken over by the government. However, everybody assumed that the government would step in and save the GSEs, should it become necessary, as it also turned out.

Table 5.3 *Investments banks' investment in ABSs as a percentage of their share capital*

Lehman Brothers	450
Bear Stearns	395
Morgan Stanley	120
Goldman Sachs	100
Merrill Lynch	90

immediate increase in the national debt of $800 billion. The state could also inject capital up to $100 billion into each of the agencies in the form of preferred stock, up to a level of 79.9 percent of their capital. For 2008, Freddie Mac reported a loss of $50.1 billion, Fannie Mae $58.7 billion.[5] The Treasury therefore decided to raise to $200 billion the amount of capital that may be injected into each agency. Since the agencies are placed under public conservatorship, their funding is part of the national debt and capital injections are not part of the TARP program for private banks (discussed further in Chapter 7).

The involved investment banks not only arranged the repackaging and issue of securitized loans, they were themselves important investors. In the middle of 2007, when the crisis hit, the investments in ABSs and MBSs in the various investment banks amounted to the amounts shown in Table 5.3.

Credit derivatives such as credit default swaps

Banks and other financial institutions in the USA and Europe have lost money not only on MBSs and CDOs, but also on credit derivatives. By a derivative is usually meant a financial instrument whose value depends on the price of another financial instrument, called the underlying – that is, the underlying instrument. The return on a future or an option on the dollar exchange rate (versus, say, sterling) depends on the development of the spot dollar–sterling exchange rate, and the yield on a bond future on the changes in yield on the underlying bond, and so on.

Neither an MBS nor a CDO made up of a portfolio of underlying mortgage loans or other MBSs should really be regarded as derivatives,

---

[5] Later figures are presented at the end of this chapter (see page 169).

but rather as spot investments. Perhaps financial products such as CDO-squared or CDO-cubed (by which is meant a CDO consisting of a portfolio of CDOs consisting of a portfolio of CDOs consisting of a portfolio of MBSs consisting of a portfolio of mortgages ...) should be treated as a derivative. There also exist "synthetic" CDOs, which are constructed from a portfolio of credit derivatives as the underlying. What, then, is a credit derivative?

There is really no major difference between a credit derivative and credit insurance; both aim to shift the risk onto a third party. A credit derivative is a financial product whose value will change with changes in the perceived or actual credit risk of the underlying security or something else. The underlying in a credit derivative is called the reference entity. This may be a country, a company or something else, whose credit rating forms the basis for the underlying. A credit derivative will give a return if and only if any of the following listed credit events[6] occurs:

- bankruptcy
- suspension of payments
- moratorium – that is, postponement of payments
- restructuring of liabilities
- lowered rating.

There are two different types of credit derivatives: those that involve a cash flow (funded credit derivative products), where credit-linked notes (CLNs) constitute the main product, and those with no underlying cash flows other than the payment of margins (collateral). Of these, the major products are credit default swaps (CDSs) and total return swaps (TRSs).

A CLN constitutes a means of increasing or diminishing one's exposure to something. If an investor owns bonds issued by a government or a company risking default, a CLN may reduce or eliminate that risk. As shown in Figure 5.2, the investor may sell a synthetic bond to a bank where the return is conditional on a credit event in the reference entity. This is tantamount to borrowing money from the bank, but the loan is eliminated if a credit event occurs in the reference entity. One could also use CLNs for pure speculation in buying synthetic bonds. These will

---

[6] In some contracts, even such factors as a suicide by a member of the reference entity's management have been judged to constitute a "credit event."

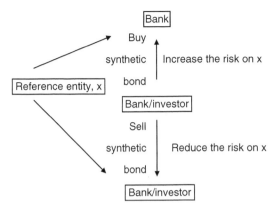

Figure 5.2 Credit-linked note

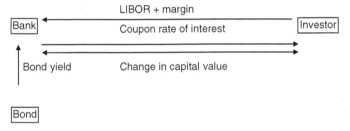

Figure 5.3 Total return swap

yield a return only if there is no credit event in the reference entity; otherwise they are worth nothing, or only a minute portion of their nominal value (see later in the chapter for prices, page 156).

A TRS, also called a total rate of return swap (TRORS), is presented in Figure 5.3. By means of a TRS, both the credit risk and the market risk are shifted to a counter-party. The bank owning the bond buys a TRS from an investor, maybe an insurance company, a hedge fund or another bank. This means that the bank abstains from all future cash flows from the bond: the coupon, as well as any future change in value. A capital gain on the bond is thus paid from the bank to the counter-party, while a capital loss is paid by the counter-party to the bank. Should a credit event such as a bankruptcy render the bond worthless, the investor will give the bank the nominal value of the bond. In return, the bank receives LIBOR plus a margin and has thus locked in a certain profit (so long as the counter-party itself does not fail, of course).

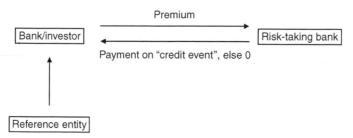

Figure 5.4 Credit default swap (= credit insurance)

In contrast to a TRS, only the credit risk is shifted in a CDS. As indicated in Figure 5.4, a bank or investor seeking protection will pay a fee to the counter-party, a bank or an insurance company (such as AIG), or a hedge fund. Should a credit event such as a bankruptcy occur, the buyer of risk will pay the originating seller of risk an amount corresponding to the principal; otherwise the CDS will mature without value. The similarity to car or house insurance is obvious. Should there be no accident, you have paid your insurance premium in vain ...

There is, however, a marked difference. One cannot purchase car insurance without having a car, whereas one may buy or sell a CDS on pure speculation, with no underlying asset to protect. Having failed to convince its European Community partners of the necessity of the regulation, Germany decided in May 2010 to ban German banks from trading so-called naked default swaps on European government bonds, as well as certain German bank stocks – that is, the situation of buying insurance (= selling the CDS) without having the underlying risk. In practice, it has been shown in the debt crisis during the spring of 2010, in countries such as Greece and Spain, that the selling of naked default swaps was minimal in relation to the size of the market and did not occasion the increased interest rates involved.

CDS contracts are traded in basis points. For obvious reasons, it costs more to insure the credit risk on a more risky company, bank or country. On November 19, 2008, when Citibank announced that it had taken over $17 billion in risky assets from its SIV, the cost of insuring against the potential bankruptcy of Citi rose from 240 to 360 basis points. This means that whoever owned $10 million of CDOs issued by Citi would have to pay an annual premium of $360,000 to purchase protection against default.

If the reference entity is judged to be extremely risky, the buyer of protection may be required to pay the premium upfront – that is, initially. A CDS on Icelandic bank Kaupthing just before its bankruptcy cost 6,250 basis points, which means that a buyer of protection must pay €6.25 million up front, plus another €500,000 per year for 5 years to cover a CDO of €10 million. Ignoring discounting, this means that the total cost of covering a risk of €10 million was €8.75 million, indicating a perceived risk of bankruptcy of 87.5 percent. The bank was taken over by the Icelandic state 5 days later and its CDOs became virtually worthless (see also below, page 156).

Purchasing protection by means of a CDS may also reduce capital requirements and hence increase profitability. Assume that you own a CDO rated BBB+ to BBB– (Standard & Poor's) or Baa1 to Baa3 (Moody's). This security receives a 100 percent risk weight – that is, the bank must hold 100 percent of a minimum capital of 8 percent according to the Basel II rules. The bank now purchases protection in the form of a CDS sold by a bank which itself has an AAA/AA rating or has its domicile in a country with this rating. The corresponding risk weight is then 20 percent, and hence 1.6 percent capital is needed. Assume a 5-year CDO yielding 80 basis points (yield minus cost of funding). The return on capital will be 10 percent if the bank keeps the asset uninsured (0.80/0.08). Supposing the CDS contract costs 60 basis points, the net yield will fall to 20 basis points. But since the position covered by a CDS draws only 1.6 percent in capital, return on capital actually rises to 12.5 percent (0.20/0.016). For this reason, most CDS contracts are used for credits rated A (risk weight 50 percent) or Baa/BBB (risk weight 100 percent). There would be little reason to buy insurance for higher-rated risks since these would anyway draw only a 20 percent risk weight (unless of course one assumes that even a AAA/AA-rated issuer will go bankrupt!).

OTC trading

While derivatives on stocks are traditionally traded on an exchange such as the CME in Chicago, Euronext LIFFE in London or EUREX in Frankfurt, interest rate and currency swaps, as well as CDSs, are mainly traded over-the-counter (OTC). This implies, first, uncertainty as to the amounts outstanding. The Bank for International Settlements (BIS) publishes semi-annual statistics on the OTC derivatives markets.

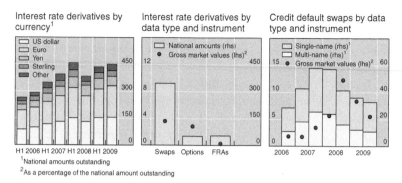

Figure 5.5 Global OTC derivatives outstanding ($ trillion), 2006–2009
Source: Bank for International Settlements

While interest rate swaps remain the biggest OTC derivative, it is the CDSs that have evidenced the fastest growth. From almost nothing at the turn of the century, they attained notional outstanding amounts of $13,908 billion at the end of 2005, $28,650 billion at the end of 2006, $57,894 billion at the end of 2007, only to fall back to $41,883 billion at the end of 2008 and $32,693 billion at the end of 2009. This figure may be compared with total OTC derivatives outstanding of $614,674 billion at the end of 2009. Hence CDS contracts were then only 5 percent of the total. See Figure 5.5.

These are the notional amounts, but the gross market value was still $6,118 billion at the end of 2008. It fell back sharply to $1,801 billion at the end of 2009, not least because of the closing-out of AIG's positions. Gross market value means the amount remaining to settle after correction for double counting and netting. A bank may have both bought and sold CDSs on the same underlying reference entity. The numbers are still huge. No wonder insurance companies such as AIG, Ambac and MBIA got into trouble. AIG had written (= guaranteed) CDSs on $527 billion, MBIA $126 billion and Ambac $61 billion when they went bankrupt in 2008.[7] And since the latter two were monolines, they had no other business that could buffer the effect.

AIG announced in March 2009 that it had paid out $91 billion (of money lent to it by the government and the Fed) to close out the

---

[7] Ambac rose from bankruptcy only to falter again in 2010, this time on insuring municipal bonds. See And then there was one, *The Economist*, November 6, 2010.

majority of its CDS contracts. The recipients included Goldman Sachs ($12.9 billion), Société Générale ($11.9 billion), Deutsche Bank ($11.8 billion) and Barclays ($8.5 billion). Most money was paid to European banks, to the great annoyance of US politicians and supervisory authorities, not to mention the general public.

AIG's total notional position in credit derivatives was over $2.7 trillion, encompassing over 12,000 individual contracts, but $1 trillion was with just twelve institutions as counter-parties. Calculations by Bloomberg have indicated that European banks were saved from raising as much as $16 billion of fresh capital on account of the pay-out from AIG. It was (and should rightly be) questioned why the counter-parties to AIG received full payment from an organization that should technically have been bankrupt, but for Treasury and Federal Reserve support. Why should the US taxpayer pay the total amount owed rather than letting the banks share in the misery by being forced to take a loss on their positions? This treatment of saving the banks from losses while debiting the taxpayer stands in sharp contrast to the handling of the hedge fund LTCM in 1998, discussed further in Chapter 8. Then the Federal Reserve Bank of New York called together the major swap parties of the failed institution and told them to fix it among themselves, which they did. A major difference in the AIG case, which may have determined the government's action, was that AIG had been very active in selling credit insurance, hence their position was one-sided and netting would not have helped much. Still, it would have been better to let the counter-party banks take (part of) the loss, enforcing the old principle of *caveat emptor* (buyer beware). The counter-parties were not innocent, uninformed private investors, but highly sophisticated financial institutions that should have known better.

It was noted that the counter-parties of a much smaller organization, Security Capital Assurance (SCA), which had also gone under as a result of writing CDS protection, received just 14 cents on the dollar. The counter-parties to SCA were, in the main, the same as those of AIG, the only difference being that AIG was hundreds of times bigger and thus "too big to fail."

When a credit event occurs for a major player for which there are many CDSs written, the normal procedure is to hold an auction, where banks and investments banks and others may indicate what they bid for the underlying security or collateral. These auctions are arranged under the auspices of the International Swaps and Derivatives Association

(ISDA). Below are indicated some of the auctions for companies mentioned earlier.

As concerns Fannie Mae and Freddie Mac, investors got back almost the nominal sum, their liabilities being guaranteed by the US state. In the bankruptcy of Washington Mutual, there remained some assets in the holding company even after JPMorgan Chase had taken over the bank. The Lehman bankruptcy, however, left investors with almost nothing. Lehman Brothers' CDOs had been sold to many individual investors in Europe, not least through Swiss UBS, the world's largest asset manager. Even worse was the situation for investors in the CDOs issued by the three Icelandic banks, or for sellers of CDS protection on these names. The subordinated debt of Landsbanki and Glitnir gave 0.1 percent of the nominal value, while in Kaupthing, investors got at least 2.4 percent.

Inversely, writers of credit protection on Kaupthing had to pay 97.6 percent of the nominal amount to the protection buyer (recall the earlier quote on Kaupthing CDSs, which indicated an 87.5 percent chance of bankruptcy – things were even worse than was thought!). Total nominal amounts of CDS contracts were $3.8 billion for Kaupthing, $2 billion for Glitnir and $1.8 billion for Landesbanki. The extent of speculation is clearly indicated by the ISDA's "List of adhering parties" in the auction on the Icelandic CDSs. The list contains 160 names, from the Agricultural Bank of China to the German savings bank WestLB. (See Table 5.4.)

Table 5.4 *Auction prices of CDS contracts, October–November 2008*

Date	Name	Bid as % of par	Comment
6/10/08	Fannie Mae	91.5	Senior debt
6/10/08	Freddie Mac	94.0	Senior debt
10/10/08	Lehman Brothers	8.6	
23/10/08	Washington Mutual	57.0	
4/11/08	Landsbanki	1.25	Senior debt
4/11/08	Landsbanki	0.125	Subordinated
5/11/08	Glitnir	3.0	Senior debt
5/11/08	Glitnir	0.125	Subordinated
6/11/08	Kaupthing	6.625	Senior debt
6/11/08	Kaupthing	2.375	Subordinated

Source: ISDA (www.isda.org)

Clearing houses

Lack of information was one problem with the OTC character of the CDS market. Another was the lack of central clearing. If there had been a clearing house standing between buyer and seller, it would have involved having a central counter-party (CCP) taking on the risk of either party failing. This is routine in stock market trading, where the US Depository Trust and Clearing Corporation (DTCC) and the European clearing houses, Eurex Clearing (Germany), LCH.Clearnet (UK, France, Benelux), x-clear (Switzerland) and CC&G (Italy), to mention the major houses, guarantee that trades will be settled and on time. US financial futures are mainly cleared and guaranteed by The Clearing Corporation and option trades by the Options Clearing Corporation. See Table 5.5.

While almost half of the OTC-traded interest-rate swaps are standardized and centrally cleared, very little of the CDS market has yet been cleared, even though a marked change is on its way in 2010.[8]

The regulatory authorities in the USA have approved two clearing houses for the clearing of the CDS market. One is the Chicago Mercantile Exchange (CME), in cooperation with the hedge fund Citadel Investments. The other is the DTCC, in cooperation with the InterContinental Exchange (ICE) and The Clearing Corporation (a clearing company for futures, but independent of the futures exchanges). The latter project appears to have won, since CME had cleared small amounts of CDS contracts by mid-2010, while the ICE had cleared credit contracts worth more than $9,000 billion by May 2010, after only 1 year's operation. The CME has abandoned its idea to transfer the CDS market onto the exchange, but is still in the running to compete in clearing OTC trades.

As everywhere in the USA, there is the problem of overlapping supervisors. Depending on its legal status, a CCP may be regulated by the Federal Reserve, the SEC or the CFTC. ICE Trust (which, as we saw above, is the main clearer for CDSs) is supervised by the Federal Reserve Bank of New York since it is a chartered limited-purpose

---

[8] IMF, *Global Financial Stability Report* (April 2010), Chapter 3, Making over-the-counter derivatives safer: the role of central counterparties, provides an excellent exposé of problems and potential solutions.

Table 5.5 *The major clearing houses in the world*

Organization	Country	Products	Owned by
Depository Trust and Clearing Corp.	USA	US equities	Members
The Clearing Corporation	USA	Futures	ICE Trust
Options Clearing Corporation	USA	Exchange-traded options	Members
CME Group	USA	Futures, CDSs, etc.	Members
ICE Clear	USA	Commodity futures	Members
ICE Trust US	USA	CDS	Members
ICE Clear Europe	UK	Futures, swaps, CDSs	Independent
LCH.Clearnet	UK	Equities, derivatives, swaps	Members, Euronext
EMCF	Netherlands	Equities, Chi-x, BATS[1]	Fortis and NASDAQ OMX
Euro CCP	UK	Equities, Turquoise	DTCC
Eurex Clearing	Germany	Equities, derivatives	Deutsche Börse, SWX
X-Clear	Switzerland	Equities	SIX group
CC&G	Italy	Equities	London Stock Exchange

[1] Chi-x, BATS and Turquoise are the major Alternative Trading Systems in Europe for trading stocks outside regular stock exchanges, also called multilateral trading facilities (MTFs) under the new EU Markets in Financial Instruments Directive (MIFID), with the purpose of creating increased competition among stock exchanges and alternative trading systems. As much as 25 percent of all share trading in European stocks was carried out through ATSs in the first half of 2010.

liability trust company in the state of New York. Both the CCPs of the DTCC, while also based in New York, are regulated by the SEC, on account of the fact that the products cleared are securities. The two CCPs are the Fixed Income Clearing Corporation (FICC), which clears all fixed-income products – that is, bonds, debentures, bills, commercial paper – and the National Securities Clearing Corporation (NSCC), which clears mainly equities, but also US depository receipts (ADRs) and exchange-traded funds (EDFs). Finally, the CFTC has the supervisory role over the futures market and hence over the Chicago Mercantile Exchange Clearing House. The sole options clearer in the USA, the Options Clearing Corporation, is jointly supervised by the CFTC and the SEC.[9]

We will come back in Chapter 9 to the whole picture of the US regulatory authorities and the (minute and insufficient) changes undertaken in 2010 by the Dodd-Frank legislation.

In Europe, the EU Commission had threatened legislation unless the market voluntarily introduced clearing of CDS contracts. Some fifteen banks and investments banks (including Barclays, Credit Suisse, Deutsche Bank, Goldman Sachs, HSBC, JPMorgan, Morgan Stanley and UBS), in a letter to the Commission, promised to use centralized clearing. Both Eurex Clearing and LCH.Clearnet have expressed an interest. The ICE Trust Europe received regulatory approval for its European operations in July 2009, and by end-September 2009 had already cleared contracts worth $460 billion. ICE, however, has announced that it will postpone the launch of European single name CDS clearing until at least September 2010, pending regulatory approval and negotiations with market participants. Their home page[10] shows that they are normally clearing just a few CDS contracts in the iTraxx index to a volume of a few hundred million dollars per day, with occasional larger peaks.

A fourth, still open, possibility is to use the platform European Multilateral Clearing Facility (EMCF), majority-owned by Fortis bank, which clears, inter alia, for the exchange NASDAQ OMX.

Clearing experts from the Swiss bank UBS have maintained that the standardization of CDS contracts is sufficient only for the centralized clearing of about 60 percent of the market volume, while it would be very costly to try to go further.[11]

---

[9] See ibid., especially p. 22.
[10] www.theice.com/marketdata/reports/ReportCenter.shtml?reportId=98
[11] Baird, Around 60 percent CDS could clear centrally.

Consequences of the financial crisis for the world's major banks

Table A5.1 (see Appendix 5.2) indicates clearly the consequences of the financial crisis for banks all over the world. Some banks, such as Wachovia, UBS and IKB, lost much more than their initial capital, although they have since received capital injections. On average, the global banking system has lost over half of the Tier 1 capital base it had when the crisis started. In July 2008, *The Banker* reported total Tier 1 capital of the world's 1,000 largest banks at the end of 2007 of $3,900 billion. Cumulative reported write-downs by banks – that is, excluding insurance companies – globally from 2007 were some $1,700 billion by mid-2010, according to IMF calculations. By end-2009, the 1,000 largest banks reported Tier 1 capital of almost $5,000 billion.[12]

Many European banks and insurance companies bear their share of the burden for the US excesses: UBS, HSBC, RBS, Bayerische Landesbank, IKB and Credit Suisse, to name the biggest cases. The banks which were caught up in their own national mortgage euphoria are too small to be listed here, even though they are now all nationalized: Northern Rock and Bradford & Bingley in the UK, Anglo-Irish Bank in Ireland, Fortis Bank in the Netherlands, Hypo Real Estate in Germany, HGAA in Austria and Roskilde Bank in Denmark are some of the more important ones.

In April 2010, the IMF specified potential write-downs (in $ billion and percentages) as follows in Figure 5.6 and Table 5.6.[13]

Of the total amount of write-downs deemed necessary, $2,276 billion, almost $2,000 billion had already been taken by the spring of 2010, and hence "only" some $300 billion were yet to come. The ECB made its own calculation in April 2010 and warned that euro area banks would probably need to write off another €90 billion in 2010 and a further €105 billion in 2011. The figure seems reasonable, given that Europeans have so far taken over 50 percent of the global write-downs and may be expected to continue to do so.

---

[12] *The Banker*, Top 1000 world banks (July 2010).

[13] The October 2010 report lowered the projected total write-down to $2.2 trillion, but did not provide the detail as in the April issue. See, however, Figure 1.1 above (page 9).

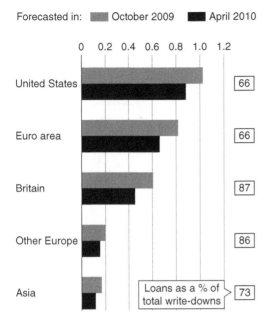

Figure 5.6 Estimated bank write-downs ($ trillion), October 2009 and April 2010
Source: International Monetary Fund, *Global Financial Stability Report* (April 2010)

The sums in Table 5.6 for write-downs correspond to 3.9 percent of world GDP for the totals involved. The write-down in the USA amounts to 6.2 percent of its GDP, in the UK 20.9 percent of its GDP, in the euro area 2.1 percent of GDP, and in Asia an insignificant amount, less than 1 percent of the region's GDP (see also Figure 1.1, page 9).

These amounts are the credit write-downs of banks. To some extent, banks have been able to charge write-downs against profits. But most write-downs have resulted in correspondingly large losses for the banks involved. A Bloomberg calculation in June 2010 showed losses in the banking sector since 2007 at $1.8 trillion. The banks had also raised $1.5 trillion in fresh capital, about one-third coming from governments. As pointed out above, banks (the 1,000 largest) have actually increased their Tier 1 capital, from $3,400 billion in 2007 to $4,900 by 2009.

Table 5.6 *Projected write-downs on loans and securities ($ billion)*

	$ billion	% of book value	% of world total
USA			
Loans	588	7.3	
Securities	296	6.5	
Sum	885	7.0	38.9
UK banks			
Loans	398	5.9	
Securities	57	3.5	
Sum	455	5.4	20.0
Euro area			
Loans	442	2.8	
Securities	224	3.2	
Sum	665	2.9	29.2
Other Europe			
Loans	134	4.1	
Securities	22	3.0	
Sum	156	3.9	6.9
Asia			
Loans	84	1.4	
Securities	30	1.8	
Sum	115	1.5	5.0
World			
Loans	1 647	4.1	
Securities	629	4.1	
Sum	276	4.1	100.0

Source: International Monetary Fund, *Global Financial Stability Report* (April 2010), Chapter 1, Table 1.2

Points to remember

- Over five-sixths of all US residential mortgages have been securitized as MBSs (as against only 18 percent in the UK).
- One may take the process one step further and construct CDOs of underlying MBSs. There are also CDOs of underlying CDOs. And CDOs of CDOs of CDOs ...
- The most secure tranches of these CDOs received the highest rating, AAA/Aaa, from rating companies such as Moody's and Standard &

Poor's, and were bought by banks, insurance companies, hedge funds, pension funds, and so on, all over the world, because they were regarded as being just as safe as government bonds, but gave a higher yield.

- Most securitized mortgages in the USA have been bought by or guaranteed by the semi-private Fannie Mae and Freddie Mac. Their losses forced them to be placed under public conservatorship in September 2008 and they will most likely be nationalized, even though no decision had been taken by October 2010.
- Even bad loans, such as subprime and Alt-A loans, may be securitized. These securities have now been written down to 20–50 percent of par, causing investors major losses.
- Investing in such securities felled large savings banks such as Countrywide and Washington Mutual. The bankrupt investment bank Lehman Brothers held CDOs for five times its core capital.
- CDSs may be used both to insure an investment in CDOs and to speculate. The insurance company AIG got into trouble writing protection on $527 billion of CDSs, thereby guaranteeing the value of the underlying bonds. AIG, having received over $180 billion in government support, paid $91 billion to counter-parties such as Goldman Sachs, Deutsche Bank and Société Générale, to close out these positions.
- A major problem in the CDS market is that it trades OTC, which means, first, that volumes and counter-parties are largely unknown and, second, that there is no centralized clearing to take over the counter-party risk.
- The major CDS actors have begun to use central counter-party clearing, although only some 60 percent of the CDS market will be covered, the rest being too non-standardized to clear centrally.

Appendix 5.1
Inherent conflicts of interest in subprime securitization

A recent paper from the Federal Reserve elegantly summarizes how a subprime mortgage is originated and securitized and the conflicts of interest that arise in the process which may lead to fraud or other unwanted consequences.[14]

---

[14] Ashcraft and Schuermann, Understanding the securitization of subprime mortgage credit.

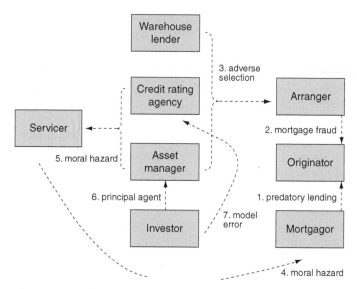

Figure A5.1 Subprime mortgages: origination and securitization

The process starts with a contact between a potential *borrower* (the mortgagor) and the *originator*. The originator may be a bank, a mortgage bank or a mortgage broker. We looked at a number of problems earlier (see pages 114, 129), which may be summarized under the heading *predatory lending* (number 1 in Figure A5.1). A subprime customer may lack the necessary knowledge of available products and the agent has no incentive to enlighten him or her, since the agent's fee (as a broker) may depend on how profitable the product sold is. The agent may also fail to adequately inform the client of the consequence of contractual arrangements such as "teaser rates," which reset at higher levels, normally after 2 years. The agent may also persuade the customer to take out a larger loan than he or she can afford.

In the next step, the mortgage is placed into a pool of mortgages to be securitized. The *arranger*, a bank or investment bank, sets up an SPV that purchases the pool of mortgages. The arranger may well be the same as the originator; failed Countrywide, for instance, was one of the major players in both origination and securitization. The legal arrangement must be such that the originator has sold off the credit risk to the SPV in the event of a borrower failing in his or her payments; otherwise the originator will still face capital adequacy requirements. The arranger should, in principle, scrutinize each individual mortgage and the connected borrower, as well as the diversification of the underlying loans (by geographic area or type of borrower or other characteristics).

The process invites a number of possibilities of *mortgage fraud* (number 2 on Figure A5.1) also called predatory borrowing. The arranger may overstate the quality of the mortgage portfolio, perhaps in collusion with the borrower, since both have an interest in the loan being granted and securitized. In general, there is the problem of asymmetric information, since the originator will have better knowledge of what is being sold than the arranger (or the investor). From a pool of mortgages, the originator may keep for its own portfolio the best assets while selling the worst assets (the "lemons"). This procedure is called "cherry-picking."

An investment bank as arranger may also withhold the information that it shorts (sold) the security for its own books while marketing it to investors. We considered a typical case earlier (see pages 75–6) where Goldman Sachs was sued by the SEC. Goldman structured and marketed a synthetic CDO (Abacus 2007-AC1) that hinged on the performance of subprime residential MBSs. The SEC alleged that Goldman did not tell investors "vital information" about Abacus, including the fact that a hedge fund by the name of Paulson & Co. was involved in choosing which securities would be part of the portfolio. Paulson simultaneously took a short position against the CDO in a bet that its value would fall. According to the SEC, the marketing materials for the CDO showed that a third party, ACA Management LLC, chose the securities underlying the CDO. Paulson & Co. paid Goldman $15 million to structure and market the CDO, which closed on April 26, 2007, the SEC said. Little more than 9 months later, 99 percent of the portfolio had been downgraded. Investors around the world, among them German IKB and Dutch ABN AMRO, lost over $1 billion.

Another instance, also at Goldman Sachs, is the now-famous Vice-President Fabrice Tourre, who marketed products to customers while internally having a negative attitude about them. In one email, he stated that "the whole building is about to collapse anytime now. Only potential survivor, the fabulous Fab." In another email he talked about both himself and customers as not "necessarily understanding all the implications of those monstrosities." The case of the SEC vs Tourre has not yet been decided as this book goes to print.

There are other parties involved in the process of creating an MBS or a CDO from an underlying set of assets: *credit rating agencies*, such as Moody's or Standard & Poor's, an *asset manager* and a *warehouse lender*. Investors, generally being restricted in what assets they may purchase, rely on these credit ratings. For instance, many pension funds are restricted to investing only in the highest qualities (AAA, AA). The process of rating will be treated in more detail in Chapter 7.

An asset manager (such as Paulson & Co. in the Goldman case above) may be involved in the process of determining which underlying assets should be chosen and is also responsible for surveying the continued quality of the assets.

The warehouse lender is a financial institution that makes a short-term loan to the SPV and/or the arranger in order to buy the underlying assets from the originator. The warehouse lender is paid off once the securities have been sold to investors. Bearing the credit risk on the borrower, it has collateral in the underlying loans, protecting against a fall in their value by over-collateralization – for example, lending $900 million against assets with a nominal value of $1 billion ("haircut"). When the subprime crisis started in 2007 and asset quality fell, the demands by lenders for more collateral felled a number of mortgage banking institutions, such as the Mortgage Lenders Network, New Century Financial (which was the then largest subprime originator), American Home Mortgage and Countrywide.

All of these may make deliberate or unintended decisions that affect the quality of the security being issued (number 3 on Figure A5.1). A rating agency may have an incentive to overstate the quality of the security being sold to investors since it may help it keep the arranging bank as its customer in competition with other rating firms. An asset manager (such as Paulson in the Goldman case) may have an incentive to pick the "lemons," since it is simultaneously shorting the security being created for its own book. A warehouse lender may be careless in its evaluation of the haircut needed for a particular set of assets (or tricked by faulty or careless information from the arranger). The lender may also use the financial weakness of non-bank mortgage originators and arrangers to charge high rates of interest.

After the originator has sold the loan, there is no further contact with the ultimate borrower. Instead, a *servicer* stands between the borrower and the investor, collecting interest and amortizations. This may be a bank or a specialized institution. Countrywide was the largest servicer in 2006, as well as the largest arranger and one of the largest origina-tors. It helps being a bank since the servicer will have to advance to investors (or rather to the SPV, which formally has issued the securities) any unpaid amounts. The servicer takes little or no credit risk and is rewarded by a fee (normally around 50 basis points).

The term "moral hazard" (number 4 on Figure A5.1), in general, means that an arrangement creates incentives that were not intended. We will come back in later chapters to the "too-big-to-fail syndrome." If a big bank knows that the government will never let it go bankrupt because its demise would have systemic implications, the bank may have incentives to take on more risk than it would do otherwise. In this instance, moral hazard is created. In the present case, moral hazard may involve several of the participants. For instance, a delinquent borrower who knows that his or her loan will be foreclosed and the property sold has little incentive to spend money on the upkeep of the house, the quality of which may thus deteriorate. Similarly, the servicer might aid the borrower by granting him or her moratoria on payments. The reason may be that being a bank it will earn interest on the loan that it makes to the SPV to make up for the missing payments. Or, it may aid the borrower to make other payments (property taxes, insurance) by giving him or her a moratorium on interest payments, since the state might be quicker to force a foreclosure on the property if taxes are left unpaid.

Similar problems of moral hazard may occur between the servicer and other involved parties (number 5 on Figure A5.1). Since the servicer is paid a flat fee on the property served, as well as expenses incurred at foreclosure, it may have an incentive to keep the property going, even though this may cause the ultimate loss to increase, to the detriment of investors, who will bear the losses, as well as rating agencies, who will lose reputation if/when highly rated securities need to be downrated. Since the servicer is also paid for expenses throughout the foreclosure process, it may have an incentive to inflate these.

By a "principal agent problem" (number 6 on Figure A5.1) is generally meant distortions in a relationship involving a superior vs a subordinate position. It may involve a manager and his or her employees, a government official in relation to the politicians mak-ing decisions or, in this case, the relationship between the ultimate owners of the securities, the investors and other parties, in particular the asset manager. The problem that arises is the question of how the employee/bureaucrat/asset manager should be rewarded for his or her services in order to feel sufficiently motivated to do a good job. We saw earlier (Chapter 4) that the major part of the compensation in banking in the USA is in the form of bonus payments (in cash or stock), while the fixed part in the form of salary is the smaller part of the remuneration. It may be doubted that employees really do a better job if they are paid $100 million in bonus than "just" $10 million or $1 million.

Individual end-investors, as well as pension funds and similar large investors, employ different kinds of asset managers. A hedge fund may in itself be regarded as an asset manager, but more usually the client invests his or her money with a manager who will invest in a variety of assets, depending on how the contract is formulated. The manager may be totally free in his or her choice of assets or, for instance, restricted to bonds above a certain rating. In the European Union, a difference is made between Undertakings for Collective Investments in Transferable Securities (UCITS), which face severe limitations on their activities, and alternative investment funds (basically hedge and private equity funds), which have more freedom to act. Normally, an asset manager will charge a fixed fee in combination with compensation for performance – for example, the performance of the portfolio above a certain benchmark index.

In the subprime crisis, the reward–risk mechanism may have been distorted by an over-reliance on ratings. Since asset managers will try to maximize yield given a certain risk, they will prefer securitized assets (MBSs, CDOs) with a certain rating to normal corporate bonds or sovereigns with the same rating, since they have a higher coupon. But ratings should really only be compared within asset classes. A AAA-rated sovereign does not have the same risk profile as a AAA-rated CDO with subprime loans as underlying assets.

The final problem in Figure A5.1, model error (7), concerns the asymmetrical information between the rating firms and the investors relying on these ratings to make decisions. It is apparent that in the subprime crisis, all the rating firms had made vastly over-optimistic assumptions as to borrower failures. Many of these errors were probably unintentional, but, as we shall see in Chapter 7, it has been stated by employees of these rating firms that they were pressured to use that model that produced the "best" result from the arranger's point of view – that is, the highest rating.

Appendix 5.2
Write-downs in banks and insurance companies, 2007–2009

Table A5.1 *Write-downs in the individual banks, investment banks and insurance companies ($ billion), 2007– 2009*

Name	Home country	Credit write-downs
Insurance companies		
AIG	USA	83
Allianz	Germany	14
Hartford Financial	USA	9
US banks and investment banks		
Citigroup	USA	160
Freddie Mac	USA	154
Fannie Mae	USA	153
Bank of America	USA	106
Merrill Lynch	USA	73
JPMorgan Chase	USA	73
Lehman Brothers	USA	30
Morgan Stanley	USA	22
Goldman Sachs	USA	11
European banks		
HSBC	UK	86
(the major part of the loss stemmed from its US operations)		
UBS	Switzerland	66
RBS	UK	44
HBOS	UK	42
(merged with Lloyds)		
ING	Netherlands	42
Barclays	UK	41
BNP Paribas	France	37
Unicredit	Italy	37
Fortis	Benelux	34
(Belgian part of bank sold to BNP Paribas)		
Deutsche Bank	Germany	33
Santander	Spain	27
Credit Suisse	Switzerland	20
Credit Agricole	France	17
Société Générale	France	17

Table A5.1 (*cont.*)

Name	Home country	Credit write-downs
Asian banks		
Mitsubishi UFJ	Japan	21
ICBC	China	16
Sumitomo Mitsui	Japan	11
Mizuho Financial	Japan	11
Sum of these	30	1,540
Sum world total		approx. 2,000

Source: own calculations from published annual accounts

6 | *Liquidity risk aspects of the crisis and a comparison with 1907 and 1929*

It has been pointed out repeatedly in the book that the present crisis started as a liquidity crisis, a lack of confidence between banks. Only at a later stage did credit write-downs and lack of capital (insolvency) become important. The liquidity aspects of the crisis are treated in this chapter, while credit risks and corresponding capital needs are discussed in Chapter 7.[1]

Appendix 6.1 presents the proposals for the supervision of liquidity risk proposed by the British FSA and the Basel group (BIS).

There are (at least) four different groups of questions to answer in this chapter, each really worth of a book on its own:

- What was the role of the Fed and, in particular, of its Chairman, Alan Greenspan, in the bubbles created in the stock market until the year 2000 and in the housing market until 2006? Should a central bank act forcefully not only against price increases for goods and services, but also against asset-price inflation?
- What conclusions can we draw from failed policies (or lack of policies) in the crises of 1907 and 1929?
- Why will "bank runs" occur and how should a safety net, deposit insurance, be set up in order to be trusted?
- What have the Fed and other central banks done so far to mitigate the collapse of interbank lending and the resulting liquidity crisis?

Greenspan's Fed and bubbles

To say the least, opinions are divided concerning the long time span of Alan Greenspan's chairmanship of the Board of Governors of the

---

[1] The crash seen from the Fed's perspective is well described in Wessel, *In Fed We Trust*.

Federal Reserve System.[2] While the chairman can, in principle, be elected for any number of 4-year periods, all members of the Board of Governors are limited to a single 14-year term, during which period they may only be removed for corruption or breach of trust. But by utilizing the fact that Greenspan's predecessor, Paul Volcker, had not served his full term, Greenspan could be reappointed to a full 14-year period and thus came to function as Chairman for an unprecedented 20 years, from August 1987 until January 2006. One must realize, however, that in the interest-setting committee, the Federal Open Market Committee (FOMC), the Chairman has but one vote.[3] He must therefore persuade committee members with excellent academic qualifications to see things his way. Not only sycophantic reasons may therefore have been behind the choice of the title that Bob Woodward gave his book on Greenspan, *Maestro*. The similarity with the orchestra conductor who has to lead brilliant, arrogant and frequently self-willed members of the orchestra is evident.

Greenspan's years at the Fed were stamped by crises: "Black Monday," October 19, 1987, when US stock markets fell by 22 percent on a single day; the Asian crisis of 1997; the Russian and LTCM crisis of 1998; the worries concerning the new century, "Y2K" in 1999–2000; the dotcom bubble in the 1990s and the resulting fall in share prices in 2000–2; the terrorist attacks on September 11, 2001; the beginning of the housing bubble from the mid-1990s, which burst only after Greenspan's departure. The title of his autobiography, *The Age of Turbulence*, is indeed well chosen.

In reading Greenspan's memoirs, one is struck by his modesty concerning his own role in the handling of these crises. During the crash of 1987, he argued for a position of wait and see, while banks were shouting for help, the White House was stricken with panic and the New York Stock Exchange wanted to close down the markets.[4]

---

[2] The references on this issue are: Batra, *Greenspan's Fraud*; Fleckenstein, *Greenspan's Bubbles*; Greenspan, *The Age of Turbulence*; Woodward, *Maestro*; Andrews, Greenspan concedes error on regulation.

[3] Members of the FOMC are the seven Governors of the Board of Governors and five of the twelve regional central bank presidents on a rotating basis. The President of the New York Fed, however, which is responsible for carrying out monetary policy in practice, has a permanent seat.

[4] The crash of 1987 is well described and analyzed in Barro *et al.*, *Black Monday*.

Greenspan was against closing the stock market, as throughout his life he systematically sought to protect the free market and argued for a world as free as possible from regulations and public interference. He writes about the stock market in his memoirs (page 107): "Shutting down a market during a crash only compounds investors' pain. As scary as their losses on paper may seem, as long as the market stays open, investors always know that they can get out. But take away the exit and you exacerbate the fear." Hence the Fed's only reaction was a straightforward announcement to the effect that "[T]he Federal Reserve, consistent with its responsibilities as the nation's central bank, affirmed today its readiness to serve as a source of liquidity to support the economic and financial system."

But just as he would do in all later crises, Greenspan actually did much more than the meager words indicated: he increased sharply the amount of liquidity in the system. And the one percentage point temporary fall in the Fed Funds rate was sufficient to restore confidence in the market place (see Figure 6.1). The stock market recovered and finished the year at exactly the same index value as at the beginning (see Figure 6.2). It would take another year, however, before the index was restored to the value before the crash. Greenspan and his colleagues knew that market valuations, as indicated by the P/E ratio, were quite normal given the phase of the business cycle, and were only marginally

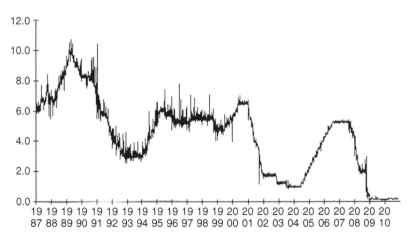

Figure 6.1 Federal Funds Rate (daily), 1987–2010
Source: Economagic Time Series

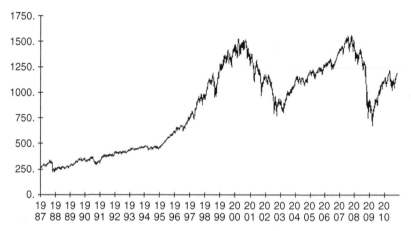

Figure 6.2 S&P 500 share price index (daily), 1987–2010
Source: Economagic Time Series

higher than the historic average of 15.[5] This fact also indicated to them that the crash was not occasioned by fundamental factors, but by market forces themselves and hence nothing that should lead to a reaction from the Fed. Indeed, the real economy was largely unaffected by the crash; GDP growth in the fourth quarter (1987) was above 7 percent. Greenspan and his colleagues could thus resume the restrictive stance of monetary policy which brought the Fed Funds rate to double-digit figures by 1989.

The handling of the crisis of 1987, occurring just 2 months after his accession, was to be characteristic of the two factors for which Greenspan has been criticized over his many years as Chairman: his predilection for market solutions and his propensity to add liquidity in great amounts when needed. The first point is criticized by Ravi Batra (*Greenspan's Fraud*), who makes Greenspan personally responsible for all evils in society: the failures of the health care system, income inequalities, the deficit in the trade and current account balances, and unemployment. Fleckenstein (*Greenspan's Bubbles*) is more to the point in criticizing Greenspan and the Fed for their deficient handling of the financial bubbles. The criticism is well taken, since Greenspan's own

[5] The P/E ratio (price-earnings ratio) shows how many times the annual profit one needs to pay for a share. The P/E ratio may also be used for evaluating a sector or the entire market.

attitude to bubbles is remarkably inconsistent. He devoted a long chapter in his autobiography to "irrational exuberance," a term he himself coined in his daily bath and which was used as the title for a well-known book by Bob Shiller.[6] The Dow Jones share price index had broken through one resistance level after another, 4,000, 5,000, 6,000. Greenspan wanted to direct the market's attention to the risk that the increase in stock market prices was only an unjustified bubble and that prices would, sooner or later, reverse their rise. He did this in a lecture before the American Enterprise Institute on December 5, 1996, in which he asked the rhetorical question of which prices the Fed was supposed to influence. Prices of goods and services? Or also futures prices on commodities? Or perhaps also the prices of future means of consumption, such as the prices of stocks and property?

Greenspan finished his speech: (page 177 in his memoirs):

But how do we know when irrational exuberance has unduly escalated asset values, which then become subject to unexpected and prolonged contractions, as they have in Japan over the past decade? And how do we factor that assessment into monetary policy? We as central bankers need not be concerned if a collapsing financial asset bubble does not threaten to impair the real economy, its production, jobs, and price stability. Indeed, the sharp stock market break of 1987 had few negative consequences for the economy. But we should not underestimate, or become complacent about, the complexity of the interactions of asset markets and the economy.

Words that would turn out to be prophetic 10 years later, 2007!

Others have been more forceful in pointing out that the Fed was responsible for the housing bubble. John B. Taylor, father of the "Taylor rule," has argued that the Fed should already have raised the Federal Funds rate at the beginning of 2002, as the economy started to recuperate from the "dotcom crisis." Instead, interest rates were gradually lowered well into 2004. "This deviation of monetary policy from the Taylor rule was unusually large; no greater or more persistent deviation of actual Fed policy has been seen since the turbulent days of the 1970s. This is clear evidence of monetary excesses during the period leading up to the housing boom."[7]

---

[6] Shiller, *Irrational Exuberance*.

[7] Taylor, *Getting Off Track*, pp. 2–3. The "Taylor rule" suggests Fed interest policy from a reaction function, based on deviations of GDP growth and inflation from

If Greenspan had thought that his words would calm the market, he was mistaken. The Dow Jones index did fall by 1 percent on the day he gave his speech, but it continued upwards, breaking through 7,000 (13/2/1997), 8,000 (16/7/1997), 9,000 (13/4/1998), 10,000 (5/4/1999), 11,000 (7/5/1999), and almost breaking through 12,000 in January 2000, before the fall began. The index had quadrupled in 10 years. The P/E ratio stood at over 40, the highest level ever recorded and far higher than even at the peak of 1929 (see below). The downturn of 2000–2 would make Dow Jones fall by 38 percent and NASDAQ by 61 percent. The bubble had indeed burst! And perhaps Greenspan's Fed helped it in so doing, since they continued to raise interest rates for another half-year after the collapse of stock market prices.

Why did Greenspan stop worrying about bubbles? There may be three separate reasons. First, he had never been a market participant himself and perhaps was too much influenced by those who had. The then Treasury Secretary Robert Rubin came from a post as Chairman and CEO of Goldman Sachs.[8] His comments on bubbles are quoted with approval by Greenspan (page 175): "First, there's no way to know for certain when a market is overvalued or undervalued ... Second, you can't fight market forces, so talking about it won't do any good. And third, anything you say is likely to backfire and hurt your credibility. People will realize that you don't know any more than anybody else."

Rubin's words and the continued rise in stock market prices led Greenspan to the following laconic summing up of the bubble, the greatest stock market bubble ever (page 179):

In effect, investors were teaching the Fed a lesson. Bob Rubin was right; you can't tell when a market is overvalued, and you can't fight market forces. As the boom went on – for three more years, it turned out, greatly increasing the nation's paper wealth – we continued to wrestle with productivity and price stability and other aspects of what people had come to call the New Economy. We looked for other ways to deal with the risk of a bubble. But we did not raise rates any further, and we never tried to rein in stock prices again.

In this quote, Greenspan himself indicates the second reason why he stopped worrying, namely the current debate about productivity and

target values. This means that if the rate of growth of GDP and/or the rate of inflation are higher than their trend values, the Fed Funds rate should be increased.

[8] After being Treasury Secretary, he returned to Wall Street where he became Chairman of Citigroup.

inflation. The theory called the "new economy" or the "dotcom revolution" claimed that the introduction of computers, the internet, mobile phones, and so on, had permanently lifted productivity growth and hence made possible higher non-inflationary GDP growth rates. The measured inflation fell back from 6 percent in 1990 to 1 percent in 1998. Moreover, the Boskin Commission Report claimed that the measured inflation rate overestimated real inflation since it did not capture the effects of the new economy of new products, increased quality and new means of distribution, such as factory outlets. And hence, as Greenspan writes, the Fed left the rate of interest alone, since there was no inflationary pressure.[9]

In addition, there occurred a number of crises which, on the one hand, did not lead to lower interest rates, but, on the other hand, did not encourage the Fed to raise rates either. In July 1997, Thailand was forced to devalue, which became the beginning of a more general crisis in those Southeast Asian countries which had financed a rapid growth of domestic investment, to a large extent in property, in dollars. The Fed stayed in the background and let the IMF play the role of lender of last resort. We will come back to this crisis in Chapter 8. In the next crisis, however, the Fed played a leading role, for the suspension of payments by Russia in August 1998 unearthed a phenomenon so far unknown, so-called hedge funds,[10] and, in particular, Long-Term Capital Management (LTCM). However, it was not Greenspan who led the rescue team, but Bill McDonough of the New York Fed. The consequences had the LTCM dumped $129 billion in assets on already nervous bond markets could have been catastrophic. Moreover, the LTCM had a portfolio of derivatives, mostly interest rate swaps, of no less than $1,250 billion, one-tenth of the total amount outstanding. Since it had had a good reputation, most of its management coming from Wall Street firms such as Salomon Brothers, and since it had two

---

[9] Boskin *et al.*, *Toward a More Accurate Measure of the Cost of Living*.

[10] The definition "hedge fund" differs between the US and Europe. In Europe, a hedge fund is a fund which does not fall under the UCITS directive (85/611/EEC) and is thus in contrast to UCITS allowed to shortsell, sell futures, write options, borrow money etc. In the US a hedge fund is a fund of no more than 100 individuals or companies with stakes of, at least, one million dollars each. Such a fund has hithertofore not had to be licensed by the SEC, nor does it have to present any kind of public reporting of its activities. This situation will change with the new legislation adopted in 2010, to be discussed in Chapter 9.

winners of the Nobel Prize in Economics on its board, it had not been required to pose normal margins or collateral. The result was that Wall Street banks and investment banks were to be found as counter-parties of all of LTCM's deals. Netting the deals under pressure from the New York Fed, it was found that additional capital of no more than $3.5 billion from the sixteen banks involved made it possible to wind down the company in an orderly way. No money from the Fed was involved – only coffee and sandwiches, and patience.

In the coming of the new century and the "Y2K" problem, Greenspan was far more personally involved. The problem at hand was that many computer programs had written dates with only two digits instead of four (86 instead of 1986) and hence must be rewritten to accommodate four digits.[11] Greenspan and the Fed worried that the transfer of funds through the Fedwire system would be affected. In this market, enormous amounts ($2,700 billion was the daily average in 2007) change owners every day, and if one link in the chain is broken the effects could be disastrous. As Greenspan writes (page 205), "The FOMC had released billions of dollars in liquidity into the financial system using options and other innovative techniques. And in the event America's credit card or ATM networks broke down, the Fed had even positioned stockpiles of extra cash at ninety locations around the United States." The consequence was an increase in money supply (M3) by $147 billion in 2 months, September to November 1999, which led to a rate of growth of money of over 14 percent, when nominal GDP was growing at only 6–7 percent.

Figure 6.1 (page 173) shows the result. Despite the economic boom, and despite the fact that no formal decision had been taken, the Fed Funds rate fell back by almost 2 percentage points on New Year's Eve and the days after. The injected liquidity also fed the stock market bubble. A market that was already overvalued exploded. Share prices on NASDAQ rose from end-September to the peak on March 10, 2000 by 85 percent. Some European stock markets, such as the Swedish OMX, doubled in the same period. Greenspan is remarkably and perhaps understandably silent about these developments in his memoir.

---

[11] Consulting firms that I used to work with in those days, in particular EDS, said that customers went to the larger consulting firms because that was the only way to get hold of good COBOL programmers.

The preparations for the Y2K problem would yield an unexpected reward a year later. On Tuesday September 11, 2001, terrorists from the al-Qaida group crashed two airplanes into the two well-known buildings of the New York World Trade Center, 110 stories high. When the two towers collapsed an hour or so later, a number of the adjacent buildings were destroyed as well. The risk of future collapses led to a large area of downtown Manhattan being sealed off. The New York Stock Exchange, the American Stock Exchange and NASDAQ were all in forbidden territory and did not open that day; they would open only the next Monday. Worse for the payments system was the fact that one of the major banks in the chain of payments was Bank of New York (today Bank of New York Mellon). This bank was and is specialized in trans-actions, as well as in clearing and settlement. It is also the world's largest global custodian. This bank happened to be within the sealed-off area and, what was worse, so was their back-up site, where copies of all transactions are kept and where the back-up computer stands. The problem was solved by giving a technician access to the building in order to retrieve a tape copy which could be run in a safe place in New Jersey. In the meantime, the Fed guaranteed all payments that should have been made by Bank of New York, several hundreds of billion dollars. With regard to the securities markets, some participants agreed to cancel trades. In this way, the flow of payments could run smoothly, and on Thursday, two days after the attack, trades done on Monday were settled normally on T+3. A remarkable achievement indeed!

But it did have a negative side effect. The Fed's actions had created the impression that the central bank was predictable, that the Fed would always react by lowering interest rates and give banks liquidity support in any situation of financial unrest. The market coined the expression "the Greenspan put," to indicate the situation that owners of securities had a free put option, so to speak, which de facto guaranteed the price of the securities from falling. The Fed reinforced this impression by lowering the Fed Funds rate after the stock market collapse, from 6.50 percent to a low of 1 percent in the middle of 2003, the lowest level since the 1950s. And share prices responded positively. While it would take until May 2007 before the S&P 500 had returned to the earlier peak (see Figure 6.2, page 174), in the background a new bubble was forming. As Fleckenstein (*Greenspan's Bubbles*) writes critically but correctly (page 181), "Greenspan bailed out the world's largest equity bubble with the world's largest real estate bubble."

In his memoirs, Greenspan briefly discusses the problem of subprime and Alt-A loans, but concludes (page 233): "I was aware that the loosening of mortgage credit terms for subprime borrowers increased financial risk, and that subsidized home ownership initiatives distort market outcomes. But I believed then, as now [note that this was written before the crash of 2007], that the benefits of broadened home ownership are worth the risk. Protection of property rights, so critical to a market economy, requires a critical mass of owners to sustain political support."

Greenspan was equally positive to new products such as CDSs. He writes (page 371):

A market vehicle for transferring risk away from these highly leveraged loan originators can be critical for economic stability, especially in a global environment. In response to this need, the CDS was invented and took the market by storm ... The buffering power of these instruments was vividly demonstrated between 1998 and 2001, when CDSs were used to spread the risk of $1 trillion in loans to the rapidly expanding telecommunications networks. Though a large proportion of these ventures defaulted in the tech bust, not a single major lending institution ran into trouble as a consequence. The losses were ultimately borne by highly capitalized institutions – insurers, pension funds, and the like – that had been the major suppliers of the credit default protection. They were well able to absorb the hit. Thus there was no repetition of the cascading defaults of an earlier era.

Greenspan's optimism as to the market's ability to sustain losses would get a real blow during 2007–8, when the CDS market turned out to be the vehicle that had shifted risks to the most improper actors, and where even "highly capitalized institutions," such as AIG and Citigroup, would have foundered but for state intervention. Again, even in his new chapter in the memoirs Greenspan is very taciturn on this point. Yet he had to admit his mistakes during a severe session in the Committee on Oversight and Government Reform of the House of Representatives. On answering the question whether he had found that the market forces could occasionally be misleading, Greenspan said: "Yes, I've found a flaw. I don't know how significant or permanent it is. But I've been very distressed by that fact."[12]

How would Greenspan's successor, Ben Bernanke, have reacted? Is there any reason to believe that a Bernanke-led Fed would have handled

---

[12] *New York Times*, October 24, 2008.

rising property prices differently? Probably not. Bernanke has long been a proponent of an explicit inflation target for the central bank, as used in Euroland, the UK, Sweden, Australia, and so on. He is of the opinion that the successes that the Fed has had under his predecessors Volcker and Greenspan are due to the fact that they had a logical framework for their actions which was similar to an inflation target.[13] He has claimed that movements in asset prices and the price level of goods and services are sufficiently correlated that it suffices to have a target for the "ordinary" inflation. This means that the central bank should not attempt to influence asset prices unless their movements would be expected to influence the general inflation rate. Bernanke writes:

Trying to stabilize asset prices *per se* is problematic for a variety of reasons, not the least of which is that it is nearly impossible to know for sure whether a given change in asset values results from fundamental factors, non-fundamental factors or both. By focusing on the inflationary or deflationary pressures generated by asset price movements, a central bank effectively responds to the toxic side effects of asset booms and busts without getting into the business of deciding what is fundamental and what is not. It also avoids the historically relevant risk that bubbles, once "pricked", can easily degenerate into a panic. Finally, because inflation targeting both helps to provide stable macroeconomic conditions and also implies that interest rates will tend to rise during (inflationary) asset price booms and fall during the (deflationary) asset price busts, this approach may reduce the potential for financial panics to arise in the first place.[14]

We may note that the increase in the Fed Funds rate from 1 percent in 2003 to 5.25 percent in 2006 did not prick the bubble in the housing market. Nor did a rate of 7 percent in Australia suffice to influence house prices down under.[15]

Incidentally, we can dismiss the idea that the low interest rates in the USA and other countries were the result of a claimed global savings glut.[16] While the savings–investment balance has certainly become

---

[13] Bernanke *et al.*, *Inflation Targeting*.

[14] Bernanke and Gertler, Monetary policy and asset price volatility.

[15] Minsky, *Stabilizing an Unstable Economy*, p. 328, was one of the first to suggest that the central bank increase its interest rate to combat speculation and "Ponzi finance."

[16] Interestingly enough, the term was coined by then Governor of the Federal Reserve Board Ben Bernanke, today its Chairman, in a speech on March 10, 2005, labeled "The global savings glut and the US current account deficit."

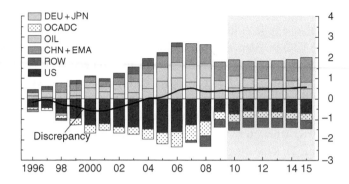

Notes: DEU+JPN: Germany and Japan

OCADC: Bulgaria, Croatia, Czech Republic, Estonia, Greece, Hungary,
Ireland, Latvia, Lithuania, Poland, Portugal, Romania, Slovak
Republic, Slovenia, Spain, Turkey, UK

OIL: Oil exporters

CHN+EMA: China, Hong Kong SAR, Indonesia, Korea, Malaysia,
Philippines, Singapore, Taiwan Province of China, Thailand

ROW: rest of world

US: USA

Figure 6.3 Current account balances (% of world GDP)
Source: International Monetary Fund, *World Economic Outlook* (October
2010), page 29

unhinged in individual countries (deficit in the USA, the UK, Spain and
Portugal; surplus in China, Japan, Germany, Norway and Switzerland,
to mention the most glaring examples), there is no evidence of a global
imbalance between savings and investment. Both rates have been falling
since the 1970s, but in tandem.[17] (See Figure 6.3.) Given data deficiencies, the deficits and the surpluses do not sum to exactly zero for the
world as a whole, as they should theoretically.

1907 and 1929

Greenspan and Bernanke are both eminently educated in economic
history, and were able to draw the right conclusions from studying the
monetary policy failures of 1907 and 1929. Both these crises were

---

[17] See, for instance, Wolf, *Fixing Global Finance*.

fundamentally the result of a wanting or erroneous monetary policy and the consequent lack of liquidity in the banking system.[18]

The 1907 crisis was not the first to affect the young USA. In his classic book on financial crises, *Manias, Panics and Crashes*, Kindleberger enumerates several earlier crises, such as 1792, 1819, 1837, 1857, 1873 and 1893. They were similar to the crisis of 1907 in the absence of a "lender of last resort" – that is, a central bank. Treasury Secretary Alexander Hamilton's creation, The First Bank of the United States, had been buried in 1811, opposed by Thomas Jefferson (the third President of the USA, 1801–9), who saw the bank as "a tool of special interests and an unhealthy concentration of economic power, part of a design to promote moneyed interests at the expense of farmers."[19] The friend and follower of Jefferson, James Madison (the fourth President of the USA, 1809–17), the father of the US Constitution, regarded the introduction of a central bank as inconsistent with the spirit of the Constitution and the rights of the states.[20] Nor did the bank's successor, The Second Bank of the United States, suffer a different fate. Its charter was allowed to expire in 1836 by Jefferson's and Madison's successor and political partisan, Andrew Jackson (the seventh President of the USA, 1829–37) in 1836.[21] The result was a system of 7,000 competing currencies circulating in the republic. Up until the Civil War, there existed only state banks. In 1863, national banks were finally created, with a national banking license, supervised by the Office of the Comptroller of the Currency (OCC).[22] Banks funded themselves by issuing currency, notes which by law were covered by government bonds. All national banks were obligated to accept one another's notes in order to create a common currency.

---

[18] References to this section are: Bairoch, *Economics and World History*, Chapter 1; Bernanke (ed.), *Essays on the Great Depression*; Bruner and Carr, *The Panic of 1907*; Eichengreen, *Golden Fetters*; Ferguson, *The Ascent of Money*; Friedman and Schwartz, *A Monetary History of the United States*; Friedman and Friedman, *Free to Choose*; Galbraith, *The Great Crash*; Kindleberger, *The World in Depression*; Kindleberger and Aliber, *Manias, Panics and Crashes*.

[19] Cunningham, *The Life of Thomas Jefferson*, p. 167. Jefferson was himself a farmer at his beloved Monticello in Virginia.

[20] Ketcham, *James Madison*, p. 320.

[21] Jackson was the first to use the party name "Democrats" for the party originally founded by Jefferson and Madison under the name "The Republican party."

[22] As will be noted in Chapter 8, "national license" did not mean that they could operate in several states, interstate banking being generally forbidden, but that their supervisor was a federal agency.

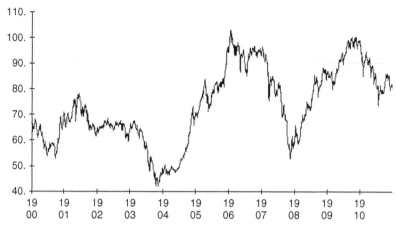

Figure 6.4 Dow Jones share price index (daily), 1900–1910
Source: Economagic Times Series

But there was no "lender of last resort." The lack would be disastrous
when the rapid growth in the young country was shaken by the devas-
tating earthquake on April 18, 1906, which more or less effaced San
Francisco. The stock market fell by almost 20 percent over the following
year under worries from investors, but recovered by the next summer,
1907. (See Figure 6.4.) The huge insurance payments (the damages
corresponded to almost 2 percent of the US GDP) went from London,
the insurance capital of the world, to the USA. The corresponding loss
of gold (both England and the USA had been on a gold standard since
1873) forced the Bank of England to a marked increase in interest rates.
The money flowed into the reconstruction of San Francisco, however,
with the result that the banks in New York were starting to feel a credit
squeeze. Even the city of New York itself was headed towards bankruptcy. In the absence of a central bank, the Treasury deposited
$12 million in New York's national banks, which gave momentary
relief. It helped little when England, in the summer of 1907, prohibited
the use of US bills of exchange, which were used to finance the import of
gold to the USA. Perhaps more than anything else, this act became the
factor to trigger the crisis.

From its new peak in July 1907, stocks had already fallen by 28 percent
when, on October 22, the Knickerbocker Trust Company suspended its
payments. A "trust company" was the investment bank of that period, an

institution which managed securities holdings for its customers, as custodian as well as a broker-dealer trading in securities, but it also let clients borrow money with the securities as collateral. The trust itself was financed by deposits, since it did not have the right to issue currency. Knickerbocker was one of thousands of trusts, but it was the third largest in New York. Its president, Charles Barney, had become involved in an attempt to create a corner in the market for copper, which failed.[23] When the second largest bank in the USA, National Bank of Commerce (today part of Commerce Bancshares in Kansas), which functioned as a clearing house in the absence of a central bank, refused to honor checks issued by Knickerbocker, a classical "run" on the bank ensued. There was no deposit insurance in those days and the reserves of the bank were totally depleted in 3 hours. On the afternoon of October 22, it had to proclaim a moratorium. The result was – just as in 2008 – a panic on the interbank market, where the rate of interest rose to, at most, 70 percent, as banks refused to lend to one another and one bank after another went belly up. Names such as Empire City Savings Bank, Hamilton Bank of New York and First National Bank of Brooklyn, vanished forever. Even the bank whose actions had triggered the events, the National Bank of Commerce, was subjected to a run, but survived after being recapitalized by its owners.

Even the largest trust companies were beginning to feel the pain. On the morning of October 23, the Trust Company of America asked John Pierpont Morgan (1837–1913), the head of J. P. Morgan & Company, to intervene.[24] Morgan was a pioneer in what today is called mergers and acquisitions (M&A) and had been the leading figure in creating such giants as General Electric, AT&T, Nabisco and US Steel. J. P. Morgan was also active in venture capitalism and had financed the Edison Electric Light Company, where the first light bulb was invented in 1879. This had made him one of the richest men in the USA. J. P. Morgan & Company used the National Bank of Commerce as its major bank, and Morgan himself was a long-standing member of the Board of

---

[23] By a corner is meant creating a dominating position in an asset, enabling the owner to dictate prices to other potential buyers. Barney became one of many suicides in the crisis.

[24] J. P. Morgan & Company lives on today in the form of the commercial bank JPMorgan Chase and the investment-bank-turned-commercial-bank Morgan Stanley in the USA and the investment bank Morgan Grenfell in London, since 1990 a part of Deutsche Bank.

Directors of the bank. Morgan called together the managers of the major trusts and also the CEO of the National City Bank of New York, the predecessor of today's Citibank. The group decided on a loan to the Trust Company of America in order to keep the bank afloat.

On the next day, October 24, the problems accelerated. The President of the New York Stock Exchange called on Morgan to tell him that the exchange would have to close since prices were falling dramatically. The problem was again lack of liquidity in the interbank market, where the rate of interest was now 100 percent. Morgan considered – as did Alan Greenspan 80 years later, almost to the day – that closing the exchange would aggravate the panic. Indicative of his dominating position among New York's bankers, he summoned the heads of the fourteen largest banks to his office, telling them that if they had not in 10 minutes agreed to lend at least $25 million, the clearing of the trades on the exchange would fail, leading to chaos and to the bankruptcy of some fifty broker-dealers. He got the money and the exchange was temporarily saved. Share prices continued to fall for another month and a few more banks went belly up, but the worst panic had been warded off. However, during this time Morgan had to personally intervene several times to persuade the banks to lend more money and the clearing houses to honor one another's checks. From end-November, a stock market rally began which almost doubled the index in 2 years. But the continued fear hit the real economy. Industrial production fell and unemployment rose from 2 to 8 percent.

Less well known is that the city of New York was very close to having to suspend its payments the same week as the Knickerbocker Trust went bankrupt, after an issue of bonds failed to attract a sufficient number of investors. Aware of the negative signal that the bankruptcy of the financial center of the USA would send around the world, Morgan had his own company buy bonds to the tune of $30 million and the city was saved.

One effect of the 1907 crisis was the formation of the Federal Reserve, charged with creating and upholding a common and generally accepted currency, and also supervisor of the financial stability of the banking system. All national banks were obliged to become members of the Fed, which undertook the role as their main supervisory authority. The Federal Reserve and its twelve regional district banks also took over the payments system, in particular the clearing of checks, from the private clearing houses, as well as becoming the lender of last resort, whose task it is to see that the interbank market functioned smoothly.

Monetary policy should operate with, as the term went, an "elastic currency," which could be increased or decreased after the needs of the economic cycle. In practice, this type of rule of operating on the money supply was impossible, since it was inconsistent with the fact that the USA was on a gold standard until March 1933 (excepting the war years), implying rigid rates of exchange. A fixed exchange rate, by definition, means the loss of monetary independence, something that would become apparent in the next crisis, 1929–33.

The 1920s were to become a prosperous period for the USA. One talked about "a new era," just as one coined the term "the new economy" in the 1990s. "The chief business of the American people is business," said President Calvin Coolidge. GDP grew almost 4 percent per year on average and stock prices mirrored the successes in the real economy. After a few disappointing years after the war, share prices took off from the end of 1920. As shown in Figure 6.5, the stock exchange had almost quintupled in value until the peak in August 1929. On August 30, a minor decline set in which had lowered prices by some 20 percent until the fateful days of October 28–29, when the stock market (measured by the Dow Jones index) fell by 24 percent in 2 days of trading. After a recovery until September 1930, the real panic set in, and by July 1932 share prices had fallen by incredible 89 percent from the 1929 peak.

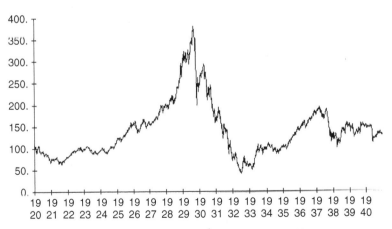

Figure 6.5 Dow Jones share price index (daily), 1920–1940
Source: Economagic Time Series

During the four years 1930–3, GDP fell by over one-quarter and unemployment rose to 25 percent. The declines in GDP were –8.6 percent (1930), –6.4 percent (1931), –13.0 percent (1932) and –1.3 percent (1933). Hundreds of books have been written on the Great Depression (some of which were cited in note 18). There is no unanimity of opinion among economists as to the causes behind the Depression, but the role played by the financial factors is generally accepted, even though the interpretations may differ from one school to another.

The immediate worry concerned the falling share prices. That the stock market collapse in 1929 involved the bursting of a bubble is evident. The P/E ratios had reached levels over 35, way above the 15–20 which is normal in an expansion phase of the business cycle. The year 1929 was a bubble almost of the dignity of the vintage 2000 dotcom bubble. Moreover, purchases of stock had often been short-term and speculative, financed by borrowing. Households therefore had to cut down on consumption and increase their savings, since lower share prices led to margin calls. Brokers' loans had amounted to $8 billion at the peak of the bubble. This may be compared with a total capitalization on the New York Stock Exchange in September 1929 of $141 billion, but also with total consumer expenditure of $77 billion and GDP of $103 billion in 1929.

It should be noted that the real economy was already in a declining phase when the stock market crashed. Perhaps, despite the stock market collapse, 1930 would have seen only a minor recession had not four factors intervened. First, the USA unleashed an international trade war by the tariff increases enacted by the Hawley-Smoot Act of July 1930. This war led to a fall in world trade of one-third in the coming years, a loss of exports which hit the USA itself the hardest in percentage terms. Real exports halved in 3 years. Fortunately, foreign trade at that time accounted for only a minute part of the economy and the effect on total demand was the loss of only a few tenths of a percent. The effect on other countries, more dependent on trade, such as the UK, was far worse.

The second factor was the wave of corporate bankruptcies and bank failures which followed the stock market collapse. Just as today, the credit quality of loans had been lowered during the expansion phase of the cycle. Add to this that the 1920s saw a wave of public issues of bonds, financed by credit as well as by the inflow of gold which took place after the return of the UK to the gold standard in 1925 at the pre-war parity, despite the inflation of the war years. The result of this decision by then-Chancellor of the Exchequer Winston Churchill was a loss of exports and purchasing power in England and led to the general strike of 1926.

The third factor was monetary policy, or rather its absence. Banks had to hold gold in a certain proportion to their demand deposits. An outflow of gold led to declining deposits and lending, since the Federal Reserve could not counteract the effect of bank failures on money supply. From the stock market collapse in October 1929 until September 1931, the money supply (M2) had already fallen by $7 billion, or 15 percent. This month, the UK abandoned the gold standard, letting its currency float downwards. In order to check the outflow of gold resulting from this act, the Fed raised the discount rate, which led to a further wave of bank failures. Between September 1931 and January 1932, 1,860 banks, with deposits totaling $1,450 million, failed. From September 1931 until President Roosevelt took office in March 1933, money supply fell by another $11 billion, or 26 percent. During 1929–33, money supply fell by over one-third.[25]

Deposits in failed banks in 1929–33 amounted to $6,830 million, corresponding to almost 7 percent of the GDP level of 1929. The corresponding figure for the present crisis, 2007–9, is $446 billion, but "only" 3.1 percent of GDP (so far). (See Table 6.1, which states the situation until June 2010.)

An alternative (Keynesian) way of stating the same thing would be to point out that interest rates rose sharply. Certainly, nominal rates had fallen. The rate on 3-month Treasury bills was at its lowest 0.03 percent, just as during the fall of 2008. But the price level fell from an index level of 17.0 in March 1929 to 12.6 in March 1933 (1983 = 100), or by an average of –7 percent per year (and –10 percent during the worst year, 1932). Hence the real rates of interest (nominal rates minus inflation) became sky high, which, together with falling demand, led to a collapse of investment: –33 percent in 1930, –37 percent in 1931 and –70 percent in 1932. The result was an impact on the GDP growth rate of approximately –5 percentage points in 1930, as well as in 1931 and 1932.

In *Free to Choose*, Milton Friedman has elegantly summed up the role of monetary policy during the Great Depression:

---

[25] All money supply data are taken from Friedman and Schwartz, *A Monetary History of the United States*, Table A-1.

Table 6.1 *Number of banks, failed banks and deposits in failed banks, 1929–1934 and 2007–2009*

Year	Number of banks (31/12)	Number of failed banks	Deposits in failed banks ($ million)
1929	24,633	659	231
1930	22,773	1,350	837
1931	19,970	2,293	1,690
1932	18,397	1,453	706
1933	15,015	4,004	3,597[1]
1934	16,096	61	
Sum		9,812[2]	
2007	8,534	3	2,400
2008	8,305	25	211,200[3]
2009	8,012	140	160,500
2010 (to June)	7,830	86	71,600
Sum 2007–2010:II		254	

Note: In 2008, Washington Mutual alone was responsible for $188 billion, the largest bank failure in US history.
Source:
1. Bernanke (ed.), *Essays on the Great Depression*, p. 48.
2. Historical Statistics of the United States, Colonial Times to 1970, p. 912; Friedman and Schwartz, *A Monetary History of the United States*, p. 438.
3. FDIC (www.fdic.gov/bank/statistical/stats /2010jun/fdic.html).

[T]he recession only became a crisis when these failures spread to New York and in particular to this building, then the headquarters of the Bank of United States. The failure of this bank had far reaching effects and need never have happened ... Only a few blocks away is the Federal Reserve Bank of New York. It was here that the Bank of United States[26] could have been saved. Indeed, the Federal Reserve System had been set up 17 years earlier precisely to prevent the worst consequences of bank failures ... It was all a question of reassuring the public that they could get their money. The Federal Reserve

---

[26] It should be noted that the Bank of United States has only the name in common with the earlier attempts to create a central bank. The bank was a privately owned commercial bank, the fourth largest in New York. Its demise in December 1930 was the largest bank collapse witnessed so far.

System was there to ensure that this happened by supplying cash to the banks ... Why didn't this system prevent The Great Depression after 1929? Because from 1929 to 1930 after the stock market crashed, the Federal Reserve system allowed the quantity of money to decline slowly thereby throttling the monetary structure ... If the Federal Reserve had stepped in, bought government securities on a large scale, provided the cash, the depositors would have found that they could've got their money and they would have stopped asking for it ... Despite excellent advice from New York, the system refused to buy government bonds, something which would have provided cash to the commercial banks with which they could have met more easily the insisted demands of their depositors. Instead, believe it or not, the system stood idly by while banks crashed on all sides. As the head of one of the [regional Federal Reserve] banks put it, the reserve system had to keep its powder dry for a real emergency.

Nor was fiscal policy engaged to give support to the falling demand level, which is the fourth factor behind the Depression. "Prosperity cannot be restored by raids upon the public Treasury," President Herbert Hoover declared. Total public expenditures were lowered by about 3 percent in real terms in both 1932 and 1933, in the vain hope of balancing the budget. Only after Roosevelt's accession was this policy reversed, and public expenditures rose in 1934 by 13 percent.

The Banking Act of 1933 – enacted during the height of the Great Depression – created the Federal Open Market Committee (FOMC) in order to prevent monetary policy from being conducted as passively as hithertofore. However, only after the USA went off the gold standard in 1934 could a more active monetary policy be conducted. After the Second World War, the Bretton Woods system again created fixed exchange rates, but restrictions on capital flows still gave monetary policy some leeway. After exchange rates became convertible in 1958, it took only 13 years before the USA was forced to devalue, and 2 years later let the dollar float.

The gold standard was not the only factor that pinioned the hands of the central bank. There was no formal goal set up to be achieved by monetary policy. Only with the Employment Act of 1946, updated and extended in 1978 by the Full Employment and Balanced Growth Act, usually called the Humphrey-Hawkins Bill after its promoters, were goals formulated for the conduct of monetary policy. In this legislation, as well as in later revisions of the Federal Reserve Act, the Fed is given a role both as concerns the real economy (growth and unemployment), as well as for the monetary economy (inflation and interest rates). The targets are not quantified, however. The present Chairman of the Federal Reserve Board, Ben Bernanke, as we saw earlier, has suggested the introduction of an explicit target for inflation, where "core prices" (changes in the consumer price index, excluding changes in the prices of food and energy) would not be allowed to rise faster than 2 percent in annual terms.[27]

"Bank runs" and deposit insurance

Liquidity is the access to liquid, risk-free, short-term funding, as well as the ability to sell assets at or close to their nominal value. *Solidity* is the access to long-term, risk-bearing capital. As we shall see in the next chapter, it was not primarily lacking solvency that felled or threatened to fell a number of banks in the USA in the present crisis, but lacking liquidity. One of the banks' major roles on the financial markets is to function as transformers of maturity. Borrowers seek the safety of long-term loans with fixed rates of interest. In the USA, 15- to 30-year fixed rate mortgages remain the most common type of mortgage lending in the prime market.[28] Depositors want flexibility and the ability to withdraw their funds without notice. This situation creates a natural conflict of interest and a risk, which must be managed by the supervisory authorities prescribing a certain minimum relationship between a bank's short-term assets and short-term liabilities. But just as important is the ability for a bank subjected to abnormally large withdrawals of depositors' money to be able to access liquidity from other banks or from the central bank.

Depositors are well aware of the fact that bank reserves only cover a fraction of their short-term liabilities (fractional reserve banking). A rumor doubting a bank's solidity and long-term capability of survival will lead to rational people trying to withdraw their deposits.[29] The first known example of such a "bank run" occurred in Sweden in 1668. The Palmstruch Bank (also called Stockholm Banco) had pioneered the

---

[27] Bernanke *et al.*, *Inflation Targeting*.

[28] One of the problems with subprime loans, as we saw earlier (pages 129ff.), was that not only was their credit quality lower, but they generally had a variable rate of interest, adjustable rate mortgages.

[29] The classic article on why bank runs occur remains Diamond and Dybvig, Bank runs, deposit insurance and liquidity. See also Diamond, Banks and liquidity creation.

practice in Europe of financing itself by issuing currency notes, or rather certificates of deposit, stating the amount of gold and silver deposited with the bank. These bills were traded and used as means of payment. The gold would obviously not have remained on the bank's books, but would have been used for new credits. A rumor led to a bank run of people wanting their gold back, with bankruptcy as the inevitable end. The bank was taken over by the government and constitutes what is today the Bank of Sweden.[30]

Deposit insurance was introduced in the USA after almost 10,000 banks failed during the Great Depression. Deposit insurance promises to repay depositors should the bank fail. The very introduction of such a scheme should provide depositors with added confidence, thereby lessening the risk of a run on the bank. Deposit insurance in the USA was instituted as part of the Banking Act of 1933. Temporary from the beginning, it was made permanent in 1935. The Federal Deposit Insurance Corporation (FDIC) was set up to charge fees from the insured banks in order to fund the system, as well as dismantle failed banks under orderly conditions. The original level of coverage was $2,500 per depositor, raised to $5,000 (1934), $10,000 (1950), $15,000 (1966), $20,000 (1969), $40,000 (1974), $100,000 (1980) and, in 2008, to $250,000 (per depositor and bank). The new higher limit was originally said to be of temporary character, but has since been made permanent. All banks that are members of the Federal Reserve System must also be members of the FDIC. Other banks were encouraged to seek membership. In just 6 months, more than 97 percent of all deposits were covered. Today all banks are covered. Since the inception of the FDIC, no depositor has lost a single dollar on insured deposits!

From 1934 until the bankruptcy and nationalization of Continental Illinois in 1984, only a small number of banks had become insolvent and had to be closed. The background to this financial stability was not only a greater macroeconomic stability during the 1950s and 1960s. Until 1976, US banks were restricted to conducting business in one state only, interstate banking being forbidden. Many states also restricted banks to having only one branch office. Except in the major cities,

---

[30] Since the Bank of Sweden did not function as a central bank until much later (1897), perhaps the Bank of England, started in 1694, should be regarded as the world's oldest central bank. Its corresponding monopoly on the issue of bank notes stems from 1844 in England and Wales.

banking was a highly local business. Deposit brokers, chasing deposits for banks far away from the depositor's home by offering attractive rates on certificates of deposits (CDs), were not allowed, nor were mortgage brokers. The thrift crisis (to which we return in Chapter 8) ensued when these restrictions were lifted in the 1980s.

Since fees were far superior to payments after the thrift crisis ended, the Deposit Insurance Fund (DIF) had a balance of $52 billion at the end of 2007, corresponding to 1.22 percent of insured deposits. A year later, this balance had shrunk to $19 billion. The sum may be compared with deposits in banks that failed during 2007–8 of $213 billion. This did not mean the DIF was itself bankrupt. First, not all deposits were covered, and second, most bank failures were solved by another bank accepting responsibility for the failed bank's deposits and depositors. Still, the FDIC has doubled the fee it collects from the insured banks for the guarantee. From 2009, banks have to pay an amount of between 12 and 45 basis points (0.12–0.45 percentage points) of insured deposits, depending on their perceived risk, as measured by their capital strength, rising by 3 basis points in 2011. Moreover, in the third quarter of 2009, all banks were charged a non-recurrent sum of 0.20 percent in order to restore the insurance fund. By law, the fund may not fall below 1.15 percent of insured deposits; at the end of 2008, the relation stood at only 0.40 percent. At the end of 2009, the DIF was in negative territory and is not expected to be restored to the required ratio until 2017. This does not affect the short-term stability and liquidity of the institution, since it is guaranteed by the USA and can borrow up to $100 billion from the Treasury.

During the thrift crisis in the 1980s, the Resolution Trust Corporation (RTC) was set up to administer and sell nationalized banks. Until it was closed in 1995, it had handled around 1,000 banks. Today the same role is played by the FDIC itself. Of the (so far) 254 banks which had failed (as of June 30, 2010), all but IndyMac Bank and some small banks were sold without delay to new owners, who took over the viable parts of the bank or alternatively, the whole bank, with a guarantee from the FDIC on future losses.[31] The bankruptcy of IndyMac on July 11, 2008 was the largest in the USA since 1984 (but the record would be broken by a wide margin a few months later by Washington Mutual). To indicate

---

[31] The FDIC has a list of failed banks at www.fdic.gov/bank/individual/failed/banklist.html

the identity of the new owner, the bank continued operations under the name IndyMac Federal Bank. The sale of the assets of IndyMac caused the FDIC to lose some $10 billion, its largest single loss.

Despite deposit insurance, a number of bank runs have taken place during the crisis. IndyMac lost $1.3 billion in withdrawals in just a few days (out of total deposits of $18.9 billion). IndyMac specialized in selling risky Alt-A loans. Already by the end of 2007, non-performing loans comprised 6.5 percent of total loans. The triggering factor behind the run was a (careless) letter from the Chairman of the Congressional Joint Economic Committee, who questioned the survival capacity of the bank. In 2007, IndyMac was the 44th largest bank in the USA and number 283 in the world (measured by the size of its Tier 1 capital).

Like IndyMac, Washington Mutual (WaMu) was a savings bank whose shares were listed on the stock exchange. The bank was number 7 in the USA and number 39 in the world, with total assets of $327 billion. WaMu's problems were related not only to the housing market, but even more to a series of aggressive purchases. Despite an injection of new capital from the owners, rumors persisted. WaMu had financed the purchases by money obtained through deposit brokers. The fact that the bank lacked a faithful customer base contributed to a run: $17 billion in deposits were withdrawn in a couple of days.[32]

The UK was long spared the financial crises which hit not only the USA, but Japan, Asia, Russia, the Nordic countries and many developing nations in the 1980s and 1990s (these are taken up in Chapter 8 and compared with today's crisis). The Bank of England closed down the Bank of Credit and Commerce International (BCCI) in 1991 and sold Barings Bank to ING Bank in 1995 (for £1!), but neither failure had anything to do with a general financial crisis. On September 14, 2008, the specialized mortgage bank Northern Rock was subjected to a run after the BBC reported that the Bank of England had secretly given the bank liquidity support to the tune of £21 billion. This was the first bank run in the UK since 1830![33] It was later revealed that the Bank of England had at the same time secretly lent £25 billion to the mortgage bank HBOS (now merged with Lloyds TSB) to avoid an acute liquidity crisis.

---

[32] All bank data are taken from *The Banker*, Top 1000 World Banks (July 2008).

[33] Although the bank run of 1830 was motivated more by political reasons than financial failures. To stop the Duke of Wellington from hindering the passage of the Reform Act, citizens were encouraged to act by "to stop the Duke, go for gold!"

Northern Rock was nationalized early in 2009, since no willing buyer could be found. In late September 2008, the FSA seized the mortgage lender Bradford & Bingley, after a run on the bank had cost it tens of millions of pounds. The bank got a bridge loan from the Bank of England of £17.9 billion. The branch offices and deposits were sold to Abbey National (owned by the Spanish bank Grupo Santander) for £612 million, while the troubled mortgage book was taken over by the state. The holding company UK Financial Investments (UKFI) was set up on November 3, 2008, for the purpose of being the formal owner of nationalized banks. Apart from the two mortgage banks, Northern Rock still remaining under government control, the UKFI also manages the British majority stake in RBS and its minority stake in the Lloyds TSB-HBOS group (more on these later).

One could imagine that in a world of deposit insurance, depositors would feel safe and hence no bank runs occur. But there are at least three reasons why a run is still logical:

• Many people are probably unaware of the existence of deposit insurance or else do not trust the promise by the government.
• Part of deposits – that is, amounts above the limit, at present $250,000 in the USA and £50,000 in the UK (per person per bank) – are uninsured.
• There may be instruments not covered by the guarantee. This applies, for example, to Money Market Mutual Funds (MMMFs), despite the fact that they are similar to certificates of deposit. A run on an MMMF started on September 15, 2008, after the Lehman bankruptcy. Many MMMFs had invested in commercial paper issued by Lehman. A similar run had already occurred on March 11 that same year on the investment bank Bear Stearns, which also had financed its operations by issuing ABCP, which was not included in the guarantee by the FDIC. In only 2 days, the bank's capital base shrank $17 billion, to $2 billion. It was sold over the weekend to JPMorgan Chase, in order to prevent further chaos.

In Europe, deposit insurance was (relatively) harmonized by Directive 94/19 EC (1994), in which the member states were enjoined to introduce a system of deposit insurance covering at least 90 percent of at least €20,000. On October 7, 2008, the heads of state and government raised the limit to €50,000. Some countries, led by Ireland and Greece, introduced unlimited deposit insurance. Protests from the European Commission forced Ireland to extend the guarantee to British subsidiaries in Ireland. After some other countries (Denmark, Germany, Austria, Hungary, Slovenia and Slovakia) had followed Ireland's example, the criticism from the Commission ceased.

An unresolved question in the wake of the financial crisis is how to treat subsidiaries of banks incorporated in other countries. If the foreign-owned bank subsidiary has a local license, it is obviously included in the scheme. But what if it does not? The British position is the following:

If you have an account with a UK branch of a bank incorporated in the European Economic Area (EEA) that becomes insolvent, it should be covered, since all member states of the EEA are required to have established a deposit guarantee scheme. A bank established in another EEA state should be a member of that state's compensation scheme, which is designed to protect depositors in that EEA country, and those with accounts at branches in other EEA countries. Where the bank's home state scheme provides a lower limit of compensation than in the UK – that is, less than £50,000 – the bank may choose to join the British system of deposit guarantee to "top up" the level of protection offered by the home state scheme. This was done by the Icelandic banks Kaupthing and Landsbanki (see below), while Kaupthing Singer and Friedlander was a subsidiary with a British banking license, and hence covered by British deposit insurance.[34]

In the event of a failure of one of these banks, there would be a two-step process, as the home state scheme would have lead responsibility for claims and would be responsible for paying the first part of any compensation. The Financial Services Compensation Scheme (FSCS) is only responsible for paying compensation for the topped-up element to £50,000 on deposits with the UK branch. FSCS would, wherever possible, try to assist claimants in their dealings with the home state scheme – for example, by putting them in contact with the home state scheme, or helping them understand the process that the home state scheme will follow. FSCS would then deal with any 'top-up' claims.

Some countries have chosen to cover also the deposits of foreign branches. Hence bankrupt bank Kaupthing's so-called "Edge" accounts were covered by Swedish deposit insurance, despite the fact that they had been booked in Iceland. In Germany, the Netherlands and the UK, a

---

[34] The information is taken from the home page of the responsible agency, the Financial Services Compensation Scheme (www.fscs.org.uk/what-we-cover/questions-and-answers).

dispute erupted concerning Kaupthing's Edge, as well as Landsbanki's Icesave accounts. In order to put pressure on the Icelandic government to accept responsibility (recall that both banks had "topped up" the levels), the UK froze all British assets of Landsbanki under the Anti-terrorism, Crime and Security Act of 2001. The UK and the Netherlands also opposed a credit of $2 billion by the IMF to Iceland. The situation was seemingly cleared up by an agreement, whereby Germany, the UK and the Netherlands extended a credit to Iceland of a size corresponding to the amounts that should be paid to depositors of the Icelandic institutions in these three countries, against the acceptance of responsibility by the Icelandic government. The deal was overturned, however, by a popular referendum, after the president vetoed parliament's decision, and the question remains unsolved (October 2010). The cost to the British taxpayers of repaying British depositors in the Icelandic banks was over £8 billion (two-thirds of Iceland's GDP).

Kaupthing Singer and Friedlander was taken into administration by the British state, and its 170,000 Edge accounts, worth £2.5 billion, transferred to the Dutch bank ING Direct. ING also took over 22,000 customers and £538 million of deposits from Heritable Bank, part of Landsbanki. The other 4,350 accounts booked in the UK by Singer and Friedlander cost the FSCS £145 million in compensation to depositors.

In its response to the financial crisis, the British FSA has severely criticized the ability of a small country such as Iceland to misuse its EEA membership to offer deposits through branches rather than through (British-supervised) subsidiaries. As the report writes, "host regulators in the EEA should have clearer powers to restrict (or even halt) the business of EEA branches where they perceive a significant emerging risk to depositors and are not satisfied with the regulatory arrangements relating to supervision[35] and/or DGS [depository guarantee schemes] in the bank's home country".[36]

To prevent future bank runs and to encourage the banking sector to pay for its own mistakes, it is important that the safety net of deposit insurance be made wide. It may be discussed whether the system of banks

---

[35] Sometimes the words "regulation" and "supervision" are erroneously used synonymously. However, regulation refers to the creation of rules, and supervision to the process of seeing to it that banks follow the rules.

[36] Financial Services Authority, A regulatory response to the global banking crisis, p. 146.

being able to buy additional insurance (discussed in the next section) from the government should not also be made permanent, provided that the fees are set at a level that really corresponds to the bank's actual risk, as measured, for instance, by the pricing of its CDSs, if available. As noted below, the system of bank guarantees during the crisis has given large subsidies to the banks in Europe as well as in the USA.

The European minimum coverage on deposit insurance was raised to €100,000 (equivalent, i.e. $85,000) by Dir. 2009/14/EC, to be implemented by December 31, 2010. It is still far lower than the $250,000 in the USA, but it is at least a step in the right direction.

What to do when deposit insurance is not enough

By means of deposit insurance, risks incurred by one type of claimants, namely depositors, are eliminated, or at least diminished. But this is not sufficient if banks have lost confidence in one another and the interbank market has stopped functioning normally. Not lending to other banks in the interbank market is the equivalent of a bank run in the deposit market.

The Federal Reserve and other central banks have normally engineered the volume of liquidity in the interbank market, and hence the price of short-term credits (the Fed Funds rate for the Fed, the refi rate for the ECB, the Bank Rate for the Bank of England, and so on), by three means. First, by open market operations, the Fed (or rather the Federal Reserve Bank of New York) buys and sells securities from/to its "primary dealers." These banks and investment banks number around twenty and are the only institutions allowed to trade with the Fed. The current list includes several British-owned institutions: Barclays Capital Inc., Greenwich Capital Markets (RBS) and HSBC Securities. The securities used in such operations include government paper as well as bonds issued by federal agencies (GNMA, FNMA, FHLMC; see pages 141ff.). Operations will most often not be outright, but conducted through a repurchase agreement, a "repo," whereby the Fed sells/buys securities to/from its primary dealers, with repurchase/resale a number of days (maximum 65 days) later. Repos will normally be of much shorter duration, normally a week. A repo is essentially a loan or borrowing, with the securities used as collateral.

By means of repos, the Fed guides the Fed Funds rate to the level decided by the FOMC. In excess of amounts borrowed in the Fed Funds market, all banks who are members of the Federal Reserve

System have the right to borrow from the Fed at the discount rate, a rate of interest set by the Board of Governors on the recommendation of the twelve regional central banks. The discount rate is normally set marginally above the Fed Funds rate. Presently (October 2010), the target for the Fed Funds rate is 0–0.25 percent. The discount rate is 0.75 percent. Part of the policy for "the discount window" also lies in the decision on which securities are accepted as collateral. This point is elaborated below. A third, less common way of influencing the liquidity in the system is to change the reserve ratio – that is, the ratio of reserves held in cash or at the Federal Reserve to deposits. At present, this ratio is 10 percent for demand deposits and 0 percent for time deposits. Traditionally, this percentage is not changed, but the Fed influenced the market by starting to pay interest on these reserves in October 2008.[37]

US actions taken

Which additions have the Fed, the ECB and other European central banks made to their toolbox this time to alleviate the liquidity crisis in the interbank market? TARP, TAF, PDCF, TSLF, MMIFF, AMLF, TALF, TLGP ... it is easy to get lost among all these acronyms. But they all refer to attempts to revitalize the interbank market and other short-term money markets.

The Troubled Assets Relief Program (TARP), at least as the program came to be utilized in practice, will shift from this chapter on liquidity and instead be taken up in the next chapter on capital. The $700 billion allocated by Congress have so far been used solely to recapitalize financial institutions, and not, as originally planned, for stabilizing the prices of securities such as mortgage-backed securities (MBSs), collateralized mortgage obligations (CMOs) or collateralized debt obligations (CDOs). We will return later on to a full presentation of the TARP funds spent and repaid.

Term Auction Facility (TAF) was the first of the new initiatives, created in December 2007. As the name indicates, it sought to complement the existing repos by extending lending over longer periods, 28 and 84 days respectively. The Fed also widened the list of securities

---

[37] In economies with less developed banking systems, such as China, changes in reserve ratios are frequently used to influence the lending capacity of the banking system.

allowed as collateral, to include also AAA-rated CDOs and CMOs. As the crisis widened, so did the allowable collateral, being extended also to high-quality lending by banks. All assets accepted were subjected to a mark-down for safety, a "haircut." Another difference is that TAF is directed at all member banks, whereas the normal open-market operations only take place through the primary dealers. Through the TAF program, European central banks, such as the ECB and the Swiss central bank (SNB), swap in dollars in exchange for their own currency and could then lend dollars in their own jurisdictions.

In March 2008, two programs were added to facilitate the conduct of monetary policy. By the Primary Dealer Credit Facility (PDCF), the Federal Reserve Bank of New York may lend money to all its primary dealers, whether banks or not. Through the Term Securities Lending Facility (TSLF), primary dealers may exchange less liquid AAA-rated bonds (MBSs, CMOs, and other asset-backed securities) against government paper, up to a volume of $200 billion. At the same time, the swap arrangements with the European central banks were increased in size. These swap arrangements have since also been concluded not only with the ECB and the SNB, but also with the Bank of England and the Bank of Japan. Since October 13, 2008, these central banks may draw an unlimited amount in dollars in currency swaps and can hence in principle lend a similarly unlimited amount in dollars. A number of other central banks (Bank of Canada, Reserve Bank of Australia, Bank of Sweden, Bank of Denmark, Bank of Norway, and so on) have concluded similar swap arrangements with the Fed, but with maximum amounts.

In October 2008, the Fed started activities to try to enhance the liquidity in short-maturity securities. By the Money Market Investor Funding Facility (MMIFF), the Fed will lend to SIVs which intend to purchase certificates of deposits (CDs) or commercial paper (CP) from MMMFs. This will enhance the secondary market in these securities, while also giving the MMMF the funds to repay customers who want out.

Simultaneously, the Fed took some initiatives to revitalize the commercial paper market, both for unsecured CP and ABCP. In the USA, CP is normally issued with very short maturities, 90 days or less, meaning that the existing stock has to be "rolled" frequently when maturing paper is to be replaced by newly issued. One consequence of the financial crisis has been greater difficulty in issuing new paper. A CP in the USA is always supported by a promise from a bank to extend a loan of the same size if the issue cannot be placed at that particular point in time, so-called "back-stop" or "swing-line" credits. A number of banks risked seeing their balance sheets swollen by such credits, with corresponding demands for more capital in an already difficult situation.

Under the programs Commercial Paper Funding Facility (CPFF) and ABCP MMMF Liquidity Facility, all members of the Federal Reserve system may borrow against collateral in the form of ABCP with the highest rating (A1, F1, P-1; see also Chapter 7), and non-financial corporations may issue paper to the Fed if there are no other buyers. Hence the Ford corporation, with a normal stock of outstanding CP of $16 billion, sold $4 billion to the Fed instead of having to rely on their back-up banks headed by JPMorgan Chase. Highly rated CP may also be used as collateral for loans in the central bank. Potentially, this meant that the Fed was guaranteeing a market of almost $2,000 billion (even though only a few hundred billion were eventually used).

Finally, November 2008 saw the introduction of the Term Asset-Backed Securities Loan Facility (TALF), which supports the market for longer securities with AAA-rating in that the Fed will lend up to $200 billion against collateral in the form of such ABSs, which have educational loans, credit card loans, car loans, and so on, as underlying loans. The purpose was to get private consumption expenditures going again. The Treasury helped by promising to take the first $20 billion of losses from money allocated under the TARP program. In March 2009, the Fed announced that the program would start on March 25, with the limit raised to $1,000 billion, and the support by the Treasury to $100 billion in potential losses.

In February 2010, the Federal Reserve closed the ABCP MMMF Liquidity Facility, the CPFF, the PDCF, and the TSLF, as well as the temporary liquidity swap arrangements between the Federal Reserve and other central banks.[38] The Federal Reserve was also simultaneously in the process of winding down its TAF: $50 billion in 28-day credit was offered on February 8, and $25 billion in 28-day credit at the final auction on March 8. The expiration dates for TALF was set at June 30, 2010 for loans backed by new-issue commercial mortgage-backed

---

[38] Swaps with some central banks were reintroduced in May 2010, as the budgetary crisis in Greece led to a renewed increase in the perception of counter-party and liquidity risk on the short-term money markets.

securities, and March 31, 2010 for loans backed by all other types of collateral.

Without any acronyms, the Fed has also lent money on other occasions. The insurance giant AIG was given a line of credit of up to $85 billion. The rate of interest, however, was set at 850 basis points above LIBOR, in order to force AIG to repay the loan as soon as possible by sale of assets. Through warrants, the Fed also has the vast majority of AIG stock as collateral. Some of the mentioned mergers (Bear Stearns, Wachovia) have also required financial support from the Fed. In November 2008, the Fed promised to purchase up to $500 billion of MBSs guaranteed by Fannie Mae and Freddie Mac, and to purchase $100 billion of their own bonds. The immediate consequence was a drop in long-term mortgage rates to unprecedented levels, below 5 percent for a 30-year mortgage. Together with the Treasury, the Fed also guarantees CDOs of doubtful quality, up to a value of $306 billion, held by Citibank. The Fed also announced that it intended to buy MBSs outright for $1,450 billion and government bonds for $300 billion during the first half of 2009.

The last acronym in the list at the beginning of this section, TLGP, is not a Fed program, but should be mentioned in this chapter anyway. The Temporary Liquidity Guarantee Program implies that the FDIC guarantees banks' new borrowing on senior securities (subordinate debt thus being excluded) up to $1,400 billion. Banks will pay a fee of 50–100 basis points, depending on maturity. The incentive for the banks is obviously to achieve lower funding costs, since the rating of the issue will be the AAA of the USA. The program also includes deposits from corporations which will, for obvious reasons, be way above the $250,000 limit covered by deposit insurance. Major FIDC-insured banks are forced to join the program (thousands of small banks have opted out), which differs from Europe, where participation has usually been voluntary. As of March 31, 2009, banks had issued bonds worth $190 billion covered by the FDIC guarantee, rising to $305 billion by May 31, 2010. From its inception, the FDIC also collected over $10 billion in fees from banks utilizing the guarantee. The program formally ended on June 30, 2009, and the resulting guarantees will end on June 30, 2012.

These various lending programs led to a doubling of the Fed's balance sheet, to over $2,000 billion. Total assets of "the monetary authority" stood at around $2,200 billion in June 2010, as contrasted to $950 billion in June 2008, before the acute phase of the crisis started in the fall (according to the Board of Governors of the Federal Reserve System, Flow of Funds data). Factors affecting reserve balances (purchases of bonds, lending to primary dealers and lending under other programs) rose from $985 billion in mid-September 2008, just before the Lehman crash and the fall of AIG, to $2,270 billion at the end of the year – an increase of more than 130 percent.[39] The Fed held some $1,300 billion of mortgage-related securities in mid-2010, as compared to zero until the end of 2007.

Despite being sued by some news agencies and newspapers, the Fed has consistently refused to reveal which banks have used the various programs and in which amounts, all in order to avoid creating additional uncertainty as to the (in-)stability of individual banks. A wise compromise was found in the Senate discussions on the government's financial action plan, namely that there would be a one-time audit of the lending programs extended in the crisis. Release of data on borrowing institutions or audits on a continuing basis would in the future be delayed until after 3 years.

European actions taken

In Europe, many countries have given liquidity support to banks in need. The Bank of England opened up extraordinary facilities for Northern Rock in the fall of 2007. We saw above that both Northern Rock and Bradford & Bingley had borrowed substantial amounts from the Bank of England before they were placed into administration (see pages 31, 148). On October 8, 2008, the Bank of England promised under its Special Liquidity Scheme to place up to £200 billion at the disposal of the banking system, the scheme having begun on a small scale in April. The Scheme allows banks to swap illiquid mortgage securities for marketable Treasury bills and government bonds. The credit and market risks remain with the originating bank, however. As of March 2009, thirty-two banks and building societies had borrowed £185 billion through the scheme. The operation was completed in February 2010, when the £200 billion target level was reached. The Bank also started a Discount Window Facility, whereby adhering banks can swap a wider

---

[39] See www.federalreserve.gov/releases/h41

range of securities for Treasury bills. In January 2009, the maturity of the Discount Window swaps was extended from 30 days to 364 days.

Central banks have also introduced facilities to allow the central bank to expand money supply directly, corresponding to the above-mentioned US acronyms. The following is how the Bank of England presented its Asset Purchase Facility (APF):

The Bank is today publishing details about how it intends initially to operate the Asset Purchase Facility agreed with HM Government and described in an exchange of letters between the Chancellor and the Governor, dated 29 January [2009]. The broad aim of the Facility is to help improve financing conditions for companies.

The Bank has been authorised to purchase up to £50 billion of high-quality private sector assets under the Facility. The following sterling assets are initially eligible for purchase: commercial paper, corporate bonds, paper issued under the Credit Guarantee Scheme (CGS), syndicated loans and asset-backed securities created in viable securitisation structures. In order to control the financial risks associated with such transactions, the Bank is authorised to purchase only high-quality assets, broadly comparable to investment grade. The Bank's operations will vary according to the structure of, and conditions prevailing in, particular markets; and will evolve through time, in the light of experience with operating the Asset Purchase Facility and feedback from the market.[40]

In addition, the APF was also extended to allow its use in monetary policy in order to enable the Monetary Policy Committee to meet the 2 percent target for CPI inflation. The range of assets eligible for purchase by the Facility on behalf of the Committee included only government debt. For this purpose, the Facility was initially authorized to purchase up to £150 billion. As noted above, the target £200 (50 + 150) billion was attained in February 2010 and was maintained throughout that year at that level.

The European Central Bank joined the Federal Reserve and the Bank of England in purchasing bonds by a decision taken in May 2009. €60 billion were to be devoted to buying mainly covered mortgage bonds, in Germany called *Pfandbriefe*.[41] These actions have swollen the balance

---

[40] News release, 6 February 2009, www.bankofengland.co.uk/publications/news/2009/009.htm

[41] Like mortgage-backed securities, covered bonds are backed by individual mortgages. But they have to be carefully selected and the loan-to value must not exceed a certain, supervised level, normally 75 percent for residential mortgages and 60 percent for commercial mortgages. These levels can vary between countries.

sheet of the central banks and hence money supply. Reserve balances held in the Bank of England trebled, from £24 billion at the end of 2007, to £36 billion in September 2008, to £71 billion in April 2009, and doubled again to £151 billion in June 2010. In the euro area, securities held by the included central banks (including the ECB) rose from €97.6 billion at the end of 2007 to €300.6 billion in June 2009 and €304.5 billion in June 2010. Total assets increased from €1,472 billion in 2007 to €2,099 billion in June 2010, an increase of 43 percent. In the same period, the total financial assets of the Fed went from $797 billion to $2,339 billion, an increase of 193 percent. The figures indicate very clearly the depth of the financial crisis in the USA and the euro area.

The difference, however, lies in the fact that the US financial crisis is believed to have been over by the beginning of 2010, even if some small banks still continued to go belly up. The renewed financial worries during May 2010 forced the ECB to take renewed actions to restore liquidity in the euro area. First, the normal requirement on collateral to be investment-grade rated was lifted, to allow for Greek government bonds to be used as collateral by Greek banks in their dealings with the ECB, Greece as a sovereign state having been lowered to junk status. Second, on May 10, 2010, the Securities Markets Programme was reopened, whereby the ECB attempts to restore liquidity in the bond markets by purchasing securities when necessary. Third, banks were allowed to borrow indefinite amounts (subject to collateral requirements) at the refi rate. Fourth, the temporary swap line with the Federal Reserve was restored to allow for the possibility of the ECB to lend also in dollars.

In October 2008, the Bank of Sweden extended a special credit of SEK 5 billion to the Swedish subsidiary of the Icelandic bank Kaupthing. In Germany, the ailing mortgage Hypo Real Estate received support to the tune of €50 billion from a consortium including the ECB, the Bundesbank and some private banks.[42] Denmark has had the tradition, like Germany, that it is the central bank in consortium with other banks who aid ailing banks, rather than the government. Hence, in September 2007, Roskilde Bank, the eighth largest, received support to the tune of DKK 4.5 billion from the central bank. Its branch network was later sold to other banks, among them Nordea, the largest bank in

---

[42] Capital support is discussed in Chapter 7.

the Nordic region. Other small banks, such as Ebh Bank, were bailed out by the central bank at the same time. In February 2009, it was Fionia Bank in Odense, the 11th largest in the country, which received support; it also was absorbed by Nordea. The Bank of Spain was forced in March 2009 to begin its first bank liquidity support operation, giving a loan of €9 billion to the ailing savings bank Caja Castilla & La Mancha. One year later, it took over the Cajasur in Andalusia, another savings bank.

Countries have also introduced guarantees for new bank borrowing other than deposits. Ireland, as usual, was first, on September 30, 2008, in guaranteeing the total liabilities of the six Irish banks, excluding only so-called "perpetuals" – that is, perpetual subordinated debt which forms part of a bank's Tier 2 capital (discussed more in Chapter 7). The banks paid a fee of €1 billion over a 2-year period to cover costs. In other European countries, new bank borrowing has also received guarantees in order to unfreeze the interbank markets. The amounts have been maximized to £250 billion in the UK, €320 billion in France, €400 billion in Germany, €75 billion in Austria, €100 billion in Spain, €200 billion in the Netherlands, €15 billion in Greece and SEK 1,500 billion in Sweden, to give a few examples. In principle, participation in the guarantee programs is voluntary, though some countries such as Sweden have exerted pressure on the banks to participate. Maturities have been maximized in individual countries to 3 years in the UK and Germany, and up to 5 years in France.

The fee was established by the European Commission as 50 basis points plus a margin, varying from bank to bank according to its riskiness, as established by the price of CDSs written on that bank, if available. This is in sharp contrast to the USA, where the TLGP charged a fee independently of bank risk. It has been calculated that this feature implied a transfer of taxpayer wealth to the US banking system of between $13 billion and $70 billion. For instance, the fee charged to Citigroup for a 3-year guarantee should fairly have been priced at 238 basis points; the actual fee charged was 75 basis points.[43]

Even the European scheme involved a clear and intended subsidy, however, in that the banks could borrow at cheaper terms than

[43] Acharya and Richardson (eds.), *Restoring Financial Stability*, p. 326.

otherwise, making a profit even considering the fee. An example is the issue by Swedish Swedbank (the only Swedish bank to participate in the scheme) of a 3-year note with government guarantee, where the Swedish state's AAA rating replaced the bank's own AA–/Aa3 rating. It has been calculated that the bank gained around 200 basis points, even taking into account the fee paid (83 basis points). This may be compared with the UK, where even the best bank, HSBC Holdings, paid 109 basis points, and Nationwide, the worst, 178 basis points, much closer to fair prices.[44]

Conclusions

As a summary of this chapter, we may note that the extension of deposit insurance and the saving of a number of banks have prevented further runs. Depositors obviously feel safer today. Interbank interest rates indicate that the markets in dollars as well as euros have recovered in the sense that the spread to the Fed Funds rate and the refi rate, respectively, are almost back to normal. Uncertainty concerning which banks still faced losses may explain why it took so long. When the authorities took over the credit risk of $306 billion of "toxic assets" in Citibank, the natural question popped up about what would happen if there were similar problems in other banks. After the bankruptcy of Lehman, there was also some uncertainty as to which banks would be regarded as "too big to fail." Why was Bear Stearns too big to fail and not Lehman? Gradually, the market realized that the Fed and the FDIC regretted their (non-)action in the Lehman case. Since then, no bank, whatever its size, has been allowed to fail in such an uncontrolled manner.

In Europe, the problems with US mortgage-related securities have been concentrated to a small number of banks, in general outside Euroland: Swiss banks such as UBS and Credit Suisse, and British banks like Barclays and HSBC. The rise and fall of house prices in countries like Ireland and the UK created home-made problems, similar to those in the USA, in mortgage banks such as Northern Rock, HBOS (now part of Lloyds TSB) and Bradford & Bingley. The problems witnessed in Dutch-Belgian Fortis and RBS were mostly a consequence

---

[44] Ibid., p. 331.

of the fact that they bought and dismembered the Dutch bank ABN AMRO at the worst possible time. In the Euromarket, only the German *Landesbanken*, IKB and some insurers, such as AXA and Allianz, have faced severe problems on account of so-called "toxic products" created on the US market.

Points to remember

- Today's crisis has many similarities to the crises of 1907 and 1929 in that they also began as a liquidity squeeze – that is, a marked lack of confidence among the actors in the interbank market. Only at later stages in the crisis would banks experience large credit write-downs and lack of capital.
- But there may also be too much liquidity. Both the stock market (or dotcom) bubble of 2000 and the housing bubble of 2006 were engineered by the low interest rate policies of the Federal Reserve.
- There are highly diverging opinions as to the possibilities open to the central bank to counteract such bubbles in asset markets. Some hold that it is impossible, while others, like the Fed Chairman Ben Bernanke, are of the opinion that asset prices may be influenced even if the interest rate is set to attain a certain inflation in the prices of goods and services.
- Experiences during the last few years do not support the hypothesis that high interest rates can subdue house price speculation. At least in countries like the UK and Australia, effects appear absent, despite their floating exchange rate giving them the possibility of an independent monetary policy. Countries such as Ireland and Spain could not conduct a monetary policy appropriate to their needs, the rate of interest in the euro area being set by the European Central Bank. Euroland is not an "optimal currency area," in particular as concerns the possibility to attack bubbles in house prices.
- In order to get interbank lending moving again, central banks have undertaken several actions, from guaranteeing new borrowing by banks to buying illiquid assets. Bank "runs" have been prevented by doubling the coverage of deposit insurance.
- Central banks in the USA, the UK and some other countries have also sought to influence long-term interest rates by buying government debt as well as mortgage-related bonds.

Appendix 6.1
The liquidity-risk framework proposed by the FSA and the BIS

British proposals

As described in the proposal[45] (page 4), the recent crisis revealed a number of deficiencies in banks' liquidity management and in the role played by the supervisory authorities:

- inadequate quality and quantity of liquid asset buffers, leading to firms' inability to liquidate them in a stress event;
- poor liquidity risk management capabilities – that is, inadequate stress testing, contingency funding planning and senior management oversight;
- over-reliance on short-term, credit-sensitive wholesale funding markets;
- large pipelines of new business with limited or no ability to fund them;
- over-reliance on funding on securitization markets;
- inability to meet significant retail outflows;
- insufficient data to assess properly firms' liquidity positions or to form sector- and industry-wide views.

The new proposed liquidity regulation applies to the larger banks (113), building societies (9) and investment firms (97), and also to branches and subsidiaries of international banks (197), while smaller institutions face simplified rules. It was scheduled to enter into force on September 1, 2010. It is estimated that the liquid portion of total assets would rise from 5 percent to 15 percent in the major banks and involve banks' holding an additional £110 billion in government bonds.

Liquid assets are defined as central bank reserves and high-quality securities issued by certain listed governments or multilateral development banks (such as the World Bank, the European Bank for Reconstruction and Development or the European Investment Bank). The framework for liquidity management is to have available liquid assets sufficient to cover 2 weeks of liquidity needs in a stressed environment.

---

[45] Financial Services Authority, Strengthening liquidity standards.

I have purposely not gone into detail concerning the requirements, since they can be supposed to be superseded by the BIS rules.

Basel proposals

The main tool proposed by the Basel group is the Liquidity Coverage Ratio.[46] It identifies certain high-quality liquid assets that the bank needs to hold in order to meet unforeseen net cash outflows in a stressed situation. Outflows are to be measured over a 30-day period (compare this with the 2-week period in the British proposal).The stress test includes both institution-specific and systemic factors. The Basel proposal also seeks to streamline the liquidity monitoring of the financial supervisory authorities, having found that at least twenty-five different measures of liquidity are currently used by the various authorities.[47]

The specific stress factors that the institution must take into account are:

- a three-step downgrade in the bank's rating, e g from AA– to A– (see Chapter 7);
- a runoff of a proportion of retail deposits;
- a loss of wholesale unsecured funding;
- a loss of secured short-term financing – for example, the inability to sell assets;
- increases in market volatilities that requires posing more collateral, but also impacts on the quality of the collateral and requires larger "haircuts" – that is, mark-down on assets;
- unforeseen draws on the bank's committed lines of credit.

High-quality liquid assets in the numerator of the Liquidity Coverage Ratio are those assets which have both a low credit risk – that is, high-quality issuer, such as a AAA-rated government – and a low market risk – that is, short remaining maturity, low price volatility, low foreign exchange risk, if foreign. It must also be easy to value and mark to market, even in a stressed situation. In practice, this means cash and reserves held with the central bank, marketable securities issued by such entities that are assigned a 0 percent risk weighting under the Basel II

---

[46] Bank for International Settlements, *International framework for liquidity risk measurement*.

[47] The introduction of a parallel net stable funding ratio to align maturities of assets and liabilities over a longer term was scrapped at the G-20 meeting in June 2010, at the request of the banking system, as overly cumbersome and expensive.

rules – that is, AAA- and AA-rated securities issued by governments, central banks and multilateral development banks. In addition, AAA- or AA-rated corporate bonds and covered mortgage bonds may be included, but only up to a certain proportion of liquid assets and subject to deep haircuts (20–40 percent).[48]

Net cash outflow in the denominator of the Liquidity Coverage Ratio is determined both by unexpected losses of deposits and funding, and unforeseen increases in lending, such as committed credit facilities which would be used to the full extent possible by the bank's customers in a stressed situation. The assumptions to be taken into account are:

- 7.5 percent runoff of stable, personal deposits (even though they are insured);
- 15 percent runoff of less stable deposits, such as those exceeding the deposit insurance limits, those held by high net worth individuals, internet deposits;
- 25 percent runoff of unsecured wholesale deposits from sovereigns, central banks;
- 75 percent runoff of deposits from non-financial large corporate customers;
- 100 percent runoff of deposits from other financial entities, including banks, insurance companies, development banks, securities firms, special purpose vehicles, and so on.

In addition, the bank would have to factor in:

- the increase in collateral required after a downrating of three steps;
- 20 percent reduction in the value of posted collateral;
- 100 percent loss of funding from ABCP, SIVs, and so on, which is tantamount to saying that the market for refinancing disappears;
- 100 percent of the bank's debt maturing within the 30-day period;
- 10 percent drawdown of committed loan facilities by retail clients;

---

[48] Rating is presented and discussed in the Chapter 7. Both Denmark and Germany protest against these proposals, which would threaten the use of covered bonds (Danish *pantebreve* and German *Pfandbriefe*) as liquid assets. Danish banks held €140 billion of covered bonds at the end of 2009, as contrasted with only €11 billion in government bonds. A restriction to a maximum of 50 percent of liquid assets would hit the Danish banks hard, as would the tough haircut. See Jenkins and Hughes, Danish banks urge changes to Basel III.

- 100 percent drawdown of liquidity facilities granted to both financial and non-financial corporate customers;
- not using any of its own lines of credit that have been granted from other financial institutions.

The net outflow resulting from these assumptions must be met by at least 100 percent by the above-stated liquid assets. However, banks have until 2015 to comply.

7 | Credit risk aspects of the crisis, rating and solvency

Chapter 6 discussed the liquidity aspects of the financial crisis and the actions taken by governments to enhance liquidity in the interbank market and in the securities markets. In the present chapter, we will take a look at the solvency aspect – that is, the demand for and supply of risk-bearing capital. This theme may be subdivided into five sections, with the questions posed being answered as we go along:

- Why did the rating companies fail in their task of measuring credit risks, especially on securitized subprime loans?
- Must (or should) banks in crisis be nationalized?
- Did the solvency of the major banks appear inadequate before the crisis?
- Why were the capital ratio requirements, as set up under the Basel I and II accords, so inadequate?
- Does mark-to-market valuation induce an undesirable procyclicality?

Appendix 7.1 gives an account of the measures taken by various countries to resupply banks with capital and raise their solvency ratios. Appendix 7.2 shows the proposed revised capital framework under Basel III.

Rating companies and the supervision of credit risks

Rating means a professional examination of the creditworthiness of countries or firms, conducted by an approved rating company.[1]

---

[1] For literature, see, inter alia: Langohr and Langohr, *The Rating Agencies and their Credit Ratings*; Levich, Majnoni and Reinhart, *Ratings, Rating Agencies and the Global Financial System*; Hull, Predescu and White, Credit default swap spreads, bond yields and credit rating announcements; Sinclair, *The New Masters of Capital*; Moody's Investor Services, *Sovereign Ratings Lists* (http://v2.moodys. com/moodys/cust/content/loadcontent.aspx?source=staticcontent/businesslines/ sovereign-subsovereign/ratingslistgbr.htm&param=all); Moody's Investor

Issuers, as well as individual bond issues, may be rated. In the USA, issues of preference shares are also usually rated, since they are more similar to debt than to equity in that their yield is fixed and they are non-voting, in contrast to most parts of Europe.

The issuer pays for the rating, which has led to the critique that rating firms have lowered their standards to get more deals in competition with a gradually larger number of rating companies.

The two most well-known rating companies are Standard & Poor's and Moody's Investor Services. Both have their origin in the nascent US bond market during and after the First World War, but have only recently acquired the dominant role they possess today. Since 1966, S&P (which also publishes the well-known stock price index S&P 500) has been part of the McGraw-Hill group. Moody's is owned by a listed company with the same name.

In the USA, since 1975, a rating institute must be a Nationally Recognized Statistical Rating Organization (NRSRO), approved by the Securities and Exchange Commission (SEC), the authority charged with supervising exchanges and securities markets and which also approves prospectuses. Some ten rating companies have been approved. Besides Moody's and S&P, we find the French-owned Fitch Ratings, part of the Fimalac group. By its purchase in 1998 of the International Bank Credit Analyst (IBCA), Fitch is important not least in the rating of financial firms.

The importance of the rating companies, not least in Europe, has increased considerably with the introduction of the new solvency rules according to Basel II (more on these rules in the following sections). Under Pillar 1, banks are supposed to place their assets in certain categories after risk (credit quality steps). The simplest variety of the rules uses external ratings to achieve this allocation, rating companies being called External Credit Assessment Institutions (ECAI) in EU-speak. The Financial Services Authority (FSA) has approved four companies for the British market: S&P,

Services, Rating Methodologies, *Actively Managed Synthetic CDOs*, September 2008 (available at www.moodys.com); Moody's Investor Services, Rating Methodologies, *Sovereign Bond Ratings*, September 2008 (available at www. moodys.com); Standard & Poor's, *Annual Global Corporate Default Study and Ratings Transition*, February 2008 (available at www.standardandpoors.com/ratings/en/us).

Table 7.1 *Summary of rating assessments for bonds*

	Moody's	S&P/Fitch	Definition
Investment grade	Aaa	AAA	Extremely strong capacity
	Aa (1–3)	AA (+, 0, –)	Very high capacity
	A (1–3)	A (+, 0, –)	Somewhat more susceptible
	Baa (1–3)	BBB (+, 0, –)	Adequate protection
Speculative grade	Ba (1–3)	BB (+, 0, –)	
	B (1–3)	B (+, 0, –)	
	Caa (1–3)	CCC (+, 0, –)	Gradually more speculative
	Ca	CC	
	C	C	
Default	D	D	In default

Moody's, Fitch and the Canadian Dominion Bond Rating Services (DBRS).[2]

Table 7.1 summarizes the assessments given by the institutes as concerns long-term borrowing. The highest grade AAA/Aaa corresponds to the highest class in the issuing of MBSs and CDOs (super senior tranche). The first four classes together are commonly called investment grade, since US pension funds are not allowed to invest in bonds of lower quality. Below investment grade, we find speculative grade bonds (also called high-yield bonds or junk bonds). An indication of the seriousness of the present financial crisis is that the spread between the rate of interest on AAA-rated government bonds in the USA and junk has never been greater. Even in the crisis of 2002, the maximum spread attained was 12 percentage points. This time round, the junk bond spread reached almost 20 percentage points in December 2008, as contrasted with 4 percentage points at the beginning of the year.[3] (See Figure 7.1.)

There exist grades for short-term paper as well (commercial paper, asset-backed commercial paper), where the highest level is normally

---

[2] EU countries' financial services authorities have so far been free to choose which companies they authorize, something that will change with new rules adopted in April 2009, whereby authorization becomes European Union business.

[3] The junk bond spread has historically more than compensated investors for the larger credit risk in junk, which means that, over time, a better yield than on government paper has been achieved by a well-diversified portfolio of junk bonds. Figure 7.1 shows bonds rated B in comparison with the government's AAA rating.

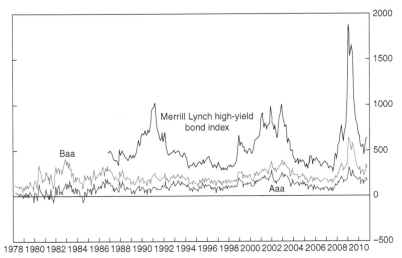

Figure 7.1 Spread between a speculative grade ("junk") bond rated B, Baa-rated corporate bonds and Aaa-rated corporate yields, all measured against Aaa-rated governments, 1978–2010
Source: International Monetary Fund, *Global Financial Stability Report* (October 2010), Appendix

needed for a successful issue: A1+ or A1 (S&P), P-1 (Moody's) and F1+ or F1 (Fitch). Lower prime levels are A2/P-2/F2 and A3/P-3/F3. Everything below is non-prime and utterly unsellable.

A major difference between today's financial crisis and those of the 1990s (the Nordic countries, Asia, Russia) is that most of the countries involved had a AAA/Aaa rating, at least to start with. This is important, not least since a bank can never have a higher rating than the country in which it is incorporated. Moody's, in a very important declaration of intent, stated on September 22, 2008, and repeated on May 27, 2009, that its view on the US economy was unchanged. Despite budget deficits of over 12 percent of GDP, Moody's regarded the political and economic stability, the flexibility and the strength of the US economy as still worth a Aaa rating. On March 15, 2010, Moody's sounded a warning, however, declaring that "on balance, we believe that the ratings of all large Aaa governments remain well positioned, although their 'distance-to-downgrade' has in all cases substantially diminished" – a clear warning to both the UK and the USA.

Standard & Poor's placed the UK's AAA rating on a negative outlook in May 2009, with regard to the exploding budget deficits and a debt level approaching 100 percent of GDP. Some commentators feared that the USA was headed the same way. By the end of 2010, no action had been taken. S&P, however, declared that its action towards the UK should in no way be construed as an implied warning to the USA, in some contrast to Moody's opinion.

The major criticism of the rating companies stems from their abject failure to rate structured mortgage-related products (such as MBSs, CMOs, CDOs and CDSs) issued in later years. Unexpectedly high rates of failure have triggered lowered ratings. During 2007 and 2008, Moody's lowered the rating on over 40 percent of the MBSs issued in recent years. The situation was even worse for bonds issued with subprime loans as underlying. Standard & Poor's gave an account, in a publication of October 20, 2008, of "rating transitions" in MBSs with underlying subprime loans issued during the period from the first quarter of 2005 to the third quarter of 2007. Despite the fact that only 1 or 2 years had passed since issue, two-thirds of the bonds saw their ratings lowered.[4] In a similar tabulation, Moody's has shown that 19.1 percent of newly issued structured loans had received a lowered rating within 1 year of issue. This may be compared with a 1-year transition rate of only 3.8 percent for the 15 years 1993–2007.[5]

The situation has continued to deteriorate. A report from Standard & Poor's in August 2010 reported that out of $3,300 billion of structured finance securities issued in 2005 to 2007, $2,400 billion, or almost three-quarters, had been downgraded.

A lowered rating on a bond is equivalent to a higher risk, which must be compensated by a higher yield. But since the coupon rate of interest is fixed for bonds that are already on the market, a higher yield can only result from a fall in the price of the bond.[6] For a company such as a bank, which is forced to mark assets to market, this gives rise to a direct effect on profits. Since there are investors with restrictions on which risk classes they may invest in, a downrating often triggers sales, which

---

[4] Standard & Poor's, *Ratings transition matrix for US RMBS Subprime*, October 2008.

[5] Moody's Credit Policy, *The Performance of Structured Finance Ratings: Full-Year 2007, Report*, July 2008.

[6] The investor who buys the bond since the price has fallen receives a higher yield than the coupon rate, since the price is now lower than 100 percent and will give the investor a capital gain as the bond climbs back to the 100 percent paid at maturity.

further lower the price. This applies in particular if the bond is down-rated from investment grade to speculative grade (as Greece was by Moody's in June 2010). A lowered rating may also give rise to chain effects if it leads to a higher price on those CDSs normally connected with the issue of CDOs.[7] The rating companies hence risk aggravating a cyclical downturn. Rating becomes procyclical instead of a tool to foresee and counteract downturns.

In the USA, the critique against the rating firms has centered on their profit interest. An academic study found that both Moody's and Standard & Poor's raised their ratings in order to retain customers when a new competitor, Fitch, entered the stage.[8] Employees have testified before Congress that the two oligopolists also competed by utilizing those models that gave issues to be rated the most advantageous rating. Moody's has also acknowledged that a programming error caused billions of dollars of CDOs to obtain an inappropriate Aaa rating.

The financial reform bill discussed in the US Congress during spring 2010 originally proposed that a government agency be set up to choose which rating company should undertake the rating of a certain bond issue or borrower. In this way, profit-driven competition between the various rating firms would be avoided and, hopefully, more objective ratings attained. The proposal was dropped from the final bill, however, and the question of rating is to be studied separately.

The European Union issued a Regulation concerning the role of rating companies in April 2009 (1060/2009). They now have to be approved by the Committee of European Securities Regulators (CESR), the group coordinating the European Union's financial supervisory authorities, rather than by individual country financial supervisory authorities. They also have to become more transparent in disclosing their models and their methodologies. Their conflict of interest is hopefully minimized by the fact that they are no longer allowed to provide advisory services to their clients.[9] However, the proposed changes did not impress the financial markets or the supervisory

---

[7] Hull, Predescu and White, Credit default swap spreads, bond yields and credit rating announcements.

[8] Becker and Milbourn, Reputation and competition.

[9] "Approval of new Regulation will raise standards for the issuance of credit ratings used in the Community," IP/09/629, April 23, 2009 (available at http://europa.eu/rapid/pressReleasesAction.do?reference=IP/09/629).

authorities. The European Association of Corporate Treasurers claimed that the proposals would make rating even more expensive, without any improvement in quality or objectivity. The CESR itself has noticed drily that "CESR and market participants believe that there is no evidence that regulation of the credit rating industry would have had an effect on the issues which emerged with ratings of US subprime securities and hence continues to support market driven improvement."[10] Still, this skeptical group (or rather, its successor, ESMA; see Chapter 9) has become responsible for the regulation of the rating companies.

The conclusion appears to be that nobody could have made a better evaluation of the risks than the criticized rating companies. In the future, however, one should be careful not to place too much faith in a rating assessment. This conclusion has implications for the next sections, namely the excessive role given to the rating companies in the new solvency requirements (Basel II and III).

A mitigating circumstance in the critique is that, in the main, the rating companies rate only credit risk, while the present crisis, at least in its infant stage, involved a classical liquidity risk, even though it may be difficult to separate the two kinds of risk in a situation where there are no market quotations for some assets. Both the British FSA and the Basel group have tried to rectify this problem with the proposals presented in Chapter 6.

Should (or could) banks in crisis be nationalized?

Since banks seek to maximize return on capital (subject to constraints), it is in the nature of things that they will tend to have too little capital if left to their own devices, without restrictions imposed on their behavior by their supervisor. It is likewise quite natural for a bank to behave procyclically – that is, to expand lending in good times when risks appear low, and cut down on lending in troughs when the creditworthiness of borrowers falls and credit write-downs on existing loans diminish their capital bases. The purpose of supervising banks' risk-taking and imposing certain minimum capital ratios is to guarantee that a bank has such a strong capital position that its solvency (= survival) is not threatened even during a deep recession. Hopefully, this capital strength will lead the bank to continue lending even in the downturn phase of the

---

[10] Committee of European Securities Regulators, The role of credit rating agencies in structured finance.

business cycle, in order not to aggravate further the seriousness of the situation in the real parts of the economy.

However, in delving more deeply into the question of supervision and capital, what precise purposes do they serve? Is the aim to guarantee that all banks always have such a strong capital base that they never risk bankruptcy, not even in a crisis as deep as the one we have just been through? In that case, the capital bar must be placed much higher than it is today. Or can one accept that some banks, those with the worst management, those with the least capital, go bankrupt? But how to manage a situation where the entire banking system is subjected to such a shock that both badly managed and well-managed banks risk failure? Is nationalization of the whole banking system, or parts of it, the answer or are there alternatives?

The problem really breaks down into two parts: which banks should be saved and how should they be saved?

The first problem is usually analyzed under the headline "too big to fail" – that is, the fact that some banks are so large in relationship to the financial system or the economy as a whole that there is no alternative but to save them. The Bank of England has pioneered the use of stress tests to analyze the capability of banks to sustain major shocks. These tests are reported twice annually in the Bank's *Financial Stability Report*. In the UK (with data from *The Banker*, July 2008), three British banks had assets of about the same size as the UK's GDP: RBS at 126 percent of GDP, HSBC at 98 percent of GDP, and Barclays at 94 percent of GDP. These three banks together held (and still hold) over 60 percent of total assets of banks domiciled in the UK. These three, together with Lloyds TSB, HBOS and Nationwide (the world's largest building society), were stress-tested in the 2008: II issue of the *Financial Stability Report* as to potential credit losses. The worst outcome of the tests was £130 billion in credit write-downs over a 5-year period, which corresponded to about three-quarters of the capital base (Tier 1 capital) held by these institutions at the end of 2007. It should be rather obvious that these banks were too big to be allowed to fail!

Still the tests were not sufficiently pessimistic. The predicted outcome of the stress tests, a loss of £130 billion or $220 billion (using an exchange rate of 1.7, the average for 2008), may be contrasted with the forecasts by the International Monetary Fund. Even having scaled down potential write-downs from earlier elevated levels, the IMF found in April 2010 that British banks would face write-downs during the crisis on loans and securities of $455 billion, or over twice the amount predicted as the "worst case" by the FSA's stress test. This goes to show the severity of the recent crisis and the inability of even clever people and institutions to imagine the depth of the oncoming crisis.

Which banks to save also depends on the general picture. The UK could afford to let BCCI go bankrupt in 1991 and Barings in 1995, not only because these banks were small, but also because of the stability of the general banking system at that time. Today, the supervisory authorities hesitate to let even a small bank fail uncontrollably, since it would increase further the uncertainty in the system when depositors and other investors try to figure out which banks are deemed too big to fail and which will be let go.

After the shock created by the Lehman bankruptcy, US authorities have saved all banks, small as well as large. Most have been merged with stronger partners, even though some, like IndyMac, were temporarily placed in conservatorship under the FDIC. In the UK, Northern Rock and Bradford & Bingley received liquidity support from the Bank of England before being placed in administration by the state in the form of UK Financial Investments. In Germany, the Munich-based mortgage bank Hypo Real Estate was nationalized in October 2009. Fortunately, the other major German problem banks – the *Landesbanken* – are already state-owned in the main and thus need not be nationalized.

In Sweden, two gravely mismanaged banks, Kaupthing Sweden and Carnegie, received liquidity support from the Bank of Sweden and were later nationalized under the authority of the National Debt Office (which also administers the deposit insurance system). Both have since been sold back to the private sector.[11] In Denmark, the Bank of Denmark, acting in consortium with the other commercial banks, has saved even the smallest institutions from failure, such as Ebh Bank, with total assets of DKK 10 billion ($2 billion).

There is, however, the risk that banks will be tempted by the implicit guarantee from the state to take bigger risks. If the gamble succeeds, the bank, its owners and its management take the profit; if it fails, taxpayers will pick up the tab.[12] For this reason, known as moral hazard, it is important that the bank is saved in such a way that its management lacks the incentive to behave in this manner. This leads us to the second question: how are ailing banks to be saved, if/when they are to be saved?

---

[11] The viable parts of Kaupthing Sweden is today the Finnish-owned Ålandsbanken. Carnegie was sold to a consortium of private equity firms.
[12] The problem is discussed at length in Stern and Feldman, *Too Big to Fail.*

As shown in Appendix 7.1, countries have taken different approaches in recapitalizing their banks. In Germany, Commerzbank has received an infusion of common stock, bringing public ownership to 25 percent. The German federal state has also been given the legal right to forcibly nationalize banks, even when minority shareholders oppose. The case in question was the mortgage bank Hypo Real Estate, where the state owned 50 percent of the capital plus one share before the bank was nationalized totally, despite objections from the minority shareholders.[13] It was the first bank nationalization in Germany since 1931, when the Depression forced the second largest bank in the country, Darmstädter und Nationalbank (Danat-bank), to close after a run. The bank was later merged with Dresdner Bank.

In the UK, mortgage banks Northern Rock and Bradford & Bingley have been totally nationalized (although in the latter only the mortgage book remains state-owned, the rest having been sold to Santander). The government's stake in RBS amounts to 84 percent after the state's preference shares were converted to ordinary shares. The state's stake in the merged Lloyds TSB-HBOS stayed at 43 percent, however, since the bank preferred to issue new stock worth £22 billion in November 2009 rather than becoming majority-owned by the government. A new issue of £3 billion in early 2010 brought down the stake of the British crown to 41 percent.

Ireland nationalized totally the third largest bank, Anglo-Irish Bank, and took an 18.7 percent minority ownership stake in Allied Irish Banks (AIB) and 13.6 percent in the Bank of Ireland (later increased, as shown in Appendix 7.1). In the Netherlands, the Dutch part of Fortis (ex-ABN AMRO) has been nationalized, whereas the majority of the nationalized Belgium-Luxembourg part of Fortis was sold to BNP Paribas.

As spelled out in more detail in Appendix 7.1, countries in the European Union have allocated some €300 billion for recapitalization of their banks.

In the USA, with some exceptions, the Treasury has chosen to recapitalize banks with non-voting preference shares which do not dilute the ownership by the present shareholders. Instead, the banks have had to pay a high rate of interest on what is in practice a loan. The main exception to the rule so far has been the savings bank IndyMac, which was nationalized and placed under the conservatorship of the FDIC, which continued operations under the name IndyMac Federal Bank. It was sold to a private

---

[13] See Wilson, Hypo reality.

equity group in January 2009. Perhaps there is a change of attitude under way. When the government's stake in Citigroup, the world's second largest bank by Tier 1 capital in 2007, was converted to ordinary shares, the Treasury came to hold 36 percent of its capital. Under the second portion of TARP (to be discussed below), the government has gained the specific right to convert preference shares into common stock.

From the banks' point of view, government ownership in the form of preference shares is to be preferred. The main advantage is that management keeps control of the organization, since preference shares do not give any influence in the form of votes at the shareholders' annual general meeting. Present owners are not squeezed out and hence also prefer this solution. The disadvantage lies in the purposely set high rate of interest.

As viewed from the authorities' and the taxpayers' point of view, contributions in the form of preference shares are of highly doubtful value. The interest or dividend received is small, after all, taking into account the fact that preference shares are also risk-bearing. And taxpayers have no part in the upside. To compensate for this absence, the Treasury has received warrants in those institutions that have needed support. These warrants may be called (repurchased) by the bank. As seen in the detailed presentation below, these warrants turned out to be highly lucrative investments for taxpayers.

Strong criticism has been directed at the way the first half of the TARP money ($350 billion) was spent. Until end-February 2009, $250 billion had been allocated to inject capital into banks in need (see Appendix 7.1); $195 billion had been paid out. On top of this sum, Citigroup and Bank of America had each received an additional $20 billion. The organization put in place by Congress to evaluate the financial stability program, the Congressional Oversight Panel (calling itself COP!), found in its first report that TARP money had not been used to increase lending to housing or modify existing loans for borrowers who risked losing their homes. Instead, the banks had used the TARP money in the main to build up reserves for future credit losses, pay back other (more expensive) loans or make aggressive bids for other banks.[14] In its report from January 9, 2009 (Accountability for the Troubled Asset Relief

---

[14] The material is available at http://cybercemetery.unt.edu/archive/cop/ 20110401223205/http://www.cop.senate.gov Nasty tongues have suggested that TARP should be an acronym for "To Already Rich Plutocrats" or "The Act Rewarding Plutocrats."

Program), the COP found that the Treasury, in its eagerness to stabilize the banking system, had "forgotten" to include in the agreements requirements on the receiving banks to account for how the money had been spent. On demand by the Treasury, some banks even refused to give an account of how they had spent taxpayers' money. A further critique is that the TARP program has aided large banks to a higher degree than small banks, which have had difficulty accessing capital markets in order to repay the received TARP money.[15]

The original thought behind TARP was to purchase banks' "toxic assets": CDOs, CMOs, MBSs with underlying mortgages, especially subprime mortgages – hence the name Troubled Assets Relief Program. The difficulty in agreeing with the selling banks on the price at which the government would buy these assets led to the idea being abandoned. Instead, the two banks with the largest investments in "toxic assets" received guarantees from the government. Bank of America (BofA) received guarantees from the Treasury and the FDIC on securities booked at $118 billion, emanating in the main from its purchase of Merrill Lynch. The guarantee covers "unusually large losses," whatever that means. BofA takes the first $10 billion in losses, and taxpayers take the rest. In a similar deal with Citigroup concerning assets worth $306 billion, Citigroup accepted bearing the first $37 billion of loss. The FDIC will thereafter bear 90 percent of remaining losses. The state was compensated by $27 billion in non-voting preference shares at an interest rate of 8 percent. The Congressional panel found, however, that the risk that taxpayers had been forced to accept was not adequately compensated.

What about total nationalization instead? You might have read a lot during the recent crisis about "the Swedish way."[16] In its crisis in the 1990s, Sweden nationalized two banks in trouble, Nordbanken and GOTA Bank, and set up "bad banks" (called Securum and Retriva, respectively) to handle the toxic assets of each one. The two ailing banks were merged and today form the Swedish part of the Nordea group, where the state still retains a 20 percent stake as a result. The assets in the bad banks were gradually disposed of in such a way that taxpayers (considering the value of their remaining stake in Nordea) were actually

---

[15] www.bloomberg.com/news/2010-07-14/warren-says-bailouts-didn-t-help-small-u-s-banks-while-aiding-wall-street.html

[16] For instance, Dougherty, Stopping a financial crisis.

repaid with interest the entire sum injected into the banks. More will be said on this in Chapter 8.

When the failed bank is nationalized totally, as in the Swedish case, the transfer of assets to a bad bank is simplified since the transfer price does not matter. The Swedish Bank Support Agency (*Bankstödsnämnden*) transferred the assets at nominal value, wrote them down in the bad banks and then recapitalized the selling institutions. In relationship to the Swedish solution, the US (or British) situation is much more difficult, for (at least) three reasons. The first one is that the banks in the Swedish case, while large, were still at that time relatively small in relationship to the size of the economy. Today's banks are giants, as noted above for the three largest British banks. They are simply too large to be nationalized. The problem may be illustrated by what happened when the mortgage bank Northern Rock was nationalized. When its £100 billion in liabilities were added to the British national debt, the debt rose from 37 to 45 percent of GDP. Thus it would be very difficult, nay impossible, for the British authorities to take over more than the 84 percent they already have in RBS, the world's largest bank measured by assets in 2008 and with liabilities twenty times those of Northern Rock.[17] Lloyds TSB presents a similar problem in being ten times the size of Northern Rock.

The USA has an identical situation. When Freddie Mac and Fannie Mae were placed in conservatorship, the Federal government potentially took over debts of $5,000 billion, which would have increased the national debt by 50 percent. The problem has been postponed since there are still private owners.[18] Congress decided in June 2010 to postpone again the question of whether these GSEs should be nationalized or re-privatized. Until then, they remain in limbo.

---

[17] Northern Rock was bank number 85 in the world measured by assets in 2007, while RBS was number 1.

[18] According to Peter Orszag in a statement of February 27, 2009, it had not yet been decided whether to integrate Fannie and Freddie in the national debt or not. In his capacity as Director of the White House Office of Management and Budget, he has the main deciding capacity. He was earlier head of the Congressional Budget Office. Should Fannie and Freddie have been on the budget in 2009, the deficit would have risen by $291 billion, or from 11 to 13 percent of GDP. When the Financial Accountants Standards Board forced the decision in March 2010, some $400 billion were added to the Federal debt, though without adding to the deficit.

But let's assume that the state wanted to take over completely the (probably) weakest of the megabanks, Citigroup. Its total assets on September 30, 2010 were $1,983 billion. On November 4, 2010, at 9:25AM (when I looked), the US national debt stood at $13,679,074,902,367, or almost $14 trillion, according to "The National Debt Clock" on 6th Avenue,[19] over 92 percent of GDP (which was $14,730 billion in the third quarter of 2010 at annual rates). A takeover of the liabilities of Citi by the US government would raise the national debt by almost 15 percentage points – all for the sake of a single bank which is not even the biggest bank in the USA anymore, either by assets or by capital.

The second and third differences are really two sides of the same coin. In the case of Securum/Retriva, the toxic assets consisted in the main of corporate loans, relatively few in number and easy to administer by a small staff. In the USA, the toxic assets consist of mortgage bonds and similar products, with millions of individual loans underlying, each of which will have to be evaluated. The Swedish case, as noticed, consisted of loans carried at a certain nominal value, whereas the US toxic products are bonds which need to be marked to market on a daily basis.

The problem may be illustrated in the following way, which also explains why the IMF in 2008 could come up with such a gigantic forecast of future write-downs, over $4,000 billion. (See Table 7.2.)

Banks in the USA have granted residential mortgages to the tune of some $11,000 billion ($11 trillion; see Table 4.3, page 124). Of this sum, $1 trillion was subprime and $1 trillion was Alt-A, while the rest was prime loans. At the end of 2008, some 3 percent of prime loans were delinquent and could be expected to fail ("probability of default", or PD, to use the terminology of Basel II, to which we will return below). For Alt-A and subprime customers, the figures were 6 percent and 12 percent respectively.

The percentages were expected to rise during 2009. Let us assume a pessimistic picture at that date, which gives rise to the delinquency PDs in Table 7.2: 10, 20 and 50 percent. Assume also that the auction result that is realized after a foreclosure and auction sale amounts to 40 percent of the nominal value, meaning that "loss given default" (LGD), is 60 percent and hence recovery 40 percent.[20] The multiplication of these

---

[19] www.usdebtclock.org
[20] The recovery rate of 40 percent is Moody's assumption, as reported in Tett, *How greed turned to panic*. Actually foreclosed homes have sold an average of 27 percent under market values for a recovery rate of 73 percent.

Table 7.2 *Expected losses before and after securitization*

Type of loan	Outstanding	Expected loss "PD"	Recovery (1-"LGD")	Loss "EL"
Before securitization				
Prime	9,000	10%	40%	540
Alt-A	1,000	20%	40%	120
Subprime	1,000	50%	40%	300
Sum	11,000	15%		960
After securitization				
Retained as loans	2,000	15%	40%	180
Securitized	9,000	35%[a]		3,150
Sum				3,330

Notes: PD = probability of default, LGD = loss given default, EL = expected loss. These data do not include investment banks.
[a] Write-down to market value of CDOs and MBSs.
Source: Author's calculations.

two numbers gives us "expected loss" (EL) of $960 billion, an amount quite consistent with actual write-downs at the end of 2008.

These figures can be compared with the vastly optimistic figures that the issuing investment banks and rating companies used for subprime loans at that time. The expected default rate was generally taken to be 6 percent (it became 15 percent) and the loss given default was set at 10–20 percent.[21]

As we saw earlier, over 85 percent of mortgages have been securitized. The resulting bonds must be marked to market by banks or other investors, in contrast to loans which may be carried at nominal value as long as the borrower is not delinquent. In Table 7.2, banks have retained $2,000 billion of loans, with an average probability of loss of 15 percent, as above. But the rest, $9,000 billion, has been securitized and the market value has fallen by an average of 35 percent (much higher, of course, for MBSs with subprime underlying, but lower for prime loans). Mark to market gives rise to an unrealized loss of

---

[21] Charles W. Calomiris, The subprime turmoil: what's old, what's new and what's next, presented to the Annual Federal Reserve Economic Symposium in Jackson Hole, Wyoming, 2008, cited in Akerlof and Shiller, *Animal Spirits*, p. 37.

$3,150 billion. It is the presence of these securitized loans that gives us the large numbers of potential losses in the banking system of $3,000 or even $4,000 billion.

So what to do? Should the government bail out banks' holdings of toxic assets? At what price? If the bank sells the asset at current market value, it loses the entire upside. It is highly likely that sooner or later the valuation of mortgage-related bonds will rise again. So long as the issuer is not bankrupt, the nominal value of the bond will be repaid at maturity. Issuers are in general guaranteed by the government (remember that Fannie Mae and Freddy Mac have three-quarters of the market!). Still, Merrill Lynch chose to sell off parts of its holdings of CDOs with subprime loans as underlying for 22 percent of the nominal value, rather than wait for a return to prosperity.

The advantage of nationalizing a bank in trouble, or at least taking a majority stake, is that the authorities get to decide the bank's policies vis-à-vis acquisitions, lending, dividend policy, salaries and bonuses, and so on. The board of directors and management may be expected to place their seats at the disposition of the new owner(s), as happened at RBS. Thereby one has hopefully reduced the risk of "moral hazard" for the future, as the delinquent board and management are punished and publicly stigmatized. The new policy announced for the second half of the TARP money, whereby preference shares held may be exchanged for common stock, is thus a big step forward compared with how the first half was spent. On top of this may be added the restrictions on salaries and bonuses in firms receiving support. It is interesting to note that restrictions on remunerations and the consequent flight of senior staff appears to have been very effective in making banks want to return the TARP money as soon as possible (discussed below).

It is somewhat surprising that no separate agency has been created in the USA to handle nationalized banks and sell off their assets. Unlike the UK, the USA has been content with letting the FDIC run the show. In the thrift crisis in the 1980s, a separate agency, the Resolution Trust Corporation (RTC), was set up, as in Sweden in the 1990s. In the UK, UK Financial Investments (UKFI) holds the government's stake, and in Ireland it is the National Asset Management Agency (NAMA).

We will come back in Chapter 9 to the issue of what to do with too-big-to-fail banks, since we need the discussion of capital ratios below and the historical background in Chapter 8 before pursuing the matter further.

One could say that in this chapter, we have studied the "positive," descriptive side of the question of what to do with big banks that fail. In Chapter 9 and in the Conclusion, we return with a "normative" approach: what people have suggested that we do about the problem of banks deemed "too big to fail." Should they be broken up?

Solvency ratios in the major banks prior to the crisis

The events during 2007, such as they were described chronologically in Appendix 2.1, did not seem alarming to most observers (including the intrinsically optimistic author of this book). Some mortgage banks in the USA and the UK, and selected other countries such as Spain, Ireland and Australia, were experiencing problems, hardly surprising in view of the growth of house prices in those countries. Some major banks, such as HSBC and UBS, had been forced to write off credit losses related to the US property market. For 2007 as a whole, the twenty-five largest banks in the world wrote down some $70 billion, but had basically recovered their capital base by issuing new (ordinary) shares. These twenty-five banks had a capital base (Tier 1)[22] of $1,454 billion at the end of 2007; the 1,000 largest banks in the world had $3,399 billion in capital. It seemed satisfactory.

Not that Cassandras were missing. An article in the *Economist* on November 24, 2007, with the title "Tightening the safety belt: banks' capital needs could end tying them up in knots," would prove prescient. It predicted a need for write-downs of mortgage-related bonds (CDOs) and CDSs by another $100 billion. It was regarded as unduly pessimistic, but would still understate reality by a factor of 10. Still, Table 7.3 shows that the major banks in the world appeared reasonably solvent at the end of 2007. The Basel rules (about which more below) prescribe that a bank must hold a minimum ratio of 4 percent of primary (Tier 1) capital to risk-weighted assets and a total capital ratio of at least 8 percent. In the USA, a bank is considered well-capitalized if its Tier 1 ratio exceeds 6 percent and its total capital ratio 10 percent.

Banks in *italics* in the table have received financial support or been nationalized, while those in **bold** have been merged with a stronger

---

[22] A definition of core capital (Tier 1) and supplementary capital (Tier 2) is given below.

Table 7.3 *Solvency ratios in the world's largest banks end 2007*

Bank	Country	Tier 1 (%)	Total ratio (%)
HSBC Holdings	UK	9.3	13.6
Citigroup	US	7.1	10.7
RBS (Royal Bank of Scotland)	UK	7.3	11.2
JPMorgan Chase	US	8.2	12.6
Bank of America	US	6.9	11.0
Mitsubishi UFJ Financial Group	Japan	7.6	11.3
Crédit Agricole	France	8.1	9.6
ICBC (Industrial and Commercial Bank of China)	China	11.0	13.1
Santander Central Hispano	Spain	7.7	12.7
Bank of China	China	10.7	13.3
BNP Paribas	France	7.3	10.0
Barclays Bank	UK	7.6	12.1
CCB (China Construction Bank Corp.)	China	10.4	12.6
HBOS (Halifax Bank of Scotland)	UK	7.4	11.1
Mizuho Financial Group	Japan	n/a	11.7
UniCredit	Italy	5.8	10.1
ING Bank	Netherlands	7.4	10.3
Sumotomo Mitsui Financial Group	Japan	6.4	10.5
Wachovia Corp.	USA	7.4	11.8
Rabobank Group	Netherlands	10.7	10.9
Deutsche Bank	Germany	8.6	11.6
Fortis Bank	Belgium	9.5	10.1
Wells Fargo Bank	USA	7.6	10.7
Crédit Mutuel	France	9.3	11.0
Intesa San Paolo	Italy	6.5	9.0
Groupe Caisse d'Épargne	France	8.7	n/a
Société Générale	France	8.0	8.9
Resona Holdings (ex-Daiwa)	Japan	9.5	14.3
Credit Suisse	Switzerland	11.1	14.5
BBVA (Banco Bilbao Vizcaya Argentaria)	Spain	5.3	10.7
UBS	Switzerland	8.8	12.0
Lloyds TSB	UK	8.1	11.0
Sberbank	Russia	13.9	14.5
Royal Bank of Canada	Canada	9.4	11.5
Caja de Ahorros-la Caixa	Spain	9.8	12.1

Table 7.3 (*cont.*)

Bank	Country	Tier 1 (%)	Total ratio (%)
Commerzbank	Germany	6.9	10.8
Groupe Banque Populaire	France	9.1	12.7
Norinchukin Bank	Japan	n/a	12.8
Washington Mutual	USA	6.7	12.3
Dexia	Belgium	9.1	9.6

Note: Banks are ranked by the total size of their Tier 1 capital.
Source: The Banker, Top 1000 world banks (July 2008) (total ratio) and annual reports (Tier 1)

partner. Note that there are some banks in both italics and bold (Fortis and HBOS).

Looking first at the Tier 1 ratio, we may note that only two of the forty banks fell short of the 6 percent ratio characterizing a well-capitalized bank: one Italian (Unicredit) and one Spanish (BBVA).[23] Even those four banks which would fail during 2008 had Tier 1 ratios of 7 percent and solvency ratios of 11–12 percent. Fortis even had a Tier 1 ratio of 9.5 percent. The highest ratios are found in the Asiatic banks, in particular the Chinese ICBC, Bank of China and CCB, but also in the Russian state-owned savings bank Sberbank. In Europe, only Dutch Rabobank and Swiss Credit Suisse had double-digit primary capital ratios. Rabobank is also the only privately owned bank in Europe to have the highest rating from both rating companies, Standard & Poor's and Moody's (AAA/Aaa); it still had this rating in June 2010 – very impressive after the crisis.

The last year when banks reported their capital under a common accounting framework, Basel I, was 2007. In 2008, banks within the European Union had changed to Basel II. The US and Asian banks (except Japan) continue on Basel I, which precludes direct comparisons such as those in Table 7.3, above. There is more on this topic later in the chapter.

[23] Unicredit issued €6.3 billion in common stock in the fall of 2008 to raise solvency ratios.

Why were the solvency ratios in Basel I and II inadequate in the crisis?

The discussion regarding solvency (capital adequacy) ratios for banks started after the collapse of the Herstatt Bank in 1974 and led to what is usually called the Basel Accord in 1988. The work was undertaken within the group of developed countries called G-10, led by the Bank for International Settlements (BIS) in Basel; hence the alternating uses of the terms the Basel rules or the BIS rules.[24]

The Basel I rulebook was adopted primarily for internationally active banks where a common regulatory framework was regarded as necessary to maintain a level playing field. In practice, the rules have come to be applied on all banks and bank-like organizations (finance companies, credit companies, broker-dealers, investment banks) in over a hundred countries. The BIS rules are formally only a recommendation, but became law within the European Union with the "Own funds" directive 89/299/EEC, which defines what is capital in banks, and the "Solvency" directive 89/647/EEC, which sets forth the measurement of risk-weighting of assets and prescribes the minimum ratios. The original framework focused solely on credit risk, market risks have been added through the so-called CAD directives 93/66/EEC and 98/31/EEC ("Capital adequacy" directive).

Tier 1 capital (or primary capital) consists in the main of common stock and preference shares, excluding cumulative preference shares where unpaid dividends are saved for later payments, as well as this year's profit or loss and reserves. Tier 2 capital (also called supplementary capital) consists of remaining preference capital as well as subordinated loans with an original maturity of at least 5 years. In particular, we note "Upper Tier 2," consisting of "perpetuals" – that is, perpetual subordinated loans which may have a call (redeemable by the borrower), but not a put (redeemable by the investor). The inclusion in Tier 1 of hybrid capital will be discussed (and criticized!) below.

A bank must have at least 4 percent of its risk-weighted assets in the form of Tier 1 capital and at least 8 percent in total capital. Tier 2 capital must not exceed Tier 1 capital, irrespective of the total. Hence a bank with, say, a 12 percent total solvency ratio must have a Tier 1 ratio of at

---

[24] G-10 actually included 11 countries, since the host country Switzerland was also a member.

least 6 percent. Table 7.3 above (page 231) shows that banks generally have decided to hold substantially more capital than required. The average Tier 1 ratio at end 2007 was 8.4 percent and the total ratio 11.3 percent. Still it was insufficient in the crisis.

In the original Basel I, assets were allocated into only five risk categories:

0 percent: claims on OECD governments and local authorities, some international organizations;

10 percent: covered mortgage bonds;

20 percent: claims on OECD banks and credit institutions, claims on other banks provided that the maturity is less than 1 year;

50 percent: claims with collateral in the form of residential property (in Germany it also includes commercial property);

100 percent: other credits, in particular commercial and industrial loans.

The interpretation of these figures is the following. A capital charge of 20 percent means that at least 1.6 percent of the value of the asset (20 percent times 8 percent) must be held as capital; 50 percent implies a ratio of capital to assets of 4 percent, while 100 percent capital charge means 8 percent, the "normal" minimum.

The Basel rules were an important step forward in the management of risk for the banks in the world, not least among the developing countries. They came to focus on their credit risks and the average capital ratios were raised sharply. Today's financial crisis would have been far worse but for these new rules. It is instructive to note that the Southeast Asian countries which had their own financial crisis in the late 1990s (to which we will return in Chapter 8) have generally held capital far above the required minima, and also avoided the toxic assets purchased by many European banks, such as UBS and the German *Landesbanken.*

While Basel I has had many positive effects, criticisms have not been lacking. A first critique is that the categories have not been sufficiently well diversified to take into account differing attitudes towards risk in different organizations. A financial supervisory authority should be able to prescribe higher ratios for those banks deemed more risky – for example, with a high degree of trading activity. This regulatory freedom has become an important part of Pillar 2 in the Basel II rulebook and was already used under Basel I by the British FSA.

Another criticism is that capital requirements for market risks (interest rates, share prices, currencies, commodities) were lacking. This led to the European Union installing its own market risk framework in the form of the Capital adequacy directive, 98/31/EEC. Market risks as well as operational risks are now covered under Pillar 1 in Basel II.

A third critique is that Basel I actually encourages banks to take on more risk. This may come about in (at least) two ways. First, a bank has an incentive to lend to more risky activities where one may expect to be able to charge a higher rate of interest, but where the capital charge is the same, 100 percent, irrespective of actual risk. Second, banks have an incentive to securitize the best credits, mortgages or business loans. These have capital charges of 50 and 100 percent, respectively, but when repurchased in the form of MBSs, ABSs or CDOs, they require only 20 percent capital charge if the issuer is an OECD bank. The securitization will often lead to a deteriorating quality of the remaining loan book if the best credits have been sold off ("cherry-picking").

The risk weights also introduce strange anomalies in that a AAA-rated country like Singapore was not a member of the OECD and hence received a risk weight of 100 percent, while countries like Turkey or Mexico, with far worse creditworthiness and rating, were OECD members and hence received a risk weight of 0 percent. The fact that short-term credits to banks in non-OECD countries had lower weights than long-term credits also encouraged speculation and a focus on short-term capital movements. The bank could save on capital by rolling over short-term credits rather than by extending a long-term credit.

Hence the aims of the new framework, Basel II, were the following:

- allow the financial supervisory authorities a more flexible choice of capital levels to take account of the bank's level of (in)competence as well as its riskiness;
- introduce more variable risk weights that better reflect the assets' actual risks;
- introduce capital charges for other risks, such as operational and organizational risks;
- use modern models, such as Value at Risk (VaR) for the measurement of risk;

- bring about a better agreement between the banks' internal capital charges ("economic capital") and the authorities' "regulatory capital" by allowing competent banks to use their own models in measuring risk levels;
- force banks to become more open in their accounting in order that "peer review" would provide incentives for better risk management.

The result of this ambition was the new proposals from the Basel committee, "A Revised Framework on International Convergence of Capital Measurement and Capital Standards" (1999). It was introduced into European Union law by Directive 2006/49/EC.

Basel II is founded upon three principles: *Pillar 1* sets forth the quantitative requirements as regards capital charges for credit risks, market risks and operational risks; *Pillar 2* regulates the interaction between a bank and its supervisor; and *Pillar 3* spells out the requirements of the information which a financial organization must make public.

Pillar 1, in its simplest form (the standardized approach), utilizes information from rating companies in order to establish risk weights for different assets. These are set out in Table 7.4. Note that in relation to Basel I, a new risk weight of 150 percent has been introduced. This means that a credit to a low-rated company of £1 million requires a minimum capital charge of 150 percent times 8 percent, or £120,000. Note also the risk weights for securitized assets. While highly rated issuers get off with 20 percent just as any other bank, CDOs and other securitized credits require capital to be held in full (1,250 percent times 8 percent = 100 percent – that is, the bank must hold capital corresponding to the entire value of the asset) if they are rated B+ or below. This applies in particular to the "equity" tranche of a securitization.

There exist special rules for small unrated borrowers. An unrated company receives a risk weight of 100 percent, just like under Basel I. Retail products, by which is meant credits to household or small companies (credit cards, overdrafts, auto loans, personal finance and small business) not exceeding €600,000 receive a risk weight of 75 percent. Loans with collateral in the form of a residential mortgage get a risk weight of 35 percent if the loan is within 75 percent of the assessed value of the property (the basis underlying covered bonds) and 75 percent for the portion above that value. Under Basel I there was only one common risk weight of 50 percent.

Table 7.4 *The standardized approach for establishing risk weights under Basel II (%)*

Borrower	AAA to AA– and A1/F1/P-1	A and A2/F2/P-2	BBB and A3/F3 /P-3	BB and non-prime	B and non-prime	C, CC, CCC and non-prime
Sovereign	0	20	50	100	100	150
Banks, long-term exposure	20	50	50	100	100	150
Banks, shorter than 3 months	20	20	20	20	20	20
Corporate long-term exposure	20	50	100	100	150	150
Corporate short-term exposure	20	50	100	150	150	150
Securitized assets	20	50	100	350	1250	1250

Note: See Bank for International Settlements, Basel Committee on Banking Supervision, Capital requirements regulations 2006 and www.fsa.gov.uk/pubs/international/ecais_standardised.pdf

In two more advanced methods (internal ratings-based approach, or IRB), banks are allowed to use their own models, in conjunction with assumptions specified by the financial supervisory authority, to establish for a borrower or group of borrowers, PD (probability of default), M (maturity) and LGD (loss given default), which together yield EL (expected loss).

The risk weights for securitization (for example, MBSs) and resecuritization (for example, CDOs) were made more detailed, but also toughened, in the summer of 2009 by an addition to the Basel II framework.[25] For instance, the lowest investment grade, BBB–, still receives a risk

[25] Bank for International Settlements, Enhancements to the Basel II framework.

weight of 100 percent under securitization. If resecuritized, however, the risk weight becomes 200 percent for senior securities and 350 percent for non-senior securities. A securitized asset rated AAA still has a risk weight of 20 percent if it is senior after resecuritization, but the ratio rises to 30 percent if it is non-senior (even though it is still rated AAA).

The capital requirements for market risks are almost identical to those specified under CAD and contain capital charges for the market risks in interest rates, exchange rates, share prices and commodities, as well as charges for the credit risk in these instruments. Here external ratings normally exist, since we are dealing with publicly traded instruments.

Not content to wait for Basel III, in June 2010 the Basel group also toughened substantially capital ratios for trading positions.[26] The main and most dramatic change is that banks must calculate losses under a 12-month holding period in a stressed situation such as that which prevailed in 2007–9. The capital requirement is set at the higher of the Value-at-Risk calculation and the latest stressed scenario with the current portfolio. In both cases, the results are to be multiplied by a factor set by the respective financial supervisory authorities at a level not less than 3. It was estimated by the BIS that large international banks would find the capital requirements for their trading books increase by a factor of at least three – that is, they would be required to hold three to four times more capital than before.

A novelty under Basel II is the capital charge for operational risk. Under the basic indicator approach, banks are told to hold 15 percent of their operating revenues as capital for operational risks. In the standardized approach, the charges are specified according to type of revenue, with charges varying from 12 to 18 percent, depending on business line. There is also an advanced measurement approach (AMA), where banks are allowed to use their internal models.

There are many things in Basel II which mark a step forward from Basel I. In particular, one should emphasize the stronger role and greater possibilities of observation allocated to the supervisory authorities, in that they will in the future:

---

[26] Bank for International Settlements, Adjustments to the Basel II market risk framework.

- approve banks' systems and models for the evaluation of risks and capital;
- verify how these models function in real life;
- evaluate major risks, such as concentration and liquidity risks;
- demand additional capital if the bank's level of risk appetite and (in) competence so require.

There remain, however, a number of problems. *The first problem* concerns the overly large role given to external rating companies. This was criticized in the statement by the CESR quoted earlier: "CESR recognizes that the use of ratings in the regulatory and supervisory framework, such as the ECAI in the CRD [capital requirements directive], could induce uncritical reliance on ratings as a substitute for independent evaluation." It is difficult to say it more explicitly!

The second problem has to do with the effects on capital of the transition from Basel I to Basel II. Some US studies have shown substantially lower capital requirements as a result of banks using their own models, in some cases over 50 percent.[27] Other developed countries have shown decreases of between –7 and –27 percent. This does not appear to be the case in the UK. Two of the major banks, Barclays and HSBC, have presented in great detail how the transition from one system to the other affected their solvency ratios for the transition year, 2007.

Barclays saw a minor fall in its Tier 1 ratio, from 7.8 to 7.6 percent. With the introduction of the advanced IRB approach under Basel II, risk-weighted assets fell in both the banking book (mainly as a result of a lower charge for residential mortgages) and in the trading book. This was offset, however, by the new charge for operational risk, meaning that total risk-weighted assets were virtually unchanged.

For HSBC, the Tier 1 capital ratio fell from 9.3 to 9 percent and the total solvency ratio from 13.6 to 11.8 percent. One reason was the new way of handling expected losses vis-à-vis impairment allowances. Under Basel II, banks have to deduct the expected loss from allowances already made, half of the difference being deducted from Tier 1 capital and half from Tier 2. This led to lower total regulatory capital. As was the case with Barclays, total risk-weighted assets were virtually

---

[27] Benink and Kaufman, Turmoil reveals the inadequacy of Basel II.

unchanged, as lower risk in the banking book and the trading book was offset by the new charges for operational risk.

It should, however, be recalled that the UK, in contrast to most EU countries (but similarly to Spain), has forced banks to set aside a capital cushion over and above the 4 and 8 percent respective ratios. Also, the British FSA has focused on Core Tier 1 capital – that is, common stock and reserves – much earlier than its continental colleagues, playing down the role of hybrid capital and supplementary capital.

The capital cushion demanded by the FSA might be the reason why British banks are affected less by the transition to Basel II. The FSA sets individual capital guidance (ICG) for each UK bank, calibrated by reference to its capital resources requirement (CRR), broadly equivalent to 8 percent of risk-weighted assets and thus representing the capital required under Pillar 1 of the Basel II framework. Also, a key input into the FSA's ICG setting process (which addresses the requirements of Pillar 2 of the Basel II framework) is each bank's internal capital adequacy assessment process. The FSA's approach is to monitor the available capital resources in relation to the ICG requirement. All banks have been given individual ICGs by the FSA, and their boards have also agreed a formal buffer to be maintained in addition to this requirement. Any breaches of the formal buffer must be notified to the FSA, together with proposed remedial action. The FSA has made it clear that each ICG remains a confidential matter between each individual bank and the FSA.

The current crisis and capital shortages in banks such as RBS, now nationalized to over 80 percent, have shown clearly, however, that Basel II provides an inadequate answer to the measurement of banks' capital needs. A possibility is to complement the Basel ratios by leverage ratios, as in the USA – that is, the ratio between a bank's Tier 1 capital and its total (unweighted) assets.[28] In the USA, a well-capitalized bank is supposed to have a leverage ratio of at least 5 percent, while 4 percent is regarded as only "adequate."

Switzerland is so far the only European country to have introduced this concept, which is, however, proposed in the new Basel III regulation (see Appendix 7.2). Table 7.5 (page 243) indicates that only twelve out of the forty largest banks in the world (measured by capital) were well capitalized, using data from 2007, and only twenty-three were even

---

[28] Larsen, Basel outlines stricter limits.

adequately capitalized. European giants, such as Deutsche Bank, had a capital asset ratio of 1.4 percent, which, inversed, means that it had a gearing ratio (assets/capital) of seventy times! Among the other problem banks, UBS had a gearing ratio of sixty-nine and RBS had a ratio of forty-three. The average leverage ratio for the 1,000 largest banks in the world is a meager 4.3 percent, implying a gearing of twenty-three times.[29]

An unweighted average of the ten largest European banks in Table 7.5 (page 243) gives a Tier 1 capital asset ratio of just 3.1 percent, much lower than the world average. It therefore comes as no surprise that Basel III, yielding to protests from the European banking community, has proposed setting thirty-three as the maximum allowed gearing ratio (a leverage ratio of 3 percent). This does not even correspond to an "adequately" capitalized bank in the USA.[30] According to research by CA Chevreux, an imposition of a 4 percent leverage ratio maximizing gearing to twenty-five times, as originally proposed, would hit banks such as Credit Suisse and Deutsche Bank especially hard. The major banks would need to raise an additional €28 billion, and their return on equity would fall from 13.6 to 11.3 percent.[31] Hence their screams, and hence the softening by the BIS.

Washington Mutual's strong ratio of 6.59 percent, however, shows that this measure also has its insufficiencies. (See also Figure 7.2.) It is apparent that gearing has been brought down substantially (leverage increased), in particular in the USA. Many banks, however, are still in the forty to fifty range.

The ratio also needs to be verified by the supervisors. Lehman Brothers conducted so-called "regulatory arbitrage" in utilizing differences between US and British regulations. By the internal program Repo 105, the bank transferred bonds at the end of each quarter to its British subsidiary. This subsidiary then sold the bonds with repurchase agreed just at the beginning of the new quarter, at a slightly higher price. In this way, Lehman had hidden $50.4 billion of unknown assets at the end of the second quarter of 2008, just before its collapse, a substantial

---

[29] Data from *The Banker*, Top 1000 world banks (July 2008).

[30] To some extent the comparison is unfair since the BIS ratio will include off-balance asset while the data in Table 7.5 applies only to on-balance assets.

[31] Masters and Murphy, European banks to face capital demands; Ishmael, European banks to face capital demands.

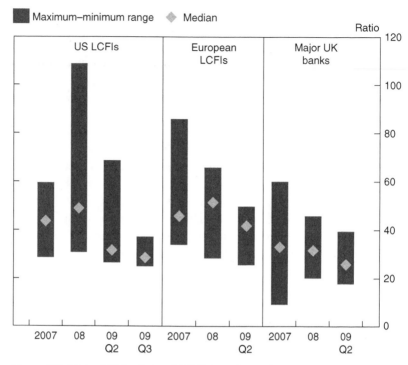

Figure 7.2 Major UK banks' and LCFIs' gearing ratios
Note: LCFI = large and complex financial institution
Source: Bank of England, *Financial Stability Report* (June 2010), Chart 12(a)

fraction of its $275 billion of assets under management. Lehman's CEO, Dick Fuld, as well as several CFOs (Chief Financial Officers) risk being charged for breach of fiduciary duty in not revealing to investors the true leverage of the firm. The firm's auditors, Ernst & Young, may also be negatively affected by this charge.

Figure 7.3 shows how the USA and the UK got into this mess. One hundred and thirty years ago, the ratio of equity to total assets stood at 25 percent in the USA and over 15 percent in the UK. But the trend was downwards, and already by the end of the Second World War the leverage ratios had attained the low levels seen today. But the constantly low equity asset ratio does not tell the whole story, since the riskiness of assets has increased tremendously over this period and off-balance derivatives have been added.

Table 7.5 *Leverage ratios in the world's forty largest banks, end 2007*

Bank	Country	Leverage ratio
HSBC Holdings	UK	4.46
Citigroup	USA	4.08
RBS (Royal Bank of Scotland)	UK	2.33
JPMorgan Chase	USA	5.68
Bank of America	USA	4.86
Mitsubishi UFJ Financial Group	Japan	4.56
Crédit Agricole	France	3.03
ICBC (Industrial and Commercial Bank of China)	China	5.57
Santander Central Hispano	Spain	4.35
Bank of China	China	6.85
BNP Paribas	France	2.22
Barclays Bank	UK	2.23
China Construction Bank Corp. (CCB)	China	5.79
HBOS (Halifax Bank of Scotland)	UK	3.66
Mizuho Financial Group	Japan	3.26
UniCredit	Italy	3.18
ING Bank	Netherlands	2.99
Sumotomo Mitsui Financial Group	Japan	4.08
Wachovia Corp.	USA	5.56
Rabobank Group	Netherlands	4.99
Deutsche Bank	Germany	1.40
Fortis Bank	Belgium	3.35
Wells Fargo Bank	USA	6.37
Crédit Mutuel	France	4.41
Intesa San Paolo	Italy	4.24
Groupe Caisse d'Épargne	France	5.03
Société Générale	France	2.02
Resona Holdings (ex Daiwa)	Japan	8.00
Credit Suisse	Switzerland	2.55
BBVA (Banco Bilbao Vizcaya Argentaria)	Spain	4.11
UBS	Switzerland	1.44
Lloyds TSB	UK	3.95
Sberbank	Russia	12.60
Royal Bank of Canada	Canada	3.97
Caja de Ahorros-la Caixa	Spain	6.71

Table 7.5 (*cont.*)

Bank	Country	Leverage ratio
Commerzbank	Germany	2.65
Groupe Banque Populaire	France	5.54
Norinchukin Bank	Japan	4.35
Washington Mutual	USA	6.59
Dexia	Belgium	2.41

Note: Countries are ranked by the size of their Tier 1 capital in 2007.
Source: The Banker, Top 1000 world banks (July 2008)

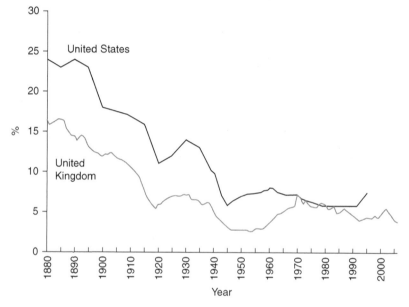

Figure 7.3 Capital asset ratios for US and UK banks, 1880–2010
Source: Haldane, Banking on the state

A third problem is that the Basel II construction reinforces the inherent tendency towards procyclicality in banks. In recessions, the lowered ratings (internal or external) of firms will lead to higher capital charges, forcing a reduction of lending. In particular, if the bank had a weak capital base to begin with, this can create severe problems.[32] A possible solution is to

---

[32] Kashyap and Stein, Cyclical implications of the Basel II capital standards.

return to Basel I, but with the rectified risk weights – that is, 35 percent for residential mortgages, 75 percent for other household and small business loans and 100 percent for all other credits. These risk weights are unaffected by the business cycle and hence do not create procyclicality.

Another way forward would be to demand that rating should encompass at least one business cycle, implying that it is the borrower's long-term prospects that are rated, not a temporary good or bad situation. A third possibility is to follow the CESR and force banks to evaluate the borrowers' creditworthiness by their own methods rather than relying on external ratings. A fourth possibility would be to rely more on stress tests to determine the capital necessary. (More on stress tests below.)

Small comfort may be drawn from the fact that the capital charge for operational risk is actually weakly countercyclical. When revenues from a certain business line, say, trading, fall, so does the capital requirement.

A fourth problem, and an important one, lies in the short databases required and the assumption that the world is normally distributed. This criticism applies in particular to the use of Value-at-Risk (VaR) models for the measurement of credit and market risks in Pillar 1. VaR models provide a confidence interval stating how much a bank will lose at most, with a probability of, say, 99 percent. But the period of observation need only be 1 year, not a full business cycle. And anyway, VaR models should not be used in determining a bank's solvency requirements. These short-term models have their uses in a bank's internal work, in allocating capital to various business lines (by expected revenue vs risk, so-called Sharpe ratios).

VaR models also build on the normal probability distribution, the Gaussian bell curve, which means symmetrical chances of higher or lower returns. But the probability distribution in a recession is skewed towards the negative side, meaning that the chance of a loss is much larger than the chance of a positive return. Also, chances of an abnormally high or low outcome are larger than what the normal distribution implies ("fat tails"). You can modify the distribution to account for these facts, but this in turn leads to the fact that concepts like standard deviation and confidence interval cannot be calculated theoretically, but have to be deduced by simulation methods.[33]

[33] Good introductions to VaR are Choudry and Tanna, *An Introduction to Value-at-Risk* and Jorion, *Value at Risk*. See also the company Riskmetrics, originally part of J. P. Morgan, pioneering the daily famous "4:15 report."

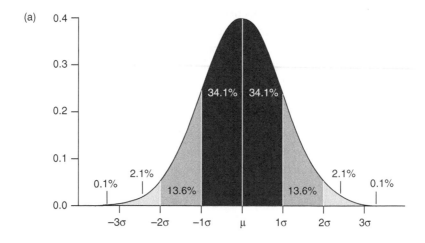

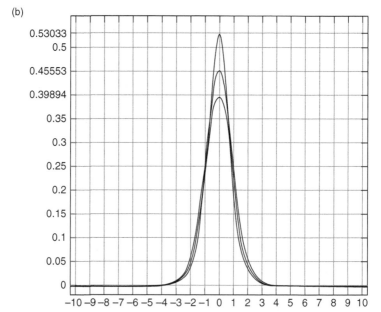

Figure 7.4 A normal distribution and a leptokurtic distribution

Figure 7.4a shows the widely used normal distribution, where only 0.1 percent of the distribution is located outside of three standard deviations (σ). Figure 7.4b shows a more realistic distribution of events, where many more observations than normal are located at the center, but also in the tails (leptokurtosis). But even this distribution is symmetric, which the world is not, particularly not in a stressed situation.

Nassim Nicholas Taleb, a Lebanese-born "quant" (quantitative analyst) with a US Ph.D. in Finance, has shown how decision-makers in financial organizations let themselves be guided by the normal distribution, ignoring events that were unlikely but possible, not captured by the negative tail in the normal distribution. He calls these events "black swans."[34]

He was hardly the first to criticize the use of the normal distribution though.[35] The FSA, in its earlier referenced Discussion Paper (09/2, page 78) showed the VaR risk for a number of London-based investment banks. Between March 2007 and June 2008, the capital charge for market risk based on the VaR measure increased by a factor of more than 2.5 times, a clear indication of the abject failure of VaR risk measures to handle evolutions over longer periods, in particular in the transition to a recessionary period. And by June 2008, the worst was still to come; remember that Lehman and AIG crashed in September 2008.

Instead, much more focus should be placed on stress tests and scenario analyses. In order to evaluate their need for more capital, the Federal Reserve in the USA, in conjunction with the other supervisory authorities (FDIC, OCC and OTS; see also Chapter 9), conducted stress tests in April to May 2009 for the nineteen major banks – that is, those with assets over $100 billion. The main scenario assumed a brief recession in 2009, followed by a recovery in 2010. In a more negative scenario, GDP fell more in 2009 and was flat in 2010, while house prices continued to fall and unemployment rose to above 10 percent. These scenarios, together with the assumption concerning interest rates, share prices, and so on, were fed into the banks' own models to yield data on credit exposures, delinquent loans and credit write–downs, as well as the value of the various investment portfolios and off-balance activities. Banks found to be undercapitalized had half a year to rectify the situation or be forcibly recapitalized by the government. Ten of the nineteen firms were ordered (and did) to raise more Tier 1 capital, to the tune of $75 billion.[36]

---

[34] Taleb, *The Black Swan*.

[35] For instance, Lux and Marchesi, Scaling and criticality.

[36] Board of Governors of the Federal Reserve System, The Supervisory Capital Assessment Program: overview of results, May 7, 2009 (available at www.federalreserve.gov/newsevents/press/bcreg/bcreg20090507a1.pdf).

In addition to national tests, the coordinating committee, the Committee of European Banking Supervisors (CEBS), has run coordinated, Europe-wide stress tests. These aim to evaluate the resilience of the European banking system as a whole rather than focusing on individual banks or individual countries. At the beginning of October 2009, results from stress-testing the twenty-two largest banks in the area showed that even under adverse conditions, no bank's Tier 1 ratio would fall below 6 percent, and the average would be 8–9 percent, depending on assumptions.[37]

In July 2010, a wider sample of European banks was stress-tested. Ninety-one lenders, accounting for 65 percent of the EU banking industry by assets, were selected, covering at least 50 percent of the market in each EU member, including fourteen German banks, twenty-seven Spanish savings banks, six Greek banks, five Italian banks, four French banks and four British banks. The stress test included both credit and market risk, but focused on mark-downs in the trading book. This assumes a market shock to valuations but no sovereign default, which would have led to write-downs also in the banking book.[38]

The assumptions were a mild recession in 2010–11, instead of a predicted mild recovery in the benchmark simulation, GDP growth being some 2 percentage points lower than forecast in 2011 and unemployment rising. Banks were told to assess the consequence of an average fall in the value of sovereign bonds by 8.5 percent, ranging from a 23 percent fall in Greece, to 14 percent in Portugal, 12 percent in Spain, 10 percent in the UK and just 6 percent in France and 4.7 percent in Germany. The yield curve was stressed upwards, rising seventy-five basis points for the 10-year maturity. The Tier 1 ratio resulting from the stressed situation must not fall below 6 percent, else the banks needed to raise more capital.

The result was that only seven banks fell below a 6 percent Tier 1 ratio. Among the banks were (state-owned) Hypo Real Estate in

---

[37] Kubarych, *Stress Testing the System*, discusses another but equally important type of stress test, which should really be called a war game, wherein a number of people from central banks and banks are confronted with various unpleasant scenarios in real time and expected to react in a coordinated and consistent manner.

[38] Morgan Stanley has found that, on average, European banks would hold Greek sovereign bonds to 90 percent in the banking book and only 10 percent in the trading book.

Germany, (state-controlled) ATE Bank in Greece and five small Spanish savings banks (*cajas*). Some other banks were close to the limit, such as Norddeutsche Landesbank and Deutsche Postbank in Germany, and Allied Irish Banks.

Even before the results were published the assumptions were criticized as being extremely lenient. CDSs were indicating a 40 percent loss on Greek bonds in the event of a default or restructuring of debt, rather than 23 percent. Some observers had predicted a capital shortfall of up to €85 billion; the actual result was an immediate capital need of only €3.5 billion. The figure may be compared with the required capital increase that was the result of the stress-testing of the US banking system, $75 billion. Should the minimum accepted Tier 1 ratio have been set at 8 percent rather than 6 percent, thirty-nine of the ninety-one banks would have failed, needing to raise €27 billion.

A further indication of the mildness of the stress test is that the effect on the average Tier 1 ratio was a fall from 10.3 to 9.2 percent, instead of the ratio rising to 11.2 percent in the baseline simulation. These small decreases in capital ratios may be contrasted with the outcome of the financial crisis of 2007–9, which cost the world's largest banks, on average, half of their initial capital.[39]

This type of stress test, undertaken in the USA and in Europe, is perhaps not even very useful. Since it was announced in advance that the results would be made public, the stress tests were bound to show that some banks were adequately capitalized, while some banks needed more capital. A situation where all the banks were judged to need more capital could have precipitated a stampede. On the other hand, had all banks been given the green light, the stress tests would not have been believed and could also have set off a negative reaction.

Instead, stress tests should be an integral part of the evaluation of a bank by the supervisor and the results should definitely not be made public, just as the extra capital required by the financial supervisory authority (under Pillar 2 of Basel II) of a certain bank is not made public.

As well stated in the presentation on stress-testing by the British FSA,[40] stress tests have the following uses:

[39] Jenkins, Stress test results underwhelming; Cadman *et al.*, Interactive: EU stress test results by bank.
[40] See Financial Services Authority, Stress testing.

(1) Determining a firm's risk profile

Stress testing can be used by firms to determine their risk profile. Stress testing of a range of different exposures to particular counterparties may identify risks which, when aggregated, are not picked up at an individual exposure or business unit level. Firms may also use stress tests to calculate the sensitivity of a firm's portfolio to large changes in risk factors, such as moves in the yield curve or foreign exchange market shifts. Stress testing is, in addition, useful for evaluating risks where VaR models are of limited use. Risk managers have found stress testing helpful for setting limits and monitoring new products where little historical data is available.

(2) Setting a firm's risk appetite and capital allocation

A key function of senior management is the identification of a firm's risk appetite which can be articulated into a meaningful strategy to guide those responsible for conducting the day to day business of the firm. Risk appetite is normally specified in the context of a firm's preferred risk/return trade off, typically referenced to relatively "normal" business conditions – with a modest "confidence interval" for events to turn out better or worse than a central case. In this context, a key function of stress testing is to sensitize senior management to the concept of the "stressed risk appetite". A well thought out and conducted stress test can help senior management focus on whether it would be comfortable with the risk/return consequences of a set of extreme, but plausible, business conditions. If the likely outcomes are outside management's stressed risk appetite, some adjustment to the business/risk profile of the firm may be warranted. This also provides an important link for effective capital allocation by senior management.

(3) Evaluating the impact of extreme, but plausible, large loss events

Existing risk management tools such as VaR tend to reflect price behaviour in everyday markets. Stress tests aim to simulate portfolio performance in abnormal market periods. They can therefore provide information about risks that fall outside those typically captured by VaR methodologies. Such risks would include those associated with extreme price movements, and those related to forward-looking scenarios that are not reflected in the recent history of the price series used to compute VaR. One particular area where there is benefit in developing closer dialogue with firms is in relation to the more extreme, forward-looking scenarios that firms use as part of their risk management process. One possibility would be for us to initiate a more structured comparison of the "hot-topic" scenarios identified by firms, and our own identification of possible risks to financial stability.

Stress-testing of liquidity risks was discussed in Chapter 6. The increased focus on stress-testing capital adequacy in the Basel III framework is discussed in Appendix 7.2.

As a result of the current financial crisis, the FSA has stated that it expects banks to have at least 4 percent Core Tier 1 capital (also called tangible common equity, TCE, or Tier 1 Core Equity) in relation to risk-weighted assets, even in a stress situation.[41] The total Tier 1 ratio required should be raised from 4 to 8 percent. The macroeconomic scenario in the FSA's stress tests is also much harsher than the one used in the USA. The current stress scenario models a recession more severe and more prolonged than those which the UK suffered in the 1980s and 1990s, and therefore more severe than any other since the Second World War. It assumes a peak-to-trough fall in GDP of over 6 percent, with growth not returning until 2011, and only returning to trend growth rate in 2012. It models the impact of unemployment rising to just over 12 percent, and, crucially, the impact of a 50 percent peak-to-trough fall in house prices and a 60 percent peak-to-trough fall in commercial property prices.

On average, US banks lost some 7 percent of the underlying assets in write-downs during the crisis of 2007–10, or $885 billion, according to the IMF forecasts discussed earlier. This amounts to over half the equity base of the banks in 2007, $1,646 billion.[42] The US banks had a Tier 1 ratio in 2007 of 9 percent on average. This probably translates to some 6 percent TCE (see also Table 7.6, page 252). If half were lost, the banks would find themselves at 3 percent TCE ratio, which is below the absolute minimum tolerated under the new rules already being adopted in the UK, while the new Basel III requirements for Core Tier 1 capital has landed at 7 percent. The conclusion is that, in order to be safe, in the future a bank must hold Tier 1 capital at some 12–16 percent of risk-weighted assets to survive the 7 percent minimum requirement even in a deep downturn.

It is also important that "capital" should be transparent. The Financial Accounting Standards Board (FASB) in the USA undertook in November 2007 a revision of what should constitute "capital" and "liabilities," respectively. According to the FASB, share capital should be limited to capital taking the first hit if a bank loses money. Thus only common stock and retained earnings and other reserves should be

---

[41] See also Financial Services Authority, Definition of capital.
[42] Board of Governors of the Federal Reserve System, Flow of Funds, Tables L.109–L.115.

Table 7.6 *Tier 1 and Core Tier 1 ratios for selected financial institutions, June 30, 2009*

	Tier 1 ratio (%)	Core Tier 1 ratio (%)
Morgan Stanley	15.8	10.6
Credit Suisse	15.5	10.4
State Street	14.5	12.5
Goldman Sachs	13.8	n a
UBS	13.2	10.1
SEB	13.1	11.3
Citigroup	12.7	8.7
Bank of New York Mellon	12.5	11.1
Bank of America	11.9	6.9
Barclays	11.7	8.8
Deutsche Bank	11.0	7.8
HSBC	10.1	8.8
Wells Fargo	9.8	4.5
JPMorgan Chase	9.7	7.7
Société Générale	9.5	7.3
US Bancorp	9.4	6.7
BNP Paribas	9.3	7.2
Royal Bank of Scotland	9.0	6.4

Source: Published quarterly statements

called capital and enter Tier 1, while preference shares and all kinds of hybrid capital should be classified as liabilities. Unfortunately, the financial crisis has prevented a similar international discussion in the International Accounting Standards Board (IASB) and decisions following this direction.[43]

The question has become topical not least because of the preference shares purchased with TARP money. Banks have tried to repay this money as soon as possible, and some banks started to do so in June 2009, with the authorization of the relevant supervisory authority. In that case, it is a question not of capital but liabilities, according to the FASB classification.

Table 7.6 shows that transforming from the BIS Tier 1 ratios to Core Tier 1 ratios can create quite different pictures when you strip out

---

[43] Financial Accounting Standards Board, Financial instruments.

preference shares and hybrid capital. The data apply to June 30, 2009. HSBC and Wells Fargo have almost identical Tier 1 ratios, whereas in terms of Core Tier 1, HSBC has double the ratio of Wells Fargo, which, at 4.5 percent, is barely above the suggested required minimum of 4 percent.[44]

The situation is similar in the UK. Between 1998 and 2008, banks in the UK issued some £100 billion in hybrid Tier 1 capital, accounting for two-thirds of all Tier 1 capital raised externally – that is, excluding retained earnings. For this reason, the FSA suggested that in the future banks be subjected to a 4 percent minimum ratio of their Core Tier 1 ratio, while the requirement for total Tier 1 capital is to be raised from 4 to 8 percent.[45]

Does the principle of mark-to-market lead to procyclicality?

A bank has several types of assets. On one hand, it has the portfolio of loans and other assets intended to be held to maturity, carried on its books at nominal value unless delinquency of the borrower forces a write-down. This portfolio is called the banking book or the investment book. The other portfolio is the trading book, containing assets that may be sold and which are revalued (marked to market) daily, or even more frequently. Rules requiring market valuation have been prescribed by the codes FSA 115 and 157 by the FASB in the USA, as well as by the international code IAS 39 from the IASB, which was adopted by the European Union in 2004.

Marking to market is an obvious and simple rule for securities where there exists a continuous market, for instance, for government bonds. But how to value complex securities like CDOs, where the market has ceased to operate? The recent financial crisis in Europe may be judged to have started in August 2007, when BNP Paribas closed some of its funds for withdrawal, since they could not establish reliable prices for some of these securities where there was no longer a market. An intermediate situation may exist if the market is still open but illiquid, meaning that a sale may push prices sharply downwards. In the crisis, even once liquid markets may be affected. When the bank Société Générale decided to close out unauthorized positions taken by the trader Jérôme Kerviel in

---

[44] See also *The Economist*, Stress-test mess, February 28, 2009.
[45] Financial Services Authority, Strengthening capital standards 3.

only 3 days in January 2008, it turned a potential loss of around €1 billion into an actual loss of almost €5 billion. Not even the highly liquid futures market for the DAX, Eurostoxx and Footsie indices could take sales of futures worth €60 billion without a severe drubbing!

Marking assets to market implies a built-in procyclicality. Asset revaluations during the expansion phase of the business cycle lead to capital gains and profits, which enhance the size of the portfolio, leading to purchases of assets and further price increases. Falling prices in recessions shrink the size of the portfolio, forcing sales of assets and further price falls. In combination with rating, market valuation leads to an evil circle of downratings, forcing sales of assets, leading to price falls and capital losses, triggering further price falls and perhaps further downratings.[46]

As a temporary measure, the USA has given the SEC the possibility, under the Emergency Economic Stabilization Act (section 132), to suspend mark-to-market valuation. The FASB decided in April 2009 to allow banks to use their internal models to establish a fair price where market prices were lacking. This rule change led to a 20 percent fall in the required mark-down of assets in the accounts for the first quarter of 2009.

In Europe, the European Commission has given the banks the option of carrying assets at original value instead of market value – that is, moving them from the trading book to the banking book. Deutsche Bank avoided write-downs of €3.2 billion as evaluated from the third quarter of 2008 to the first quarter of 2010 by using this option, shifting €38 billion of assets from one book to the other, thereby also avoiding the necessity of applying for the government capital support extended to, inter alia, its main competitor Commerzbank. The Dutch ING Groep similarly reclassified assets worth €24.4 billion, as did Société Générale, with assets worth €25.3 billion, thereby saving €2.8 billion in paper losses.[47]

---

[46] The well-known bank economist Henry Kaufman (called "Dr Doom"), one of the few to predict the oncoming financial crisis, issued a warning back in 1994 that excessive reliance on mark-to-market could trigger a systemic financial crisis. He would be proved right, even if it took more than 10 years! See Kaufman, *The Road to Financial Reformation*.

[47] MacAskill and Kirchfeld, European banks' hidden losses may threaten EU stress tests.

	Historic-cost value, $bn	Fair value, $bn	Difference as % of tangible common equity
Regions Financial	83.0	70.2	160
KeyCorp	53.5	47.3	89
Huntington Bancshares	35.5	33.4	71
Fifth Third	73.6	70.4	44
Wells Fargo	742.3	721.1	30
Bank of America	908.0	884.1	20
Citigroup	670.4	658.3	10
JPMorgan Chase	675.6	674.7	nil

Figure 7.5 Loans in selected US banks (historic cost vs fair value), 2010
Source: *The Economist*, June 12, 2010

As shown by Figure 7.5, carrying the loan book at historic costs or at a marked-to-market fair value implies a drastic difference, not least for the effect of the necessary write-downs on capital. Regions Financial, the 14th largest bank in the USA by Tier 1 capital, would have had to take a write-down of $13 billion on a Tier 1 capital base of $18 billion, and Wells Fargo write-downs of $21 billion on an equity base of $114 billion. It is no wonder that the major banks are lobbying against the fair-value proposals of the FASB.[48]

The attempt by the FASB in May 2010 to force US banks to value more of their assets at market value has been undermined by the IASB moving the other way, dominated as it is by the interests of the major European banks, especially German. No international accord on accounting appears likely in the near future.[49]

---

[48] Westbrook and Katz, US banks recruit investors to kill FASB fair-value proposal.
[49] Sanderson, Guerrera and Thomas, Divide over accounting standards set to widen.

Points to remember

- A bank needs to have adequate capital to protect it from bankruptcy in the event of credit losses. International agreements in the Basel group decide how much.
- If a bank loses capital to an extent where it is no longer viable, the authorities face a dilemma: letting the bank go bankrupt or nationalizing it wholly or partly.
- A bank whose failure risks the collapse of the entire banking system is judged to be "too big to fail" and must be protected by the state, by recapitalization or outright nationalization.
- Nationalization implies full government control of the bank and its development and also means that taxpayers will be able to recover their investment when the bank is sold back into the private sector.
- The problem with the concept of "too big to fail" is that the implicit promise of help may create incentives for the management to take greater risks than they would otherwise have done ("moral hazard").
- For this reason it may be necessary to let individual banks fail, as happened with BCCI and Barings Bank in the UK in the 1990s. In today's crisis, it was obviously wrong to let the investment bank Lehman Brothers go bankrupt, since it created uncertainty as to the future behavior of the authorities. Since then no bank has been allowed to fail, either in the USA or Europe. Instead, problematic banks have been merged with stronger partners, with the support of the FDIC, recapitalized by the government or placed in administration – that is, nationalized.
- The creditworthiness of banks and other borrowers is established by a process called rating, by such companies as Moody's and Standard & Poor's. The highest grades for long-term securities are called AAA or Aaa.
- The rating companies have greatly underestimated the risks connected with bonds with underlying mortgages, in particular subprime loans. Of recently issued mortgage bonds, three-quarters have been downrated. A lower rating leads to falls in the prices of these bonds and hence to losses for the investors.
- Since 1989, EU countries must hold capital in a certain proportion to their risk-weighted assets. Government bonds issued by a highly rated country are judged to have no risk and hence a zero risk weight.

Residential mortgages are weighted at 35–75 percent and commercial loans at 75–150 percent.

- Since the minimum capital (solvency) ratio allowed is 8 percent, this is tantamount to saying that a bank must hold at least 2.8 percent capital for a residential mortgage (35 percent times 8 percent) and at least 6 percent for commercial loans. In practice, banks have elected to hold much higher capital ratios.
- US banks lost approximately half their original capital during the crisis. If, in the future, they are required to hold at least 7 percent TCE (basically, common stock), this implies a minimum TCE ratio in good times of at least 12–15 percent.
- In new rules from 2007 (Basel II), banks may use their own internal models to establish the amount of capital necessary, which in some cases may lead to a sharp fall in the amount of capital required. Discussions are under way in the relevant supervisory bodies to raise capital standards in relation to today's requirement, and also attempt to make capital ratios less procyclical (see Appendix 7.2).

Appendix 7.1
Government support activities for banks' capital ratios, 2007–2010

German actions taken

Its strong capital base allowed Landesbank Baden Württemberg (LBBW) to take over its smaller colleague Landesbank Sachsen in September 2007. The latter had sustained losses of €2.8 billion on US CDOs and derivatives related to the US subprime market through its Irish subsidiary. This company had an intimate relationship with Lehman Brothers, selling as well as investing in Lehman's CDOs. The bank had a high rating supplied by its main owner, the state of Sachsen, enabling it to finance the investments by issuing asset-backed commercial paper (ABCP). As a condition for LBBW taking over the bank, taxpayers in the poor state of Sachsen had to bear the losses, €2.8 billion, corresponding to €650 per inhabitant, irrespective of age.

The next bank with problems related to the subprime market was IKB (Deutsche IndustrieBank), whose main owner was the state-owned Kreditanstalt für Wiederaufbau (KfW). IKB had started an SIV in Dublin called Rhinebridge, with assets of €15 billion, funded by issuing commercial paper. One of their investments was in a CDO structure called Abacus, issued by Goldman Sachs, which became worthless (discussed earlier, page 165). IKB is one of the investors cited in the lawsuit by the US SEC against Goldman Sachs (see Appendix 2.1, 16 April 2010, pages 75–6).[50]

IKB received a liquidity support from its owner and from a consortium of German banks, but still needed a capital injection of €1.5 billion from the federal state to counter losses. IKB has since been sold to Lone Star Funds, a US private equity group domiciled on Bermuda. One may wonder what use KfW, founded to channel Marshall Aid after the Second World War and later used to rebuild the former East Germany, had for investing in US subprime paper, securitized and issued by Lehman Brothers. Even after selling IKB, KfW itself continued to invest in Lehman's CDOs. Indeed, the last payment of €350 million was made on the same morning (Central European Time) that Lehman filed for bankruptcy in the USA (Eastern Standard Time). This led to KfW being given the title "der dummeste Bank Deutschlands" (the most stupid bank in Germany) by the newspaper *Frankfurter Allgemeine Zeitung*. KfW also had claims amounting to €288 million on the three bankrupt Icelandic banks.

Germany decided in October 2008 that an amount not exceeding €80 billion could be used to recapitalize banks by purchasing (preferably) preference shares. Moreover, €400 billion were allocated to guarantee bank liabilities. Commerzbank, which had recently bought Dresdner Bank from the insurance company Allianz, received €8.2 billion in capital from the federal state and another €10 billion at the beginning of 2009. The German state thereby holds 25 percent of the bank through its investment agent SonderFonds Finanzmarktstabilisierung (SoFFin). Deutsche Bank, however, has so far avoided state support (in part by reclassifying assets, as noted above, page 254).

The fifth largest bank in Germany, Bayerische Landesbank, had also invested in US CDOs to the tune of €24 billion, leading to a loss of €4.3 billion, on top of which came losses related to the Icelandic banks of €1.5 billion. Its main owner, the state of Bayern, which owns 94 percent of the bank, refrained from asking for federal support and

---

[50] See, for instance, http://blogs.reuters.com/felix-salmon/2010/04/16/goldmans-abacus-lies/

instead raised new capital together with the other owners, the local savings banks.

Bayern Landesbank was also affected severely by the failure of the Austrian mortgage bank Hypo Group Alpe Adria International (HGAA). It purchased a majority share in May 2007 for €1.6 billion, a further €440 million in December and another €700 million in December 2008. HGAA also received a capital injection of €900 million from the Austrian state. Austria nationalized the bank in December 2009, paying Bayern Landesbank €1 for its 67 percent ownership. The bank's total loss on the investment was €3.7 billion. Bavarian taxpayers have had to cough up a total of €10 billion to save the *Landesbank* from collapse. Ten years earlier, it had been the only AAA-rated *Landesbank* in Germany.

The mortgage bank Hypo Real Estate has received capital injections, loans and guarantees from the federal state and Bundesbank totaling €110 billion and was nationalized in October 2009 (as noted above).

Westdeutsche Landesbank (WestLB) is the only one of the state-owned regional banks to have received federal support, a capital injection of €3 billion.

The largest of the *Landesbanken*, Baden-Württemberg, has sued Goldman Sachs over losses in a CDO structure called Davis Square Funding VI, which the seller characterized as "safe, secure and nearly risk free," while simultaneously buying protection – that is, speculating that the bond would fail.

All together, Germany has injected €38 billion into its banking system and allocated €50 billion of guarantees (out of a possible maximum of €480 billion). In its April 2010 assessment, the IMF placed German banks' ultimate write-down needs at €314 billion, equivalent to 9 percent of GDP. By mid-2010, the federal state had spent 5 percent of GDP in capital injections and asset purchases, according to the IMF.

Austrian actions taken

The Austrian federal state has injected €1 billion in preference shares into Erste Bank, the second largest bank in Austria. As noted above, it also gave Hypo Group Alpe Adria International €900 million before nationalizing it.

Hence the total amount spent was €2 billion. The decided maximum amounts were €15 billion in new capital and €75 billion in guarantees.

British actions taken

The British government has nationalized two mortgage banks, Northern Rock and Bradford & Bingley. The core parts of the latter, mainly the deposits, were later sold to Abbey National, part of the Spanish Grupo Santander. Shares in the nationalized banks are held by the holding company UK Financial Investments. The compensation to the shareholders, if any, has yet to be decided (October 2010). The costs to the taxpayer may be assessed only after the banks have been sold back to private investors. The Bank of England has claims amounting to £55 billion on Northern Rock (including guarantees).

The British state set aside £109 billion to recapitalize banks. Of this sum, £37 billion had been used by 2008 – that is, £20 billion in RBS and £17 billion in Lloyds TSB. The state thereby became majority owner, with 60 percent of RBS, and the largest owner of Lloyds, with 40 percent. Lloyds TSB had already contracted to purchase the mortgage bank HBOS (Halifax Bank of Scotland) for £12 billion. In January 2009, the state extended its ownership of RBS to almost 80 percent by exchanging preference shares for ordinary shares. At the same time, the state guaranteed assets worth £325 billion.

In March 2009, a similar agreement was made with Lloyds TSB. After the conversion, the government would own 77 percent of the bank, while guaranteeing assets worth £260 billion. As a result, the bank's Tier 1 ratio would rise from 6.4 percent to 14.5 percent. This deal, however, was never consummated, the state ownership remaining at 43 percent, purchased at a cost of £20 billion.

Royal Bank of Scotland (RBS) has been forced to sell off its insurance division and some bank branches after decisions from the European Commission's competition commissioner and the UK Treasury. The bank has sold its RBS branches in England and Wales, as well as its NatWest branches in Scotland. RBS also agreed to put £282 billion of assets into the government's Asset Protection Scheme and take an additional £25.5 billion of investment from the Treasury. As a result, the government will increase its stake in RBS to 84.4 percent. RBS increased the first loss on the assets protected under the government insurance program to about £60 billion, from the £42.2 billion initially agreed.

All in all, the British government has spent £78.5 billion on capital injections into RBS and Lloyds Banking Group, out of the £109 billion set aside for banks' capital support. To this amount should be added an unknown sum resulting from promising the Bank of England to indemnify it for its liquidity support to the banks in trouble, which may be established only when the two building societies have been sold and their toxic assets disposed of. The Treasury has also undertaken to guarantee up to £250 billion of new securities issued by banks. The cost to the Treasury so far in mid-2010 is 6.5 percent of GDP.

Irish actions taken

The seriousness of the Irish financial crisis is evidenced by the fact that the country has spent a total of €33 billion recapitalizing its banking system, a sum corresponding to 15 percent of GDP. In a first step, €5.5 billion was injected into the Bank of Ireland, Allied Irish Banks and Anglo Irish Bank. In Anglo Irish Bank, the state came to own 75 percent, raised to 100 percent by total nationalization in January 2009. In Allied Irish Banks the state owned 18.7 percent and in Bank of Ireland 13.6 percent by mid-2010. Of the €32 billion spent, €22 billion has gone into Anglo Irish Bank. The government has warned that the total might rise to €50 billion.

Ireland was also the first country to set up a "bad bank" to take over and manage impaired assets from the banking system. The National Asset Management Agency (NAMA) planned to buy loans for a maximum of €81 billion, applying an average "haircut" of 47 percent – that is, loans will be purchased from the banks for just about half of their nominal value.

The continued banking problems in Ireland, together with its budgetary consequences, has led Standard & Poor's to lower Ireland's rating two notches from the AAA level. Moody's has also downgraded Ireland two notches to Aa2 and with a negative outlook (by October 2010).

French actions taken

French banks have in general made it through the crisis without major problems. The losses sustained by Société Générale in early 2008 were not a direct consequence of the subprime crisis, but of unauthorized trading positions in conjunction with a remarkably weak risk function ("middle office"). The loss of €4.9 billion was offset by a share issue.

Its strong position allowed BNP Paribas to purchase 75 percent of the Belgian and Luxembourg parts of the bankrupt and nationalized Fortis Bank, paying with its own shares. This makes BNP the largest bank in Euroland, at the same time as Belgium becomes its largest owner, with 13 percent of the capital. The Belgian government has also set aside €740 million for a "bad bank," into which toxic assets worth €11.4 billion were placed. On top of this, the Belgian government guarantees future delinquent loans coming from Fortis after BNP pays the first €3.5 billion. Belgium will also underwrite a share issue of €2 billion by BNP if necessary. By the end of 2009, BNP Paribas was the world's largest bank, with assets at almost $3 trillion, according to *The Banker*.

French and Belgian authorities have also given the French-Belgian bank Dexia (ex Crédit Local and Crédit Communal) an injection of capital of €6.4 billion, raising its Tier 1 ratio to 14.5 percent.

France has also set up a support fund encompassing €40 billion to recapitalize its banks. As a start, France wanted to invest a total of €10.5 billion: Crédit Agricole (€3 billion), BNP Paribas (€2.55 billion), Société Générale (€1.7 billion), Crédit Mutuel (€1.2 billion), *caisses d'épargne* (savings banks; €1.1 billion) and Banque Populaire (€950 million). The capital would be supplied on condition that the banks increase their lending by 3–4 percent. The program was initially rejected by the European Commission on grounds of competition (did the banks really need the capital?). After the program had been approved in December, the same banks received another €10.5 billion in capital support.[51]

The total amount spent on capital injections is thus some €28 billion, to which may be added a possible €320 billion of guarantees. In terms of GDP, the Treasury has spent just 1.1 percent. Only Italy, of the major European powers, has been even luckier, spending but 0.3 percent of GDP in capital injections.

Actions taken by the Benelux countries

The Belgian-Dutch bank Fortis got digestion problems (like RBS) after buying and carving up the Dutch bank ABN AMRO. The three Benelux

---

[51] Xiao, French banks amid the global financial crisis.

countries took over the main part of the bank in September 2008 for €11.2 billion. The Netherlands pulled out of the agreement 2 weeks later, however, and purchased the Dutch parts of the bank, plus the insurance business, plus the parts of ABN AMRO yet to be integrated, for a total of €16.8 billion. This forced the above-mentioned sale of the Belgian-Luxembourg parts to BNP Paribas.

In November 2009, the Dutch residual of ABN AMRO received €4.4 billion in capital support to facilitate its merger with the Dutch residual of Fortis.

The Netherlands has also set up a fund for capital injections into banks in need of €20 billion, of which the other major Dutch bank, ING, received €10 billion in October 2008. Another €7.5 billion was injected in a rights issue in 2009, but repaid later in the year, together with an additional €5 billion of government-held shares being rebought. The Dutch government has also underwritten 80 percent of ING's portfolio of Alt-A loans, amounting to €28 billion.

The Belgian KBC Bank also received capital support to the tune of €3.5 billion.

The Netherlands is also authorized to guarantee up to €200 billion of newly issued bank liabilities.

Swiss actions taken

UBS, the bank in Europe most severely affected by the subprime crisis (with write-downs corresponding to $66 billion, most of which was on US mortgage securities; see Appendix 5.2), has received its support mainly from the central bank, Schweizerische Nationalbank (SNB). It also issued shares to the Swiss state of 6 billion Swiss francs, which were used to capitalize a "bad bank" formally run by the SNB into which toxic assets to the tune of 60 billion Swiss francs were placed. Switzerland thereby came to own 9.3 percent of UBS. The other major bank, Credit Suisse, has avoided state interference, instead relying on a private issue of capital of 10 billion Swiss francs.

Spanish actions taken

Spain long avoided the crisis, despite its building boom and subsequent crash, perhaps as a result of its demands that banks build up extra capital in the boom – "dynamic provisioning." In 2009, however, it had to allocate €10 billion to recapitalize its ailing savings banks, *cajas de ahorro*, in order to facilitate mergers among these small-size institutions. Two banks have also had to be bailed out, Caja Castilla la Mancha and Caja Sur. The number of *cajas* has been reduced by mergers from forty-five to eighteen. The total amount spent has been only €11.2 billion, corresponding to 1 percent of GDP, as of July 2010. Spain has also set up a bank guarantee scheme worth potentially €100 billion.

Danish actions taken

In Denmark it is the central bank (Nationalbanken) which has the major role in saving banks in trouble. The tab is for the most part picked up by the other banks. Roskilde Bank, the eighth largest, received new capital of DKK 4.5 billion. Smaller banks with problems, such as Ebh Bank, have been merged with stronger partners. In January 2009, the Danish government changed its mind, however, and announced a fund (Finansiel Stabilitet) of up to DKK 100 billion to be used for recapitalizing banks. One of the first recipients was Fionia Bank in Odense. The continued gravity of the crisis can be seen in June 2010, when Amagerbanken entered an agreement with Finansiel Stabilitet to have DKK 17 billion in liabilities guaranteed by the state until 2013.

Swedish actions taken

The Swedish program for "stability-enhancing actions" also includes the possibility of allocating a maximum of SEK 50 billion (€5 billion) for recapitalizing needy banks, provided their capital ratios rise no more than 2 percentage points. No bank expressed an interest, even though Swedbank, as noted in Chapter 6, participated in the guarantee part of the program (encompassing up to €150 billion, equivalent). The law also provides for the possibility of forcibly nationalizing banks if necessary. Carnegie Investment Bank and the Swedish subsidiary of Kaupthing were nationalized and later sold back to the private sector, the National Debt Office being stuck with the bad assets of the latter.

Nordea Bank happened to be a recipient of SEK 5 billion in support capital without having asked for it. In order to save money in the budget, the state participated, in its capacity as owner, in Nordea's issue of common stock in May 2009, using the support money instead of taking money from the budget, an action criticized by the National Debt Office in its capacity as formal owner. Its objections, however, were overruled by the Treasury.

Summary for the EU countries

Summing the data for individual countries, we find that the above-mentioned countries in the European Union, at the peak of the crisis, had allocated some €360 billion for potential capital injections into their banking systems and extended some €1,900 billion in bank liability guarantees. Adding purchases of "toxic assets," as well as liquidity support and bank funding support, brings the total for the EU to over €3,700 billion, corresponding to well over $5,000 billion, or 33 per cent of the EU's GDP. For the euro area, the figure is slightly lower, at 30 per cent. (See Table A7.1 below and Figure A7.1, page 266). Even higher numbers could be achieved if one also includes deposit guarantee schemes (as I do for the USA in Table A7.2). Out of twenty-seven member states, eighteen introduced bank liability guarantees, fifteen approved recapitalization measures and eleven gave liquidity support to their banks.

Table A7.1 shows the commitments of the major European governments in May 2009, ranked by the percentage of each country's GDP represented by the contributions. The totals include capital injections, guarantees granted, effective asset relief and liquidity interventions, but excluding deposit insurance.[52]

US actions taken

Of the $350 billion authorized under the first part of TARP, $250 billion were allocated to recapitalize banks. In October 2008, nine large banks split $125 billion: JPMorgan Chase ($25 billion), Wells Fargo ($25 billion), Citigroup ($25 billion), Bank of America ($15 billion), Merrill Lynch ($10 billion), Goldman Sachs ($10 billion), Morgan Stanley ($10 billion), Bank of New York Mellon ($3 billion) and State Street Bank ($2 billion). Fifteen medium-sized banks accepted support totaling $38 billion, while a number of small banks received

---

[52] The data in the text and in the table are taken from Louis, Bank rescue costs EU states $5.3 trillion.

Table A7.1 *Major European governments'*
commitments

	€ billion	% of GDP
Ireland	385	229
Belgium	265	76
Austria	165	59
UK	781	49
Sweden	142	47
Netherlands	246	42
Germany	554	22
France	350	18
Spain	130	12

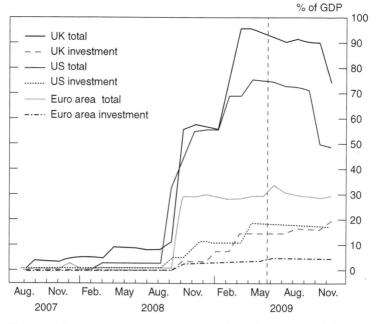

Figure A7.1 Public sector interventions in the USA, the UK and the euro area
(% of GDP), August 2007–November 2009

Note: The figures do not include the deposit guarantee system, in contrast to
Table A7.2, which explains the difference between the 70 percent for the US
reported in the graph vis-à-vis the 100 percent of GDP shown in Table A7.2.
Source: Bank of England, *Financial Stability Report* (December 2009)

support that was important to them but insignificant for the overall total. Some of them are listed here: PNC Financial Services ($7.7 billion), Capital One ($3.55 billion), Fifth Third ($3.5 billion), Regions Financial ($3.5 billion), Suntrust ($3.5 billion), BB&T ($3.1 billion), Key Corp. ($2.5 billion), Comerica ($2.25 billion), Marshall & Ilsley Corp. ($1.7 billion), Northern Trust Corp. ($1.5 billion), Huntington Bancshares ($1.4 billion), Zions Bancorp. ($1.4 billion), First Horizon National ($866 million), City National Corp. ($395 million), Valley National Bancorp. ($330 million), UCBH Holdings Inc. ($298 million), Umpqua Holdings Corp. ($214 million), Washington Federal ($200 million), First Niagara Financial ($186 million), HF Financial Corp. ($25 million) and Bank of Commerce ($17 million). In all, some 350 banks participated in the TARP program for capital support.

Citibank, however, needed another $20 billion in support just a month later, on top of which the FDIC and the Federal Reserve have guaranteed $306 billion of its toxic assets. Bank of America also needed another $20 billion in support in January 2009 after its merger with Merrill Lynch, over and above the $25 billion that the two institutions had already received. The state also guaranteed $118 billion of toxic assets.

The TARP program was originally directed exclusively at banks. Merrill Lynch could participate as a part of Bank of America. Goldman Sachs and Morgan Stanley had been accepted by the Federal Reserve as banking corporations, hence changing their supervisor from the SEC to the Fed. But insurance companies could also access TARP money if the financial group included a bank. By purchasing the small bank Federal Trust in Florida for $10 million, the gigantic insurance company Hartford Financial Services, one of the largest in the USA, with total assets of $450 billion, changed itself into a banking group, thereby gaining access to the Fed's TAF lending facility. It also received $3.4 billion in new capital under TARP in June 2009. A similar amount from TARP was received by the Lincoln National Financial Group after the purchase of the Newton County Loan & Savings Bank. Lincoln had assets of $200 *billion*, while the bank had total deposits of $3.8 *million* ...

It should be noted that while capital injections in Europe have been given in the form of common stock or voting preference shares, the US contributions have mainly been given as non-voting preference shares, with warrants being added to give the taxpayer part of the upside. The conclusion is that in the USA, the authorities in general preferred to leave the running of the banks to the existing management, while European authorities have opted for a more hands-on approach. Perhaps this principle changed as the government exchanged its preference shares in Citi for common stock, making it Citi's biggest owner, with 36 percent of the stock. The stake was brought down to 18 percent by July 2010, by selling shares on the market.

Many countries have placed restrictions on salaries and bonuses in their support programs. In the USA, institutions receiving support may not deduct for tax purposes "golden parachutes" or salaries and bonuses exceeding $500,000 per annum. This restriction is only applicable, however, to the CEO, the CFO and the three best-paid executives. The levels of compensation may be compared with those given in Chapter 4. President Obama decided that banks participating in any of the support programs must restrict salaries to their top executives to $500,000 per annum. Any exceeding amount must be given in the form of stock, to be sold only when all government support has been repaid.

The European Union took decisions in July 2010 on new rules for remuneration in banks as well as hedge funds. At least 40 percent (or 60 percent for large bonuses) of the bonus must be postponed for 3 to 5 years and the payment upfront must be limited to half the amount, the rest being paid in stock. The cash portion is thus reduced to 20–30 percent of the total. Some EU countries already have similar rules, following the previous recommendation by the EU Commission, K (2009) 3159.

These direct limitations on remuneration may have clear negative effects if crucial staff decide to leave for unrestricted firms – that is, those firms not receiving government support – or unregulated activities. A more productive way to control excessive bonuses is probably for the supervisory authorities to demand higher capital ratios for those firms whose remuneration systems are judged to be excessively focused on short-term profits, and hence risky. This way forward is open already under Pillar 2 of Basel II.

Some countries have also introduced taxes on bonuses. The British Chancellor of the Exchequer imposed a one-time 50 percent tax for 2009 on bankers' bonuses above £25,000. The tax was paid by the banks as a surcharge on income. Coming on top of the increase in the

British top marginal tax rate, from 40 to 50 percent on incomes over £150,000, the measure threatened an exodus of bankers from London. France was the only country to follow the British example. The tax apparently had no effect, as one would expect from a one-time tax. Banks preferred to pay the surcharge out of profits than to lose key personnel.

In various programs (capital injections, loans, purchases of securities, guarantees, swap arrangements), the US government has accepted potential costs at a total of over $16 trillion, more than the entire GDP and far more than the existing size of the national debt. Of this potential sum, less than $3,000 billion had been used by September 2009, at the height of the crisis. (See Table A7.2.) The sum of $16 trillion may be compared with a European figure of $5.3 trillion (if one adds the deposit guarantee system to the above-quoted figure of $4.4 trillion).

In direct outlays on capital injections and asset purchases, the Treasury has spent 4.8 percent of GDP – that is, less than the UK, but about the same as Germany.

Compare also Figure A7.2 for US, UK and Euro totals. Note the development over time. After September 2009, the amounts drop off. Hence I have purposely not updated the data in Table A7.2, wanting to show what the supports were at the height of the crisis.

It is not altogether obvious which government programs should be included in "support to the financial system." The Special Inspector General for the Troubled Asset Relief Program (SIGTARP) found in his report to Congress in July 2009 (his Table 3.4) that the potential amount at stake was $23.7 trillion, or over 150 percent of GDP. He achieved this high number by adding several other agencies, such as Veterans' Administration and Federal Housing Finance Agency, and also assuming much wider potential losses on securities acquired by the Federal Reserve.[53] The question, though, is whether all potential support to housing should be regarded as costs of the financial crisis?

---

[53] Pozen, *Too Big to Save*, p. 337, has a similar presentation of maximum exposure and actual payments. He has missed some programs, in particular the government guarantee for FDIC-insured deposits. He reaches a number similar to Table A7.2, since the $3,200 billion guarantee for money market funds was still in force as of March 25, 2009, the date of his table.

Table A7.2 *Potential and actual amounts in the various US financial support programs by September 2009 ($ billion)*

Program	Maximum amount	Amount used
FDIC		
Guarantee for insured deposits	4,800	n/a[1]
Guarantee for uninsured deposits	700	n/a
Guarantee for public private investment	800[2]	0
Temporary Liquidity Guarantee (TLGP)	1,500	308
Guarantee GE debt	65	55
FDIC part Citigroup guarantee	10	0
FDIC part Bank of America guarantee	3	0
FDIC cost of bank takeovers	n/a	45
SUM FDIC	7,878	408
Federal Reserve		
Primary discount window	111	29
Secondary credit	1	0
Primary dealer facility	147	0[3]
Liquidity support ABCP	146	0
Commercial Paper Funding Facility (CPFF)	1,800	14[4]
Term Securities Lending Facility (TSLF)	250	0
Term Auction Facility (TAF)	500[5]	110[6]
Overnight securities lending	10	9
Term Asset-Backed Securities Loan Facility (TALF)	1,000	44[7]
Money Market Funding Facility	600	0[8]
Purchases Bear Stearns assets[9]	29	26
Purchases AIG assets[10]	53	35
Credit AIG	60	39
Purchases of Fannie/Freddie MBSs	1,250	776[11]
Purchases of Fannie/Freddie debt	200	150

Table A7.2 (*cont.*)

Program	Maximum amount	Amount used
Citigroup bailout, Fed portion	220	0
Bank of America bailout, Fed portion	97	0
Commitment to buy Treasuries	300	295[12]
Foreign exchange swaps	unlimited	29
SUM Federal Reserve	6,774+ unlimited swaps	1,556
Troubled Assets Relief Program (TARP)[13]		
Bank capital purchase program	218	205
GM, Chrysler	80	78
Auto suppliers	5	4
AIG[14]	70	70
"Make home affordable"	50	27
Bank of America	20	20
Citigroup	20	20
Citigroup asset guarantee	5	5
Bank of America asset guarantee	8	0
Guarantee for TALF	20	20
Guarantee for public private investment	100	27
Consumer lending initiative	50	0
Available for additional initiatives	54[15]	0
SUM TARP	700	476[16]
Government		
New capital Fannie Mae/Freddie Mac	400	111
"Hope for homeowners"	320	20
"Neighborhood stabilization"	25	0
Treasury guarantee MMF[17]	0	0

Table A7.2 (*cont.*)

Program	Maximum amount	Amount used
SUM *Government*	745	131
SUM *TOTAL*	16,097	2,571[18]

Notes:

[1] The report is available at www.sigtarp.gov/reports/congress/2009/
July2009_Quarterly_Report_to_Congress.pdf

[2] Not applicable, since uses are paid by the insured banks themselves through fees.

[3] A maximum amount of $1,000 billion, with $100 billion in capital from TARP and a similar amount from private sources, implies private borrowing with FDIC guarantee of $800 billion.

[4] Peaked at $147 billion in October 2008.

[5] Maximum utilized was $152 billion, in January 2009.

[6] Previously authorized maximum amounts had been $2,000 billion.

[7] Peaked in November 2008 at $415 billion.

[8] The amount was raised from $200 billion to $1,000 billion in March 2009, at the same time as the Treasury's support for losses was raised from $20 billion to $100 billion, money taken from the TARP program. A new feature added in March was that already issued mortgage bonds were included if they had originally carried a AAA rating.

[9] Peaked at $152 billion in October 2008.

[10] "Maiden Lane."

[11] "Maiden Lane II and III."

[12] The program was terminated in April 2010.

[13] The program was terminated in October 2009.

[14] The maximum allocated by Congress was $700 billion.

[15] The total money allocated to help AIG was $182.5 billion, of which $70 billion was new share capital. A total of $127 billion was drawn as of September 2009.

[16] Congress decided in July 2010 to use parts of the residual TARP money, $19 billion, to pay for the added cost of supervision, after Republican senators had blocked the proposed bank levy.

[17] Or one could say $358 billion, since banks had repaid $118 billion (see below).

[18] The Treasury guarantee program for Money Market Funds was allowed to expire in September 2009. The government collected $1.2 billion in fees without spending a single dollar. The guarantee reached a maximum of $3,200 billion.

Source: CNN, September 25, 2009; Congressional Oversight Panel; press releases from Freddie Mac and Fannie Mae; TARP announcements at www.financialstability.gov/docs/transaction-reports/transactionReport051209.pdf and www.financialstability.gov/docs/transaction-reports/transactionReport051209.pdf; own calculations for deposit insurance

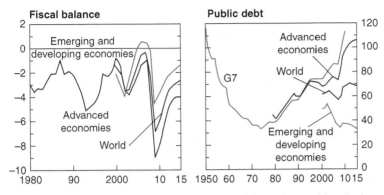

Figure A7.2 Budget balances and government debt in the world and advanced economies (% of GDP), 1980–2015
Note: Fiscal policy will become contractionary in 2011, following significant expansion mostly during 2009. Nonetheless, public debt ratios are projected to continue to rise, unless further action is taken. Although fiscal and household consolidation can be expected to lower demand in advanced economies, domestic demand in key emerging economies is not projected to compensate for this. Similarly, the change in fiscal policies in emerging and advanced economies with low debt and external surpluses is not expected to differ much from policy elsewhere.
Source: International Monetary Fund, *World Economic Outlook* (October 2010), page 18

It would be wrong, I think, to include also the various stimulus programs, such as the American Recovery and Reinvestment Act, student loan guarantees, Advanced Technology Vehicles and Car Allowance Rebate System, none of which was directly linked with aiding the financial sector. In all, these programs added another $1.2 trillion in potential expenses by the government, of which about half had been drawn by September 2009.

By September 2009, the date of Table A7.2, $118 billion of TARP money had been repaid, of which $25 billion was from JPMorgan Chase and $10 billion each from Goldman Sachs and Morgan Stanley, $5.5 billion from US Bancorp., $3.1 billion from BB&T and $2 billon from State Street Bank.

One major consequence of bailing out the financial sector, and the negative effect on growth and government revenues that followed in the wake of the crises, is a dramatic build-up of government debt. The

IMF estimated in April 2010 that the advanced countries (G-7) would experience an increase of government debt of 40 percentage points of GDP.[54] This estimate might prove too low. Reinhart and Rogoff showed that the average effect on debt-to-GDP ratios from all the financial crises during the period after the Second World War was 86 percentage points. Their data base, however, is dominated by events in developing countries, where the effects on the budget of financial crises have been much more severe than in developed countries (as shown in Chapter 8).[55]

Individual country examples are the USA, where the IMF has calculated that the ratio of gross government debt to GDP would rise from levels around 60 percent before the crisis to 110 percent by 2015, levels unheard of in peacetime. In the UK, the gross debt-to-GDP ratio would rise from 40 to over 90 percent of GDP. For both these countries, the increase is then 50 percentage points (of GDP). For the euro area as a whole, debt to GDP would rise from 65 to 95 percent of GDP, or by 30 percentage points (increasing by 15 percentage points in Germany, 30 percentage points in France and 20 percentage points in Italy). Less developed EU countries will fare even worse. The Greek debt ratio is forecast (by the IMF) to rise from figures below 100 percent of GDP to 149 percent of GDP before the situation stabilizes and ameliorates.

Appendix 7.2
The proposed new capital requirements under Basel III

On July 7, 2010, the European Parliament voted overwhelmingly in favor of the proposal concerning new and higher capital requirements in banks. These measures, proposed by the Basel group in December 2009, were finalized by November 2010.[56] The G-20 meeting in Toronto in June 2010 supported unanimously the higher ratios, but the members were inclined to delay their introduction to avoid a new credit crunch. The actual numbers were presented by the Basel Committee in September 2010, but will be subjected to a quantitative impact study (QIS 6).[57]

---

[54] International Monetary Fund, A fair and substantial contribution, p. 2.
[55] Reinhart and Rogoff, *This Time Is Different*, pp. 170 and 232.
[56] Bank for International Settlements, Strengthening the resilience of the banking sector.
[57] Bank for International Settlements, Higher global minimum capital standards.

There are basically five issues deemed problematic under Basel II that are to be rectified:

- The quality and quantity of the capital base is to be raised and it should become more transparent.
- The risk coverage is to be increased, in particular as concerns the counter-party credit risk arising from derivatives, repos and security financing activities.[58]
- In order to simplify international comparisons across regulatory systems and to set an overall limit on banks' risk-taking, an overall leverage ratio (Tier 1 capital/total assets) will be introduced.
- The tendency to procyclicality will be addressed by the creation of counter-cyclical buffers ("forward-looking provisioning").
- A 30-day stressed liquidity standard will be added to the Basel II framework. (This has already been presented and discussed in Chapter 6.)

The quality and quantity of the capital base is to be raised and become more transparent

Under Basel II, there have been three types of capital, in descending order of usefulness to absorb losses: Tier 1 capital (basically, common equity, reserve funds and retained earnings, but also non-cumulative preference shares); Upper Tier 2 capital (basically, other preference shares and perpetual subordinated debentures); Lower Tier 2 capital (other subordinated debentures with an original maturity of at least 5 years); and Tier 3 capital, which was only allowed for the coverage of market risks, not credit risks (subordinated debentures with an original maturity of at least 2 years).

The formalized required minimum ratios were 4 percent for Tier 1 capital and 8 percent for total capital. Some jurisdictions, such as the UK, also enforced a 2 percent ratio on Core Tier 1.

The distinction as well as the interpretation of the various forms of capital was made highly unclear by the use of hybrid forms of capital, varying between countries. Hybrids could encompass a maximum of 30 percent of Tier 1 capital. The problem with such hybrid capital is

---

[58] Capital requirements for the trading book and resecuritizations have already been raised, as noted earlier.

that their availability to absorb losses has never been tested, and hence it becomes a matter for the courts to decide when, how and to what degree they will be loss-bearing. Their transparency was also not very high.

The main problem with the definition of capital in the Basel II framework was the focus on what kind of capital could absorb losses when the firm was bankrupt. In Basel III, the focus is on defining the capital base that can absorb losses *in a going concern*. For this reason, Tier 3 capital is abolished altogether and hybrids phased out. The focus is changed from total capital to the capital that can best absorb losses – that is, Tier 1 capital and, in particular, Core Tier 1 capital.

An interesting new capital product, used by Lloyds Banking Group for instance, is the CoCo bond, contingent convertible Core Tier 1 securities, also called enhanced capital notes (ECNs). These bonds, with normal tax-deductible interest so long as they are bonds, are automatically and irrevocably converted to common equity should Lloyd's Core Tier 1 ratio fall below 6 percent.

The required capital ratios will also be increased sharply. Focusing on Core Tier 1 capital, basically equity and reserves, the new rules demand an increase of the absolute minimum from 2 percent to 4.5 percent. In order to guarantee this minimum, a conservation buffer of 2.5 percent is added, making the effective rate 7 percent. Banks below this level will face restrictions on dividend and bonus payments. Other buffers under discussion (and hence not yet decided by September 2010) are a counter-cyclical buffer of up to 2.5 percent (as used already in Spain), and an additional buffer of 1–2 percent placed on banks deemed to be systemically important ("too big to fail").[59] The total Tier 1 ratio is raised from 4 to 6 percent, while the overall capital requirement is maintained at 8 percent (not counting the buffer capital). The new rules will be phased in gradually. The 4.5 percent minimum must be attained by January 1, 2015, while the buffer capital has until 2019. The new liquidity standard also has to be fulfilled by 2015. The use of hybrid capital in Tier 1 capital will be phased out gradually over a period not ending until 2023.

---

[59] The FSA in the UK has indicated that it will force at least the major banks to hold an absolute minimum of 10 percent true core equity. See *Financial Times*, UK signals tougher bank capital regime, September 22, 2010; Masters and Jenkins, FSA poised to set tougher capital rules.

Banks will also have to subtract from Core Tier 1 capital items such as good will, some tax credits and minority investments. Calculations indicate that for many banks this will correspond to an increase in the minimum Core Tier 1 ratio to around 10 percent.

Previously, certain highly risky positions (such as certain securitization and equity exposures, significant investments in commercial entities, and late payment exposures on non-DvP and non-PvP transactions,[60] were deducted 50–50 from Tier 1 and Tier 2 capital. In the future, they will receive a 1,250 percent risk weight, which is basically the same thing as saying that they are to be fully deducted from (Core) Tier 1 capital.

The risk coverage is to be increased, in particular as concerns the counter-party credit risk

The recent financial crisis exposed several problems with understated risks in banking. In particular, the focus in Basel II was on the effects of a bankrupt counter-party firm, not a firm whose securities issued fell sharply in value. Two-thirds of experienced losses in the financial system were due rather to valuation adjustments and only one-third to actual default (see Table 7.2).[61]

Four initiatives are to be undertaken to counteract these deficiencies. First, and most importantly, in the future, the basis for capital requirements will be the result of stress tests under the scenario spelled out earlier for the proposed liquidity ratio.

Second, banks are encouraged to supplement the official ratings of securities and counter-parties with their own assessments.

Third, resecuritizations (CDOs) will in general be subject to higher capital requirements than first securitizations, as spelled out earlier.

---

[60] DvP = secured Delivery vs Payment in central counter-party clearing (CCP) in houses such as Eurex Clearing, LCH.Clearnet or the clearing subsidiaries of the Depository Trust Company; PvP = corresponding secured Payment vs Payment in clearing houses such as CLS Bank for foreign exchange transactions or CHIPS in the USA for domestic payments (Clearing House Interbank Payments System).

[61] This statement from the Basel Committee (Bank for International Settlements, Strengthening the resilience of the banking sector, p. 30), however, is inconsistent with the findings of the IMF concerning write-downs. Table 5.6 showed that write-downs on loans in the world were 70 percent of the total and write-down on securities 30 percent. Perhaps the Basel Committee meant losses in the trading book.

Fourth, banks will be encouraged to clear OTC derivatives through a recognized clearing house (CCP). Clearing houses fulfilling the recommendations set out by the Committee on Payment and Settlement Systems (CPSS) and the International Organization of Securities Commissions (IOSCO) will receive a zero percent risk weight. Bilaterally cleared OTC derivative trades will receive much higher capital requirements than today, and also higher requirements as to the higher marginal requirements that will result from a stressed situation (remember that it was counter-parties' demands for more collateral after AIG's downrating that felled the firm).

In order to simplify international comparisons across regulatory systems and to set an overall limit on banks' risk-taking, an overall leverage ratio (Tier 1 capital/total assets) will be introduced

While US banks are required to have leverage ratios of total assets to equity above 4 percent, and hence are restricted to a gearing ratio below twenty-five, we saw earlier that one German and one Swiss bank had gearing ratios above seventy in 2007, two French banks and one British bank were geared forty-five times (see Table 7.5, page 243). The introduction of a leverage ratio à la USA would thus mean a dramatic change for European banking. Banks have defended themselves by pointing out that European banks hold much more assets with low-risk weights than US banks (government and covered mortgage bonds in particular), and that risk-weighted assets rather than total assets thus provide a better idea of the riskiness of a certain bank. In particular, the argument applies to so-called covered bonds (used in particular in Germany, Denmark and Sweden). Banks have succeeded in postponing the new leverage requirements, which will now be tested from 2013. Also, they succeeded in getting the ratio lowered from an original 4 percent to 3 percent, implying an allowed gearing of thirty-three instead of twenty-five.[62]

---

[62] Ishmael, Banks win battle to tone down Basel III; Basel Committee on Banking Supervision, The Basel Committee's response to the financial crisis: report to the G20 (October 2010). See Bank for International Settlements, Basel Committee on Banking Supervision, Capital requirements regulations 2006.

The tendency to procyclicality will be addressed by the creation of counter-cyclical buffers ("forward-looking provisioning")

In only one country in Europe, Spain, did the supervisory authorities force banks (under their Pillar 2 competence) to hold special capital buffers to have spare capital in the downturn. This may explain the relative health of the Spanish bank giants Santander and BBVA.

To force a more forward-looking behavior in setting capital requirements, the Basel Committee supports the IASB move to an expected loss approach – that is, loans are to be written down even though the borrower is not delinquent if there is a suspicion that the loan may become impaired as a result of a financial crisis. The write-down as a result of expected loss is to be taken in total from Tier 1 capital.

There may also be changes in the way the probability of default (PD) is measured. To prevent procyclicality, PDs may be set at ratios corresponding to a full business cycle.

8 | *Financial crises in modern history: similarities and differences*

Let us begin this chapter with a summary of the magnitude of the major crises in order to have a "tree" onto which we may attach the later "branches" about events and explanations of causality.[1] In Chapter 6, we discussed the financial crisis of 1907 and the Great Depression 1929–33 and the conclusions one could draw from these events. "Black Monday" – that is, the stock market crash of 1987 – does not deserve to be called a financial crisis, since it affected only the share market, with little or no impact on other markets or the real economy. The same goes for the dotcom crisis of 2000–2. Laeven and Valencia from the IMF have recently written an excellent comparison of 124 banking crises with systemic elements for the period 1970 to 2007.[2] Most of these occurred in developing economies and have been contained nationally. Similarly, the 138 financial crises identified by Reinhart and Rogoff in sixty-six countries were also dominated by those in developing nations.[3] The crises in Japan, Southeast Asia and Russia are well worth discussing, however, as well as the savings and loan crisis in the USA in the 1980s and the banking crises in the Nordic countries in the 1990s.

In Table 8.1, the first column indicates the main year(s) of the crisis. This does not mean that the crisis was officially pronounced over at the later date. The Swedish crisis was, for all practical purposes, over in 1993, even though the blanket guarantee from the state for all banks' liabilities was in force until July 1996, and the Bank Support Agency was not dismantled until that very year. Similarly, the thrift crisis in the

---

[1] Paul Krugman, the Nobel Prize winner in Economics of 2008, has recently written a highly readable book on the crisis: Krugman, *The Return of Depression Economics*.
[2] Laeven and Valencia, *Systemic banking crises*.
[3] Reinhart and Rogoff, *This Time Is Different*.

Table 8.1 *Cost of different banking crises*

Year	NPL/loans (%)	Cost (% of GDP)	No. of bankrupt banks
Japan 1990–2002	35	24	180
Asia 1997–9			
Indonesia	33	57	83
Thailand	33	44	64
Korea	35	31	312
Iceland 2008–?	60?	80	4
Russia 1998	40	6	720
USA 1980–94	4	3.7	3,700
Sweden 1990–3	13	3.6	2–10
Norway 1988–91	16	2.7	7–15
Finland 1991–4	13	12.8	4
USA 2007–10	7	6.2	306+3[1]
UK 2007–9	6	9.1	4

Notes: Countries are listed in the order in which they are discussed in this chapter.
NPL = non-performing loans. Cost is the gross cost to the budget without consideration
to later repayments and disposals of assets.
[1] Meaning 306 banks and 3 investment banks.
Source: IMF and own calculations

USA was over in 1991, while the Resolution Trust Corporation that
handled failed thrifts was not abolished until 1995. Column 2 shows
non-performing loans as a percentage of total loans at the height of the
crisis. Column 3 shows the gross cost to taxpayers as a percentage of
GDP, thus not including repayments to the state, as toxic assets and
nationalized banks were sold back to the private sector. Column 4
shows the number of banks that were seized by the supervisory authorities, went bankrupt or were forcibly merged.

The table will be discussed further at the end of this chapter.

There are probably as many definitions of a systemic crisis as there are
economists who have tried their hand at such a definition. The important point is that it relates to problems on many financial markets which
interact and reinforce one another and which also create serious dis-
turbances on the real markets for goods and services. By this definition,
neither the crash of 1987 nor the dotcom crisis of 2000 was a financial
crisis, "only" market crashes. Mishkin (1995) has defined systemic risk

as "the likelihood of a sudden, usually unexpected, event that disrupts information in financial markets, making them unable to effectively channel funds to those parties with the most productive investment opportunities."[4]

This definition may suffice for the time being. Now over to the reality of banking crises.

Japan, 1990–2002

The drawn-out Japanese financial crisis[5] was engendered by the deregulations in the 1980s and the 1990s, and released by the fall in share prices and house prices from 1989, as well as by the Asian financial crisis in 1997.[6] A total of almost 200 financial institutions were closed at a cost to the government of 24 percent of GDP; seven banks were nationalized. Until 1997, the problems were of such a magnitude that they were handled within the resources of the banking system itself. From the middle of the 1990s, the housing crisis mainly affected the so-called "long-term credit banks," which earlier had had a monopoly on certain forms of borrowing, such as bank bonds, a separation of powers between commercial banks and long-term credit banks which was now abolished. The credit banks, having lost their raison d'être by this measure, were saved for the time being. Nippon Credit Bank, the third largest, received support from the Bank of Japan, but was nationalized when its problems continued. Two years later, the second largest, Long-Term Credit Bank of Japan (LTCB), was also nationalized. The largest credit bank, Industrial Bank of Japan (IBJ), merged in 2002 with Dai-Ichi Kangyo Bank and Fuji Bank, forming the Mizuho Financial Group, after this new type of financial conglomerate had been permitted.

---

[4] Mishkin, Comment on systemic risk, in Kaufman (ed.), *Research in Financial Services.*

[5] See Nakaso, The financial crisis in Japan; Posen and Mikitani (eds.), *Japan's Financial Crisis*, in particular Ben Bernanke, Japanese monetary policy: a case of self-induced paralysis?, and Benjamin M. Friedman, Japan now and the United States then: the lessons from the parallels.

[6] At the peak in 1990, the Japanese stock market was valued at almost four times Japan's GDP. This may be compared with the US dotcom bubble in 2000, when the stock market was valued at "only" twice GDP.

The year 1997 saw the first bankruptcy among the twenty largest so-called "city banks," which had hitherto been judged to be "too big to fail." Hokkaido Takushoku Bank, the tenth largest bank in Japan, was allowed to go bankrupt. As did the bankruptcy of Lehman Brothers 11 years later, this bankruptcy raised a question mark as to the intentions of the authorities, thereby making the crisis more acute than before. The Asian crisis in the summer of 1997 also created problems for the securities houses (corresponding to US investment banks), where Yamaichi Securities (the fourth largest) and Sanyo Securities became the first victims. The deregulation ("Big Bang") had increased competition both from domestic commercial banks and from foreign banks when prices were deregulated. The separation between banks and investment banks (§65 in the Japanese Securities Act, the equivalent of the Glass-Steagall Act in the USA) was also abolished. The surviving securities houses, however, are strong today. Nomura Securities took over the Asian and Japanese parts of bankrupt Lehman Brothers in October 2008. Through its subsidiary Instinet, Nomura Holdings also owns Chi-x in the UK, an Alternative Trading System (ATS), or multilateral trading facility (MTF) in EU-speak.

Until 1998, the main actions taken by the government had taken the form of liquidity support from the Bank of Japan. The fall in share and house prices revealed a weakness in the calculation of capital by Japanese banks. In sharp contrast to other countries, Japanese banks had been allowed to include 45 percent of surplus values in shares and property as Tier 2 capital. When the index Nikkei 225 had fallen from at most 38,000 in 1989 to 16,000 in the mid-1990s, there were no longer any excess values. The halving of property values in the first half of the decade made the situation even worse. Prices on commercial property in Tokyo fell by 70 percent. The OECD calculated the total capital loss in Japan for the years 1990–7 at 1,000,000 billion yen, corresponding to twice Japan's GDP.

The acute phase had also been postponed by the fact that a loan under Japanese rules did not become non-performing until after 6 months of non-payment of interest and amortizations, as contrasted to 3 months in the USA and Europe. During this drawn-out period, delinquent loans rose exponentially. In February 1998, new legislation allowed capital support to banks in trouble. This change was important, not least for maintaining the confidence of international investors and counter-parties.

Measured by total assets, six of the world's ten largest banks were at this time Japanese: Bank of Tokyo-Mitsubishi (number 1 in the world), Sumitomo (4), Dai-Ichi Kangyo (6), Fuji (7), Sanwa (8) and Sakura (9).

The first real solutions to the question of problem loans came in 1999. For the first time, an independent financial supervisory authority was created by breaking out its activities from the Treasury. Japan also instituted the program Prompt Corrective Action (PAC), including the adoption of the Western definition of delinquent loans, even when this meant an immediate rise in such loans. Prime Minister Hashimoto (Reuters, May 27, 1998) made clear that badly managed banks would be allowed to fail, while a total of 13,000 billion yen could be used to recapitalize well-run banks with capital deficiencies. A government agency, a bad bank, Resolution and Collection Bank Corporation (RCB), was set up to purchase bad loans from bankrupt banks, as well as from other banks with capital needs. The support fund from the government was increased dramatically, and, in contrast to earlier measures, the state could now also inject Tier 1 capital. The total funds available still only amounted to 30,000 billion yen, while delinquent loans were calculated at 100,000 billion yen and necessary write-downs at perhaps half this amount.

The government also saw through the merger of the twenty largest banks into five banking groups. As a result of the crisis, Japanese banks have lost their predominant position on the world market. Among the twenty-five biggest banks in the world (by total assets at end-2007) when the crisis started, one would find only three Japanese: Mitsubishi UFJ (number 9), Mizuho (14) and Sumitomo Mitsui (21). The last mentioned bought 2.1 percent of the share capital in Barclays Bank in July 2008. Mitsubishi UFJ invested $9 billion in Morgan Stanley in October 2008.

As a summary, we may note from Table 8.1 that the Japanese financial crisis was much more serious than the Nordic crises or the US thrift crisis, or, for that matter, today's US crisis, measured by non-performing loans and cost to the government in support. The main reason was the slow reaction by the government and the authorities. It took almost 10 years before the crisis was attacked in earnest. Financial crises must be resolved quickly! Compare this with today's financial crisis, which became acute in October 2008 and was over by the end of 2009.

The Asian crisis, 1997–1999

Like so many crises, the Asian crisis started undramatically but was to have dramatic consequences.[7] The devaluation by Thailand in July 1997 was in no way unexpected, having regard to the rapid growth of the country and the consequent rising deficit in the current account. Many observers had seen a devaluation coming, but the side effects became far worse than expected. The high growth rates of the Asian countries had given them the name "tiger economies," and just as was the case in the "new economy" in the USA, many believed the high growth rates were there to stay. Between 1990 and 1996, GDP grew by an average of 7.7 percent in Thailand, by 7.4 percent in (South) Korea and by 7.2 percent in Indonesia. Inflation was basically under control in Thailand and Korea, but accelerated to double digits in Indonesia. Growth was mainly generated by a wave of investments. The share of fixed investment in GDP was around 40 percent in both Thailand and Korea, a situation reminiscent of China today. The main difference, however, lies in the current account deficit. While China's investments have been aimed at the export industry, leading to a massive current account surplus and the world's largest currency reserves by far, the expansion in Southeast Asia was funded by borrowing, and the investments had taken place, in the main, in a gradually more overvalued property sector rather than in the real economy. In addition, the Chinese currency, the yuan, is still seen to be undervalued by some 30–40 percent, despite the revaluations of the last few years (as of October 2010), while the Asian currencies were sharply overvalued, as later development would show.

The current account includes not only exports and imports, but also interest payments to foreigners, which were accelerating. In 1996, Thailand had an external deficit of −8 percent of GDP, while corresponding figures were −5 percent in Korea and −4 percent in Indonesia. The exchange rates were pegged to the dollar, which made a gradual adjustment to changed conditions impossible. Instead, identical to the situation in the UK and Sweden in 1992, a change towards a more realistic rate of exchange came abruptly and forcibly. Borrowing in all three countries had basically taken place in dollars at low rates of interest while the money had been lent and invested in local currencies.

---

[7] This section draws on, inter alios: Delhaise, *Asia in Crisis*; Hunter, Kaufman and Krueger, *The Asian Financial Crisis*; Radelet and Sachs, The East Asian crisis.

The foreign debt levels had thereby attained 30–50 percent of GDP, and the borrowers were not the states but privately owned banks and finance companies. Another factor of importance was the maturity gap, with massive short-term borrowing, which needed to be rolled over frequently, financing lending at longer maturities.

At the beginning of 1997, capital movements turned outwards, not least because of rising yields on dollar-based assets. After some months of febrile but futile defense of the exchange rate, the central bank of Thailand gave up and, on July 2, 1997, allowed the baht to float. Some observers have claimed that it was the handover by the British government to China of Hong Kong the day before which created uncertainty as to the future of the region and triggered the final and decisive speculative attack. The consequence was an immediate fall in the baht of 20 percent. Half a year later, the baht had fallen by 55 percent. The foreign debt in local currency as well as interest payments became correspondingly more expensive and rose to 90 percent of GDP. On July 28, Thailand asked the IMF for assistance and on August 11 was granted support totaling $17 billion. The conditions for the loan will be discussed below.

The victims of the financial crisis in Thailand were not primarily banks, but independent as well as bank-owned finance companies. Finance One, the largest of the finance companies, in reality being one of the ten major banks, was the first to collapse, with liabilities of over $4 billion. On August 5, the central bank closed forty-eight finance companies. Before the crisis was over, fifty-nine of the original ninety-one finance companies, as well as five of fifteen banks, would be closed or nationalized. The Bank of Thailand also undertook to guarantee all liabilities of the remaining banks. A "bad bank," Radhanasin, was set up to manage and sell the bad loans of the banking system. At the peak, it owned 30 percent of total assets in the banking system.

The cost of the crisis to taxpayers would amount to 44 percent of GDP (according to the IMF), more than ten times the cost of the US thrift crisis or the Swedish or Norwegian crises. The rapid expansion in the area, with China as the main locomotive, helped to resolve the problem. By 2003, Thailand had repaid the loan to the IMF in advance, and by 2009, the exchange rate against the dollar had almost returned to the level it had in July 1997.

As a result of the fall of the baht, speculation ensued against the other currencies in the area. The Philippines was forced to abandon the dollar peg on July 11 and Malaysia on July 14. On August 14, Indonesia let its rupiah float; over the coming year it would fall by 70 percent. The country received a loan from the IMF of $23 billion at the end of October. Korea managed for the time being, but was felled by the stock market crash in Hong Kong at the end of October, which led to a fall of 23 percent in the Korean stock market index Hang Seng in just a few days. On November 17, Korea gave up and let the won float. The consequence was a depreciation of almost 40 percent. On December 4, Korea and the IMF signed the largest loan ever given by the IMF, $57 billion. Korea could not be allowed to fail. In economic terms, the country was as big as Thailand, Malaysia and Indonesia put together, and with regard to the threatening neighbor, North Korea, the economic and political stability of South Korea was vital to the entire region.

Korea's problems emanated from well before the financial crisis, but were exposed and released by the crisis. In April 1997, one of the major family-owned industrial conglomerates (*chaebol*), Hanbo Steel, had gone bankrupt. It revealed that one of the major banks, Korea First Bank, had exposures on Hanbo amounting to 60 percent of its equity, despite "creative accounting," which had artificially raised the perceived size of its capital. The true exposure far exceeded the bank's equity. The maximum according to international agreements ("large exposures") is 20 percent of capital. As a result of the undeveloped domestic capital market, the *chaebols* had debt-equity ratios of 7–8, most of the liabilities being in foreign currency. The third largest car manufacturer, Kia, had already gone bankrupt in July 1997 (but has since been resuscitated); Samsung Motors was bought by Renault. Daewoo Motors was purchased by GM, while its former president landed in jail for 10 years as a result of fraud and untruthful accounting.

The apparent stability of Korea was a result of the definition of non-performing loans. Just as was the case in Japan, a loan was only declared delinquent after 6 months of non-payment. While the official statistics claimed that only 4.5 percent of total loans were non-performing, foreign observers placed the figure at 12–15 percent of total loans as early as 1996, and the figure was predicted to rise to 30 percent within a couple of years. As a result, equity was already negative in the banking system as a whole, while the official BIS ratio was 9 percent, as against a required minimum of 8 percent.

Korea also set up a bad bank, Korea Asset Management Corporation, to handle the bad loans. A total of 312 financial institutions were closed.

Most of these were small credit unions, but four banks were nationalized, among them the two biggest, Korea First Bank and Seoul Bank. Five
banks were forcibly merged with stronger partners. The banking crisis is
estimated by the IMF to have cost more than 30 percent of GDP. Ten
years after the crisis, before the recent global crisis, the GDP per capita of
Korea had grown to $26,000 (to be contrasted with $8,500 in Thailand,
$3,900 in Indonesia, $47,000 in the USA and $36,600 in the UK, using
CIA data from 2008). By 2008, the exchange rate had basically returned
to pre-crisis levels, only to fall by 40 percent in the renewed crisis in
2007–9.

Indonesia is the fourth largest country in the world measured by
population, but it was number 20 in GDP terms. The reason for the
speculative attack which felled the rupiah was just as much political
unrest as economic problems. Indonesia also had a more deregulated
economy than its neighbors, which aggravated capital flight and hence
the depreciation. In 6 months, the rupiah fell by 85 percent, from 2,350
to almost 15,000 rupiah per dollar. President Suharto fired the governor
of the central bank, but was himself forced into exile in mid-1998. It was
claimed that the Suharto family had $40 billion invested abroad, which
may be compared with total currency reserves after the devaluation of
$140 billion.

The dramatic depreciation made the consequences of the crisis much
more severe in Indonesia than in the other affected countries. GDP
growth changed from 5 percent in 1997 to –14 percent in 1998, and
inflation exploded, from 12 to 47 percent. Out of 237 banks originally,
70 were closed down and 13 nationalized. The Indonesian Bank
Restructuring Agency was set up to handle bad assets of both private
and state-owned banks. The total cost of the crisis has been estimated by
the IMF at over 50 percent of GDP.

Despite the fact that the countries in the regions were saved by IMF
loans amounting to over $100 billion, the conditions for the loans led to
a situation where the IMF came to be blamed for the crisis, or at least its
aggravation. The financial crisis is still called "the IMF crisis" in Korea
and Indonesia. IMF came to stand for "I aM Fired." Some of the IMF
conditions were quite reasonable in view of the weak banking sector
and the accounting tricks that the previous legislation had allowed –
conditions such as recapitalization of surviving banks, restructuring
and mergers among the banks, the introduction of a separate financial
supervisory authority and a bad bank to handle the bad loans, the

abolition of all currency regulations, the introduction of a floating exchange rate, greater transparency in banks' accounts and new bankruptcy legislation.

But the IMF also required a prompt return to budget balance and measures to bring down the inflation rate, which in countries that had had huge savings ratios and budget surpluses before the crisis seemed strange, not to say cruel. The budget deficits were a natural consequence of the crises, just as the inflation was a natural consequence of the depreciations. Through its demands, the IMF forced countries to lower consumption standards, lower imports and hence balance the current account. But the price in terms of lower standards of living and higher unemployment was high. The critique has been merciless from such observers as Joseph Stiglitz, then Chief Economist at the World Bank and later Nobel Prize winner in Economics, and Jeffrey Sachs, professor at Harvard University and advisor to Russia and many other developing countries in transition to a market economy.[8]

Another factor contributing to the acute crisis was the actions by the ratings companies. Between January 2007 and December 2008, Moody's lowered the rating of Indonesia by five notches (from Baa3 to B2 – that is, junk), Korea by six notches (from A1 to Ba1 – that is, junk) and Thailand by five notches (from A2 to Ba1 – that is, junk). It is hardly an impressive performance by rating companies to treat all these countries as investment grade months before the crisis, only to sink them by these gigantic steps during the crisis.

Iceland, 2008–?

The Icelandic financial crisis is instructive for its own sake, but it may also serve as a summary of the Asian crises, since Iceland committed exactly the same errors as the Asian countries 10 years later and at twice the scale (in relationship to the size of the economy). On the macroeconomic plane, Iceland grew faster than surrounding countries in the first years of the new century, or by 4–6 percent per year. The focus of the government was aimed at achieving a better diversification of the economy, where the fishing industry still accounted for 20 percent of exports and 8 percent of employment. On the industrial side, Iceland

---

[8] Weisbrot, Ten years after, summarizes the critique. See also Feldstein, Refocusing the IMF.

wanted to utilize its cheap hydroelectric and geothermal energy for such energy-demanding industries as aluminum production. Service sectors such as tourism and banking were also in focus. The investment ratio in GDP was almost 30 percent and investments grew by over 20 percent annually.

The program was a spectacular success on the surface. Unemployment was negligible and Iceland rose in the "rich man's league" to position number 9 in the world, well above countries such as Sweden, Denmark or the UK. But the high growth rate had a drawback. Just like in Asia, there appeared a deficit in the current account which skyrocketed to –25 percent of GDP in 2006, only to fall back somewhat to –15.5 percent in 2007. The reason was improved exports, not least by the financial sector. Also just like in Asia, capital imports led to increases in house prices, which doubled between 2001 and 2007, rising 35 percent in individual years.

The three major Icelandic banks had seen spectacular growth. Kaupthing was started in the 1980s as a local broker-dealer, but grew to bank number 124 in the world by 2007, with total assets of $86 billion through a series of aggressive mergers. JP Nordiska Bank was acquired in Sweden, in Norway the broker Sundal, in the UK the bank Singer & Friedlander, in the Netherlands NIBS and in Belgium Robeco Bank. The bank had activities in thirteen countries. Funding was through the internet in the main, under the name of Kaupthing Edge (which alluded to "cutting edge"); accounts were booked in Iceland even when acquired locally.

Landsbanki and Glitnir, with assets of $49 billion and $48 billion, respectively, were somewhat smaller than Kaupthing, but still number 177 and 232 in the world. Like Kaupthing, Glitnir was really a broker-dealer with ambition. It purchased BN Bank in Norway, the brokerage firm Fischer Fondkommission in Sweden and FIM in Finland. Landsbanki had the different background of having been the central bank of Iceland, issuing currency notes, and through mergers it became a private bank as late as 2003. Just like Kaupthing, it then started purchasing aggressively, which led to its presence in fifteen countries. Like Kaupthing, the main funding was through the internet, under the brand name Icesave. An attraction to British customers was the promise to always pay at least twenty-five basis points better interest than the Bank Rate.

All together, at the end of 2007, the three banks had total assets of $184 billion. This may be compared with Iceland's GDP of $20 billion.

Liabilities in foreign currency were five times Iceland's GDP, and even netting out foreign currency assets, Iceland had liabilities in foreign currency amounting to 250 percent of GDP, over $40 billion of foreign debt. This may be compared with foreign exchange reserves of $2 billion. How Iceland's central bank, Sedlabanki, could stand passively and witness this development is incredible. The mismatch in currency is evidenced by the foreign indebtedness. The mismatch in interest rate was just as severe, with investments in residential mortgages funded by short-term deposits.

On the surface, the banks were stable and efficient, with BIS ratios of 11–12 percent and cost-income ratios of 0.47–0.56 (2007), fully in line with the major British banks having BIS ratios of 11 (Lloyds TSB) to 13.6 (HSBC) and cost-income ratios of 0.47 (HBOS) to 0.57 (Barclays). But the problem was that a central bank cannot be lender of last resort in foreign currency. As stated well by Mervyn King, Governor of the Bank of England, banks may be international in life, but they are national in death. The financial crisis was to expose mercilessly the mismatches in currency and interest of the Icelandic banks. Their subsidiaries in Europe were subjected to runs, in particular the British Singer & Friedlander. On October 7, the Icelandic financial supervisory authority nationalized Landsbanki and Glitnir, and the day after the Icelandic parts of Kaupthing. The Swedish subsidiary of Glitnir (ex Fischer FK) was sold to HQ Bank and its Norwegian subsidiary to the SpareBank 1 Group. Kaupthing's British subsidiary Singer & Friedlander was declared bankrupt and placed into administration by the Treasury, acting on advice from the FSA and the Bank of England. Its deposits were transferred to ING Direct, as were the deposits of Hardibanki, the British subsidiary of Landsbanki. Kaupthing Bank Sweden was nationalized under the National Debt Office and later sold to the Finnish bank Ålandsbanken, which thereby entered the Swedish market. The continued legal battles as to Kaupthing's Edge and Landsbanki's Icesave have been discussed earlier (pages 197ff.). In June 2009, Iceland declared itself legally responsible for depositors in these accounts, but lacking the possibility to repay. The issue of responsibility remains unsolved in late 2010.

From the middle of 2007 until June 2009, the Icelandic stock index OMXI15 fell by 97 percent, from index 9,000 to 270. On the other hand, it had risen 800 percent from 2001 to 2007. The currency has fallen from ISK 90 to the dollar to 181 (by October 2010), a depreciation of

50 percent, having been as low as ISK 340 to the dollar. As a result of the crisis, GDP fell by 7 percent in 2009, while inflation rose to 12 percent. The IMF projected the cost to the taxpayer at a stunning 80 percent of GDP, twice the cost of the Asian crisis and twenty times the US thrift crisis or the Nordic crises.

The Russian financial and economic crisis of 1998

Looking up the words "Russian crisis" on the internet, you find only articles on the crisis of 2007–9. But the recent crisis is irrelevant for this book, since it is a direct reflection of falling oil prices and not a result of financial imbalances per se. The fall in the price of oil from a maximum of $147 per barrel to $40 led to a fall on the Russian stock exchange (RTS index in dollars) of, at the trough, 78 percent. Russia has to a large extent survived the fall by its accumulated currency reserves of $600 billion (in August 2008). Not surprisingly, *The Economist* carried the headline "Russia resurgent" in its issue of August 16, 2008. The reserves still stood at $429 billion at end-May 2010, and the stock market had recovered a large part of the loss.

A more relevant systemic crisis to be compared with the others discussed in this chapter was the crisis of 1998, the one that triggered the collapse of LTCM in the USA.[9] The background to the problems was the fall of the Soviet Union in 1991. According to calculations by the statistical office (Goskomstat), GDP fell by 40–50 percent until 1996. The decline was very disparate in different parts of the economy, with industrial production falling more (50–60 percent) than services (20–30 percent), even though exact calculations are difficult to make, since the contribution to GDP of the "unproductive" service sector was not measured during the Soviet era. All calculations are made even more difficult by the size of the black economy, placed by Western sources at 40–50 percent of GDP. This fact had consequences, not least for tax collection. Another worrying trait was that fixed investments had fallen to a quarter of the level in 1990.

---

[9] A few instructive articles on the Russian crisis are listed below. Organisation for Economic Cooperation and Development, *Economic Survey of the Russian Federation*; Kharas, Pinto and Ulatov, An analysis of Russia's 1998 meltdown; Pinto, Gurvich and Ulatov, Lessons from the Russian crisis of 1998 and recovery.

The Asian crisis and the sharp fall of oil prices in 1997 and the first half of 1998 pointed the world's attention to the weaknesses of the Russian economy, and in particular to its dependence on oil exports. The RTS index halved in the first half of 1998 and the short-term rate of interest was raised to 150 percent to defend the rouble. Russia received a loan of $1.5 billion in the summer, when it was forced to pay a spread 650 basis points over US treasuries, contrasted with 250 points a year earlier. Moody's downgraded Russia's rating from Ba2 to B1. The national debt was still low by Western standards. The Federal debt was only 25 percent of GDP, but was growing fast. Over half of the debt consisted of short-term Treasury bills (GKO) and short-term bonds (OFZ), which had to be rolled over. Foreign investors owned 20 percent of the debt and were getting more and more unwilling to continue to invest in rouble-denominated assets. A rapidly increasing share of the debt (25 percent in 1997) consisted of foreign currency (OVZ, also called "taiga bonds"). The high nominal rates of interest, 200 percent just before the collapse, made the debt burden impossible. In July 1998, monthly interest payments on the national debt exceeded the total monthly revenue of the state.

Russia had had high ambitions for its banking sector, insolvent banks being allowed to fail. During the four years until 1997, 700 banks (out of a total of 2,000) had seen their licenses revoked. The central bank had already decided by 1999 that solvency ratios should be at Western levels – that is, a minimum of 8 percent of risk-weighted assets. A deposit-guarantee system was put in place. But the banking sector was hurt by the sky-high interest rates and by increasing lack of confidence from foreign depositors. Inadequate data increased the concerns. When the medium-sized Toko Bank (with the European Bank for Reconstruction and Development, or EBRD, as part-owner) was closed in May 1998, it turned out that its borrowings in foreign currency were at $125 million, far above what its accounts had indicated.

Political factors aggravated the situation. President Yeltsin had fired the popular Prime Minister Chernomyrdin in March 1998, together with the entire government, and in his place nominated the only 35-year-old energy minister Kiriyenko. He succeeded in arranging a loan from the IMF and the World Bank of $22.6 billion. This loan had just started to be paid out when speculation against the rouble forced the central bank to give up the fixed exchange rate on

August 17, 1998. The main reason behind the speculation was that parliament (the duma) had turned down the government's proposed tax hikes. The new exchange rate also turned out to be difficult to defend, and from September 2, the rouble floated, falling 45 percent against the dollar in a couple of months. Inflation rose to almost 100 percent. Simultaneously, a moratorium was declared on interest payments in dollars as well as roubles. As a result, Standard & Poor's downrated Russia to CCC with negative outlook – that is, only a notch above D, or default. The moratorium gave the central bank some breathing space, and the deposits by foreigners in failing banks were shifted to the state-owned savings bank Sberbank. Half of the remaining banks, 720 banks, were closed by the supervisory authorities. Among them was Oneximbank, the largest private bank in Russia, with $2 billion of deposits from foreigners, as well as the second largest, Inkombank, with EBRD as both part-owner and lender. The bankrupt banks together had accounted for one-third of all bank deposits. But thanks to the speedy closing down of failed institutions, the cost of the banking crisis came to be set at a relatively modest 6 percent of GDP.

Several factors contributed to solving the Russian problem much faster than anticipated. First, the duma changed its mind and accepted the tax raises, pushed by the IMF as a condition for further payments of the granted loan. Second, the IMF loan improved liquidity in dollars. Third, the weak and unpopular Kiriyenko was replaced by Yevgeny Primakov. He had altogether a different standing to Kiriyenko and the unique background of having been a professor of economics, general and deputy head of the security services, the KGB, speaker of Parliament and foreign minister. Fourth, the depreciation of the currency led to an increase in exports, aided also by the renewed increase in oil prices. As a consequence, Russia was already able to resume interest payments on November 15. GDP growth accelerated and the government budget was balanced in 2000. The government debt was reduced from at most 94 percent of GDP in 1999 to 42 percent in 2002. Russia today (October 2010) has a Baa1 rating with a stable outlook from Moody's.

The lesson is that even in a financial and economic crisis, speedy and decisive action to close down insolvent financial institutions is not only necessary, but may help in restoring confidence in the leadership and in the economy, and thus also turn the macroeconomy around.

The US "savings and loan" (thrift) crisis, 1980–1994

During the long period from the end of the Second World War until 1970, only twenty-five commercial banks failed in the USA. The 1970s saw the failure of seventy-nine banks – not a very large number, but among them were some big banks. In October 1973, San Diego National Bank went bankrupt. With deposits of almost $1 billion, it was the largest bank failure so far. The record was quickly broken in October 1974, when the New York-based Franklin National Bank, with deposits of $1.5 billion, failed and its assets were bought by the European American Bank. At the beginning of 1975, Security National Bank in New York was forcibly merged to avoid bankruptcy. The reason for the failure of these two banks (as well as Herstatt Bank in Germany) was the currency unrest created by the oil price increases in 1973–4 and the dollar's transition to a floating exchange rate from February 1973. The dollar fell (against the D-mark) by 15 percent in 1973 and by a total of 45 percent until 1980. Both Franklin National and Herstatt were important actors in the exchange market and had been long dollars. Difficulties for the city of New York in the mid-1970s accentuated problems for banks based in that city.

A clear indication of the lack of confidence in the banking system was that the interest spread between Treasury bills and certificates of deposits widened, from an average of 45 basis points in the 1960s to a maximum of 470 points in July 1974 (Franklin's difficulties became known in May). This was one of the reasons why the authorities in the USA and other countries decided on a more hands-on approach to problem banks. Banks would not be allowed to fail uncontrollably. During the far worse banking crises in the 1980s, this attitude led to the spread staying at around 100 basis points.

The crises in Franklin National and Security National had had a specific origin. A deeper and more general banking crisis began spectacularly in 1982 with the failure of Penn Square Bank in Oklahoma City, with $0.5 billion in deposits. It was vastly overshadowed when Continental Illinois in Chicago, then the seventh largest bank in the country, with $30 billion in deposits, was saved from bankruptcy by being nationalized by the FDIC in 1984. It would be sold only 10 years later, to Bank of America. During the years 1980–94, more than 1,600 commercial banks failed, the peak being 206 banks in 1989. Problem banks (according to FDIC criteria) varied between 600 and 1,000 at the end of the 1980s.[10]

The cost of the banking crises is related not only to the number of failed banks, but also to their sizes. From 1986, average assets in failed/merged/saved banks rose to $30 billion in 1989 and to over $60 billion in 1991, under the influence of such failed banks as Bank of New England in Boston, which by itself cost the FDIC $5.5 billion to take over.[11] To the failure of 1,600 commercial banks was added the far more serious thrift crisis. From 1980 to 1994, about a thousand savings banks were wound down, corresponding to one-third of the number at the beginning of the period.

The problem in the commercial banks was largely dependent on the Third World debt crisis. At the end of the 1970s, US banks, especially major ones, had extended credits to developing countries, mainly in Latin America. The reason was a lack of demand for loans from the domestic market following the low activity after the second oil price increase in 1979. Lending took place under a full understanding with the supervisory authorities and the government, which saw with pleasure that the deposits invested in dollars by the newly rich OPEC countries ("petro dollars") were transferred to the South American developing countries. The Chairman of Citibank, Walter Wriston, also declared that lending was risk-free, since a sovereign country cannot go bankrupt.

Around 1980, two events occurred which changed the situation radically for borrowers. First, the real rate of interest (the nominal rate minus inflation) rose sharply, from low or even negative numbers to 4–5 percent. Second, US rates of interest became extremely volatile after the change in monetary policy in 1979, to focus on money supply instead of interest rates. The focus on keeping a stable rate of growth in money supply led to all volatility being transferred to the rates of interest. Short rates of interest rose to 18 percent, and even long-term bond yields reached 15 percent at the peak. The problem was accentuated by the increased spreads paid by Latin American borrowers. Low demand for exports and high rates of interest led to gradually more

---

[10] Swary and Topf, *Global Financial Deregulation*, Table 13.4; Friedman, The risks of financial crisis, p. 20.

[11] While the bank's depositors were saved, investors in the bank's bond lost $914 million, according to Banks, *Volatility and Credit Risk*, p. 11.

difficult situations for the borrowing countries. Mexico failed on its payments in August 1982, when interest payments had risen to 34 percent of the country's export revenues. In the wake of Mexico, some forty other developing nations soon followed.[12]

The stabilizing factor (apart from the explicit abandoning of the failed monetary policy experiment on October 6, 1982) was the Brady plan, named after the then Treasury Secretary.[13] Agreements were made with Mexico, Argentina, Brazil, Venezuela and a number of smaller countries, as well as with their creditors. Banks faced a choice of three alternatives in order to get their lending guaranteed by the US government. One was to keep the nominal claim unchanged, but lower the rate of interest to 6.5 percent. A second option was to receive an accord of 35 percent of the loan, but guaranteed by the USA. The third option was to give new loans as the price for the total amount being guaranteed. In summary, we may point out that banks, as well as their supervisors, showed a surprising naivety towards "Third World debt." Interest rate margins were deceptively attractive, but were in fact far too low to compensate for the actual credit risk, a situation clearly reminiscent of the origins of today's crisis.

The next crisis was to be more difficult to resolve. The thrift crisis occurred in savings banks, in the USA being either exchange-listed savings and loan associations (S&L) or mutual savings banks.[14] These banks had long been entangled in regulations regarding the levels of deposit rates of interest ("Regulation Q"), maturities and direction of lending. Loans could only be given at 20- to 30-year fixed interest rates, and only to residential, 1–4 family houses within the state or within a radius of 100 miles (160 kilometers) from the head office. From the end of the 1970s, the savings banks were deregulated. In 1978, they were allowed to issue "money market certificates", the yield being tied to the Treasury bill rate. By the Depository Institutions Deregulation and Monetary Control Act (DIDMCA) in 1981, competition was opened up for competition with other savings banks, as well as with commercial banks. By using deposit brokers, a local savings bank in Texas

---

[12] Sachs, Managing the LDC debt crisis.
[13] See, inter alios, Sachs, Making the Brady plan work.
[14] This section builds on, inter alios, Barth, Trimbath and Yago (eds.), *The Savings and Loan Crisis*; Brumbaugh, Carron and Litan, Cleaning up the depository institutions' mess; Brumbaugh, *Thrifts Under Siege*; White, *The S & L Debacle*.

could reach new depositors in, say, Boston, New York and Los Angeles.

Deposits thus came to take place at variable money market rates. Lending, however, continued at long-term fixed rates. Savings banks in California had already been permitted to lend at variable rates (adjustable rate mortgages, or ARM) in 1975. These loans, however, were always restrained as concerned rate variations, both for individual years and over maturity ("lifetime rate cap"). The consequence of variable deposit rates and – in principle – fixed lending rates was a gigantic negative maturity gap. By this is meant that the rate of interest on liabilities adjusted more quickly than the rate of interest on assets. When the CD rate increased from 8.20 percent in 1978 to 15.91 percent in 1981, the loss to the savings bank sector could be calculated to be $20–30 billion per year. The total cost over the period has been calculated at some $100 billion.[15]

The sensitivity to interest rates was also increased by the fact that half the volume of residential mortgages had been collateralized as mortgage-backed securities (MBSs) and collateralized mortgage obligations (CMOs). The savings banks bought these bonds with the proceedings of the sold loans. But the exchange of assets had a drawback. A loan may be carried at nominal value so long as the borrower is not delinquent. Bonds must be marked to market, however, and they fall in value as interest rates rise. Bryan has calculated that the increase in interest rates during spring 1987 led to a fall in the value of mortgage bonds owned by savings banks corresponding to two-thirds of the banks' equity.[16]

The second reason behind the thrift crisis took place in 1983, when savings banks were allowed to lend without restrictions. So a Texas-based savings bank could chase deposits in Boston and New York and lend the money to residential as well as commercial property in Los Angeles and Chicago. The Garn-St Germain Depository Institutions Act (1982) had given savings banks the authority to lend 40 percent of total loans to commercial property. The effect was huge losses, as oil prices collapsed from $40 to below $10 a barrel. For the industrial world as a whole, the lower oil prices were a bonanza. For the US oil states it was an unmitigated disaster, as property prices fell. Losses in the savings

---

[15] Benston, Carhill and Olasov, The failure and survival of thrifts, p. 309.
[16] Bryan, *Breaking up the Bank*, p. 47.

bank industry were thus heavily concentrated regionally. One-quarter of the losses were in Texas alone and three-quarters came from just six states: Texas, Arizona, California, New York, New Jersey and Pennsylvania. Between 1986 and 1989, 296 thrifts were closed by their supervisory authority, the Federal Savings and Loan Insurance Corporation (FSLIC). The failed savings banks had assets of $125 billion. Having paid some depositors in these failed banks, the FSLIC was itself bankrupt.

The Financial Institutions Reform, Recovery and Enforcement Act (FIRREA) of 1989 created the Resolution Trust Corporation (RTC) to handle and sell assets of failed savings banks. The FSLIC was dismantled and its role transferred to the FDIC. The supervisor of the savings banks, the Federal Home Loan Bank Board, which had failed miserably in its mission, was also dismantled. Instead, an authority within the Treasury Department, the Office of Thrift Supervision (OTS), was formed.[17] The RTC dismantled a total of 747 savings banks, with assets of $394 billion, until 1995, when it was itself retired from service. The bill for resolving the crisis was set at $166 billion in 1989, rising to $325 billion according to the General Accounting Office (GAO) in 1990. This sum corresponds to 4 percent of GDP, virtually identical to the IMF figure in Table 8.1. The figure is also virtually identical to the cost of the Norwegian and Swedish crises (see below). A re-examination by the FDIC in 2000 reduced by half the gross amount, to $152 billion.[18]

The thrift crisis also led to several charges of corruption and embezzlement. Most well-known was the scandal in Lincoln Savings and Loan in Irvine, California. Its CEO, Charles Keating, had quintupled the bank's assets in as many years. The bank was formally a subsidiary of Keating's own building corporation. When both the holding company and the bank suspended payments in April 1989, it turned out that many investors had purchased commercial paper issued by the building contractor, not CDs issued by the bank, and hence this was not covered by deposit insurance. Nevertheless, it cost the FSLIC $3 billion, as the bank's assets were transferred to the RTC and sold off. Keating himself landed in jail for several years for fraud. Keating had also received

---

[17] Bankruptcies in such giants as Countrywide, Washington Mutual and IndyMac in the recent financial crisis would show clearly that the OTS was hardly better at its task than its predecessor.

[18] Curry and Shibut, The cost of the savings and loan crisis.

political support from a number of US senators, who themselves had received financial contributions from him. These were condemned by the Senate's ethics committee for poor judgment, but were not suspended or impeached. Among these "Keating Five" was found the 2008 Republican presidential candidate, John McCain.

The Nordic financial crises, 1987–1995

The crises in the Nordic countries were highly similar. The origin was deregulation of credit markets leading to a lending boom and "bubbles." The only major difference between the countries was the form of speculation: mainly residential real estate in Norway, commercial property in Sweden and stocks in Finland. The solutions involved widespread nationalizations in Norway, while in Sweden only two banks were nationalized, with the rest saved by a blanket guarantee from the government covering all bank liabilities. In the Finnish case, only one bank was formally nationalized, while the others were saved by the injection of hybrid capital instruments by the government. Aggravating the crisis in all three countries was a fixed rate of exchange which had to be abandoned. The crises can be treated in a relatively perfunctory manner, since they were entirely local and affected no other markets or countries. They are taken up here mainly to contrast origins and solutions, as well as comparing the magnitude of the crises and of the costs to taxpayers.

Sweden

The second half of the 1980s had been a period of extreme growth and high profitability in Swedish financial institutions: banks, mortgage banks and finance companies. After quantitative restrictions on both interest rates and lending volumes were lifted in 1985, lending expanded briskly. The volume of total loans doubled in the banking sector between 1986 and 1989, and increased by 60 percent in the mortgage banks. Just as in the present boom, homeowners used their new liberty to sharply increase consumption, with savings ratios falling into negative territory. Also like the present crisis, interest rates were not set at levels to compensate for the increasing risks, and banks were unaccustomed to setting rates of their own accord, so continued to shadow the discount rate. Indeed, several banks, such as the later failed

GOTA Bank, aggressively targeted volume growth rather than profit-ability, doubling its balance sheet in 2 years.

The first indications of a crisis came in September 1990, when one of the major finance companies was unable to roll over its commercial paper.[19] Rumors about losses in the sector, which had lent heavily to commercial property, spread rapidly and led to an acute liquidity crisis in the entire finance company sector. The three biggest companies were ultimately to fail, while the bank-owned finance companies were saved by their owners.

The rapid deterioration in the real economy from the autumn of 1990, with a fall in GDP by 5 percent over the next 3 years, was aggravated by several instances of interest rate shocks from the central bank to prop up the exchange rate: in October 1990 and December 1991. When the central bank took the unprecedented step in September 1992 of raising the overnight rate of interest to 500 percent, the collapse of the entire banking sector was seen as entirely possible. Even 3-month rates landed at over 30 percent, meaning that credit markets were effectively closed. The solution to the situation came with the next speculative wave, forcing the abandoning of the fixed exchange rate regime on November 19, 1992, letting the krona float.

Credit write-downs in the banking sector in 1990 rose to 1.1 percent of the stock of loans, a figure considered normal with regard to the oncoming recession. Some banks, however, were more affected than others. In particular, banks with no local knowledge, which had lent to the booming property sector in the major cities, lost heavily. Little Tomelilla Savings Bank succeeded in losing two-thirds of its entire loan stock in a single year. The big numbers, however, came from Nordbanken and GOTA Bank. The situation worsened at the beginning of 1991, and Nordbanken had to issue new shares to its major owner, the Swedish state, increasing the government share of ownership to 77 percent. In April 1992, the bank was nationalized completely. A "bad bank," Securum, was set up to handle the non-performing loans. Transfer of assets was easy, since the government owned both institutions and no haggle about a fair price was needed.

---

[19] Some books on the Swedish crisis are: Lybeck, *Finansiella kriser förr and nu*; Lybeck, *Facit av finanskrisen*. See also the more recent Jonung *et al.* (eds.), *The Great Financial Crisis in Finland and Sweden*.

The second problematic bank was GOTA Bank. After relatively modest credit write-downs in 1990 and 1991, they exploded to 20 percent of outstanding loans in both 1992 and 1993. Additional capital was urgently required, something which its owner, the insurance company Trygg Hansa, was unable to supply. The bank was nationalized in December 1992 and its non-performing loans transferred to a bad bank, Retriva. In 1993, the two state-owned banks were merged to form the Swedish part of what is today Nordea, where the Swedish state remains the major owner, with 20 percent of the share capital as a result of the crisis almost 20 years ago.

In 1992 and 1993, the crisis peaked, with credit write-downs of an average of 7 percent both years for the banking sector. At the peak, some 13 percent of all loans were non-performing, a figure which may be compared with 9 percent in the USA in June 2009. Table 8.2, however, shows that there were sharp differences between well-managed banks such as Handelsbanken and the banks that were ultimately to fail, Nordbanken and GOTA Bank. Ailing savings banks were saved by merging into what is today Swedbank, without any other support from the government than a guarantee for its interest payments. The small banks in trouble where credit write-downs were large in relative terms were saved by their owners (JP-Bank by the cooperatives, Östgöta

Table 8.2 *Credit write-downs per bank (SEK billion), 1990–1993*

Bank	Write-downs (SEK billion)	Percent of loans
Nordbanken	46.0	21.4
Sparbanken Sverige (Swedbank)	38.8	17.6
GOTA	29.1	37.3
SEB	24.5	11.7
Handelsbanken	16.5	9.5
Föreningsbanken	10.7	16.6
Other savings banks	4.3	9.7
Foreign-owned banks	2.2	13.6
Östgöta Enskilda Bank	1.6	10.6
JP-Bank	0.6	35.2
Bohusbanken	0.4	22.9
Total	174.7	16.8

Source: Jan Wallander in Bankkriskommittén, *Bankkrisen*, p. 80.

Enskilda Bank by the Lundberg group, and Föreningsbanken by the Farmers Association).

The total write-down was financed in equal parts by capital injections by the government, additional capital from the owners and the increased profitability in the banking sector from 1993. In addition, in September 1992, the government undertook to guarantee all liabilities of the banking system except perpetuals – that is, undated subordinated notes being a part of the banks' Tier 2 capital.

In total, SEK 65 billion was injected by the government into the two ailing banks, including Securum and Retriva, corresponding to the 3.6 percent of GDP indicated in Table 8.1 (page 281). Jennergren and Näslund found that the cost to taxpayers had already been halved to SEK 35 billion 5 years later, as a result of asset sales.[20] Given the remaining government interest in Nordea which it plans to sell, the government support has been repaid totally, with no cost to the taxpayer.

Norway

Norway started its process of deregulation a few years before Sweden, and hence the crisis also came earlier.[21] Credit write-downs had already reached the 1 percent mark in 1987 and continued to accelerate until 1991, the year when all three major commercial banks were de facto nationalized. Problems were aggravated in oil-rich Norway by the abrupt fall in oil prices in 1987. A few aggressive smaller banks were placed under observation by the local financial supervisory authority, Kredittillsynet. Losses doubled in the system as a whole in 1988, and one of the smaller banks, Sunmörsbanken, was taken over by the Deposit Insurance Fund and merged with Kreditkassen, the second largest bank. Likewise, the savings banks' Deposit Insurance Fund and the Bank of Norway recapitalized and helped to engineer mergers of several savings banks in trouble. A failing commercial, Norion, was placed in administration and wound down, the first such event in Norway since 1923.

During 1987–90, the two deposit guarantee funds had helped to recapitalize three commercial banks and twelve savings banks, and

---

[20] Jennergren and Näslund, Efter bankkrisen.
[21] This section builds on, inter alia, the official investigation Norges Offentliga Utredningar, *Bankkrisen*.

were themselves bankrupt. The Norwegian state thus set up a government deposit guarantee fund for both savings banks and commercial banks. Its funds being depleted already, the following year it was supplemented by a government fund especially set up for government ownership of banks. On October 14, 1991, the second largest bank, Kreditkassen, notified the supervisory authorities that its capital was entirely depleted, despite earlier capital injections by the state funds. The bank was nationalized in its entirety and recapitalized. Only a few weeks later, the proceeding was repeated with Focus Bank, number three. Later that autumn, the largest bank, Den Norske Bank, received capital support and became 85 percent owned by the government.

From 1992, the economic situation ameliorated and credit write-downs fell from 6 percent in 1991 to 4 percent in 1992 and 2 percent in 1993. The savings bank sector became profitable in 1992, and in 1993, the entire banking system was back in black. The total cost of the crisis to taxpayers came in at 30 billion Norwegian crowns, or 4 percent of GDP, virtually identical to the Swedish case, despite the fact that the crisis had been far more widespread.[22] The two crises are also similar in terms of causes and developments. From deregulation, it took 3–5 years to build up a stock of non-performing loans sufficiently large to overwhelm the system. In Norway, the stock of loans doubled between 1984 and 1987; in Sweden, it doubled between 1986 and 1989.

One reason why Norwegian banks had to rely more on government support lay in the construction of loss reserves. Swedish banks had been able to use their profitability to build up reserves for expected losses. Until 1988, Norwegian banks were only allowed to deduct 1 percent of the loan stock each year until the loss reserve fund had attained 5 percent, and their contributions to the deposit guarantee funds turned out to be totally inadequate.

Focus Bank is today part of the Danish Danske Bank, Kreditkassen, a part of Nordea. Den Norske Bank is today DnB NOR, after its 2003 merger with the insurance company Gjensidige NOR. The Norwegian state still owns 34 percent of DnB NOR, but has no remaining ownership in Nordea or Danske Bank.

---

[22] The IMF study in Table 8.1 (page 281) indicates a slightly lower figure, 2.7 percent.

Denmark

In contrast to its Scandinavian neighbors, and in contrast to today, Denmark did not experience a financial crisis in either the 1980s or the 1990s. There were several reasons for this. First, the Danish credit markets were never regulated by means of quantitative restrictions as the other three countries were. Second, Denmark adopted a hard-currency policy in the early years of the decade, shadowing first the D-mark and then the euro. Hence the economy never overheated and there were no speculative excesses or bubbles. Instead, Danish banks faced continuous problems on a smaller scale, related to economic problems in the household sector caused by the strong currency.

A further contrast is that Denmark had started a system of deposit guarantees well before the others. This bank-financed fund saved three small banks in 1992. Problems in the tenth largest bank, Vardabanken, were solved by the central bank in cooperation with the other banks, a system which, as we saw above, was used initially in today's crisis, but which turned out to be inadequate in a major crisis.

Finland

Credit write-downs in Finland were negligible until 1991.[23] The comparison with the Scandinavian countries is unfair, however, since Finnish banks were only allowed write-downs on realized credit losses, not expected losses. Deregulation also took place later in Finland than in Sweden or Norway. The Finnish crisis erupted abruptly in September 1991, when the fourth largest bank, Skopbank (which was the head of the savings bank system), had to be taken over by the Bank of Finland. The situation was aggravated by the collapse of the Soviet Union and the consequent fall in Finnish exports. GDP fell by over 6 percent in 1991. The currency was devalued by 12 percent in 1991 and by another 12 percent in the general currency crisis in 1992 (which also felled the UK and Sweden), and the markka was allowed to float.

Anticipating further problems, a government fund was started which took over the ownership of Skopbank. The Finnish savings banks which had merged into Sparbanken Finland ran into problems of such magnitude that the only solution was for the state to take over

---

[23] See Koskenkylä and Vesala, Finnish deposit banks 1980–93.

and divide the bank into four equal parts, which were sold to the four major banking groups, which were still relatively stable: Kansallis Osake Pankki (KOP), Föreningsbanken/Union Bank of Finland (UBF), Postipankki and OKO-Bank. The non-performing loans in the savings banks were placed in a government-owned bad bank, Arsenal. KOP, however, had to accept a government capital injection to be able to afford the purchase.

Credit losses continued in 1992 and 1993, together with a gradually worsening economic situation. GDP fell by 13 percent in 3 years, 1991–3, and unemployment rose to 20 percent. When the danger was finally over in 1995, the banking crisis had cost Finnish taxpayers 12.8 percent of GDP, three times the cost of the crisis in Norway or Sweden. As a result of the crisis, the Finnish state still owns 14 percent of the insurance company Sampo, which had bought (and later sold) Postipankki. In the other banks, the capital needed was injected in the form of subordinated debt, which has since been repaid. KOP and Föreningsbanken (which had merged to form Merita Bank) today form the Finnish part of Nordea Bank. OKO Bank is today Pohjola Bank.

Summary and a comparison with today's crisis

There are many similarities between the Nordic banking crises and the US thrift crisis. Deregulations and new instruments or environments (MBSs, pricing policy) which the banks could not handle were behind the crises, which were very similar in development as well as costs. It takes 4–5 years for a critical level of non-performing loans to be built up, and an equally long period to sort out the problems.

The RTC in the USA was started in 1989 and abolished in 1995. The Swedish Bank Support Agency, as well as the "bad bank" Securum, were set up in 1993 and abolished in 1996 and 1997, respectively. The Finnish bad bank Arsenal was established in 1993, and even if it was not wound down until 2003, the crisis was over, in the main, by 1998. The costs were similar in the USA, Norway and Sweden, but higher in Finland as a result of the Soviet collapse. None of these crises reached the heights of the Asian (not to mention the Icelandic!) crises, however.

In the fragmented US banking system, many more banks failed in the 1980s (3,700) than in the more concentrated Asian banking system, and even more so in the Nordic financial system.[24] In Table 8.1, I have stated two to ten failed banks in Sweden, depending on how one wants to make the calculation. Only two banks were nationalized, and formally, only the holding company GOTA AB went bankrupt. We reach the higher figure by adding those savings banks which would have failed had they not merged into Swedbank. More banks were nationalized in Norway, and, as in Sweden, we reach the higher figure by adding the ailing but merged savings banks. In Finland, the included banks are Skopbank, STS-banken, Sparbanken Finland and KOP, while, as mentioned, the state did not put any equity into the other banking groups.

Can we compare these crises with the present (US) crisis? Most definitely! In the US banking system, non-performing loans amounted to 5 percent of all loans at the end of 2009, if we use the 90-day delinquency rate, and 9 percent if we use the 30-day delinquency rate (see Figure 4.5, page 132). Since the beginning of 2007 until September 2010, 306 banks had failed, to which we may add the investment banks Bear Stearns, Merrill Lynch and Lehman Brothers (see www.fdic.gov/bank/individual/failed/banklist.html).[25]

The cost to the taxpayer of the present US crisis, however, has been negligible so far. The FDIC has been involved in a number of mergers, as well as the nationalization of IndyMac and some smaller banks, later sold back to the private sector. The guarantees given to the new owners of IndyMac have been calculated to amount to between $8.5 billion and $9.4 billion. In the various mergers, the deposits were taken over by the acquiring bank, but the toxic assets were left with the FDIC and sold off. As a consequence, the Deposit Insurance Fund fell, to become negative by 2010. As noted earlier, fees have been raised sharply to restore the

---

[24] Denmark differs from its Nordic neighbors in still having around 150 banks, some of them very small, not counting subsidiaries or branches of foreign banks.

[25] See also the comparisons in Reinhart and Rogoff, Is the 2007 sub-prime financial crisis so different? The five "big crises" which the authors use as a comparison with today's crisis are Spain (1977), Norway (1987), Sweden (1991), Finland (1991) and Japan (1992). The authors do not underline the fact that the Nordic crises were aggravated by a fixed exchange rate system, in contrast to today. It is also difficult to have an opinion about Spain, where the Franco regime had just disappeared in the 1970s and which was not yet a member of the European Community, which was to give political stability as well as economic aid.

size of the fund. These losses are the only losses realized so far and they are borne not by taxpayers but by the banks themselves, via the Deposit Insurance Fund.

The Federal Reserve has lent a couple of trillion dollars under the various programs presented in Chapter 6. It should be remembered that all securities bought or guaranteed have been evaluated with a "haircut" – that is, there was a margin for future losses. According to its own accounts, the Federal Reserve actually made a gain through 2009 on securities acquired from bailing out Bear Stearns and the insurer American International Group (AIG). Securities with a face value of $62 billion were purchased for $30 billion in September 2008. After falling to $22 billion at the lowest point, they were calculated to have a market value of $45 billion at the beginning of 2010. At the end of March 2010, these securities, taken as collateral and placed in SIVs called Maiden Lane I, II and III, were worth $6 billion more than the underlying loans granted.[26] In the fall of 2010, AIG was allowed to draw unused TARP funds in order to allow a total repayment of the Federal Reserve loans.

The US state has helped with capital injections and guarantees. Of the $700 billion of TARP money, $476 billion had been spent by September 2009 (see Table A7.2):

- Around 600 banks have sold preference shares to the government. The amount outstanding was $205 billion. The sums invested per bank varied between $25 billion and $442,000.
- Citibank and Bank of America had each received an extra $20 billion, plus a guarantee to Citi worth $5 billion.
- AIG had received an injection of $70 billion in preference shares, now converted to common stock.
- $20 billion had been promised to cover losses on the Fed's TALF-program.
- GM and Chrysler, and their finance companies GMAC, turned bank, and Chrysler Financial Services received a total of $82 billion.
- Various public programs had spent $54 billion.

---

[26] See Board of Governors of the Federal Reserve System, *Credit and Liquidity Programs and the Balance Sheet* (published monthly).

The total sum to be spent, $700 billion, corresponds to some 5 percent of GDP. But there is reason to believe that most of the funds will be repaid.[27] (See below.)

The Reconstruction Finance Corporation (RFC) was started in the 1930s to give capital aid to banks with solvency problems. A total of 6,000 banks received $1.3 billion, corresponding to 2–3 percent of the GDP of 1933. This would be equivalent to some $200 billion of today's dollars. Taxpayers received repayments corresponding to basically the entire sum.

During the thrift crisis of the 1980s, the Resolution Trust Corporation (RTC) was set up to handle failed savings banks. A total of 747 banks, with total assets of $394 billion, were wound down and their assets sold. The cost to the taxpayer at the end of the crisis, of $124 billion, corresponding to 2 percent of GDP, should be compared with the gross expense of 3.7 percent of GDP, as stated in Table 8.1.[28]

The TARP program was initially calculated to cost $341 billion. In April 2010, these estimates were later cut to $127 billion by the President's Office of Management and Budget, corresponding to less than 1 percent of GDP. Indeed, the $205 billion invested in the banking sector had been largely repaid, with a profit to the Treasury of $19 billion. The remaining calculated losses were hence attributable to the insurance company AIG ($50 billion), the two rescued auto firms and their finance companies ($31 billion) and $49 billion for the Home Affordable Modification Program.[29] In September 2010, the Congressional Budget Office lowered the estimated final cost of TARP even further, to $66 billion, or a minute 0.5 percent of GDP. At the same time, the Treasury Department estimated the final cost at an even lower $51 billion ($17 billion to the auto industry, $46 billion to the home-owner program, minus the gain on bank support).

---

[27] Since the mortgage institutions Fannie Mae and Freddie Mac have been placed under public administration, capital injections and loans to these institutions no longer count as an expense to the state, but as a transfer between different agencies. The limitation lies instead in the ceiling decided by Congress on the total size of the Federal debt, raised to $14.3 trillion in February 2010.

[28] Curry and Shibut, The cost of the savings and loan crisis.

[29] Reuters, December 12, 2009; *The Economist*, January 16, 2010; Guerrera, US collects $10.3bn from Citi bail-out; SIGTARP, Quarterly Report to Congress, April 20, 2010.

Taxpayers have also received a nice return on their investments. When Goldman Sachs repaid its $10 billion of TARP money, the government cashed in $318 million in dividends on the preferred stock, and an additional $1.1 billion for the warrants held by the government and repurchased by the bank. The firm calculated that the TARP investment gave the taxpayer an annualized return of no less that 23 percent.

Regarding the bank where the government was and is most heavily involved, Citigroup, by June 2010, the Treasury had offloaded in the market half of its holdings of common stock, bringing its ownership down to 18 percent, while cashing in a $2 billion profit, to which must be added the $3 billion it has received in dividends from its holdings of preferred stock. The value of these securities, which the government got for free, is over $5 billion.

For 2009, the Treasury calculated a gross profit on the sold warrants from thirty-four banking organizations at $2.9 billion. The average return on the TARP investment in these institutions, including dividends and profit on warrants, was 8.8 percent. In October 2010, Bloomberg calculated a similar 8.2 percent return on all money spent on banks and insurance companies over the 2-year period. On top of these profits, the Federal Reserve earned capital gains of several billions on CDOs, as noted above, the actual profit being determined only when the bonds have been sold.

In the UK, the Chancellor initially calculated that the government was likely to lose about £60 billion from the rescue of British banks, including RBS, Lloyds TSB, Bradford & Bingley and Northern Rock. However, the IMF stated in its *Global Financial Stability Report* in the spring of 2009 that the eventual cost to British citizens would be a lot higher, amounting to some £140 billion, or almost £5,000 for every UK taxpayer. The loss is related to the fact that the banks were set to lose money throughout this crisis, and the value of the shares bought by the government was unlikely ever to recover fully. At 9.1 percent of GDP, this total cost was among the worst of any major industrialized nation, even though the IMF has since scaled it down, to 6.5 percent of GDP in April 2010.

It should be pointed out, however, that, just like in any other crisis, this sum will in all likelihood turn out to be much smaller when the final result is published. Indeed, a new British report in December 2009 set the total cost at an astonishingly low £8 billion, or 0.5 percent of

GDP.[30] Whether the IMF or the British Treasury will ultimately prove right remains to be seen. Given the verdict of earlier crises, my money is on the Treasury.

Points to remember

- The recent financial crisis has many similarities with earlier crises in history. The similarities with the crises of 1907 and 1929 were discussed in Chapter 6. In this chapter we have presented, discussed and compared crises during the last 20 years.
- Financial crises have most often occurred as a result of an external event. The Nordic crises, the crises in Asia and Japan, and the US thrift crisis were all the result of deregulation, the consequences of which neither the banks nor their supervisors could master. The Russian crisis of 1998 was mostly the result of falling oil prices, but had serious financial effects.
- Some crises, such as the Nordic and Asian crises, have been aggravated by the defense of a fixed exchange rate.
- Today's crisis has been aggravated by the presence of instruments which have shifted the risk away from the loan originator. But MBSs and CMOs were already present in the thrift crisis of the 1980s. Many banks had securitized loans to create more liquid assets, buying them back in the form of bonds. These had to be marked to market, however, in contrast to the loans. As a result of rising interest rates, losses in savings banks were mostly as a result of the interest rate risk rather than the credit risk.
- It takes time for a crisis to develop and it takes time for it to be resolved. From the releasing events, it takes 3–5 years to build up a critical level of non-performing loans, and a similar period to address the problems.
- Today's financial crisis may be expected to cost several times the thrift crisis or the Nordic crises. The earlier Asian crises, not to mention today's Icelandic crisis, however, are vastly worse.

[30] *The Economist*, January 16, 2010.

9 | *Worldwide changes in regulation and supervision as a result of the crisis*

Many things have been, or are in the process of being, changed as a result of the recent financial crisis. Some of these changes have already been discussed in earlier chapters, such as new rules for *capital requirements* and *liquidity ratios*, and ceilings on *bonus payments* in banking. While the higher demands on banks' capital and liquidity ratios may be postponed until 2012 or even later, they *will* come, say the leaders of the G-20 countries, and this, after all, is the important factor in influencing banks' decision-making and, in particular, risk-taking. It is mainly in the USA, after the Republicans' control of the House of Representatives as a result of the mid-term election of 2010, that doubts remain about how harshly the decisions already taken will be implemented. Detailed decisions that have to be made concern such things as the role of proprietary trading, capital requirements, derivatives trading and clearing, and, not least, the power to break up firms that are "too big to fail."

The financial crisis of the first decade of the twenty-first century would have been vastly more serious without the experiences from earlier crises, which led to changes in the financial system and in the supervision of the financial markets. *Deposit insurance* to prevent bank runs was introduced in the USA directly after the Great Depression, but in Europe only in the 1990s in most countries. Luckily, deposit guarantee schemes were in operation when today's crisis struck, else we would have seen far more bank runs.[1] They need to be improved in two ways. First, the level of protection must be made permanent, at least at the present levels, or, preferably, increased further. The European Union has proposed that the level be raised from €50,000 to €100,000 (or

---

[1] The reader who feels an irresistible urge for a strict mathematical proof of why deposit insurance is necessary is encouraged to read Repullo, Policies for banking crises.

equivalent).[2] It should be doubled to agree with US limits. The USA will keep its present limit at $250,000 rather than let it fall back to earlier levels in 2014, as originally planned. Generosity will certainly pay off; after all, it is the banking system itself, not the taxpayer, which foots the bill. Second, it is of the utmost importance that the fees reflect the actual riskiness of a particular bank, as is already the case in the USA. At least one EU member state, however, has already introduced variable deposit insurance fees.[3]

The understanding that *liquidity* is the critical factor behind most banking crises was drawn already in the crisis of 1907 by the banker J. P. Morgan, as we saw in Chapter 6. This insight appeared forgotten during the Great Depression, until its role was re-emphasized by scholars such as Milton Friedman and Anna Schwartz in the 1960s, not forgetting later work by Ben Bernanke *et consortes*. Among actions taken to enhance liquidity may also be counted guarantees given by the government to other bank creditors than depositors. Even if one should let shareholders pay the price for their ignorance and negligence when recapitalizing and/or nationalizing banks, holders of bank bonds and other priority liabilities must be saved, or confidence in the financial system will evaporate.[4]

Not least in the case of Ireland, which is the EU country hardest hit by the financial crash (relative to its GDP), there has been a discussion of where to draw the line. After equity and subordinated debt have been wiped out, should taxpayers bear the residual loss or should bondholders also participate in the losses? And what will be the consequence for future investors' demands for yield should such a loss-participation scheme be introduced?

One must, however, separate instances when a bank remains a going concern from those when it is closed down by the supervisory authorities. Subordinated debentures and other forms of "mezzanine" capital

---

[2] Tait, EU to step up compensation for fraud cases; Tait, Wilson and Masters, Banks hit at pay-out proposals.

[3] The country in question is Sweden, where banks pay a fee varying from 0.06 to 0.14 percent, depending on their capital-adequacy ratios. See the Swedish National Debt Office's home page: www.insattningsgarantin.se/sv/For-finansiella-institut/Anslutning-till-IG-och-IS/Instituten-betalar-olika-avgifter

[4] An exception, of course, is the earlier mentioned CoCo bonds, which convert automatically to common stock if the bank's Core Tier 1 ratio falls below a preset level (6 percent in the case of Lloyds).

may be available to cover losses, thus protecting depositors and other senior creditors, if the ailing bank is closed down, but not so long as it remains in business. This implies that systemically important, large banks, deemed to be "too big to fail," should face stricter conditions on the use of subordinated debt and hybrids in their capital ratios, since their liquidation is unimaginable.[5] This reinforces the view stated below that systemically important banks should have an extra capital cushion, just because they are big and may expect to be saved.

A third factor which has contributed to mitigating the effects of today's crisis is the *build-up of capital*, in particular equity capital, as a result of the Basel I rules from 1988. In the 10 years from 1998 to 2007, Tier 1 capital in the world's 1,000 largest banks doubled from $1,676 billion to $3,399 billion. It was to become sorely needed. In today's crisis, some $1,800 billion have already (July 2010) been spent in write-downs by banks on assets related to the housing market, corresponding to almost half the banks' capital base at the beginning of the crisis. Yet profitability and initial public offerings (IPOs) – that is, issues of new equity – as well as government injection, has led to a capital base (Tier 1) in the 1,000 largest banks that attained almost $5,000 billion at the end of 2009.

In this chapter, we are going to focus on the remaining issues, regulation and supervision of banking. By *regulation* is meant the formulation of the rules of the game for banks to follow. By *supervision* is meant the act of seeing to it that banks follow what has been prescribed.

The chapter is divided into the following sections:

- How should authorities react in an acute crisis?
- Banks too big to fail have become even bigger!
- Do scale economies justify big banks?
- How to limit the size of banks too big to fail
- Will bank taxes and financial stability funds alleviate the next crisis?
- How should hedge funds be supervised?
- Host- or home-country control?
- How will supervision be organized and coordinated in the USA in the future?
- How will the consumer be protected?

---

[5] See Financial Services Authority, A regulatory response to the global banking crisis, pp. 67 and 69.

How should authorities react in an acute crisis?

The unanimous conclusion from both theoretical works and practical analyses is that action needs be taken rapidly before ailing banks are able to take on yet larger risks in order to attempt to recoup their losses and in this way threaten even more banks. The longer one waits, the greater will be the costs to the Deposit Insurance Fund, to the government and, ultimately, to the tax payer.[6]

The reason for a speedy intervention is not least that a crisis may be simmering and then suddenly burst, expressed well in the following quote:

It is rather tempting to see financial crashes as the analogue of critical points in statistical mechanics, where the response to a small external perturbation becomes infinite, because all the subparts of the system respond cooperatively.[7]

The development of the financial crisis through 2007 and the beginning of 2008, and then the sudden explosion in September 2008, bears witness to this line of thought, "the last straw breaks the laden camel's back ..."[8]

A book on "safe and sound banking" summarizes the policy needed, with experiences gathered from the US thrift crisis in the 1980s:

If the bank is not declared insolvent when the market value of net worth is zero, but only after it has become negative, the consequences are likely to be more severe for the community than if it were declared insolvent sooner ... If economically insolvent banks are not declared insolvent, losses will accrue to uninsured creditors and/or the insurance agency as well as to shareholders. The timing of the declaration of insolvency affects the identities of the parties,

---

[6] Some economists from the World Bank have challenged these conclusions in an interesting and provocative article. They have analyzed financial crises in thirty-two countries. They find that in the cases where the government interfered with unlimited guarantees for the banking system and with ample liquidity support, the end result was both greater public expenses and larger economic loss in terms of production than in other countries. One wonders, however, if their econometric results do not depend on inverse causality – that is, in countries where the crises have been more severe for other reasons (such as a fixed rate of exchange or falling oil prices), the governments have been forced to take more extensive action. See Claessens, Klingebiel and Laeven, Resolving systemic crises.

[7] Aguilar *et al.*, Are financial crashes predictable?

[8] This well-known saying is actually a quote from Charles Dickens, *Dombey and Son* (1848).

including the insurance agency, who will bear the losses ... Moreover, as net worth becomes smaller and eventually negative, ... the bank is progressively encouraged to increase its risk exposure in the hope of winning big and staying alive.[9]

Hence the insolvent bank must be taken over and closed by its supervisor, its deposits being sold to another – but solvent – bank. Alternatively, the insolvent bank may itself be merged with another bank. The deposit guarantee fund (the FDIC in the USA) will usually have to bear the cost for the non-performing loans, either taking them onto its own books in order to sell them later on or guaranteeing the purchasing bank from the future losses involved. A third alternative, if the bank is believed to be viable in the longer run, is to recapitalize it partly or fully with government – that is, taxpayer – money.

The Harvard professor Benjamin Friedman has drawn similar conclusions in contrasting how the financial crises in the USA and Japan, respectively, were handled:[10]

- act quickly;
- do not allow insolvent organizations with inadequate capital adequacy to continue;
- force ailing banks to merge;
- sell the assets which have been placed under public administration;
- punish the shareholders, not the depositors or the holders of bank bonds;
- monetary and fiscal policy must both be expansive in order to facilitate the restructuring of the banking system.

Similar thoughts echo from the Swedish financial crisis in the 1990s:[11]

- A clear coordination between the political system and the supervisory authorities guaranteed that measures were carried out in an effective and efficient way and were regarded as credible. The setting-up of a Bank Support Agency (*Bankstödsnämnden*) facilitated the coordination between the Treasury, the Central Bank, the financial supervisory authority and the National Debt Office.

---

[9] Benston *et al.*, *Perspectives of Safe and Sound Banking.*
[10] Benjamin M. Friedman, Japan now and the United States then: the lessons from the parallels, in Posen and Mikitani (eds.), *Japan's Financial Crisis.*
[11] Proposition 2008/09:61, Stabilitetsstärkande åtgärder för det svenska finansiella systemet [Measures to strengthen the Swedish financial system], p. 211.

- Rapid, conclusive and measured actions to handle problematic banks were decisive for restoring confidence.
- A clear and predictable set of rules for actions to be taken gave the possibility of solutions which were aimed at the specific situation of a particular bank and were important for the efficient handling of the situation.
- Clear incentives for both bank owners and management to minimize the use of government support lowered the ultimate cost to the taxpayer.
- Government support was given in forms which gave the state precedence to repayments when the situation for the bank receiving support improved. State "bad banks,"[12] such as Securum and Retriva, were set up to administer and claw back the delinquent loans in banks and the underlying collateral.
- Even in the case where the state becomes an important owner in a bank, that bank is to be run on strictly commercial grounds. The state should use its influence to ascertain that the bank acts according to the conditions on which the support has been given.
- There should be demands for a high level of transparency, both from the banks and from the authorities, concerning the problems, but also about taken or planned actions necessary to restore confidence.

As we saw earlier (page 303), Swedish taxpayers got their money back with a good return on the investment, even though it took some 10–15 years.

The always delightfully provocative Nassim Nicholas Taleb, whom we encountered earlier in his discussion and criticism of the excessive reliance on the normal distribution, has gone further in his conclusions about what needs to be corrected in his *Financial Times* blog on "Ten principles for a Black Swan proof world" – that is, for a more stable financial system.[13]

Banks too big to fail have become even bigger!

There are really two problems with overly large institutions. The second problem is the effect they will have on the financial system when they

---

[12] To be precise, the two "bad banks" were formally finance companies, not banks.
[13] Taleb, Ten principles for a Black Swan proof world.

crash, vide Lehman's bankruptcy. Hence they must be saved. But this very act of saving them creates the first problem, namely the effect on the risk-taking of these institutions that the public safety net encourages ("moral hazard").

It is not only bigness per se that constitutes a reason for banks being too big to fail. In the list below of institutions worldwide deemed too big to fail, we note the absence of such large banks as Crédit Agricole in France, Commerzbank in Germany and Lloyds Banking Group in the UK. The reason for their exclusion is that, while large, they are not sufficiently internationally active or interconnected with their brethren as to create systemic risk.

The Financial Stability Board (FSB) has identified thirty financial groups worldwide that are considered to be so large and so interconnected that they do pose systemic risk and should be supervised cross-border (or perhaps broken up?):

- Five US banks: Goldman Sachs, JPMorgan Chase, Morgan Stanley, Bank of America Merrill Lynch, Citigroup;
- One Canadian bank: Royal Bank of Canada;
- Four British banks: HSBC, Barclays, RBS, Standard Chartered;
- Two Swiss banks: UBS and Credit Suisse;
- Two French banks: Société Générale and BNP Paribas;
- Two Spanish banks: Santander and BBVA;
- Two Italian banks: UniCredit and Banca Intesa San Paolo;
- One German bank: Deutsche Bank;
- One Dutch bank: ING;
- Four Japanese banks: Mizuho, Sumitomo Mitsui, Nomura, Mitsubishi UFJ;
- Six insurance groups: Axa (France), Aegon (Netherlands), Allianz (Germany), Aviva (UK), Zurich Financial Services (Switzerland) and Swiss Re (Switzerland).

Not only does the too-big-to-fail syndrome increase risk-taking. At the same time, the implicit guarantee by the state lets big banks borrow on more favorable terms than smaller institutions, since the creditors are certain that the biggest banks will be bailed out by the government, while this requisite may not pertain to smaller banks. This skewed competition in funding costs leads to big banks being able to lend at lower rates than smaller banks, increasing their loan books faster and hence making them even bigger. A catch-22 situation to be rectified!

The Center for Economic and Policy Research (CEPR) has studied the impact on the funding costs of large and small banks in the USA, after the events during the last few months of 2008 made it totally clear that the big banks would be bailed out. In particular, the TARP program and the special care given to Citigroup and Bank of America convinced investors of the reversal of attitudes of a government that had let Lehman fail just a few months earlier. "Big banks" in the study were defined as those with more than $100 billion in assets, which applied to eighteen US banks at the time. The CEPR found that the effect of the measures taken was a rise in the spread of the funding costs of large vs small institutions, rising from an advantage in favor of the big banks of twenty-nine basis points on average over the period 2000–7, to seventy-eight basis points from the final quarter of 2008 through to the second quarter of 2009. This corresponds to a subsidy given to these big banks of no less than $34 billion per year, at the taxpayers' expense, thereby also distorting competition between small and large banks.[14]

The share of total bank assets in the USA owned by the ten largest commercial banks and savings institutions held still at between 10 and 20 percent from the end of the Second World War until 1998. Then the ratio exploded to 50 percent by 2004,[15] and continued to increase to 60 percent by 2007 and 63 percent by the end of 2009.[16] In the world, the ten largest banks held 26 percent of the assets of the 1,500 largest banks at the end of 2008, up from 18 percent in 1999.[17]

Hence the problem of big banks is not unique to the USA. In both absolute terms and even more so in relative terms, many countries in Europe fare far worse. Table 9.1 shows the impossible situation for the Icelandic supervisory authorities to control banks, each with assets four to six times the country's GDP; indeed, the three biggest Icelandic banks together held assets corresponding to fifteen times Iceland's GDP in 2007. The consequence in terms of the (im)possibility for Iceland to

---

[14] Baker and McArthur, The value of the "too-big-to-fail" big bank subsidy.
[15] Kaufman, *The Road to Financial Reformation*, p. 100.
[16] *The Banker*, various issues; Board of Governors of the Federal Reserve System, Flow of Funds, Historical Tables L109 and L114.
[17] Calculations by Bloomberg.

Table 9.1 *Certain banks' assets ($ billion) and as a share of the home country's GDP, 2007*

Country	Bank	Assets ($ billion)	Assets/GDP (%)
Iceland	Kaupthing	86	623
Switzerland	UBS	2,019	484
Iceland	Landsbanki	49	374
Schweiz	Credit Suisse	1,209	290
Netherlands	ING	1,463	290
Belgium-Luxembourg	Fortis	1,129	254
Belgium-Luxembourg	Dexia	889	173
Spain	Santander	1,343	132
UK	RBS	3,807	126
Netherlands	Rabobank	839	121
Ireland	Bank of Ireland	312	118
France	BNP Paribas	2,494	104
Ireland	Bank of Ireland	312	102
Belgium-Luxembourg	KBC	523	102
Ireland	Allied Irish Bank	262	99
UK	HSBC	2,354	98
UK	Barclays	2,459	94
France	Crédit Agricole	2,268	87
Germany	Deutsche Bank	2,974	86
Austria	Erste Bank	295	85
Italy	Unicredit	1,504	80
USA	Citigroup	2,187	16
USA	Bank of America	1,716	12
USA	JPMorgan Chase	1,562	11
USA	Wachovia	783	6
USA	Wells Fargo Bank	575	4

Source: The Banker, Top 1,000 world banks (July 2008) and CIA for GDP levels

repay depositors in failed banks what their legal deposit insurance entitled them to has already been discussed (page 198).

But Switzerland's two major banks are also each several times the size of the country's GDP, and that is huge in absolute terms. Not surprisingly, but quite reassuringly, by 2008 (long before the EU), Switzerland had already taken steps to reduce the size and risks of these behemoths, introducing minimum leverage ratios and higher capital requirements for the Swiss banks than what Basel II required at that time.[18] Indeed, these new rules made UBS halve its gearing (assets over Tier 1 capital) ratio, from sixty-nine in 2007 to thirty-five in 2009. Switzerland's enacting of more stringent capital requirements than the BIS proposal will be taken up below.

Not only were banks large to begin with, the crisis made the big banks even bigger, as a number of them swallowed weaker colleagues. To name but a few mergers:

- Bank of America took over Countrywide and Merrill Lynch, increasing total assets from $1.72 trillion in 2007 to $1.82 trillion in 2008 and $2.22 trillion in 2009.
- JPMorgan Chase took over Bear Stearns and Washington Mutual, increasing total assets from $1.56 trillion in 2007 to $2.18 trillion in a single year.
- Wells Fargo took over the bigger bank, Wachovia (with assets of $0.78 trillion), increasing its total assets from $0.58 trillion in 2007 to $1.31 trillion in 2008, an increase of 125 percent in a single year.
- Lloyds TSB merged with HBOS, increasing its total assets from $0.71 trillion to $1.03 trillion in 2 years.
- BNP Paribas increased total assets from $2.49 trillion in 2007 to $2.89 trillion in 2008, $2.95 trillion in 2009 and $3.5 trillion with the integration of the Belgian parts of Fortis in 2010.
- Barclays' total assets went from $2.46 trillion in 2007 to $2.99 trillion in 2008, mainly as a result of its purchase of Lehman Brothers' US business.
- Santander, having earlier purchased Abbey National, took over viable parts of the crashed mortgage banks Bradford & Bingley and Alliance & Leicester, as well as Banco Real in Brazil (from ABN AMRO). From total assets of $1.34 trillion in 2007, its balance sheet went to $1.60 trillion by 2009. In July 2010, Santander also purchased the German parts of Swedish SEB.

However, an important difference between Santander and many of the other banks mentioned is that Santander works mainly through

---

[18] The initially set minimum capital-asset ratio in 2008 was a mild 3 percent, implying a possible gearing ratio of thirty-three times. See also *The Banker*, Top 1000 world banks. The exemption in question had hithertofore exempted Swiss domestic loans from inclusion in total assets.

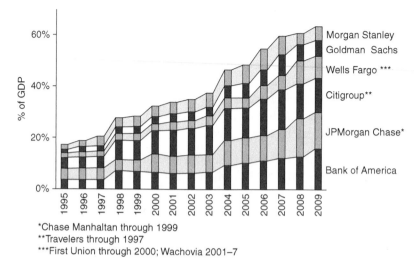

Figure 9.1 The six largest banks in the USA (assets as a % of GDP)
Source: Johnson and Kwak, *13 bankers*, page 203

subsidiaries rather than branches, meaning that the local banks are separately capitalized, and supervised by the local financial supervisory authorities. We will return below to the advantages of host-country supervision rather than home-country control.

The consequence for the concentration ratio in the USA is shown in Figure 9.1. The share of the six largest banking groups grew from 20 percent of GDP to over 60 percent of GDP during the last 10 years, the development being accelerated by the banking crisis over the last 3–4 years. Banking assets being slightly larger than GDP, this translates into the six largest banking groups having 58 percent of total banking assets.

Nominally, there exists in the USA a rule that no bank be allowed to have more than 10 percent of total deposits in the country.[19] As seen clearly in Figure 9.1, this rule has had to be suspended, with three of the six biggest banks already exceeding the limit. In the legislation enacted by Congress in July 2010, the rule comes back, but only by preventing mergers and acquisitions that would take a bank above the 10 percent limit. Organic growth is still permitted.

[19] The Riegle-Neal Interstate Banking and Efficiency Act of 1994.

Perhaps one should consider a similar rule in some European markets as well. It would certainly change the banking landscape in most countries. In the UK, the five largest banking groups (RBS, HSBC, Barclays, Lloyds Banking Group and Standard Chartered) held 89 percent of all British banking assets in 2009. In Switzerland, just two banks, UBS and Credit Suisse, had over 50 percent of all banking assets.

But there may be advantages to being large. As stated by Deutsche Bank's Chief Executive Officer, Josef Ackerman, banks need to be large in order to finance development projects and service large companies. Bigness per se is not the issue, but overall risk, said Ackerman.[20]

Do scale economies justify big banks?

Unfortunately for Ackerman *et consortes*, it appears difficult in general to justify the size of big banks by their efficiency, or their economies of scale and scope. By scale economies is meant lower cost of production per unit as the number of units produced increases. Typical economies of scale appear in capital-intensive businesses, in particular computer-dependent lines of business. A good example is the total dominance of such specialized banks as Bank of New York Mellon and State Street Bank in custodial services – that is, the safekeeping of securities. A custodian bank holds the securities if they exist in physical form, or keeps the registry of dematerialized assets, arranges clearing and settlement after purchases or sales, performs cash management, collects dividends from equities and coupons from bond holdings, performs foreign-exchange transactions, and keeps track of all business events, such as annual meetings of shareholders, new issues and stock splits.

With total assets under management in the world exceeding $100 trillion by mid-2010, the two mentioned banks, plus JPMorgan Chase and Citigroup, have 60 percent of the global market total between them, an extreme case of scale.[21] Unfortunately, most banking is labor-intensive rather than capital-intensive, so the conclusions from asset management cannot be generalized.

By economies of scope are meant lower costs of production by co-production. For instance, the same branch office staff can sell deposits

---

[20] Said on November 16, 2009, according to Bloomberg News, December 2, 2009.
[21] www.globalcustody.net/default/custody_assets_worldwide

and loans, stocks and asset management, as well as both banking and insurance products.

A third term to define is X-efficiency. While economies of scale show the *potential* reduction in cost per produced unit, X-efficiency shows the *actual* cost in relation to the most efficient bank of the same size. Banks above the minimum cost at a certain size are said to show X-inefficiencies.

The matter may be illustrated in principle by Figure 9.2. As the size of banks, as measured on the horizontal axis, increases, the average cost falls. This does not mean that all banks' costs fall to an equal degree, the curve showing the most efficient bank in each size class. This theoretical exercise leaves two, connected, questions unanswered. First, is there a certain optimal scale in banking, and, second, does the curve continue horizontally (constant returns to scale) or does it turn upwards again as we move to the right of the minimum optimal scale (decreasing returns to scale)? Such a fact may depend either on diseconomies of scale or on

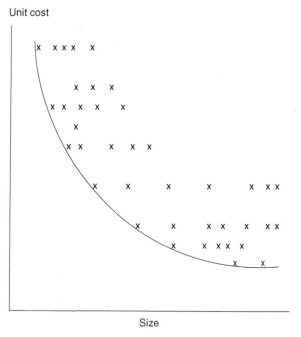

Unit cost

Size

Figure 9.2 A schematic view of economies of scale and X-(in-)efficiencies
Note: Each X represents a bank.

economies of scale being offset by the lesser flexibility and hence lower internal efficiency in large organizations.

One study of Belgian banks expressed it well: "In particular, banks and savings banks can be represented by a similar U-shaped charge curve, where the big banks and perhaps the biggest public credit institutions have grown too large, with the result that they lose their cost efficiency, their development slows down and their market share diminishes, in favor of medium sized establishments which have attained their optimal size."[22]

While there have been surprisingly few studies on efficiency in banking in the last 10 years (with some exceptions), there are a number of earlier studies, all of them being summarized in Table 9.2.

While one should hesitate to draw too strong conclusions – after all, the world of banking is changing rapidly – six conclusions would appear justified:

- The optimal scale in banking is quite small; traditional banking is a labor-intensive activity. There would appear to be no or few economies of scale above total assets of $10 billion. At the end of 2009, Bank of America, JPMorgan Chase and Citigroup were probably 200 times larger than is needed to achieve efficient scale.[23]
- Even where economies of scale exist, they are unlikely to exceed 5 percent of total costs.
- While some studies show few diseconomies of scale above optimal size, it should be remembered that big banks are subsidized by being too big to fail. Take away this subsidy and there would be diminishing returns – that is, diseconomies of scale;
- While difficult to pinpoint, there is likely to be an optimal scale, after which larger organizations lose efficiency due to inflexibility and lack of control over a large organization.
- For a given size, certain banks may have costs 20 percent higher than the industry minimum for the same scale and product mix; X-efficiency is much more important than scale economies.
- Very few mergers increase the efficiency of the two partners. "It is likely that domestic full acquisitions are motivated by managerialist motives such as size-maximization or the too-big-to-fail rationale".[24]

---

[22] Pallage, An econometric study of Belgian banking.

[23] Johnson (MIT professor and former Chief Economist, IMF), Implications of the "Volcker Rules" for financial stability.

[24] Vennet, The effect of mergers and acquisitions.

Table 9.2 *Scale and scope economies in banking*

Study	What banks and what period?	Optimal scale?
USA:		
Athanasios G. Noulas, Subhash C. Ray and Stephen M. Miller, Returns to scale and input substitution for large US banks, *Journal of Money, Credit and Banking*, 22:1 (February 1990), pp. 94–108	Banks with assets > $1 billion, 1986	$1 billion to $3 billion showed economies of scale, above $3 billion showed diseconomies
William C. Hunter, Stephen G. Timme and Won Keun Yang, An examination of cost subadditivity and multiproduct production in large US banks, *Journal of Money Credit and Banking*, 22:4 (November 1990), pp. 504–25	Banks with assets > $1 billion	Optimal scale around $2 billion
Allen N. Berger and David B. Humphrey, The dominance of inefficiencies over scale and product mix economies in banking, *Journal of Monetary Economics*, 28:1 (August 1991), pp. 117–48	Banks with assets < $1 billion	Optimal scale around $75 million to $200 million
Daniel M. Gropper, An empirical investigation of changes in scale economies for the commercial banking firm, 1979–86, *Journal of Money, Credit and Banking*, 23:4 (November 1991), pp. 718–27	Banks with assets between $10 million and $2 billion, 1979–86	Scale economies up to $200 million

Reference	Sample	Findings
Allen N. Berger, Diana Hancock and David B. Humphrey, Bank efficiency derived from the profit function, *Journal of Banking and Finance*, 17:2–3 (April 1993), pp. 317–47	All banks 1984–9	For all sizes of banks, X-inefficiencies dominate scale economies
Patrick H. McAllister and Douglas McManus, Resolving the scale efficiency puzzle in banking, *Journal of Banking and Finance*, 17:2–3 (April 1993), pp. 389–405	Three different sets of sizes	Large-scale economies up to $500 million; the result depends on the selection
Sherrill Shaffer, Can megamergers improve bank efficiency? *Journal of Banking and Finance*, 17:2–3 (April 1993), pp. 423–36	Banks with assets > $1 billion, 1984–9, were investigated by simulation techniques to distinguish economies of scale and scope and X-efficiency	Only half the number of mergers in banks > $1 billion reduces costs; only 15% of mergers > $10 billion reduces costs
Jeffrey A. Clark and Paul J. Speaker, Economies of scale and scope in banking; evidence from a generalized translog cost function, *Quarterly Journal of Business and Economics* (March 1994), pp. 1–35	Medium and large US banks	Economies of scale at least up to $1 billion
Karlyn Mitchell and Nur M. Onvural, Economies of scale and scope at large commercial banks: evidence from the Fourier flexible functional form, *Journal of Money, Credit and Banking*, 28:2 (May 1996), pp. 178–99	Banks with assets between $1 billion and $100 billion, 1990	No economies of scale or scope above $1 billion

Table 9.2 (*cont.*)

Study	What banks and what period?	Optimal scale?
Julapa Jagtiani and Anya Khanthavit, Scale and scope economies at large banks: including off-balance-sheet products and regulatory effects (1984–1991), *Journal of Banking and Finance*, 20:7 (August 1996), pp. 1271–87	The 120 largest banks 1984–91; off-balance-sheet activities included	Clear diseconomies of scale for the largest "money center banks" and the super-regionals
David C. Wheelock and Paul W. Wilson, Do large banks have lower costs? New estimates of returns to scale for US banks, Working Paper 2009–054C, Federal Reserve Bank of St Louis (October 2009) (available at http://research. stlouisfed.org/wp/2009/2009-054.pdf)	All US commercial banks, 1984–2006	Increasing returns to scale for all bank sizes, though relatively small
Europe:		
Stéphane J. Pallage, An econometric study of the Belgian banking sector in terms of scale and scope economies, Université Libre de Bruxelles, *Cahiers Economiques de Bruxelles*, 130 (1991), pp. 125–43	84 Belgian banks, 1988	Economies of scale up to $4 billion
Henry-Jean Gathon and Fabienne Grosjean, Efficacité productive et rendements d'échelle dans les banques belges, *Brussels Economic Review*, 130 (1991), pp. 145–60	Belgian banks 1983–8	Economies of scale up to $3 billion to $4 billion

Reference	Sample	Findings
Ugur Muldur, Economies of scale and scope in national and global banking markets, ir. Alfred Steinherr (ed.), *The New European Financial Market Place* (Harlow: Longman Group UK Limited, 1992), pp. 31–48	129 French banks	Ne economies of scale found, even for small banks
Sigbjørn Atle Berg, Finn R. Førsund, Lennart Hjalmarsson and Matti Suominen, Banking efficiency in the Nordic countries, *Journal of Banking and Finance*, 17:2–3 (April 1993), pp. 371–88	Around 1,000 Finnish, Norwegian and Swedish banks, 1990	44% of Finnish banks, 52% of Norwegian and 72% of Swedish banks were efficient
Asghar Zardkoohi and James Kolari, Branch office economies of scale and scope: evidence from savings banks in Finland, *Journal of Banking and Finance*, 18:3 (May 1994), pp. 421–32	43 Finnish savings banks, 1988	Economies of scale up to $250 million
Rudi Vander Vennet, The effect of mergers and acquisitions on the efficiency and profitability of EC credit institutions, *Journal of Banking and Finance*, 20:9 (November 1996), pp. 1531–58	492 mergers during 1988–92 within the EU. The study follows banks 3 years before and 3 years after the merger. 422 mergers were within the same country and 70 were cross-border	*Conclusion 1.* The buying bank is more efficient than average, while the bought bank shows worse results before the merger. *Conclusion 2.* After the merger, efficiency and profitability fall in the merged organization. "Acquirers have overestimated their ability and may have been confronted with resistance to change." *Conclusion 3.* In merging banks with similar profitability, there is no sign of increased efficiency or profitability in the merged organization. "It is likely that domestic full

Table 9.2 (*cont.*)

Study	What banks and what period?	Optimal scale?
		acquisitions are motivated by managerialist motives such as size-maximization or the too-big-to-fail rationale." *Conclusion 4.* Increased profitability only when very small banks are merged, in particular German, Spanish and Italian savings banks. *Conclusion 5.* Increased profitability in cross-border mergers; it is perhaps easier to force out the previous management than in domestic mergers.
Günter Lang and Peter Welzel, Efficiency and technical progress in banking: empirical results for a panel of German cooperative banks, *Journal of Banking and Finance*, 20:6 (July 1996), pp. 1003–23	757 Bavarian cooperative banks, 1989–92	Economies of scale in the very smallest organizations
Günter Lang and Peter Welzel, Technology and cost efficiency in universal banking: a "thick frontier" – analysis of the German banking industry, *Journal of Productivity Analysis*, 10:1 (1998), pp. 63–84	German banks	Optimal scale $1 billion to $3 billion
Dandan Zeng, Technical efficiency in European mega bank mergers and acquisitions, Working Paper, University of Birmingham (May 2006)	100 European megabanks, 1996–2003	Merger activities mostly driven by differences in efficiency

How to limit the size of banks too big to fail

- Should banks too big to fail have tougher capital requirements?
- Or should they be broken up?
- Should Glass-Steagall be reintroduced?
- Is "narrow banking" the answer?
- Can "living wills" facilitate the demise of banks?

A number of countries should ponder the question of whether their banks may have become too big, absolutely and/or relatively.[25] While financial crises have certainly been set off by the failure of individual large banks (Continental Illinois 1984, Lehman Brothers 2008), as well as by a number of smaller banks (the thrift crisis in the 1980s), the latter situation is easier to handle, since the failing organizations, being small, are also less complex.

"Too big to fail" may have become "too big to save" – hence, break it up! "If they're too big to fail, they are too big!" has been said by even such a free-market proponent as Alan Greenspan.[26] Or, as stated by US Senator Bernie Sanders (Independent, Vermont), "if it's too big to fail, it's too big to exist." At least in the USA, there already exists legislation to break up companies judged to have become too large. Under the Sherman Act of 1890, Standard Oil was broken up in 1911 into thirty-four separate companies. Perhaps the time has come to do the same thing with Citigroup, Bank of America, JPMorgan Chase, Wells Fargo, and so on. If oil companies can be broken up, why not banks? However, a specific proposal to limit the size of the largest banks – that is, make the present 10 percent rule on deposits binding, was watered down by Congress in the discussions on the Dodd-Frank Bill (see pages 81 and 366).

There are (at least) two important questions connected with such a 10 percent rule. First, why 10 percent? Why accept the status quo (in the USA)? There is nothing to indicate that this is optimal. Should the banks' market shares not be rolled back to where they were 15–20

---

[25] Lybeck, It is time to consider breaking up the banking behemoths; Morgenson, Too big to fail, or too big to handle, *New York Times*, June 20, 2009; Krugman, Too big to fail fail.

[26] Bloomberg News, October 12, 2009.

years ago – that is, to a few percentage points of the total market (see Figure 9.1)?

But today's banking is also entirely different from that of just a few decades back, not least in the fact that it is utterly international. This brings us to the second question: what do we put in the denominator in order to restrict, say, RBS's total assets to a certain percentage? Percentage of what? Of Scottish banks' assets? Of British banks' assets? Of European banks' assets? Of world banks' assets? While RBS may be a giant in Scotland and an elephant in the UK, as well as the world's largest bank by assets in 2008, it still held "only" 3.6 percent of the assets of the 1,000 largest banks in the world, and hence an even smaller share of all banking assets. Is that "big?" Is it too big?

A better alternative may be to focus on the implicit subsidy provided by the "too-big-to-fail" doctrine and try to create a level playing field between banks of different sizes. One way may be to tax big banks just because they are big, as was proposed by President Obama, but rejected by Congress. His proposal would have taxed banks with assets above $50 billion with a fee of 0.15 percent on assets put to risk – that is, excluding insured deposits. In the German proposal for a financial stability fund (see below), big banks will pay a higher charge than small banks. Germany wants to impose a progressive tax on bank balance sheets, with bank-taxable liabilities below €10 billion being taxed at 0.02 percent, those over €10 billion one basis point higher, and those above €100 billion at 0.04 percent. Deutsche Bank had €1,500 billion in total assets in 2009, and Bayerische Landesbank €416 billion, to mention a couple of the German banks which have figured in our story.

Another way to address the problem would be for supervisors to add a capital charge for big banks just because they are big. This does not require any new legislation either in the USA or in Europe. It could be done under the existing Basel II framework under Pillar 2 (as was indeed done in countries like Spain and the UK, and as is being proposed in Switzerland).[27]

The only question is how much is reasonable. We do not know what the FSA demanded from British banks, since the agreements between banks and the FSA are classified. Judging from how much the UK has had to spend to recapitalize some of its major banks, it obviously was

---

[27] See also Greenspan, We need a better cushion against risk.

not enough. In Spain, the two major banks have fared better and gone through the crisis virtually unscathed, but was this as a result of their business model or because of more stringent capital requirements ("dynamic provisioning")?

The OECD tried to assess how much more capital big banks would have to have to equalize for the implicit and explicit guarantee that they have. According to their calculation, it would imply levying a capital charge to increase their equity-to-assets ratio by 18 percentage points, to some 25 percent.[28] If this capital-asset ratio seems excessive, it corresponds to where the US banks were by the 1880s, before there was a government guarantee (see Figure 7.3, page 244). If that is the situation we want to emulate, without any government prop-ups to carry banks over the crises, that is the capital they are going to need to survive on their own, so the result should not be surprising.[29]

Another alternative to the too-big-to-fail issue may be to break up banks along product lines. After each financial crisis, there will always be someone proposing "narrow banks." After the thrift crisis in the USA, narrow banks were proposed by L. L. Bryan. This time, the proposal came from British journalist/economist John Kay.[30]

A narrow bank, by definition, is a safe bank, all risky activities having been moved to other (less regulated?) institutions. Narrow banking would restrict deposit-taking banks to holding liquid and safe government bonds and bills. Loans would instead be made by other financial institutions. The only activities undertaken by the narrow bank would be deposit-taking and payment services such as checking. The narrow bank would lend no money; it would conduct no off-balance-sheet activities, such as guarantees or derivatives; nor would it trade stocks, bonds, commodities or derivatives, either for customers or for its own accounts.[31]

---

[28] Organisation for Economic Cooperation and Development, *Economic Outlook*, 86 (November 2009), p. 46.

[29] See also Bank for International Settlements, Countercyclical capital buffer proposal.

[30] Bryan, *Breaking up the Bank*; Kay, *Narrow Banking*.

[31] Until 1983, when liquidity ratios were abolished, those banks in Sweden that acted as central banks for the savings banks and the agricultural banks, respectively, had to hold 50 percent of their liabilities in government and mortgage bonds. This might be the only historical case of true "narrow banks." The system, however, was not conducive to efficiency in these organizations, nor did it help the conduct of monetary policy, as banks could create mortgage bonds at will. See Lybeck, Commercial bank behavior and the Swedish monetary sector.

A narrow bank would obviously pay its customers much lower interest on their deposits than banks can do at present, since their ability to pay would be set by the (low) yield on short-term government bonds minus their costs and profits. A more fundamental objection to narrow banking is whether this construction really makes the financial system safer. By breaking out the safest part of the bank – deposits on the liabilities side and bond holdings on the asset side – the residual, by definition, becomes riskier. Will such risky firms be allowed to fail? Hardly! A much better safety net seems to be to create the image of a narrow bank by generous deposit insurance coverage, guaranteed by the state, but paid for by the banks themselves, and increasing sharply the requirements on the banks as concerns their liquidity coverage. This is precisely what has been proposed recently in the European Union.

A further comment would be that narrow banks miss the whole purpose of banking, which is to take controlled risks in transforming short-run deposits into longer-term lending, safe and guaranteed deposits into slightly riskier loans and investments, and so on. If narrow banks are not allowed to do this fundamental job of maturity and risk transformation, somebody else will have to do it. The need does not go away just because narrow banks are not allowed to fulfill the need.

Another proposed alternative to creating safer banks is the "Volcker rule," named after the former Chairman of the Board of Governors of the Federal Reserve System, now advisor to President Obama. The Volcker rule would take half a step back to the world of Glass-Steagall, where commercial banking and investment banking were separated. It would allow banks to undertake trading only for customers, for market-making or for their own protection (hedging positions), moving all other trades (proprietary trading, or "prop" trading), in particular in derivatives, to separately capitalized subsidiaries. Banks would not be allowed to own or run hedge funds or private equity funds, except within limits. Even this proposal has its limitations. Lehman Brothers was an investment bank, not a deposit-taking bank. Yet its failure sent shock waves across the entire global financial system. Evidently, the separation of activities is no guarantee for stability. We need higher capital cushions in both commercial banks and investment banking, as well as better supervision and control of the risks involved.

In practice, Congress watered down the Volcker rule, to the point of becoming rather toothless. Banks will in the future still be allowed to place 3 percent of their Tier 1 capital into private equity and hedge funds, provided it does not exceed 3 percent of the fund's capital. As concerns "prop" trading, it will continue to be allowed for interest and foreign-exchange derivatives. Only credit derivatives such as CDSs will have to be shifted out of the banks, if they are not centrally cleared through a CCP clearing house. The two banks mainly affected will be JPMorgan Chase and Citigroup, since the two ex-investment banks Goldman Sachs and Morgan Stanley already keep most of their derivatives trading in broker-dealer subsidiaries. Estimates made by the industry itself set the negative effect of the Volcker rule on earnings per share (EPS) at a relatively modest 1–6 percent.

Another solution to the "too-big-to-fail" syndrome has been to demand of the banks that they plan for their own orderly demise – to write "living wills." Such a plan would document which activities would or could be sold off in times of need, how other activities are to be wound down, in order to help the organizations to simplify their legal structures (which was totally impenetrable in the case of Lehman, working under 2,895 different legal identities!).[32] Indeed, as of July 2010, almost 2 years after the bankruptcy, the administrators of the Lehman estate still face $225 billion of unsettled claims, having just sold $2.4 billion of claims against Lehman in Germany for $500,000.[33]

The problem with living wills is that their usefulness depends on the judicial system, in particular bankruptcy regimes, which vary from country to country. Lehman made over 50 percent of its revenue from outside the USA. Lehman's bankruptcy was relatively straightforward in the USA, and its US operations were sold (to Barclays). It was the European and Asian operations that created problems. There is simply no such thing as an integrated global framework for dealing with failing, internationally active banks. Each country's supervisory authorities will attempt to freeze the available assets in their own jurisdiction – vide the British actions taken towards the Icelandic banks' British units, subsidiaries and branches.

The new regulatory set-up in the USA, to facilitate the winding-down of large, complex, interconnected financial institutions, is presented and discussed below.

---

[32] *The Economist*, Death warmed up, October 3, 2009.
[33] Sakoui, Hopes rise over unwinding of Lehman's assets.

Will bank taxes and financial stability funds alleviate the next crisis?

The Obama administration had originally proposed to tap the banking sector for a tax on large banks and hedge funds, to pay for the "orderly liquidation" of large banks, indicated by naming the tax "the financial crisis responsibility fee."[34] Banks and insurance companies with assets over $50 billion, and hedge funds with assets over $10 billion, were to pay a 0.15 percent fee on their risk-bearing assets (total assets minus capital and insured deposits) over 10 years, in order to build up a fund of some $90 billion to pay for the orderly disposal of banks. The fee could be kept for more than 10 years, if necessary, to claw back every cent spent on the TARP program. Thirty-five domestic banks and insurance companies and fifteen US subsidiaries of international banks were expected to be affected. Former investment banks, such as Goldman Sachs and Morgan Stanley, having few deposits, would be especially hard hit. When this proposal was shot down in Congress, Obama instead proposed a tax (note the change of terms, "tax," not "fee") that would pay for the increased cost of supervision under the financial reform bill, $18 billion. But this tax was also dropped, to secure sufficient Republican votes on the Dodd-Frank Act, with Congress instead "stealing" some of the remaining TARP funds, thereby letting taxpayers pay for the increased quality and cost of supervising big banks.

In the UK, the stability fee proposed is set at 0.04 percent initially, rising to 0.07 percent of taxable liabilities (liabilities minus core equity minus insured deposits), aiming to yield £2 billion annually, which will go directly into the budget, not building up a fund (for reasons given below). Liabilities with maturities of less than 1 year will be taxed at half the rate. Only institutions with liabilities greater than £20 billion will be taxed.

In Sweden, banks pay a fee of 0.036 percent on liabilities, excluding equity and such debentures which qualify as Tier 2 capital. The target is a fund amounting to 2.5 percent of GDP to fund future bank salvations. The fee is to become differentiated by banks' riskiness later on.

---

[34] This section discusses only stability funds. Other ways of taxing the financial sector, such as bonus taxes, "Tobin" transaction taxes and financial activity taxes (FAT), are presented and well discussed in International Monetary Fund, *A fair and substantial contribution*.

In Germany, banks will pay a fee graduated by size, as noted above; €1.2 billion is to be collected annually and, as in Sweden, used to build up a bank resolution fund. In Austria, likewise, the fee is set at 0.07 percent, to yield an annual €500 million in order to build up a stability fund.

In the European Union, the Commission has proposed the creation of "EU-wide bank resolution funds," supposed to save taxpayers' money on future bank bail-outs and to stabilize the financial system (COM (2010) 254 final). The UK has opposed the proposal on grounds of moral hazard, in that the very existence of a fund will lead banks to take even larger risks, in that banks believe that they will always be saved. For this reason, the money collected from banks under the British levy will simply go into the general budget.[35] The UK also claims that the bank levy is a tax which the EU countries must adopt unanimously, thus giving the UK a veto on its construction. The EU Commission considers it a fee where decisions may be taken by normal majority voting.

Apart from the clear risk of "moral hazard" – money available is apt to be used[36] – the proposed funds also appear small in relationship to what might be needed. In the recent crises, European countries have spent far more than the planned funds on capital injections, purchase of assets and lending by the Treasury: 6.5 percent of GDP in the UK (out of 11.9 percent potentially promised) and 4.9 percent of GDP in Germany, while in France, utilization stopped at 1.1 percent of GDP. In the USA, 4.8 percent of GDP was actually used to save banks (not counting guarantees and lending by the Federal Reserve). The US fund which Congress rejected would have attained a meager 0.6 percent of GDP.

An interesting alternative/complement has been suggested by the CEO of Italy's Unicredit, Alessandro Profumo. He proposes that European banks themselves fund a European Recovery Fund of €20 billion to bail out failed colleagues. The idea is quite similar to the existing system in countries like Germany and Denmark, namely, that the financial sector itself should bear the primary responsibility to

---

[35] If the stability fund invests its revenues in government bonds, which appears likely, it really does not matter if the stability fee goes into a fund or directly into the budget, except for the psychological difference on bank behavior.

[36] To minimize moral hazard, the resolution fund will not be used to recapitalize banks continuing to be private in principle, but used to fund bank take-overs or the transfer of assets to a "bad bank," or guarantees. It is doubtful that this distinction may be practical in a crisis. After all, why build up a resolution fund if not in order to use it to recapitalize banks?

bail out colleagues in trouble, but runs counter to the preferred socialist solutions suggested by the UK, France, Sweden, Austria, and so on.[37]

How should hedge funds be supervised?

As a consequence of the Russia-LTCM crisis in 1998, politicians as well as the general public demanded increased transparency concerning the hedge fund industry: its size, yield vs risk, management, direction of investments. It has been calculated that there were some 10,500 hedge funds in the world, with assets of over $2,000 billion before the crash on the financial markets (including commodities). Of these funds, 55 percent were domiciled in the USA, 30 percent in Europe, 5 percent in Asia and 10 percent in various offshore jurisdictions, like the Bahamas, Bermuda, the Cayman Islands and the Virgin Islands. An excellent and very perspicacious article in the European Central Bank's *Financial Stability Review* warned back in June 2006 of the potential force in these funds, which appeared to be running in the same direction in their quest for superior yields ("alpha"), in a world where risk premium had fallen almost to zero. What would happen when all these funds turned around 180 degrees and sought to exit their investments, was the rhetorical question. In the fall of 2008, we got the answer!

As noted earlier, hedge funds have been completely unregulated in the USA, on the condition that they have no more than 100 investors, individuals or companies, or that they have no more than 500 investors having at least $5 million each in financial net worth. In December 2004, the SEC ruled that hedge funds must be registered with the SEC in their capacity of investment advisors. The ruling applied to funds with capital greater than $25 million and/or more than fifteen investors. A hedge fund manager took the SEC to court and a US Court of Appeals referred the matter back to the SEC, where it died. A number of proposed pieces of legislation were put before Congress without receiving more than cursory interest. In the revised legislation in summer 2010, a statute was finally adopted that hedge funds and private equity funds large enough to pose a systemic risk must register with the SEC.

---

[37] Profumo, Europe's banks need a recovery fund.

In Europe, all investment funds must be authorized by and be subject to supervision from their respective financial supervisory authorities. They are also subject to the normal capital-adequacy requirements of financial institutions. Funds following the UCITS directive 2009/65/EU (Undertakings for Collective Investments in Transferable Securities), aimed at retail investors, face strict rules on their ability to borrow, sell short, go negative on derivatives transactions, and so on. Hedge funds, private equity funds, and so on – in EU terminology called special funds (or alternative investment funds, AIF) – have more freedom. Their main restrictions concern minimum levels of liquidity and diversification of risks in their investments. Both types of funds, however, must describe their investment strategy: types of assets, sector or geographical restrictions and other criteria. They must also state which measure of risk they utilize – for example, Sharpe ratios – and indicate a desired level of risk according to this measure. There exists also the requirement that the physical (or dematerialized) securities be held by a separate institute/depository.[38]

The UK has gone further than most other EU countries in regulating the hedge fund industry. True retail hedge funds – that is, funds with no restrictions as to shorting, borrowing or on their investments – are not permitted. The UK rules for authorized funds do permit the use of derivatives, but positions must be covered globally, hence there can be no net liabilities created. There are also constraints on borrowing (leverage); therefore any hedge-fund-like strategies are restricted. That said, a number of UK UCITS funds have been established, using what are sometimes referred to as "hedge fund light" strategies, to provide managed returns for retail investors. From the second half of 2009, funds of alternative investment funds (FAIFs) were introduced, allowing non-UCITS retail schemes to invest up to 100 percent in unregulated collective investment schemes. There were investment restrictions, substantial due diligence requirements, and potentially a number of limits on the concentration of investment, use of leverage, notice of dealing

---

[38] The activities of the recently exposed fraudster Bernard Madoff would have been revealed if he had used an independent firm as depository, which in the USA is best practice, but not legally required. His funds contained $65 billion in totally fictitious investments. During the last 13 years, he had not made one single trade; all reports were just figures on a piece of paper. New money coming in had been used to pay dividends to existing investors. He claimed to have done his trades through his own broker-dealer firm, a practice which should not be allowed, in particular since it was run by his sons.

and maximum period to settle redemptions. For example, FAIFs will only be permitted borrowing of up to 10 percent of the net asset value.[39]

The European Union, unjustly blaming hedge funds and private equity funds for the financial crisis, has sought to sharpen the restrictions on these AIFs, managing assets totaling some €2 trillion in the EU area (Commission proposal COM[2009] 207, IP[10/869]). Funds administering assets greater than €100 million would be required to seek permission from the competent authority, with rules set on an EU-wide basis. The limit will include 30 percent of the funds and 90 percent of fund assets. Since funds from outside the EU face a transitional period while their regulatory background is investigated, the proposed directive has been criticized, not least by the USA, but was adopted anyway by the ECOFIN Council and the EU Parliament in October 2010.

Host- or home-country control?

The major focus of economic legislation in the European Union has always been on competition and the creation of a "level playing field."[40] The White Book from 1985 (COM [85] 310) singled out the financial sector as the battering ram to create a single European market; indeed 25 of some 130 concrete proposals pertained to this sector. The guiding principles were mutual recognition of financial firms and home-country control of cross-border banks, insurance companies and investment firms. The major pieces of legislation for our area under study were the Second Banking Coordination Directive (89/646/EEC) and the Investment Services Directive (93/22/EEC). A quote from the latter will show clearly the aim of the legislation:

Whereas each Member State must ensure that within its territory, treatment of all investment firms authorized in any member state and likewise all financial instruments listed on the Member States´ regulated markets is non-discriminatory; whereas investment firms must all have the same opportunities of joining or having access to regulated markets; whereas, regardless of the manner in which transactions are at present organized in the Member States, it is

---

[39] The description of the hedge fund industry in the UK builds partly on the excellent survey by KPMG, Funds and fund management 2010.

[40] This section builds, inter alia, on the EU Commission staff working document, European financial supervision: impact assessment, SEC (2009) 1234.

therefore important, subject to the conditions imposed by this Directive, to abolish the technical and legal restrictions on access to the regulated markets.

In order to meet the obligations imposed in paragraph 1, host Member States shall offer the investment firms ... the choice of becoming members of or having access to their regulated markets either;

- directly, by setting up branches in the host Member States, or;
- indirectly, by setting up subsidiaries in the host Member States.

It quickly became rather obvious that this method was not sufficient. Member states could still enact their own legislation too independently of the ambition of the EU directives, and the process of changing and enforcing EU directives was too slow and too cumbersome. In the European Commission's Financial Services Action Plan of May 1999, strategic objectives were set out to create an integrated EU capital market by April 2004 (a single EU financial services market, by open and secure retail markets, state-of-the-art prudential rules and supervision). Accordingly, a "Committee of Wise Men," also called the Lamfalussy Committee, after its chairman, was set up in 2000 to make proposals as to how this was to be achieved.

The Lamfalussy Committee expressed the view that all European services and securities legislation should be based around a conceptual legislative framework of essential principles. These consist of so-called *level 1 principles*, whereby new types of directives or regulations are to be decided by normal EU legislative procedures – that is, proposal by the Commission to the Council of Ministers and the European Parliament for co-decision procedure. The European Commission should inform the European Parliament on any of these level 1 proposals and seek an understanding with the European Parliament on the scope of level 2 implementing measures. Furthermore, the European Commission should consult, beforehand, with market participants, end-users (issuers and consumers), member states and their regulators on any level 1 legislative proposal.

With respect to *level 2* decisions concerning securities, the Committee of Wise Men proposed a working method for the CESR, the European Commission and the European Securities Committee (ESC) to define, propose and decide on the technical implementing measures of level 1 directives and regulations. First, the European Commission, after consultation with the ESC, asks the CESR (a level 3 institution) to draw up technical advice for the implementing measures on the basis of a clear mandate. The CESR then sends its formal advice to the European

Commission, following a consultation with the market practitioners, consumers and end users on its draft advice. Subsequently, the European Commission presents a proposal for technical implementing measures to the ESC, taking into account the technical advice of the CESR. In the meantime, the European Commission also ensures that the European Parliament is fully informed of all these proposed measures. After approval by the ESC of these implementing measures, the Parliament is given 1 month to consider if the proposed technical implementing measures approved by the ESC should be formally adopted by the European Commission.

A similar set-up for the banking and insurance sectors was created by the European Commission, acting together with the level 2 institution, the European Banking Committee (EBC) and the level 3 institution, the Committee of European Banking Supervisors (CEBS). The level 3 institution for insurance is the Committee of European Insurance and Occupational Pensions Supervisors (CEIOPS).

Level 3 concerns a strengthened cooperation between (national) regulators to ensure consistent and equivalent transposition of level 1 and level 2 legislation. This clearly requires an active role of the CESR and CEBS in the field of common and uniform implementation of EU financial legislation. The CESR and CEBS fulfill this role by producing administrative guidelines, interpretive recommendations, common standards, peer reviews, comparisons of regulatory practice to improve consistent application and enforcement of the legislation or the standards concerned.

Strengthened enforcement of the Community rules is identified by the Lamfalussy Report as *level 4*. This is primarily the responsibility of the European Commission, but the report pointed out that member states, regulators and market participants have an important role in supplying information to the European Commission about any potential infringement of Community rules.

This four-level system of decision-making was codified by Directive 2005/1/EC.

Today's crisis has shown the inadequacy of this framework of decision-making.[41]

---

[41] See also http://ec.europa.eu/internal_market/finances/docs/committees/ supervision/communication_may2009/impact_assessment_summary_en.pdf

- There has been (and still is) too much focus on competition and too little emphasis on financial stability and macro-/micro-prudential supervision.
- The level 3 organizations (CEBS, CESR and CEIOPS) have lacked teeth to enforce their recommendations on the national supervisors. This has been detrimental for cross-border activities in particular. Home-country financial supervisory authorities have focused on the domestic financial system, not giving sufficient attention to the supervision of their foreign branches. Host-country financial supervisory authorities have generally been too cautious and too slow in reacting to obvious problems. The implicit connivance of the British FSA as regards the deficiencies of the Icelandic banks' deposit insurance coverage is a notable case in question. There have also been instances of infighting instead of cooperation between national supervisors. The breakdown of civility between the Dutch and the Belgian financial supervisory authorities (and governments!) regarding the bankrupt Fortis Bank shows supervisory cooperation at its very worst.
- The financial rule book has been very different in different EU countries, since these have been allowed too much discretion in implementing EU directives. These differences have been glaringly obvious, not least in capital-adequacy ratios, where national supervisors have diverged, for instance, on what kind of hybrid capital should be allowed in Tier 1 and to what extent. Another well-known discrepancy is the 50 percent risk weight allotted to commercial properties in Germany, with all other countries enforcing a full 100 percent risk weight. The national interpretations of what information a financial firm should publish (Transparency Directive 2004/109/EC) have also varied widely.
- There have been fragmented responsibilities for supervision of a certain financial group with cross-border operations, implying less than adequate supervision of the group as a whole.
- Worst of all, even where financial groups have been supervised on a well-functioning, cooperative, cross-border basis (the Nordic cooperation concerning the Nordea Group, for instance), the focus has been on micro-prudential issues concerning that particular group, rather than on macro-prudential questions concerning the stability or instability of the financial system as a whole.
- Inadequate attention has also been given to financial infrastructure organisms such as clearing houses and Central Securities

Depositories (CSDs), with these becoming more and more international in character. For instance, LCH.Clearnet clears equity trades emanating from the London Stock Exchange, NYSE Euronext in Paris, Brussels, Amsterdam and Portugal, the SIX Swiss exchange and la Bourse de Luxembourg, as well as from a number of fixed-income, commodities and derivatives markets. Euroclear is another case of a widespread cross-border operation, operating not only Euroclear Bank in Brussels for international trades, but also the domestic CSDs in Belgium (ex-CIK), Netherlands (ex-Necigef), Finland (ex-APK), France (ex-SICOVAM), Ireland (ex-Crest), Sweden (ex-VPC), Finland (ex-APK) and the UK (ex-Crest).

There are obviously two widely different directions that one could take in order to create clearer and more consistent supervision. One is to increase centralization, trying to move financial supervision from the domestic focus onto the European scene. The other possibility would be to move back from home-country control and supervision to host-country supervision.

The objectives when moving to a better integrated supervision at the EU level are:

- establish a more effective framework for financial supervision;
- enhance financial stability;
- foster the integration of EU financial markets, while maintaining or improving competition;
- safeguard the interests of consumers, investors and other users of financial products.

Following suggestions from a committee set up under the chairmanship of Jacques de Larosière,[42] the European heads of state and government decided in June 2009 to establish a European Systemic Risk Council (name later changed to European Systemic Risk Board) under the ægis of the ECB, to compile and analyze questions concerning financial stability. Second, a European System of Financial Supervisors is to be set up to give more power to all the level 3 organizations.

---

[42] He is a former Director of the Ministry of Finance, Managing Director of the IMF and the EBRD, and Governor of the Banque de France, and also a member of the French Academy of Science – quite an impressive CV.

When asked why the committee did not propose an EU-wide financial supervisory authority for banks, insurance companies and securities markets, Mr. de Larosière responded curtly that "we might have been accused of being unrealistic." In particular, the resistance of the UK to creating a supranational body, directed, or at least heavily influenced, by the ECB, also for non-euro members permeated the compromise solution. As stated in the British FSA Discussion Paper, A regulatory response to the global banking crisis:

a key feature of any such body or arrangement is that it would recognize that supervisory authority is inextricably linked with fiscal responsibility and political accountability. For as long as these remain national, supervisory authority must also remain a national responsibility. This means that day-to-day supervision of financial services firms needs to rest with financial supervisors. There is, however, scope for a range of regulatory activities, most specifically rulemaking, to be centralized. The FSA would support the development of an EU body that would be a radical development of the existing Lamfalussy committees. It would take on their dual functions of assisting the development of EU legislation and bringing about convergence in supervisory practice. The body would have rule-making powers covering both prudential and conduct of business requirements and would provide guidance on the meaning of the rules adopted (p. 157).[43]

One might add that an EU-wide financial supervisory authority would not only have to deal with the large cross-national organizations, but also supervise thousands of small banks with exclusive domestic presence, such as savings banks and credit unions.

Figure 9.3 shows the new framework for macro- and microprudential supervision in the EU.

At the bottom we find the national supervisors for banking, securities and insurance. These may, of course, be combined into fewer agencies, with some countries, such as the UK (FSA), Germany (BaFin), Sweden (Finansinspektionen) and Denmark (Finanstilsynet), having but one common supervisor for all three areas. Other countries have put banking supervision into the central bank, while maintaining a separate supervisor for the securities markets. Examples are Italy (CONSOB) and France (AMF). The UK and Germany are headed in this direction.

---

[43] The British position on micro- and macro-prudential supervision is also summarized at www.meuc.eu/documents/ss9_united_kingdom.doc

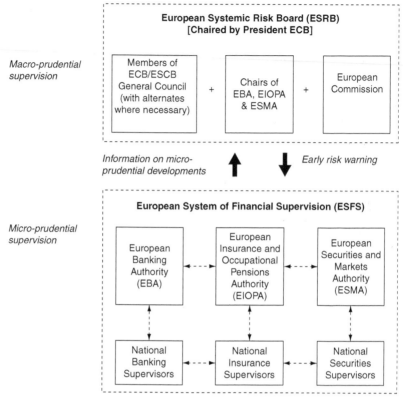

Figure 9.3 The new framework for financial supervision in the European Union
Source: European Commission, The high-level group on financial supervision, page 57

Coordinating the work of national supervisors, we find beefed-up level-3 organizations: the European Banking Authority (EBA) replacing the CEBS, the European Insurance and Occupational Pensions Authority (EIOPA) replacing CEIOPS, and the European Securities and Markets Authority (ESMA), replacing the CESR. The use of the term "authority" rather than "commission" is supposed to indicate organizations with more teeth. The national and European organisms form part of the European System of Financial Supervision (ESFS) for micro-prudential supervision. In this way, it is planned that there should be better consistency and integration, both in harmonizing the rule book in the separate EU countries and in terms of a better focus on cross-border organizations and supernational organs, such as clearing houses and securities depositories.

While the system for supervising micro-prudential risks involves minor changes in existing organizations, a whole new body is created for macro-prudential supervision, the European Systemic Risk Board (ESRB). This body should identify risks to overall financial stability, identify appropriate measures to reduce these risks and apply corrective actions when needed to enhance financial stability.

Apart from a staff of a couple of hundred people, the members ex officio of the General Board of the ESRB would be:

- Chairperson: President of the ECB for (at least) the first 5 years;
- Elected Vice-Chairperson;
- 27 (at present) central bank governors;
- President of the ECB (if after 5 years he or she is no longer chairperson);
- Chairpersons of the three European supervisory authorities;
- Member of the European Commission for financial affairs.

The chairpersons of the national supervisory authorities, as well as representatives from ECOSOC (Economic and Social Committee) and EEA country representatives, would participate in a non-voting role.

There would still be thirty-four members of the committee. We might be forgiven for doubting that such a large body could function effectively. Much will rely on the competence of the staff and on the competence, courage and prestige of the chairperson. Critique has also been levied at the ESRB for being too dominated by central banks and by euro area central banks, and the ECB in particular.[44]

Pursuant to the British objections, the EU compromise concerning the European System of Financial Supervisors spells out that this organization cannot take decisions forcing a member country to bail out a failing bank with taxpayer money, since the money used would come from national sources and hence be covered by the national prerogative of fiscal policy.

The European system of regulation and supervision will thus, in the main, continue as before. Surprisingly little attention has been given to the fact that today's crisis started as a liquidity crisis, and to the difficulty of separating a liquidity crisis from a solvency crisis. This conclusion should force an even more intimate cooperation between the central banks and their respective financial supervisory authorities. Perhaps the Latin countries (France, Spain, Italy, and so on) are right in

---

[44] See the blog by Willem Buiter, Maverecon, http://blogs.ft.com/maverecon/2009/10/the-proposed-european-systemic-risk-board-is-overweight-central-bankers

their organizational set-up, where banking supervision is a department within the central bank rather than a separate agency, as in the UK, Germany and the Nordic countries. However, the UK is moving its FSA into the Bank of England under the name of the Prudential Regulation Authority, and Germany is planning to move at least banking supervision (parts of BaFin) into the Bundesbank.

It is quite obvious that the present set-up has given too much competence and power to the home-country supervisor, to the detriment of the host-country supervisory authorities. The alternative to the proposed EU-wide supervision, therefore, would be to return to supervision by national supervisors. This, in turn, would require cross-border banks to set up locally chartered subsidiaries, rather than working through branches. As noted earlier, this is the business model practiced already by some major banks, such as Grupo Santander. There would be obvious advantages to such a supervisory model, in particular the closeness between the supervisor and the supervised, as well as the fact that subsidiaries would have to be separately capitalized, thereby increasing the financial strength of the group as a whole. It is no wonder that Santander has one of the world's highest Core Tier 1 ratios, as well as the largest number of shareholders of any international banking group. Host-country control would also mean more efficient control of the sufficiency of Deposit Insurance Funds, avoiding the havoc that the Icelandic banks wreaked in the UK, Germany and the Netherlands.

Since banks will be working as independent subsidiaries rather than branches, one of the major implications of host-country supervision will be that individual banks will be smaller. This, in turn, may solve, or at least lessen, the "too-big-to-fail syndrome," as each locally chartered bank may be allowed to fail without hurting other members of the group.

Host-country supervision would obviously strengthen the position of host-country supervisors vis-à-vis home-country supervisors in the supervisory colleges that are now and will continue to be necessary in the future to oversee cross-border banking. Obvious disadvantages with the host-supervisor model are cost aspects, less possibility to harmonize rule books and supervisory standards and models, and, not least, a much lower focus on creating a level playing field to enhance competition.

Supervision in the European Union will thus, in the main, continue to involve individual central banks and national financial supervisory authorities, as well as a few supernational coordinating bodies. In an EU of twenty-seven nations, this means almost a hundred national bodies and at least five supernational organisms (EBA, EIOPA, ESMA, ECB and ESRB). How effective and efficient the coordination between these various national and supernational bodies will be remains to be seen.

How will supervision be organized and coordinated in the USA in the future?

The situation is even worse in the USA, and the changes enacted in July 2010 do little to alleviate the situation (even if the new rules were to be implemented after the Republican mid-term victory in November 2010, which is to be doubted). As shown in Appendix 9.1, there exist no fewer than eleven federal regulatory authorities, often overlapping. State bodies for banking and insurance are obviously duplicated in the fifty states. Part of today's problems arose since banks could often choose their lead supervisor, or in some instances, such as AIG, avoid any form of supervision whatsoever for its London-based Financial Products (FP) division.

The OTS, a department within the Treasury, supervises not only individual nationally chartered savings banks, but all financial groups including a savings bank. It was generally known that the OTS was a benign supervisor. The major failures of supervision occurred, not unexpectedly, in failing large savings banks, such as Washington Mutual, IndyMac, Countrywide, Downey Savings and Loan, and World Savings Bank. All of these were based in California and had the same main supervisor, the guy who allowed IndyMac and some others to book infusion of capital months before its actual arrival, in order to save the bank from the compulsory liquidation that an insufficient capital ratio entails. "The role of the Office of Thrift Supervision, as the name says, is to supervise these banks, not conspire with them," stated Charles Grassley, the leading Republican on the Senate Finance Committee.

Nor is the situation better as concerns insurance companies. These are solely supervised by state organs, there being no national supervisor, which for obvious reasons may lack the competence to understand today's complex financial products. None of the federal authorities, such as the Federal Reserve, the FDIC or the OCC, forms part of the supervision. As concerns AIG, the OTS supervised the savings bank in the group but not the FP division, which took on risks that would never have been permitted in a bank. FP's total assets were some $1,000 billion at the end of 2007, making it half the size of the gigantic financial conglomerate Citigroup. Of its bond portfolio, 38 percent was said to be AAA-rated, but this would prove to be illusory as the crisis hit and the bonds were downrated, with huge losses as a consequence. On top of these investments, AIG had written $527 billion of CDSs, guaranteeing payments on MBSs and CDOs. Already in 2007, $11.5 billion of losses on these contracts were booked in the Annual Account, but it was pointed out that these losses were unrealized and expected to reverse as markets stabilized. This turned out not to be the case, and the loss for AIG in 2008 became almost $100 billion, the largest loss ever recorded by a publicly traded corporation anywhere in the world. It may be compared with a loss at car company GM of $31 billion the same year. Capital infused and loans extended to AIG swelled to $182.5 billion. This was the only time in the crisis that he had been mad, said Fed-chief Ben Bernanke, over how a company could so flagrantly abuse the holes in the net of supervision. The anger from the public and from politicians did not diminish when a large part of the money received from taxpayers, $91 billion, was paid out to close out positions in derivative contracts, mostly with European banks such as Société Générale, Deutsche Bank and Barclays.

The proposals by the Obama administration in June 2009, enacted by Congress in July 2010 (The Wall Street Reform and Consumer Protection Act), will do little to improve the situation. The major changes on the supervisory side are, first, the merger of the OCC and the OTS into a new National Banking Supervisor under the Treasury Department, and, second, a new Federal Insurance Office within the Treasury to provide, for the first time, nationwide monitoring of the insurance industry, previously regulated solely by the individual states. The states, however, will continue to do the actual supervision of insurance companies. The SEC and the CFTC will continue to co-exist, despite obvious overlaps and unclear boundaries. The CFTC is a clear winner, since, in the future, it will regulate and supervise all OTC derivatives, including CDSs (while the SEC is the major regulator for derivatives with underlying securities).

The power of the Federal Reserve is strengthened. It keeps its supervisory role over banks, big as well as small, with original proposals to rid it of the supervision of small banks having failed. The Federal

Reserve Board will include a new Vice-Chairman, responsible for financial stability, reporting to Congress twice a year. It gets responsibility for supervising financial holding companies deemed to pose systemic risk, even if they do not include any banks. Large bank-holding companies that have received TARP money cannot escape supervision from the Federal Reserve by dropping their banking subsidiaries ("the hotel California provision"). Large financial companies that pose a systemic risk will also become subject to more stringent capital and liquidity requirements, set out under Pillar 2 of Basel II. The new Consumer Financial Protection Bureau will be an independent part of the Fed, to police the financial industry and protect the consumers, especially as regards credit card fees and mortgage loans. Its director will be a presidential appointee, subject to confirmation by the Senate. The Fed also succeeded in eliminating the requirement that it should reveal the names of banks who have borrowed from the Fed; this will now be required only with a 2-year lag. Emergency lending by the Fed becomes more restricted, however, in that it must be approved by the Secretary of the Treasury and adequate collateral collected (vide AIG!).

The FDIC gains the right to seize systemically important financial groups, whether banks or not (AIG, GMAC ...). A new Financial Stability Oversight Council (FSOC) is created to coordinate the various agencies as regards macro-prudential supervision and systemic risks. It consists of ten members from the Federal Reserve, the new Consumer Financial Protection Bureau (see below), the FDIC, the FHFA, the National Credit Union Agency, the CFTC, the SEC, the OCC and one independent member, all chaired by the Secretary of the Treasury. With two-thirds of the vote, it may require a financial company deemed to pose systemic threats to divest assets. It will be aided by a new Office of Financial Research within the Treasury.

Several aspects of the original proposal by President Obama have been dropped or modified along the road:

- The proposed tax on banks to repay TARP funds has been dropped. The only requirement is that bailouts must never cost the taxpayer anything; all expenditures during a crisis must be recovered.
- Proposals to change the way in which rating companies such as Moody's or Standard & Poor's operate have been postponed for further study.
- The bill does not attack the "too-big-to-fail" syndrome. Banks may continue to grow organically, even though they have more than 10

percent of a particular business area, but they may not acquire or merge with a firm that would cause them to exceed the limit.
- There are few restrictions on compensation structures. Shareholders' meeting may have a non-binding vote on the company's compensation practices.
- The future of Fannie Mae and Freddie Mac is not included in the bill.
- Perhaps worst of all, nothing has been done in the USA, or for that matter in the G-20, to resolve the question of how internationally active banks shall be wound down.

How will the consumer be protected?

Together with the overhaul of the regulatory and supervisory authorities, the Obama administration also proposed creating a new stand-alone agency for consumer protection. However, the Fed succeeded in retaining and extending its present role on consumer finance in that it will house the Consumer Financial Protection Board. It has been given the following tasks:

- be accountable as the primary federal financial consumer protection supervisor;
- have broad authority to protect consumers of credit, savings, payment and other financial services, and regulate such products and services;
- have "full authority" to enforce protections through orders, fines and penalties;
- define standards for plain products and subject alternative products to greater scrutiny, ban unfair terms and practices or restrict terms and practices for products that may have benefits;
- help ensure that executive pay does not create conflicts of interest between consumers and financial firms;
- enforce fair lending laws and the Community Reinvestment Act, which requires financial institutions to serve sparsely populated or low-income areas;
- overhaul mortgage laws to make them clearer and fairer to consumers;
- require firms to offer a simple mortgage, with straightforward terms and uniform disclosure; consumers could opt for alternative loans but these would be subject to restrictions;
- ban unfair practices such as "yield spread premiums," which entitle mortgage brokers to higher fees if they steer consumers to mortgages with higher costs;

- require mortgage brokers to be paid over time, based on loan performance, rather than in a lump sum at closing;
- restrict or ban prepayment penalties;
- require loan originators or loan bundlers to retain 5 percent of credit risk;
- minimum underwriting standards are created for home mortgages; in the future, the lender is required to assess whether the borrower can repay interest and amortizations by verifying income, credit history and job status – this does away with so called Alt-A loans ("liar loans").

Many of these tasks are obviously meritworthy, but it is doubtful that a new superagency is the right answer to the problem. It should also be noted that the USA, in contrast to Europe, already has (state) rules for the authorization of loan officers in financial institutions and mortgage brokers. In order to become a licensed loan officer in Texas, for example, 1 week's training or 8 months "on-the-job-training" is required. The applicant's identity has to be verified, and his/her education, job practice, possible entries in the crime register, payment delinquencies investigated. In order to be licensed as a mortgage broker, a written exam is required, showing the applicant's knowledge of the relevant state and federal laws, knowledge about mortgage products and conditions for loans to be accepted by Fannie Mae/Freddie Mac, interest-rate mathematics, and so on.

What is lacking is better education of and greater demands on the borrower (= consumer). In making his presentation of the proposal, President Obama criticized those who took out loans they could not possibly afford. But many people did not understand that "teaser rates" would be raised; nor were they capable of simulating the effects on their budget. As Bob Shiller has so wisely pointed out in his recent book on the financial crisis, the advisory columns in the newspapers are really aimed mostly at those who *do not need* advice![45] Education is sorely needed, but there is already some movement in this direction. The private organization, Financial Industry Regulatory Authority (FINRA), has taken the initiative to create a foundation, the FINRA Investor Education Foundation, which spends an annual $20 million on education and fellowships in finance.

---

[45] Shiller, *The Subprime Solution.*

In Europe, great efforts have been made to protect investors in securities. Strict rules apply for mutual funds, both UCITS and special (hedge) funds. In the Markets in Financial Instruments Directive (MIFID) (2004/39/EC), investment firms are required to establish whether their clients are to be regarded as retail customers, professionals or counter-parties, with correspondingly different demands on information to be furnished.

Article 19 of MIFID specifies that:

1. Member States shall require that, when providing investment services and/or, where appropriate, ancillary services to clients, an investment firm act honestly, fairly and professionally in accordance with the best interests of its clients.

2. All information, including marketing communications, addressed by the investment firm to clients or potential clients shall be fair, clear and not misleading. Marketing communications shall be clearly identifiable as such.

3. Appropriate information shall be provided in a comprehensible form to clients or potential clients about:
   - the investment firm and its services,
   - financial instruments and proposed investment strategies;
   - This should include appropriate guidance on and warnings of the risks associated with investments in those instruments or in respect of particular investment strategies,
   - execution venues, and
   - costs and associated charges

   so that they are reasonably able to understand the nature and risks of the investment service and of the specific type of financial instrument that is being offered and, consequently, to take investment decisions on an informed basis. This information may be provided in a standardised format.

4. When providing investment advice or portfolio management the investment firm shall obtain the necessary information regarding the client's or potential client's knowledge and experience in the investment field relevant to the specific type of product or service, his financial situation and his investment objectives so as to enable the firm to recommend to the client or potential client the investment services and financial instruments that are suitable for him.

Of particular interest is the requirement in 19.4 that the investment firm obtain information on the client's ability to understand the product he/she is being sold. Yet, for unknown reasons, similar requirements on loan officers in banks are missing. The European Code of Conduct concerning home loans (2002), signed by the European Mortgage Federation in conjunction with the European Commission, only specifies what information a bank must provide to customers, but there is no requirement that the bank find out how much the borrower has understood of the terms. Nor are there any requirements that loan officers be licensed or authorized in any similar way to the compulsory licensing of those bankers dealing with investment products.

A further necessary change in the financial safety net must be the introduction or the lowering of the maximum allowable loan-to-value for mortgages. We saw earlier many instances of loan-to-value exceeding 100 percent, even for a newly purchased house. (Then) Prime Minister Gordon Brown suggested in 2009, on behalf of the UK, that a legal maximum loan-to-value of 95 percent be established. This could be compared with existing legal maxima of 80 percent in Denmark, 75 percent in France and 60 percent in Germany. It would seem unavoidable in a country like the UK, which has just faced a severe housing bubble, with the consequence that most of its mortgage-banking sector is nationalized, to start thinking about this problem, though probably settling on a far lower number than that suggested by the PM.[46] The Swedish financial supervisory authority has introduced a limit on loan-to-value of 85 percent, applicable from October 2010. In Norway and Finland, the corresponding limit is 90 percent. In China, the authorities have raised the minimum cash downpayment from 40 to 50 percent.[47]

Major recommendations in this book and their fulfillment to date

Banks, capital and deposit insurance

- Abolish all types of hybrid capital in banks' Tier 1 ratio, moving them to Tier 2. This has been partly done, although with an excessively long period of adaptation, until 2023.

---

[46] This point, though without numerical suggestions, was also made at a conference in January 2009, within the framework of the so-called Geneva reports. See www.voxeu.org/reports/Geneva11.pdf

[47] See also Lybeck, No one addresses real cause of crisis.

- Set the minimum Core Tier 1 ratio at 6–8 percent and raise the total Tier 1 ratio to 10–12 percent. This has also been partly done with a Core Tier 1 ratio of 7 percent and a total Tier 1 ratio at 8.5, though only from 2019.
- Since half a bank's capital may be lost in a deep crisis, such as the one we have just been through, capital ratios at the top of the cycle should, in principle, be double these ratios, say, 12–16 percent ("dynamic provisioning").
- Increase the use of stress tests to complement present VaR measures; this has been partly done, but in a very mild format.
- Introduce a stress-tested minimum liquidity ratio. This has been done, though only from 2015.
- Introduce a minimum leverage ratio (maximum gearing ratio) as an additional guide to restricting banks' risk-taking. This has been done, though only at 4 percent leverage (twenty-five times gearing), which corresponds to the US category of "adequately" capitalized banks.
- Establish more generous levels for deposit insurance. The US level is staying at $250,000; the EU level should be increased to far more than the recently decided €100,000.

Regulation and supervision

- Hedge and equity funds worldwide above a certain minimum size must be registered with their respective financial supervisory authority and supervised. This seems to have been done.
- Financial supervisory authorities (like the SEC) should approve all proposed issues of shares and fixed-income instruments, irrespective of whether these are directed at the general public or at qualified investors.
- Supervisory authorities should try to increase the transparency and minimize the complexity of financial products, perhaps outlawing such products as CDO-squared and CDO-cube. The EU proposal to ban "naked" CDSs – that is, buying protection without having the underlying risk – however, may increase rather than diminish actual financial risks.
- The originator should retain at least 10 percent of the securitized loan (rather than the proposed 5 percent).
- Supervisory authorities need to cooperate better, both within the European Union and in the USA. It is difficult to see how one can

avoid the introduction of an EU-wide financial supervisory authority, at least for the euro area.
- The alternative is the return to host-country control and supervision.
- International cooperation in financial supervision is still totally lacking, as are common rules for bankruptcies.

Consumer protection

- Demand authorization of all EU bank loan officers, as is already the case for investments.
- Introduce a parallel directive to MIFID in requiring banks to establish a customer's competence level.
- Require that mortgage brokers be registered with their financial supervisory authorities.
- Require more responsibility from borrowers also, but provide education.

Macro-policy

- Introduce a legal maximum loan-to-value ratio for new loans not higher than 85 percent, and establish a minimum rate of amortizations for existing loans above that ceiling.

Postscript

Since the book went to press, the US Financial Crisis Inquiry Commission (FCIC) has published its report (Final report of the National Commission on the Causes of the Financial and Economic Crisis in the United States, US Government Printing office, 2011).

The report builds mainly on interviews, which makes it strong on anecdotal evidence and weak on analysis. Since most of the interviewed people are from the financial industry itself or borrowers affected by the crisis, it is not surprising that the Commission puts the main blame on weak regulation, supervision and coordination between supervisory authorities. Since the report focuses exclusively on the USA, it makes no effort to explain why lending and housing "bubbles" emerged in countries with very different economic situations and dissimilar regulatory environments from the USA.

Appendix 9.1
List of regulatory authorities in the USA

Authority	Tasks	Supervised institutions, example
Federal Reserve and its Board of Governors and twelve regional Reserve Banks	Supervises financial conglomerates and member banks. Gives liquidity support and supervises the stability of financial markets; gets a bigger role as coordinator between the various agencies	Financial groups like Citigroup, JPMorgan Chase, KeyCorp, SunTrust Corp, PNC Financial Services
Office of the Comptroller of the Currency (OCC), a department within the Treasury	Supervises commercial banks with a national license (national banks), but also foreign banks in the USA	Banks like Citibank, PNC Bank, Key Bank, SunTrust Bank, National City. In all, some 1,600 banks and 50 foreign-owned banks
Federal Deposit Insurance Corporation (FDIC)	Supervises those national and state commercial banks and savings banks which are not members of the Federal Reserve; responsible for banks in administration. Shares supervision of Fed member banks with the Fed	Bancorp. South Bank, Bank of the West, GMAC Bank
Office of Thrift Supervision (OTS), a department within the Treasury (to be abolished)	Supervises individual savings banks, as well as financial conglomerates containing a savings bank	GE, Hartford, Countrywide and other groups containing savings banks; individual savings banks
National Credit Union Administration	Supervises credit unions	Navy Federal Credit Union, Pentagon Federal Credit Union, Columbia Credit Union, and so on

State Department of Financial Institutions	Supervises state banks	Most of the bankrupt banks, such as Sanderson State Bank in Texas and Security Pacific in California, had a state license, not a national license
State "Insurance Departments"	Supervise insurance companies	AIG, Hartford Financial
Federal Housing Finance Agency (FHFA)	The supervisory authority for Federal Home Loan Banks	Ginnie Mae, Fannie Mae and Freddie Mac
Securities and Exchange Commission (SEC)	Supervises securities markets, exchanges, investment banks, broker-dealers, mutual funds, clearing houses; approves prospectuses	NYSE, NASDAQ, earlier Goldman Sachs, Merrill Lynch, Lehman Brothers, and so on, New York Stock Exchange, NASDAQ, the Fixed Income Clearing Corporation (FICC) and the National Securities Clearing Corporation (NSCC)
Commodity Futures Trading Commission (CFTC)	Supervises exchange trades in derivatives like futures and options; some clearing houses	Chicago Mercantile Exchange (CME), Chicago Board Options Exchange (CBOE), New York Mercantile Exchange, Chicago Mercantile Exchange Clearing House, Options Clearing Corporation

There also exist self-regulatory organizations (SROs), in particular, the Financial Industry Regulatory Authority (FINRA), which is responsible for supervising all securities companies (banks, investment banks, broker-dealers, mutual funds), as well as NASDAQ, the US Stock Exchange, the New York Stock Exchange (NYSE), the International Securities Exchange (ISE) and the regional exchanges, in particular as concerns questions such as insider trading. It is also responsible for educating and licensing the employees of these companies. It also has the power to levy penalties on financial firms. Goldman Sachs was ordered in June 2010 to pay $20.6 million to scammed investors. The investment bank should have known about the Ponzi scheme pulled off by its subsidiary, the collapsed Bayou Hedge Funds.

Appendix 9.2
Overview of bank taxes in different countries

Country	Rate (%)	What is taxed	Start date	Annual yield (€)
Austria	0.055–0.085	Domestic assets minus equity	2011	500 million
Belgium	0.15	Bank deposits	2010	700 million
Denmark	0.20	Covered deposits	2011	n/a
Germany	0.02–0.04	Parent company liabilities	2011	1 billion
Hungary	0.15–0.50	Domestic bank assets	2011	670 million
France	0.25	Risk-weighted assets	2011	555 million
Sweden	0.036	Liabilities minus equity	2009	250 million
UK	0.075	Liabilities less insured deposits and core equity	2011	3 billion

Notes:
1. 0.02 percent for liabilities less than €10 billion; 0.03 percent between €10 billion and €100 billion; and 0.04 percent above €100 billion.
2. Only institutions with liabilities greater than £20 billion will be taxed.

10 | *Outstanding issues*

Trying to conclude or even summarize a book of the present format and size, with its wealth of information in the form of institutional facts, statistical data, discussions and analyses, is beyond human capacity – at least beyond mine! Let me focus instead on what issues remain to be fixed in order to mitigate the next financial crisis, for there will surely be one. During my 45 years as a professional economist in academia, banking and consulting, I have witnessed and participated in (and written about) a number of these crises. I expect to cover at least a couple more before I am done, though hopefully they will not be of Richter magnitude 8.0 or so, such as the one we have just been through.

Could we perhaps also speculate on which financial products and/or which institutions might trigger the next crisis? Has anything been done in the solving of the present crisis that might make things even more difficult the next time round? I leave these questions until the end.

What conclusions can we draw from the years 2007–10 and from government policies?

Hedge funds and private equity funds

Governments all around the world have attacked phenomena which have attracted popular animosity, but which were irrelevant to the present crises. Neither hedge funds nor private equity funds lay behind the crisis, yet they have been given much blame for it. This said, I think it is a good thing that funds over a certain size should be compelled to register with their supervising authority and comply with certain regulatory standards. This will prevent another LTCM crisis. Exempting small funds (under €100 million in the European Union, or under €500 million if their activities are unleveraged) keeps down the bureaucracy on both sides. Requiring the presence of a custodian, separate from the asset manager, prevents future scandals such as the Madoff hoax. It remains to be seen whether the proposed Directive on Alternative Investment Funds in the

EU is counter-competitive, as claimed by several US funds selling their products in Europe.

The remuneration system

Bonuses and greed have attracted much popular attention and ire. But no instance has been pinpointed where the remuneration system or the level of pay led to excessive speculation. The main public culprit in the crash, the investment bank Lehman Brothers, actually led its Wall Street colleagues in handing out bonuses in stock rather than cash. Many of the short-sighted attempts by politicians to rein in offensive bonuses may have had adverse effects. Banks in the USA that were subjected to pay restrictions chose to repay TARP funds early, perhaps too early, in order to escape the "pay czar." Companies like the ailing AIG lost key personnel because of the pay restrictions. In Europe, and in particular in the UK, banks chose to pay the tax on bonuses themselves rather than lose key staff.

The new restrictions on the pay-out of bonuses in the European Union seem right and fair. A system of paying huge cash bonuses in a given year, without the possibility to claw back part of them if the investment goes awry over the next few years, seems inherently wrong. Yet focusing on a few top income earners does not change the attitude that "greed is good," which has permeated the entire financial system. And the general public is just as affected by similar behavior. Speculatory "animal spirits" à la Akerlof and Shiller have characterized human beings from the beginning of mankind. It is to be doubted that a few restrictions on the highest-paid will have much impact on the behavior of the overall economy. Anyway, if EU legislation appears overly restrictive, an affected bank can always locate itself elsewhere.

It would be much better to encourage the supervisory authorities to examine in detail the remuneration system in financial organizations and add an extra capital charge under Pillar 2 of Basel II and III to punish the offenders and make them change their ways.

The government-sponsored enterprises Fannie Mae and Freddie Mac

In the USA, one of the major questions for the future is what to do with the semi-public Fannie Mae and Freddie Mac. They had already cost the taxpayer $145 billion by mid-2010. The politically independent

Congressional Budget Office (CBO) estimates the cost at $389 billion by 2019 (out of the $400 billion that have potentially been granted in new capital).[1] As was well-stated by the incoming Republican Chairman of the House Financial Services Committee, "you cannot be half pregnant. You either have a government-managed program or you have a private solution."[2] Republicans naturally favor the second alternative. It is obvious that the formally private, yet government-sponsored set-up, led the companies' counter-parties to believe that the government would step in if necessary, as indeed happened. When the Financial Accounting Standards Board (FASB) forced the decision in March 2010, recognizing the liability of the USA, some $400 billion was added to the federal debt. What happens further on is in doubt. Many politicians from both parties, such as the Democratic former Chairman of the House Financial Services Committee, Barney Frank (one of the fathers of the Dodd-Frank bill), want to abolish them altogether and subsidize mortgages directly from the budget rather than in this indirect way, by the guaranteeing of the liabilities of two nominally private enterprises.[3]

Will the FSOC and the ESRB spot systemic risk more quickly?

It remains to be seen whether the new institutional make-up in the USA and Europe will do a better job of spotting systemic risks in the future. Critical commentators have pointed out that if the ten people now joined in committee on the Financial Stability Oversight Council (FSOC) had wanted to have a meeting before, nothing would have stopped them. Why would the fact that they are formalized increase their powers of foresight? So the only real contribution in this part of the Dodd-Frank Act is the addition of a staff whose qualifications and power remain to be seen, the Office of Financial Research within the Treasury Department.

In Europe, the European Banking Authority (London), the European Securities Markets Authority (Paris) and the European Insurance and Occupational Pensions Authority (Frankfurt) will be small organizations, with forty to sixty people each, as contrasted with the British FSA's 3,000 employees or the German BaFin's 1,800. Power remains with the local financial supervisory authorities as a matter of competence and people

---

[1] Kapner, Lawmakers wary of Fannie and Freddie reform.
[2] Braithwaite, Regulators pressured to curb Wall Street reforms.
[3] Allen, Democrat Frank says abolish Freddie and Fannie.

power. As concerns the macro-stability watchdog the European Systemic
Risk Board(ESRB), it has been criticized as being solely a weaker copy of
the central bank governors, especially the ECB's. Also, the ESRB cannot
enforce decisions in member states, since a bank bail-out involves budgets
and taxes which remain the member countries' exclusive domain,
demanding unanimity in bodies such as ECOFIN. Only if its secretariat
builds up such competence that it actually adds information and analysis
over and above what is available today will there be any gain.

Basel III

As concerns capital-adequacy ratios, BIS and the G-20 are to be con-
gratulated for the sharp increase in capital requirements, as well as for
their focus on Core Tier 1 capital (true core equity, TCE) rather than on
wider but irrelevant concepts, as well as for a tighter definition of what
constitutes Tier 1 capital. An increase in the TCE ratio from 2 to 7
percent (4.5 percent plus a 2.5 percent buffer) may seem a large step, yet
there remains the politically charged discussion of a buffer for counter-
cyclicality, as well as a charge for size. It needs to be remembered that
banks lost, on average, half their capital in the recent crisis, implying
that a normal TCE ratio at the top of the cycle of some 10–15 percent
might be necessary if the minima are never to fall below 4.5 or 7 percent,
respectively. Are governments and financial supervisory authorities
prepared to force banks to achieve these levels?

It has also been questioned if the long periods of adjustment are really
necessary: 2015 for liquidity ratios, 2019 for capital ratios and 2023 to
get rid of the hybrids. The 4.5 percent minimum TCE has to be attained
by 2015, however, or the bank will face restrictions on its dividends. As
noted by the *Financial Times'* Chief Economics Editor, Martin Wolf,
even though more equity might raise direct costs, a higher capital
cushion should lower the cost of other types of funding as it becomes
less risky.[4] Martin Wolf has also suggested that while it might be
difficult to attain the prescribed capital ratios much faster than specified, relying only on retained profits and IPOs, it might be preferable to
have shorter adaptation periods and instead let governments infuse the
needed capital in the form of common stock, which can then be gradually sold to the general public over the next 5–15 years.

---

[4] Wolf, Basel: the mouse that did not roar.

As for the USA, it should be remembered that its banks are still operating under Basel I. The planned transition to Basel II for the twenty or so biggest banks with international operations was held up by the supervisors, noting the sharp fall in required capital as banks' own internal models were allowed (see Chapter 7). Hence banks were told to await Basel III. However, Basel III is in conflict with the Dodd-Frank Act, because the latter requires regulators to remove from the rule books all references to official credit ratings. But Basel III, almost to the same extent as Basel II, relies on these external ratings by Standard & Poor's and Moody's and others like them. Apparently nobody thought of this and no solution has been found (by November 2010, as this is written). Presumably, US banks will stay on Basel I for the time being.

The prop desk

Proprietary trading – that is, banks' trading for their own books and profits – is another scapegoat of the Great Crash. The "Volcker rule" would have done away with all prop trading in deposit-taking institutions, but the proposal was watered down in Congress. In the future, banks will still be allowed to place 3 percent of their Tier 1 capital into private equity and hedge funds, provided it does not exceed 3 percent of the fund's capital. As concerns in-house prop trading, it will continue to be allowed for interest and foreign exchange derivatives. Only credit derivatives such as CDSs will have to be shifted out of the banks, unless they are centrally cleared through a CCP clearing house. But while some prop traders have left for hedge funds, most of the original people are still there, although the prop desks have been shut down or reduced in size. Is it too much to imagine that the activities are being continued, only shifted to the clients' desk, it being virtually impossible for an outsider to decide when a bank is anticipating or hedging a client order and when it is acting for its own books?

Too big to fail

In order to contain the size of its two biggest banks, UBS and Credit Suisse, Switzerland proposes to work through extra capital requirements on big banks, as set out in Table 10.1.[5]

[5] Simonian and Murphy, How Swiss finish was factored in.

Table 10.1 *A comparison of standard capital requirements (%) under Basel III and those proposed by Switzerland*

Type of capital	Basel III	Switzerland
Minimum TCE (by 2015)	4.5%	4.5%
Conservation buffer (by 2019)	2.5	5.5 (equity)
		3.0 (CoCo bonds)
Counter-cyclical buffer	? (0–2.5)	?
Systemic groups buffer	? (0–2.0)	6.0 (CoCo bonds)
Sum decided TCE or similar	7.0	19.0

Switzerland will thus require a 10 percent TCE capital ratio, as contrasted with 7 percent under Basel III. The rest of the 19 percent ratio may be attained by using Contingent Convertible Capital.[6] Switzerland also introduced a minimum leverage ratio of 3 percent back in 2009, long before Basel III.

The Financial Stability Board (FSB) has identified thirty financial groups worldwide, of which twenty-four are banks, which are considered to create systemic risk and should be supervised cross-border. Since there exists no cross-border supervision, and there will be none for the foreseeable future (except the limited warning function of the IMF), one could at least hope for sharper capital requirements à la Switzerland for these twenty-four banks. But will the G-20 have the political strength to act?

What has been done in the USA to contain the megabanks from becoming even larger? The Dodd-Frank Act prevents banks from acquisitions that would lead to a market share in excess of 10 percent, though there are no restrictions on organic growth. Three groups already exceed the 10 percent limit by deposits (Bank of America, JPMorgan Chase and Citigroup). Germany is pushing legislation that would give the government powers to break up banks in a crisis. In the USA, regulators are taking a pause in deciding how the Risk Council should proceed in breaking up banks ("resolution authority"). This will probably be one aspect of the Dodd-Frank Act that the new Republican majority will (try to) shoot down. France has stated that it plans to place

[6] It should be noted that these rules are proposals to be enacted by Parliament in early 2011.

a tax on a bank's "riskiest activities," though with no specifics, in November 2010, and with no concern for size. Given that Europe's and the world's largest bank by assets is BNP Paribas (with Crédit Agricole as number three), and given France's traditional support for its industrial flagships, this laissez-faire attitude fails to surprise.

Break up big banks?

Switzerland has stated explicitly that it will not place restrictions on the size of its banks other than the required higher capital ratios, nor will it restrict their activities such as proprietary trading. In the UK, the Vickers Committee (under John Vickers, former Chief Economist at the Bank of England) is not expected to propose that British megabanks be broken up. HSBC, Standard Chartered and Barclays have threatened to move abroad should this be proposed. The Commission may propose higher capital and liquidity standards than those set by Basel III, and perhaps also limit proprietary trading.

Even if both competition aspects and the lack of economies of scale indicate the need for a break-up of the megabanks, as most recently proposed by John Kay,[7] it cannot be done by individual countries, but only by worldwide agreements, which appear highly unlikely. It seems much better to achieve limitations on size by higher capital standards à la Switzerland (and perhaps in the UK?).

Bail-out or bail-in?

An interesting debate has taken place in one of the countries that has suffered most from the financial crash, namely Ireland. Should the worst forecasts come true, the cost of cleaning up the Irish banking sector will cost the taxpayer some €50 billion, corresponding to almost 30 percent of Ireland's GDP. Should the taxpayer really shoulder this entire burden (bail-out)? Given that equity owners have been wiped out, should those next in line, bond-holders, not suffer as well, by a "bail-in?" This question will obviously have to be fought out in each country's legal system (since bankruptcy laws differ), but it strengthens the case for CoCo bonds, where the possibility of a bail-in is explicit in the contract.

---

[7] Kay, We must press on with breaking up banks.

Housing and the mortgage market

We have seen that the origin of this financial crisis lay in the US (and, to some extent, British, Irish and Spanish) housing mortgage markets, for a number of reasons:

- lack of physical contact between borrower and lender;
- unintelligible terms of loan contract (in particular, teaser rates);
- lack of restrictions on loan-to-value (LTV);
- easiness to borrow, even for subprime and Alt-A borrowers;
- historically low interest rates;
- government sponsoring of homeownership (Community Reinvestment Act);
- government protection of homeowners (Homestead Acts);
- lack of possibility for banks to claw back more than the house (non-recourse);
- explosion of the "shadow banking system," enabling the securitization of loans;
- ignorance of many international investors in US CDOs and CDSs;
- explicit or implicit connivance of the rating institutions in giving AAA ratings.

As noted in the preceding chapters, *none* of these factors has truly been changed as a result of the Dodd-Frank Act. There is still no restriction on LTV in the USA, and you can still walk away from your house and your loan scot-free. Government-sponsored Fannie and Freddie will still guarantee almost the entire mortgage market (in flow terms). The 30-year fixed mortgage rate is, at around 4 percent (November 2010), lower than ever since the 1950s, in both nominal and real terms. Even before the 2010 elections, the Obama administration could not get nomination of the proposed head of the new Consumer Financial Protection Agency (CFPA) through Congress. Instead, the highly qualified Professor Elizabeth Warren (also Chairman of the Congressional Oversight Panel) was given a job as advisor to the President, in which capacity she is supposed to write the agenda of the new agency. Given the political shifts of 2010, it seems very likely that the CFPA will either be killed outright or at least made totally toothless.

In the UK, it has been proposed (but not yet decided) to restrict LTV to 95 percent. Only Sweden has enacted a restriction of 85 percent LTV for new loans.

Housing may very well be the cause behind the next bubble and the next financial crisis.

Where will the next crisis be?

I think that there is an almost universal agreement that letting Lehman Brothers fail was a major policy mistake of the Bush administration. Not that investment banks should necessarily be saved, but the signal sent by earlier actions in saving Bear Stearns and Merrill Lynch was that these banks were also included in the public safety net. The bankruptcy of Lehman overturned this belief and led to the financial panic in September 2008 which took the world's central banks a full year to contain. Indeed, the decision by the Federal Reserve in November 2010 to buy an additional $600 billion of bonds could be interpreted as a continued liquidity-enhancing "quantitative easing," resulting from the Lehman crash.

I believe there is also a broad agreement that saving banks all over the world with taxpayers' money was not only necessary, but also beneficial. Indeed, in the USA, by 2010, taxpayers had already been repaid in full, with a handsome profit. In the UK, the net cost to the taxpayer was calculated as basically nil.

Yet there are two disturbing factors which, in conjunction, may create the next crisis. One is that some 10 percent of the entire OTC derivatives market takes place with non-financial corporations, which succeeded in being exempted from the new rules. In the USA, they are working under the umbrella of the National Association of Manufacturers (NAM), together with the Chambers of Commerce and the Business Roundtable, to form the Coalition for Derivatives End Users. The 171 members include companies from IBM to brewer MillerCoors and tractor-maker Deere & Co. In Europe, the corresponding lobby group is the European Association of Corporate Treasurers. The Dodd-Frank Act exempts non-financial corporations not only from clearing requirements (though they must report data to data repositories), but also from placing collateral to back up the transaction. Note that it was demand for more collateral (from Goldman Sachs) that felled AIG. Note also that it was the unregulated Financial Products division that brought down AIG. Nothing prevents a non-financial company from creating an in-house trading division, even in financial products, that will be just as unregulated as AIG was, and does

Table 10.2 *Total notional amounts of OTC derivatives outstanding*
($ billion), December 2009

Type of derivative	Total notional amount outstanding	Of this: With non-financial counter-party
Foreign Exchange		
Forwards	23.1	4.9
Swaps	16.5	2.1
Options	9.5	1.7
Interest rate		
Forward rate agreements (FRAs)	51.7	1.9
Interest rate swaps (IRSs)	349.2	30.2
Options	48.8	10.8
Equity-linked	6.6	1.7
Commodity	2.9	n/a
CDSs	32.7	1.6
TOTAL	614.6 (incl. unallocated)	59.8

Source: Bank for International Settlements, *Semi-Annual OTC Derivatives Statistics,*
Market activity in the second half of 2009 (May 2010)

not even have to post collateral, if its counter-parties are willing to
accept this situation.

Table 10.2 sets out the OTC derivatives situation at the end of 2009.

Now, put this information together with the bailing out of some very
large, non-financial companies in the latest crisis. Perhaps bailing out
AIG was necessary, given the number of counter-parties and the volumes involved, and the financial character of the products involved. But
bailing out GM and Chrysler may have sent a signal that any corporation large enough, and in particular a large employer in its community, would be saved. So who will be next? Boeing, with close to 100,000
employees, based in Washington state? Exxon Mobil, with its 80,000
employees? Dupont, with 60,000 employees, an important employer in
Delaware? Alcoa, similarly with 60,000 employees, mostly in
Pennsylvania? Or, more probably, a company which nobody thought
was in trouble.

There is an apt term in macroeconomics, "volatility transfer." Prevent volatility in one market (such as the exchange rate) and it will pop up in another market (for instance, in the form of unemployment). Uncertainty and volatility cannot be done away with, only transferred somewhere else. The same would appear to be true for the regulation of financial markets. Forbid speculation in one place and it will just appear somewhere else. Will Boeing, Dupont, Exxon, Alcoa and the other major non-financial corporations, not to mention commodity traders such as Cargill and Vitol, become part of the "shadow banking system" too? Nothing prevents it, and they do not have Basel III capital requirements; often they do not even have to post collateral for their derivatives transactions.

As was well-stated in a beautifully researched article in the *Financial Times*:

Yet a nagging worry is expressed by some regulators, bankers and other experts within the financial services industry that these reforms, like others in the past, risk backfiring. What if those taboo, high-risk businesses cannot be stopped in their tracks as regulators and politicians would like? What if, instead, they just move to a new home – within the sprawling mass of hedge funds, private equity firms, trading houses, even energy companies, all of which are largely unregulated and free of the capital requirements imposed on the banks?[8]

[8] Jenkins and Masters, Financial regulation.

Bibliography

Abadie, Loïc, *La crise financière de 2008/2010: mode d'emploi pour la décrypter et l'exploiter* (Paris: Éditions Valys, 2008).

Acharya, Viral V. and Richardson, Matthew (eds.), *Restoring Financial Stability: How to Repair a Failed System* (Hoboken, NJ: John Wiley and Sons, 2009).

Aguilar, J. P., Bouchaud, J. P., Cont, R., Laloux, L. and Potters, M., Are financial crashes predictable?, *Europhysics Letters*, 45:1 (January 1999), pp. 1–5.

Akerlof, George A., The market for "lemons": quality uncertainty and the market mechanism, *Quarterly Journal of Economics*, 84:3 (August 1970), pp. 488–500.

Akerlof, George A. and Shiller, Robert J., *Animal Spirits: How Human Psychology Drives the Economy and Why it Matters for Global Capitalism* (Princeton University Press, 2009).

Allen, Franklin and Gale, Douglas, *Understanding Financial Crises* (Oxford University Press, 2007, 2009).

Allen, JoAnne, Democrat Frank says abolish Freddie and Fannie: report, Reuters, August 18, 2010.

Andrews, Edmond L., Greenspan concedes error on regulation, *New York Times*, October 24, 2008.

Anson, Mark J. P., Fabozzi, Frank J., Choudhry, Moorad and Chen, Ren-Raw, *Credit Derivatives: Instruments, Application and Pricing* (Hoboken, NJ: John Wiley and Sons, 2004).

Ashcraft, Adam B. and Schuermann, Til, Understanding the securitization of subprime mortgage credit, Federal Reserve Bank of New York, Staff Report no. 318 (March 2008).

Baird, Jane, Around 60 percent CDS could clear centrally say experts, Reuters (April 16, 2010), www.reuters.com/article/idUSTRE63F13720100416

Bairoch, Paul, *Economics and World History: Myths and Paradoxes* (University of Chicago Press, 1993).

Baker, Dean, *Plunder and Blunder: The Rise and Fall of the Bubble Economy* (Sausolito, CA: PoliPointPress, 2009).

Baker, Dean and McArthus, Travis, The value of the "too-big-to-fail" big bank subsidy, Centre for Economic Policy Research Issue Brief (September 2009).

Ball, Philip, *Critical Mass: How One Thing Leads to Another* (London: Random House, Arrow Books, 2005).

Bank of England, *Financial Stability Report* (various issues). *Quarterly Bulletin* (various issues).

Bank for International Settlements, *Semi-annual OTC Derivatives Statistics* (various issues).

Basel Committee on Banking Supervision, Capital requirements regulations 2006, Statutory Instrument, SI 2006/3221 (2006).

Principles for sound stress testing practices and supervision (January 2009).

Financial Stability Forum, Addressing procyclicality in the financial system (April 2009).

Enhancements to the Basel II framework (July 2009).

International framework for liquidity risk measurement, standards and monitoring (December 2009).

Strengthening the resilience of the banking sector (December 2009).

Adjustments to the Basel II market risk framework (18 June 2010).

Basel Committee on Banking Supervision, Countercyclical capital buffer proposal, Consultative Document (July 2010).

Assessing the macroeconomic impact of the transition to stronger capital and liquidity requirements (August 2010).

An assessment of the long-term economic impact of the new regulatory framework (August 2010).

Higher global minimum capital standards (September 12, 2010).

The Banker, Top 1000 world banks (July 2008, July 2009, July 2010).

Bankkriskommittén, *Bankkrisen* (Stockholm: Finansdepartementet, 1994).

Banks, E., *Volatility and Credit Risk in the Capital Markets* (Chicago: Probus Publishing Company, 1993).

Barro, Robert J., Fama, Eugene F., Fischel, Daniel R., Meltzer, Allan H., Roll, Richard and Telser, Lester G., *Black Monday and the Future of Financial Markets* (Homewood, IL: Dow Jones-Irwin for the Mid America Institute for Public Policy Research, 1989).

Barth, James R., Trimbath, S. and Yago, Glenn (eds.), *The Savings and Loan Crisis: Lessons from a Regulatory Failure*, The Milken Institute Series on Financial Innovation and Economic Growth (Dordrecht: Kluwer Academic Publishers, 2004).

Batra, Ravi, *Greenspan's Fraud: How Two Decades of his Policies have Undermined the Global Economy* (New York: Palgrave MacMillan, 2005).

Becker, Bo and Milbourn, Todd, Reputation and competition: evidence from the credit rating industry, Harvard Business School Working Paper 09-051 (2008, revised September 2010).

Benink, Harald and Kaufman, George, Turmoil reveals the inadequacy of Basel II, *Financial Times*, February 27, 2008.

Benston, G. J., Carhill, M. and Olasov, B., The failure and survival of thrifts, in R. G. Hubbard (ed.), *Financial Markets and Financial Crises* (University of Chicago Press, 1991), pp. 305–84.

Benston, George J., Eisenbeis, Robert A., Horvitz, Paul M., Kane, Edward J. and Kaufman, George G., *Perspectives of Safe and Sound Banking: Past, Present and Future* (Cambridge, MA: MIT Press, 1986).

Bernanke, Ben (ed.), *Essays on the Great Depression* (Princeton University Press, 2000).

Bernanke, Ben and Gertler, Mark, Monetary policy and asset price volatility, National Bureau of Economic Research Working Paper 7559 (February 2000).

Bernanke, Ben and Lown, Carla, The credit crunch, *Brookings Papers on Economic Activity*, 2 (1991), pp. 205–47.

Bernanke, Ben S., Laubach, Thomas, Mishkin, Frederic S. and Posen, Adam S., *Inflation Targeting* (Princeton University Press, 1999).

Blundell-Wignall, Adrian, The subprime crisis: size, deleveraging and some policy options, *OECD Financial Market Trends*, 94:1 (June 2008), pp. 1–25.

Blundell-Wignall, Adrian, Atkinson, Paul and Lee, Se Hoon, The current financial crisis: causes and policy issues, *OECD Financial Market Trends*, 2 (2008), pp. 1–21.

Boskin, Michael J., Dulberger, Ellen R., Gordon, Robert J., Griliches, Zvi and Jorgenson, Dale, *Toward a More Accurate Measure of the Cost of Living*, Final Report to the Senate Finance Committee from the Advisory Commission to Study the Consumer Price Index (The Boskin Commission) (December 4, 1996).

Braithwaite, Tom, Regulators pressured to curb Wall Street reforms, *Financial Times*, November 4, 2010.

Brownell, Charles, *Subprime Meltdown: From US Liquidity Crisis to Global Recession* (New York: Ingram, 2008).

Brumbaugh, R. D., *Thrifts Under Siege* (New York: Ballinger, 1988).

Brumbaugh, R. D., Carron, A. S. and Litan, E., Cleaning up the depository institutions' mess, *Brookings Papers on Economic Activity*, 1 (1989), pp. 243–396.

Bruner, Robert F. and Carr, Sean D., *The Panic of 1907: Lessons Learned from the Market's Perfect Storm* (Hoboken, NJ: Wiley, 2007).

Brunnermeier, Markus, Crockett, Andrew, Goodhart, Charles A., Persaud, Avinash and Shin, Hyun Song, The fundamental principles of financial regulation, Geneva Reports on the World Economy 11, Conference Report, Centre for Economic Policy Research (2009).

Bryan, L. L., *Breaking up the Bank: Rethinking an Industry Under Siege* (New York: Dow Jones Irwin, 1988).

Cadman, Emily, Bernard, Steve, Kassel, Johanna and Jenkins, Patrick, Interactive: EU stress test results by bank, *Financial Times*, July 23, 2010.

Case, Karl E. and Shiller, Robert, Is there a bubble in the housing market?, *Brookings Papers on Economic Activity*, 2 (2003), pp. 299–362.

Chaplin, Geoff, *Credit Derivatives, Risk Management, Trading and Investment* (Chichester: John Wiley and Sons, 2005).

Choudry, Moorad and Tanna, Ketul, *An Introduction to Value-at-Risk* (Chichester: John Wiley and Sons, 2006).

Claessens, Stijn, Klingebiel, Daniela and Laeven, Luc, Resolving systemic crises: policies and institutions, World Bank Policy Research Working Paper 3377 (August 2004). Also in Honohan and Læven (eds.), *Systemic Financial Crises*, pp. 169–96.

Cohan, William, *House of Cards: A Tale of Hubris and Wretched Excess on Wall Street* (New York: Doubleday, 2009).

Committee of European Securities Regulators, The role of credit rating agencies in structured finance, CESR/08–277 (May 2008).

Cooper, George, *The Origin of Financial Crises: Central Banks, Credit Bubbles and the Efficient Market Fallacy* (Petersfield: Harriman House, 2008).

Cunningham, Noble E., *The Life of Thomas Jefferson* (New York: Ballantyne Books, 1988).

Curry, Timothy and Shibut, Lynn, The cost of the savings and loan crisis: truth and consequences, *FDIC Banking Review*, 13:2 (2000), pp. 26–35.

Delhaise, Philippe F., *Asia in Crisis: The Implosion of the Banking and Finance Systems* (New York: Wiley, 1998).

Diamond, D. and Dybvig, P., Bank runs, deposit insurance and liquidity, *Journal of Political Economy*, 3 (1983), pp. 401–19.

Diamond, D. W., Banks and liquidity creation: a simple exposition of the Diamond-Dybvig model, *Federal Reserve Bank of Richmond Economic Quarterly* (spring 2007), pp. 189–200.

Dougherty, Carter, Stopping a financial crisis, the Swedish way, *New York Times*, September 22, 2008.

Eichengreen, Barry, *Golden Fetters: The Gold Standard and the Great Depression, 1919–1939* (Oxford University Press, 1992).

Ellis, Luci, The housing meltdown: why did it happen in the United States?, BIS Working Papers no. 259 (September 2008).

Equal Credit Opportunity Act (15 U.S.C. § 1691) (1974).

European Central Bank, *Financial Stability Review* (various issues).

European Commission, The high-level group on financial supervision (de Larosière Committee), Report (25 February 2009).

Commission recommendation on remuneration policies in the financial services sector, COM(2009) 3159.

European Economic Advisory Group, The financial crisis, *Report on the European Economy* (February 2009), Chapter 2.

Federal Reserve Board, *Federal Reserve Bulletin* (various issues).

Feldstein, Martin, Refocusing the IMF, *Foreign Affairs* 77:2 (March/April 1998), pp. 20–33 (available at www.jstor.org/stable/20048786).

Housing, credit markets and the business cycle, National Bureau of Economic Research Working Paper 13471 (October 2007).

Ferguson, Niall, *The Ascent of Money: A Financial History of the World* (New York: Allen Lane, 2008).

Financial Accounting Standards Board, Financial instruments with characteristics of equity, Financial Accounting Series 1550–100 (November 2007).

Financial Services Authority, Stress testing, Discussion Paper 05/02 (May 2005).

Definition of capital, Discussion Paper 07/06 (December 7, 2007).

A regulatory response to the global banking crisis, Discussion Paper 09/2 (March 2009).

Strengthening liquidity standards, Policy Statement 09/16 (October 9, 2009).

Strengthening capital standards 3, 09/29, Consultative Paper 09/29 (December 2009).

Fleckenstein, William, *Greenspan's Bubbles: The Age of Ignorance at the Federal Reserve* (Maidenhead: McGraw Hill, 2008).

Foster, George Bellamy and Magdoff, Fred, *The Great Financial Crisis: Causes and Consequences* (New York: Monthly Review Press, 2009).

Friedman, Benjamin M., The risks of financial crisis, in Martin Feldstein (ed.), *The Risk of Economic Crisis* (University of Chicago Press, 1991), pp. 19–44.

Friedman, Milton and Friedman, Rose, *Free to Choose* (New York: Harcourt, 1980).

Friedman, Milton and Schwartz, Anna J., *A Monetary History of the United States, 1867–1960* (Princeton University Press, 1963).

Galbraith, John Kenneth, *The Great Crash, 1929* (New York: Houghton Mifflin, 1954, 1997).

Garber, Peter M., *Famous First Bubbles: The Fundamentals of Early Manias* (Cambridge, MA: MIT Press, 2000).

Gerhardt, Maria, Consumer bankruptcy regimes and credit default in the US and Europe: a comparative study, Centre for Economic Policy Studies Working Paper 318 (July 2009).

Goodman, Laurie S., Li, Shumin, Lucas, Douglas J. and Zimmerman, Thomas A., *Subprime Mortgage Credit Derivatives* (Hoboken, NJ: John Wiley and Sons, 2008).

Gorton, Gary B., *Slapped by the Invisible Hand: The Panic of 2007* (New York: Oxford University Press, 2010).

Greenspan, Alan, *The Age of Turbulence: Adventures in a New World* (New York: Penguin, 2007, 2008).

We need a better cushion against risk, *Financial Times*, March 26, 2009.

Guerrera, Francesco, US collects $10.3bn from Citi bail-out, *Financial Times*, July 2, 2010.

Haldane, Andrew G., Banking on the state, *BIS Review* 139 (2009), pp. 1–20.

Ul Haq, Mahbub, Kaul, Inge and Grunberg, Isabelle (eds.), The *Tobin Tax: Coping with Financial Volatility* (Oxford University Press, 1996).

Honohan, Patrick and Læven, Luc (eds.), *Systemic Financial Crises: Containment and Resolution* (Cambridge University Press, 2005).

Hull, J., Predescu, Mirela and White, Alan, The relationship between credit default swap spreads, bond yields and credit rating announcements, *Journal of Banking and Finance*, 28:11 (November 2004), pp. 2789–2811.

Hunter, William C., Kaufman, George G. and Krueger, Thomas H., *The Asian Financial Crisis: Origins, Implications and Solutions* (Berlin: Springer Verlag, 1999).

International Monetary Fund, *Global Financial Stability Report* (various issues).

World Economic Outlook (various issues).

A fair and substantial contribution by the financial sector, Final Report for the G-20 (June 2010).

Ishmael, Stacy-Marie, European banks to face capital demands, *Financial Times*, December 7, 2009.

Banks win battle to tone down Basel III, *Financial Times*, June 24, 2010.

Jenkins, Patrick, Stress test results "underwhelming," *Financial Times*, July 26, 2010.

Jenkins, Patrick and Hughes, Jennifer, Danish banks urge changes to Basel III, *Financial Times*, July 7, 2010.

Jenkins, Patrick and Masters, Brooke, Financial regulation: the money moves on, *Financial Times*, September 14, 2010.

Jennergren, P. and Näslund, Bertil, Efter bankkrisen, vad blev notan för skattebetalarna, *Ekonomisk debatt*, 1 (1998), pp. 69–76.

Johnson, Simon, Testimony submitted to the US Senate Committee on Banking, Housing, Urban Affairs, Executive session to vote on nominations and a hearing entitled "Implications of the Volcker Rules for financial stability," February 4, 2010.

Johnson, Simon and Kwak, James, *13 Bankers: The Wall Street Takeover and the Next Financial Meltdown* (New York: Pantheon Books, 2010).

Jonung, Lars, Kiander, Jaako and Vartia, Pentti (eds.), *The Great Financial Crisis in Finland and Sweden: The Nordic Experiment of Financial Liberalization* (Cheltenham: Edward Elgar Publishing Ltd, 2009).

Jorion, P., *Value at Risk: The New Benchmark for Controlling Market Risk* (Chicago: Richard D. Irwin, 1997).

Kapner, Suzanne, Lawmakers wary of Fannie and Freddie reform, *Financial Times*, July 21, 2010.

US housing: Sunset Boulevard, *Financial Times*, August 17, 2010.

Kaufman, George G. (ed.), *Research in Financial Services: Banking, Financial Markets and Systemic Risk* (Greenwich, CT: JAI Press, 1995).

Kaufman, George G. and Kenneth E. Scott, What is systemic risk and do bank regulators retard or contribute to it? *The Independent Review*, 7 (winter 2003), pp. 371–91.

Kaufman, Henry, *Interest Rates: The Markets and the New Financial World* (London: I. B. Tauris & Co., 1986).

The Road to Financial Reformation: Warnings, Consequences, Reforms (New York: John Wiley & Sons, 2009).

Kashyap, Anil K. and Stein, Jeremy C., Cyclical implications of the Basel II capital standards, *Economic Perspectives*, **28**:1 (2004), pp. 18–31.

Kay, John, *Narrow Banking: The Reform of Banking Regulation* (London: Centre for the Study of Financial Innovation, 2009).

We must press on with breaking up banks, *Financial Times*, September 15, 2010.

Ketcham, Ralph, *James Madison: A Biography* (Charlotteville: University Press of Virginia, 1971, 1990).

Keynes, John M., *The General Theory of Employment, Interest and Money* (New York: Harcourt, Brace and World, 1936).

Kharas, Horni J., Pinto, Brian and Ulatov, Sergei, An analysis of Russia's 1998 meltdown: fundamentals and market signals, *Brookings Papers on Economic Activity*, 1 (2001), pp. 1–68.

Kindleberger, Charles P., *The World in Depression, 1929–1939* (Berkeley: University of California Press, 1986).

Kindleberger, Charles P. and Aliber, Robert Z., *Manias, Panics and Crashes: A History of Financial Crises* (New York: MacMillan, 1978, 2005).

Koskenkylä, Heikki and Vesala, Jukka, Finnish deposit banks 1980–93: years of rapid growth and crisis, *Bank of Finland Discussion Papers*, 16/94 (August 1, 1994).

KPMG, Funds and fund management 2010, regulation, the United Kingdom (available at www.kpmg.com/Global/en/IssuesAndInsights/ ArticlesPublications/Documents/Hedge-funds-2010/United-Kingdom-HF-Regulation-2010.pdf).

Krugman, Paul, *The Return of Depression Economics and the Crisis of 2008* (New York: W. W. Norton, 2009).

Too big to fail fail, *New York Times*, January 11, 2010.

Kubarych, Roger, *Stress Testing the System: Simulating the Global Consequences of the Next Financial Crisis* (New York: Council on Foreign Relations Press, 2001).

Laeven, Luc and Valencia, Fabian, Systemic banking crises: a new database, IMF Working Paper 224 (2008).

Langohr, Herwig and Langohr, Patricia, *The Rating Agencies and their Credit Ratings: How They Work and Why They Are Relevant* (New York: Wiley, 2008).

Larsen, Peter Thal, Basel outlines stricter limits, *Financial Times*, November 21, 2008.

Levich, Richard M., Majnoni, Giovanni and Reinhart, Carmen M., *Ratings, Rating Agencies and the Global Financial System* (Dordrecht: Kluwer Academic Publishers, 2002).

Louis, Meera, Bank rescue costs EU states $5.3 trillion, more than German GDP, Bloomberg News, June 11, 2009.

Lux, T. and Marchesi, M., Scaling and criticality in a stochastic multiagent model of a financial market, *Nature*, 397 (1999), pp. 498–500.

Lybeck, Johan A., Commercial bank behavior and the Swedish monetary sector, Ph.D. dissertation, University of Michigan (1971).

Finansiella kriser förr and nu (Stockholm: SNS Förlag, 1992).

Facit av finanskrisen (Stockholm: SNS Förlag, 1994).

Finanskrisen (Stockholm: SNS Förlag, 2009).

It is time to consider breaking up the banking behemoths, *Financial Times*, March 19, 2009.

No one addresses real cause of crisis, *Financial Times*, January 29, 2010.

MacAskill, Andrew and Kirchfeld, Aaron, European banks' hidden losses may threaten EU stress tests, Bloomberg News, July 6, 2010.

Mackay, Charles, *Extraordinary Popular Delusions and the Madness of Crowds* (New York: Harmony Books, 1841, 1852, 1980, 1995, 2003).

McKenzie, George and Stephen Thomas, *Financial Instability and the International Debt Problem* (London: Macmillan, 1992).

Masters, Brooke and Jenkins, Patrick, FSA poised to set tougher capital rules, *Financial Times*, September 21, 2010.

Masters, Brooke and Murphy, Megan, European banks to face capital demands, *Financial Times*, December 6, 2009.

Milne, Alistair, *The Fall of the House of Credit: What Went Wrong in Banking and What Can Be Done to Repair the Damage* (Cambridge University Press, 2009).

Minsky, Hyman P., *Can "It" Happen Again? Essays on Instability and Finance* (New York: M. E. Sharpe, 1962, 1982).

Longer waves in financial relations: financial factors in more severe depressions, *American Economic Review*, 54:3 (May 1964), pp. 324–35.

Stabilizing an Unstable Economy (New Haven, CT: Yale University Press, 1986; reissued New York and London: McGraw Hill, 2008).

Mishkin, Frederic S., Comment on systemic risk, in George G. Kaufman (ed.), *Research in Financial Services: Banking, Financial Markets, and Systemic Risk*, vol. 7 (Greenwich, CT: JAI Press, 1995), pp. 31–45.

Morgenson, Gretchen, Too big to fail, or too big to handle? *New York Times*, June 20, 2009.

Morris, Charles R., *The Trillion Dollar Meltdown: Easy Money, High Rollers, and the Great Credit Crash* (New York: Public Affairs, 2008).

Münchau, Wolfgang, *Kernschmelze im Finanzsystem* (Munich: Carl Hanser Verlag, 2008).

Nakaso, Hiroshi, The financial crisis in Japan during the 1990s: how the Bank of Japan responded and the lessons learnt, BIS Economic Papers, no. 6 (2001).

National Audit Office, Maintaining financial stability across the United Kingdom's banking system, HC 91 Session 2009–2010 (4 December 2009).

Norges Offentliga Utredningar, *Bankkrisen*, NOU, 30 (1992).

Organisation for Economic Cooperation and Development, *Economic Outlook* (various issues).

Banks Under Stress (Paris: OECD, 1992).

Economic Survey of the Russian Federation (Paris, OECD, 1998).

Pallage, Stéphane J., An econometric study of the Belgian banking sector in terms of scale and scope economies, Université Libre de Bruxelles, *Cahiers Economiques de Bruxelles*, **130** (1991), pp. 125–43.

Paulson, Henry M., *On the Brink: Inside the Race to Stop the Collapse of the Global Financial System* (New York: Business Plus, 2010).

Pinto, Brian, Gurvich, Evsey and Ulatov, Sergei, Lessons from the Russian crisis of 1998 and recovery, in Joshua Aizenmann and Brian Pinto (eds.), *Managing Volatility and Crises: A Practitioner's Guide* (Cambridge University Press, 2005), pp. 406–38.

Posen, Adam S. and Mikitani, Ryoichi (eds.), *Japan's Financial Crisis and its Parallels to US Experience* (Washington DC: Institute for International Economics, 2000).

Pozen, Robert, *Too Big to Save: How to Fix the US Financial System* (Hoboken, NJ: John Wiley & Sons, 2010).

Profumo, Alessandro, Europe's banks need a recovery fund, *Financial Times*, July 11, 2010.

Radelet, Steven and Sachs, Jeffrey, D., The East Asian crisis: diagnosis, remedies, prospects, *Brookings Papers on Economic Activity*, 1 (1998), pp. 1–90.

Read, Colin, *Global Financial Meltdown: How We Can Avoid the Next Economic Crisis* (Basingstoke: Palgrave Macmillan, 2009).

Reinhart, Carmen M. and Rogoff, Kenneth S., Is the 2007 US sub-prime financial crisis so different? An international historical comparison, National Bureau of Economic Research Working Paper 13761 (January 2008).

This Time Is Different: Eight Centuries of Financial Folly (Princeton University Press, 2009).

The aftermath of financial crises, *American Economic Review*, 99:2 (May 2009), pp. 466–72.

Repullo, Rafael, Policies for banking crises: a theoretical framework, in Honohan and Læven (eds.), *Systemic Financial Crises*, pp. 137–68.

Rochet, Jean-Charles, *Why Are There So Many Banking Crises? The Politics and Policy of Bank Regulation* (Princeton University Press, 2008).

Rogoff, Kenneth S. and Reinhart, Carmen M., This time is different: a panoramic view of eight centuries of financial crises, National Bureau of Economic Research Working Paper 13882 (March 2008).

Roubini, Nouriel, The current US recession and the risks of a systemic financial crisis, US House of Representatives Financial Services Committee (26 February 2008).

Crisis Economics: A Crash Course in the Future of Finance (New York and London: Allen Lane, 2010).

Roubini, Nouriel and Brad Setser, *Bail-outs or Bail-ins: Responding to Financial Crises in Emerging Markets* (Washington DC: Institute for International Economics, 2004).

Sachs, Jeffrey, Managing the LDC debt crisis, *Brookings Papers on Economic Activity*, 2 (1986), pp. 397–440.

Making the Brady plan work, *Foreign Affairs*, 68:3 (summer 1989), pp. 87–104 (available at www.jstor.org/stable/20044010).

Sakoui, Anousha, Hopes rise over unwinding of Lehman's assets, *Financial Times*, July 11, 2010.

Sanderson, Rachel, Guerrera, Francesco and Thomas, Helen, Divide over accounting standards set to widen, *Financial Times*, May 27, 2010.

Santomero, Anthony M., Viotti, Staffan and Vredin, Anders, *Challenges for Central Banking* (Boston, MA: Kluwer Academic Publishers, 2001).

Santow, Leonard, *Do They Walk on Water? Federal Reserve Chairmen and the Fed* (New York: Praeger, 2008).

Shiller, Robert J., *Irrational Exuberance* (Princeton University Press, 2000, 2005).

The Subprime Solution: How Today's Global Financial Crisis Happened and What to Do About It (Princeton University Press, 2008).

A market to prop up, *Financial Times*, March 23, 2010.

Shiller, Robert J. and Case, Karl E., Is there a bubble in the housing market? *Brookings Papers on Economic Activity*, 2 (2003), pp. 299–362.

Simonian, Haig and Murphy, Megan, How Swiss finish was factored in, *Financial Times*, October 4, 2010.

Sinclair, Timothy J., *The New Masters of Capital: American Bond Rating Agencies and the Policy of Creditworthiness* (Ithaca, NY: Cornell University Press, 2005).

Sommer, Reine, *Die Subprime-Krise. Wie einige faule US-Kredite das internationale Finanzsystem erschüttern* (Hannover: Telepolis, 2008).

Sorkin, Andrew Ross, *Too Big to Fail: Inside the Battle to Save Wall Street* (London: Allen Lane, 2009).

Soros, George, *The New Paradigm for Financial Markets: The Credit Crisis of 2008 and What it Means* (New York: Public Affairs, 2008).

Statutory instrument, Capital Requirements Regulations 2006 (SI, 2006/3221).

Stern, Gary H. and Feldman, Ron J., *Too Big to Fail: The Hazards of Bank Bailouts* (Washington DC: Brookings Institution, 2003, 2009).

Sundararajan, V. and Baliño, Tomès J. T., *Banking Crises: Cases and Issues* (Washington DC: International Monetary Fund, 1991).

Swary, I. and Topf, B., *Global Financial Deregulation: Commercial Banking at the Crossroads* (Oxford: Basil Blackwell, 1992).

Tait, Nikki, EU to step up compensation for fraud cases, *Financial Times*, July 11, 2010.

Tait, Nikki, Wilson, James and Masters, Brooke, Banks hit at pay-out proposals, *Financial Times*, July 12, 2010.

Taleb, Nassim N., *The Black Swan: The Impact of the Highly Improbable* (New York: Random House, 2007).

Ten principles for a Black Swan proof world, *Financial Times*, April 7, 2009.

Taylor, John B., *Getting Off Track: How Government Actions and Interventions Caused, Prolonged and Worsened the Financial Crisis* (Stanford, CA: Hoover Institution Press, 2009).

Tett, Gillian, How greed turned to panic, *Financial Times*, May 9, 2009.

Vennet, Rudi Vander, The effect of mergers and acquisitions on the efficiency and profitability of EC credit institutions, *Journal of Banking and Finance*, **20**:9 (November 1996), pp. 1531–58.

Wæchter, Philippe and You, Martial, *Subprime, la faillite mondiale? Cette crise financière qui va changer votre vie* (Monaco: Éditions Alphée, 2008).

Weisbrot, Mark, Ten years after: the lasting impact of the Asian financial crisis, Centre for Economic Policy Research (August 2007).

Wessel, David, *In Fed We Trust: Ben Bernanke's War on the Great Panic, How the Federal Reserve Became the Fourth Branch of Government* (New York: Crown Publishing, 2009).

Westbrook, Jesse and Katz, Ian, US banks recruit investors to kill FASB fair-value proposal, Bloomberg News, July 8, 2010.

White, L. J., *The S & L Debacle: Public Policy Lessons for Bank and Thrift Regulation* (Oxford University Press, 1991).

Wilson, James, Hypo reality, *Financial Times*, March 20, 2009.

Wolf, Martin, *Fixing Global Finance* (Baltimore, MD: Johns Hopkins University Press, 2008).

Wolf, Martin, Basel: the mouse that did not roar, *Financial Times*, September 14, 2010.

Woodward, Bob, *Maestro: Greenspan's Fed and the American Boom* (New York: Touchstone, 2000).

Xiao, Yingbin, French banks amid the global financial crisis, International Monetary Fund Working Paper 09/201 (September 2009).

Zandi, Mark, *Financial Shock: A 360° Look at the Subprime Mortgage Implosion and How to Avoid the Next Financial Crisis* (Upper Saddle River, NJ: Pearson Education, 2009).

Newspaper articles etc

The Economist, various issues from July 2007

AAAsking for trouble, July 12, 2007

Bond insurers, a moniline meltdown, July 26, 2007

Asset-Backed Securities Sold down the river Rhine, August 9, 2007

A liquidity squeeze, Bankers mistrust, August 16, 2007

Banks in trouble, the game is up, August 16, 2007

American investment banks, Shots in the dark, August 30, 2007

Houses built on sand, September 13, 2007

Bank mergers, Three's company, September 13, 2007
British banks, the great Northern run, September 20, 2007
America's housing giants, Don't free Fannie and Freddie, October 4, 2007
When to bail out, October 4, 2007
Curing SIV, October 18, 2007
CDOh no!, November 8, 2007
Bank capital, tightening the safety belt, November 27, 2007
American house prices, fantasy or phobia, November 29, 2007
Central banks, A dirty job but someone has to do it, December 13, 2007
Bond insurers, Buddy can you spare us $15 billion?, January 24, 2008
Credit derivatives, gross exaggeration, January 31, 2008
Société Générale, No défense, January 31, 2008
Credit-Rating Agencies, Restructured products, February 7, 2008
Northern Rock, Now make it work, February 21, 2008
The credit crunch, mark it and weep, March 6, 2008
Credit markets, if at first you don't succeed, March 13, 2008
Wall Street's crisis, March 19, 2008
Investment banks, the $2 bail-out, March 19, 2008
The financial system, what went wrong?, March 19, 2008
American banks, Not so thrifty, April 10, 2008
Derivatives, taming the beast, April 17, 2008
Derivatives, clearing the fog, April 17, 2008
Deposit insurance, when the safety net fails, May 1, 2008
European banks, Austria 1, Germany 0, May 15, 2008
Insurance, Is AIG the Citigroup of insurance, May 15, 2008
Paradise lost, May 5, 2008
Cycle clips, May 15, 2008
Black mark, May 15, 2008
Bank of America and Countrywide, June 26, 2008
Fannie Mae and Freddie Mac, end of illusions, July 17, 2008
Aftermath of a megamerger, July 17, 2008
Bank losses, hall of shame, August 7, 2008
American housing, Ticking time bomb?, August 14, 2008
Auction-rate securities, Kick in the ARS, August 14, 2008
Capital ideas, August 28, 2008
German banking, September 4, 2008
European banks, cross-border contagion, September 18, 2008
AIG's rescue, size matters, September 18, 2008
Investment banking, is there a future?, September 18, 2008
American finance, And then there were none, September 25, 2008
Echoes of the Depression, 1929 and all that, October 2, 2008
Accounting, Fair cop, October 2, 2008
Global banks, On life support, October 2, 2008

When fortune frowned (special survey), October 11, 2008
Global finance, lifelines, October 11, 2008
America's bail-out, TARP priority, October 11, 2008
Link by link, October 18, 2008
Rescuing the banks, but will it work? October 18, 2008
Hedge funds in trouble, October 25, 2008
Mewling and puking, how damaged is the Basel 2 accord?, October 25, 2008
A helping hand to homeowners, October 25, 2008
Cracks in the crust [on Iceland], December 13, 2008
Greed – and fear, a special report on the future of finance, January 24, 2009
Move over, subprime, February 7, 2009
A ghoulish prospect [nationalization of banks], February 28, 2009
Stress-Test Mess, February 28, 2009
Rebuilding the banks, May 16, 2009
In defence of the dismal science (Robert Lucas), August 8, 2009
The toxic trio (Fannie Mae, Freddie Mac, AIG), August 15, 2009
Where it all began (house prices), August 22, 2009
Death warmed up (on letting banks fail), October 3, 2009
Over the counter, out of sight, November 14, 2009
Cheap as chips, January 16, 2010
Base camp Basel, January 23, 2010
They might be giants, May 15, 2010
Repent at leisure, a special report on debt, June 26, 2010
A decent start (US financial reform), July 3, 2010
Coming in from the cold, December 18, 2010
Chained but untamed: Special report on international banking, May 14, 2011
America's bail-out maths, June 11, 2011

Financial Times, various issues from August 2007

A crash history lesson in crashes for Wall Street, August 27, 2007
Credit write-downs, February 20, 2008
Turmoil reveals the inadequacy of Basel II, February 27, 2008
IMF points to high cost of credit crisis, April 9, 2008
Triple A rating does not guarantee against default, May 3, 2008
Credit turmoil shows how Basel II must be improved, May 8, 2008
New Basel consensus in need of fundamental rethink, May 9, 2008
Who rates the rating agencies?, May 29, 2008
Do away with rating-based rules, July 9, 2008
Brussels outlines ratings agencies plan, July 31, 2008
EU criticized for ratings proposal, September 3
Credit ratings agencies, September 28, 2008
Europe's banking crisis neeeds a common solution, October 2, 2008
Global Financial Crisis, October 11–12, 2008

Influence of ratings agencies questioned, October 17, 2008
US regulators and what they do, October 22, 2008
In the face of fragility, December 15, 2008
Britain and Spain: a tale of two house market bubbles, January 6, 2009
Error-laden machine, March 3, 2009
To nationalise or not to nationalise is the question, March 4, 2009
The Fed's moral hazard maximizing strategy, March 6, 2009 (Willem Buiter)
Hypo Reality, March 20, 2009
Ten principles for a Black Swan proof world, April 7, 2009 (Nassim Nicholas
    Taleb)
Subprime explosion: who isn't guilty? May 6, 2009
How greed turned to panic, May 9, 2009
America's triple A rating is at risk, May 13, 2009
Financial reform, respinning the web, June 22, 2009
The cautious approach to fixing banks will not work, July 1, 2009
Houses to put in order (on Fannie Mae and Freddie Mac), September 4, 2009
In defence of financial innovation (by Robert Shiller), September 28, 2009
How to tame the animal spirits (by John Plender), September 30, 2009
UK bank chief doubts curbs will stop future crises, October 21, 2009
Payback time, October 27, 2009
A three-way split is the most logical, October 29, 2009
An eclectic aviary (on the Federal Reserve), November 13, 2009
Smoke signals, November 26, 2009
Citi [of London] limits, December 14, 2009
Latest saga hardens lack of faith in Landesbanks, December 15, 2009
How America let banks off the leash, December 17, 2009
Banks face revolutionary reform, January 22, 2010
Tripped up, January 25, 2010
Government rescue packages for banks, January 25, 2010
Use of clearers to rein in OTC derivatives, January 15, 2010
The hindered haircut (on AIG), January 27, 2010
A disorderly descent, February 2, 2010
Banks concede reform is inevitable, February 4, 2010
Eroded authority (on British bank supervision), February 12, 2010
Markets fear end of easy money era, February 20/21, 2010
A business decision (on leaving your house to the bank), February 23, 2010
Lehman file rocks Wall Street, March 13, 2010
A [property] market to prop up, March 23, 2010
Goldman versus the regulators, April 19, 2010
The challenge of halting the financial doomsday machine, April 21, 2010
A new broom (on Irish banking), May 10, 2010
A wider divide [between bankers and politicians], May 26, 2010
Accounting standards divide set to widen, May 27, 2010

That sinking feeling, June 2, 2010
Leaning lenders, June 4, 2010
A tricky pick (on Goldman Sachs and Abacus CDO), June 10, 2010
Worries over [European] banking stress tests fuel anxiety, June 15, 2010
Banks win battle to tone down Basel III, June 25, 2010
A line is drawn, July 1, 2010
EU sets new pay practices in stone, July 2, 2010
Short measures, July 19, 2010
Banks find exercise relatively painless, July 24–25, 2010
Seven lenders fail stress tests, July 24–25, 2010
A test cynically calibrated to fix the result, July 26, 2010
Stressed but not blessed, July 26, 2010
Derivative dilemmas, August 12, 2010
Suspense over, August 19, 2010
Bailout doubts unnerve investors, August 26, 2010
The money moves on, September 15, 2010
Basel: The mouse that did not roar, September 15, 2010
Germany's weak link, September 28, 2010
The long hangover, October 4, 2010
The best bet to curb too big to fail, October 14, 2010
Room to improve, November 2, 2010
Paper weight, November 2, 2010
Pressure mounts over derivatives clearing, November 3, 2010
A garden to tame, November 15, 2010
A punt too far, November 20/21, 2010
America must start again no financial regulation (by Henry Kaufman),
    December 17, 2010
Brussels plans bondholder 'bail-nis', January 7, 2011
Overarching problems, January 27, 2011
Elusive information, February 16, 2011
The debt net, February 21, 2011
Visibility needed (on German banks), April 6, 2011
Lenders pressed on capital raising, April 7, 2011
A shield asunder, May 20, 2011
German regulator hits at bank stress tests, June 7, 2011

New York Times

Triple A failure, April 27, 2008
Stopping a Financial Crisis, the Swedish Way, September 22, 2008
Greenspan concedes error on regulation, October 24, 2008
Too big to fail or too big to handle, June 20, 2009
A year after a cataclysm, little change on Wall St, September 12, 2009
The Big Squander (by Paul Krugman), November 20, 2009

Index